CULTURE AND PSYCH

Culture and Psychological Development

Dabie Nabuzoka
and
Janet M. Empson

palgrave
macmillan

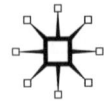

© Dabie Nabuzoka and Janet M. Empson 2010

All rights reserved. No reproduction, copy or transmission of this publication may be made without written permission.

No portion of this publication may be reproduced, copied or transmitted save with written permission or in accordance with the provisions of the Copyright, Designs and Patents Act 1988, or under the terms of any licence permitting limited copying issued by the Copyright Licensing Agency, Saffron House, 6-10 Kirby Street, London EC1N 8TS.

Any person who does any unauthorized act in relation to this publication may be liable to criminal prosecution and civil claims for damages.

The authors have asserted their rights to be identified as the authors of this work in accordance with the Copyright, Designs and Patents Act 1988.

First published 2010 by
PALGRAVE MACMILLAN

Palgrave Macmillan in the UK is an imprint of Macmillan Publishers Limited, registered in England, company number 785998, of Houndmills, Basingstoke, Hampshire RG21 6XS.

Palgrave Macmillan in the US is a division of St Martin's Press LLC, 175 Fifth Avenue, New York, NY 10010.

Palgrave Macmillan is the global academic imprint of the above companies and has companies and representatives throughout the world.

Palgrave® and Macmillan® are registered trademarks in the United States, the United Kingdom, Europe and other countries.

ISBN: 978–0–230–00888–5

This book is printed on paper suitable for recycling and made from fully managed and sustained forest sources. Logging, pulping and manufacturing processes are expected to conform to the environmental regulations of the country of origin.

A catalogue record for this book is available from the British Library.

A catalog record for this book is available from the Library of Congress.

10 9 8 7 6 5 4 3 2 1
19 18 17 16 15 14 13 12 11 10

Printed and bound in Great Britain by
CPI Antony Rowe, Chippenham and Eastbourne

*For Dabie's children, Tutsirai and Chikobwe, and
Janet's children, Rachel and James*

Contents

Acknowledgements	x
Notes on Contributors	xi
Epigraph	xii

Introduction and Guide to the Book   1
Dabie Nabuzoka and *Janet M. Empson*

    Rationale and focus of the book   1
    Structure and features of the book   3
    Overview of chapters   4

1   Culture's Influence on Psychological Development   11
    Dabie Nabuzoka

    1.1 Introduction   11
    1.2 Socialization of children and
          developmental outcomes   15
    1.3 Summary and conclusions   23

2   Approaches to Studying Human Development in
    Diverse Cultures   27
    Dabie Nabuzoka

    2.1 Introduction   28
    2.2 Cultural perspectives on human development   31
    2.3 Models and theories of development   41
    2.4 Methodological approaches   48
    2.5 Summary and conclusions   50

3   Child-Rearing Goals and Practices   55
    Cecilie Jávo

    3.1 Introduction   56
    3.2 Cultural models and parental ethnotheories   58
    3.3 Culture, childrearing and child development   63
    3.4 Acculturation and childrearing   69

	3.5 Childrearing in indigenous Sámi and majority Norwegian cultures: A comparative study	72
	3.6 General conclusions	82
4	**Social Disadvantage and Child Development** *Janet M. Empson*	92
	4.1 Introduction	93
	4.2 Subcultures of social disadvantage	94
	4.3 Poverty and social disadvantage	98
	4.4 Effects of poverty on children	102
	4.5 Individual differences in susceptibility to effects of social disadvantage	122
	4.6 A theoretical framework for child development in conditions of poverty	127
	4.7 Conclusions	130
5	**Culture and Cognitive Development** *Janet M. Empson* and *Dabie Nabuzoka*	142
	5.1 Introduction	142
	5.2 Models of the relationship between culture and intellectual functioning	144
	5.3 Theoretical perspectives	147
	5.4 Relationship between cognitive and social development	163
	5.5 Implications of the cultural context of cognitive development	169
	5.6 Summary and conclusions	171
6	**Language and Psychological Development** *Dabie Nabuzoka*	178
	6.1 Introduction	179
	6.2 Universal features and cultural variations across languages	180
	6.3 The role of language	184
	6.4 Bilingualism	189
	6.5 Summary and conclusions	203
7	**The Development of Cultural and Ethnic Identity** *Rachel Takriti*	209
	7.1 Introduction	210
	7.2 Religion and ethnicity	211

	7.3	Prejudice and children's understanding of ethnic groups	214
	7.4	Children's ethnic attitudes	218
	7.5	Religious identity	226
	7.6	Social-psychological theories	233
	7.7	Summary and conclusions	238
8		Culture in Applied Developmental Psychology	247
		Dabie Nabuzoka and *Janet M. Empson*	
	8.1	Introduction	247
	8.2	Application of theory and research findings	250
	8.3	Implications for policy and practice	265
	8.4	Issues in applied developmental psychology and research	285
	8.5	Conclusions	293

Glossary	302
Author Index	313
Subject Index	325

Acknowledgements

Our thanks go to all our friends and relatives who have experienced with us the saga of writing this book! We particularly wish to thank Peter Derlien for his help with figures and reading draft manuscript. We are very appreciative of the patience and encouragement of our editors Jamie Joseph and Neha Sharma at Palgrave Macmillan in Basingstoke.

Notes on Contributors

Dr Dabie Nabuzoka is Principal Lecturer in Psychology at Leeds Metropolitan University and Chartered Psychologist of the British Psychological Society (BPS). His research interests include cultural influences on child development and the social functioning of children with learning disabilities. He is author of Children with Learning Disabilities: Social Functioning and Adjustment (BPS-Blackwell) and co-author (with Janet Empson) of Atypical Child Development in Context (Palgrave Macmillan).

Dr Janet M. Empson is Visiting Fellow to the Faculty of Development and Society at Sheffield Hallam University, Associate Fellow of British Psychological Society (BPS) and full member of the Health Division of the BPS. Her main specialist teaching and research area is developmental psychology with a particular interest in child health and well-being. She is co-author (with Dabie Nabuzoka) of Atypical Child Development in Context (Palgrave Macmillan).

Dr Cecilie Jávo is Senior Child Psychiatrist at the Sami National Centre for Mental Health (SANKS) in Karasjok, Norway. Dr Jávo has done extensive research on childrearing and behaviour problems within a cross-cultural framework, where she has compared Norwegian and Sámi cohorts. She is also leader of the Committee of Transcultural Psychiatry of the Norwegian Psychiatric Association.

Dr Rachel Takriti is Senior Lecturer in Psychology at Leeds Metropolitan University. Her research interests include the development of identity in children from various religious and ethnic backgrounds.

Real culture lives by sympathies and imaginations, not by dislikes and disdains-under all misleading wrappings it pounces unerringly upon the human core.
>William James, American philosopher 1842–1910
>*McClures Magazine*, February 1908, p. 422

Introduction and Guide to the Book

Dabie Nabuzoka and Janet M. Empson

There is a general recognition in developmental psychology that children typically develop in rich social and cultural contexts. However, until about relatively recently, few textbooks have solely focused on the specific ways in which such contexts may impact on child development. Thus, the influence of sociocultural factors on children's social and psychological development is the main focus of *Culture and Psychological Development*. These factors relate to the general environment in which the child is developing, and include the organization, functioning and social features of institutions charged with the responsibility of bringing up children. In most societies, such institutions include the family (nuclear, extended or adopted), but can also include more formalized arrangements such as schools and other community activities. The concern of this book is on how interactions between the child and others, mostly adults but also other children, in such contexts have a significant influence on their psychological development. The focus is, therefore, mostly on social dimensions to children's development and psychological functioning.

Rationale and focus of the book

The idea to write this book came about during the course of teaching developmental psychology to undergraduate students. Initially, invited to contribute to one or two lectures on cultural influences on child development, it soon became clear that this would not be sufficient to do much justice to the topic given that culture permeates almost all domains of human functioning and development. We, therefore, introduced a module called 'Cultural Perspectives on Development'. However, this title seemed to imply a focus solely on theoretical approaches, while the intention was to have a much wider focus than that. Therefore, the module was later renamed 'Culture and Psychological Development' to reflect a focus on both theoretical perspectives and specific manifestation of cultural influences on various aspects of human development. The idea was to provide students with a module that was essentially on developmental psychology, but which emphasized involvement of cultural processes in the various domains of psychological functioning and development.

The next task was to identify textbooks that could be used by our undergraduate students. As many lecturers have found out when introducing new courses, no particular book available seemed to entirely address the specific aims of the module. Although in the past few decades a number of books have been published on the relationship between culture and aspects of psychological functioning, few have addressed this as a key feature of developmental psychology. Fewer still have been written to be accessible to a wide range of those with interest in child development including university students (undergraduates and graduates), professionals concerned with the general welfare of children, and those who simply have an interest in finding out and understanding about the various social influences on children's development. We, therefore, set out to compile a book that would address some of these concerns and be useful to such a diverse audience and also as a text on similar courses. The outcome was *Culture and Psychological Development*.

This book is, therefore, generally intended as an introduction to some of the conceptual and theoretical explanations of the role and influence of culture on the psychological development of children, and the implications of such influences for the welfare of children. It is envisaged that the issues of concern here will not only be of interest to the student of developmental psychology, but also to those concerned with promoting the welfare of children. Such people include those whose work requires an understanding of the particular ways in which cultural factors are related to children's development. Professionals working in multicultural contexts readily come to mind. But if we accept that every child at any given time is developing in a social and cultural context, then the particular ways in which such contexts are related to children's development should be of interest to all those who want to find out more about child development in general. This includes those who are on psychology courses in university, or those to whom the subject may be relevant in professions such as teaching, social work, psychiatry and law, or those with sheer curiosity about various influences on children's adjustment. The general theme of the book is 'child development and functioning in cultural context'. Specific aims of the book are, therefore, as follows:

- To provide an introduction to theoretical perspectives and approaches to the study and understanding of the influence of cultural factors on the psychological development of individuals, particularly children;
- To provide an introduction to the various ways in which culture can be constituted in different contexts, including those obtained in multicultural societies;
- To discuss and illustrate the influence of various aspects of culture on specific aspects of children's social and cognitive development; and
- To discuss some of the practical and research implications of approaches that incorporate considerations of cultural influences on children's psychological development.

The orientation of this book is in recognition of the various ways culture can be constituted. To illustrate this, different examples of the constitutions of culture are discussed: traditional, modern, ethnic background, religious affiliation and socio-economic status. A number of outcomes of such cultural factors are identified in social and cognitive functioning, language development, general outcomes in psychological adjustment (including mental health), and the development of cultural and ethnic identity. The focus is, therefore, on a selected number of social ecological factors and how these are related to children's functioning in some psychological domains.

Structure and features of the book

The book is divided into eight chapters focused on the following: conceptual and methodological issues (Chapters 1 and 2); some of the contexts and practices which influence child development (Chapters 3 and 4); cultural influences on social and cognitive domains (Chapters 5 and 6); a specific example of cultural and social adjustment in children (Chapter 7); and implications for applied developmental psychology (Chapter 8). These chapters are written by authors with interests and experience of conducting research in these areas. A number of features have been included in most chapters to make the book more useful. These include the following:

Format of contents: Each chapter presents an introduction and outline of the main subject area. Key theoretical perspectives are introduced and a discussion is presented of the key issues and conceptual frameworks applied in studying children's development in general or in a particular domain of functioning.

Discussion points: Most of the chapters include one or more discussion points, which are questions or tasks designed to encourage you to think and reflect on your understanding of the issues presented and also about some of the theoretical and practical implications.

Case studies: Boxes are spread out across the various chapters, in which case studies or examples are presented to illustrate some of the key concepts, issues or approaches. These are either summaries of studies addressing a key issue or illustrating an approach to studying a particular aspect of a domain of children's functioning or in some cases in the form of vignettes of specific scenarios or situations.

Further readings: At the end of each chapter is a short indicative list of publications for further reading on the subject. These are intended to provide further elaboration of specific aspects of the subject area and, at times, a more advanced and critical analysis of some issues on the subject matter and/or the various perspectives.

Glossary: At the end of the book is a glossary of definitions of central terms. Although the meaning of many of the terms will be apparent in the main text, this also provides a convenient way of knowing what is meant by key terms.

Overview of chapters

The organization and focus of the various chapters of this book is a reflection of the various ways culture can be defined and how it has been studied, and is focused on those domains where its influence has been most clearly demonstrated. Thus, there is a focus on conceptual and methodological issues in studying the relationship between culture and psychological development, and more specific focus is on various domains of functioning to illustrate the nature of such a relationship in the development of children.

First, in Chapter 1, the theoretical and practical rationale for studying the relationship between culture and psychological development are introduced and outlined by Dabie Nabuzoka. First, a number of questions are identified on the significance of the relationship between culture and psychological development. The rationale presented for studying this relationship starts from the premise that the majority of children in the world grow up in diverse cultural contexts far removed from those which gave rise to dominant theories in developmental psychology, and that such diversity of experiences needs to be reflected in such theories. Various approaches to studying culture's influence on psychological development are then briefly introduced and outlined. Also, briefly discussed are some of the linkages made between socialization practices and developmental outcomes in children. In particular, a point is made that child-rearing practices by and large foster capacities in children that maximize the values of a given culture. In addition to discussing variations in socialization practices across various ethnocultural groups, some domains of children's development and functioning are identified, in which the influence of culture can be demonstrated. These include language and cognitive development, and the development of cultural identity. Thus, the chapter introduces the themes and issues addressed at length in the various chapters that follow in the book.

In Chapter 2, Dabie Nabuzoka provides an outline of various approaches to studying human development in diverse cultures. First, the concept of culture is discussed, briefly looking at some definitions used in developmental psychology. Then various approaches and theoretical models in conceptualizing culture and its influence on human development are outlined. Traditions of studying culture in developmental psychology are outlined and discussed including cross-cultural psychology (Berry et al., 2002) and cultural psychology (Cole, 1992; Göncü, 1999). Also discussed is a more recent theoretical perspective that has gained prominence, that of indigenous psychologies. These approaches are introduced as not necessarily being mutually exclusive but as sharing an emphasis on the role of the context of development in terms of the physical and social environment, and also of the various structures and systems of society. Such a focus is reflected in the theoretical models introduced in the chapter. Finally, the chapter introduces specific methodological approaches associated with research reflecting some of these theoretical perspectives.

Chapter 3, by Cecilie Jávo, introduces the various ways child-rearing practices socialize children for adult life in different cultures. Childrearing has been studied from various perspectives focusing on specific parenting styles and psychological outcomes in the offspring and also on environmental and contextual factors as determinants of parenting goals and practices. Other studies have also identified ethnic factors as important determinants of such goals and practices. This chapter focuses on the individualism-collectivism (I-C) construct as one dimension of social psychological functioning considered to have antecedents in child-rearing practices. This construct is associated with differing values in different societies, which inform social behaviour in different ways at different levels. For example, a defining difference has been identified as lying in a basic concern for oneself (individualism) in contrast to a concern for the groups to which one belongs (collectivism). Using a case study comparing child-rearing practices of indigenous Sámi and majority Norwegians, Cecilie Jávo questions the assumption that traditional societies tend to be largely oriented towards practices that promote collectivism while modern societies apply child-rearing practices that promote individualism in the young. As Jávo demonstrates, the evidence from research in various ethnic cultures linking such features of child-rearing practices to socialization goals and values is not straightforward.

Chapter 4, by Janet Empson, develops further some of the issues explored in the previous chapter by Cecilie Jávo on cultural variations in socialization practices, focusing more specifically on the effects of social disadvantage on child-rearing practices and developmental progress and adjustment. Empson illustrates the complexity of relationships between poverty and social disadvantage and the cognitive, educational, social-emotional development and physical and mental health of children. Such relationships are presented as being mediated in part by the mental health and socialization behaviours of caregivers, which also vary for different ethnic groups. Also introduced in this chapter is the wide range of individual differences found within a socio-economic group regarding parents and children who show resilience to adversity. This suggests possible ways in which interventions with families in difficulties may be focused on helping them to realize more of a child's developmental potential. The chapter concludes with a discussion of the utility of the ecological-systems model (Bronfenbrenner, 2005) and the ecological-transactional model (Lynch and Cicchetti, 1998) as explanatory frameworks for linking social disadvantage to developmental outcomes, and resilience, respectively.

In Chapter 5, we (Janet Empson and Dabie Nabuzoka) present a discussion of the role of cultural factors in cognitive development. The development of cognitive functioning has been one of the main

INTRODUCTION AND GUIDE TO THE BOOK   7

concerns in developmental psychology. The chapter starts with an outline of various models of the relationship between culture and intellectual functioning proposed by Sternberg (2004). Two main theoretical perspectives with implications for culture's influence on cognitive development are then introduced: Piaget's genetic epistemology and Vygotsky's social constructivism. Key features of each of the two perspectives are first outlined, followed by a discussion of how more recent investigators following the two perspectives have elaborated on the importance of cultural context for the study of cognition. Some research evidence and examples are discussed which illustrate the various interactions between children's cognitive development and context. Amongst the perspectives discussed at length to illustrate the view that cognitive processes are embedded in culture are sociohistorical theory (Karpov, 2005), Rogoff's (2003) notion of guided participation, including also the role of cultural tools and social interaction in cognitive development (Gauvain, 2001). In addition, the relationship between social and cognitive development is discussed with illustrations of how social contexts influence performance on cognitive tasks. The roles of social cognitive factors, relationships and affective factors are also discussed. The chapter concludes with a discussion of wider implications of the cultural context of children's cognitive development.

In Chapter 6, Dabie Nabuzoka introduces language development as a mediator between culture and social as well as cognitive development. The evidence is discussed for the link between the acquisition of different languages in various cultural contexts and aspects of psychological development and functioning. First, an outline is provided of some universal features and cultural variations in languages, including aspects of the structure of different languages, the particular ways in which they develop and how children come to acquire language as a part of their socialization. Then the role of language is discussed in terms of how its transmission is considered to be a means of socialization and, in particular, how it has been linked with psychological outcomes such as thought processes. Another focus is on the role of language socialization as a mediator between culture and the transmission of aspects of behavioural attributes in the young. Finally, Nabuzoka discusses the fact that most people in the world learn and speak more than one language, increasingly making bilingualism or multilingualism the norm and not an exception. An outline is provided of some aspects of the acquisition of more than one language in children, adolescents and adults. Then the consequences of bilingualism are discussed in terms of cognitive functioning and psychosocial adjustment. The chapter concludes with an overview of the relationship between language, culture and psychological development of individuals.

In Chapter 7, Rachel Takriti discusses the development of children's cultural and ethnic identity including a focus on the development of religious beliefs. Cultural identity has been an active area of research for some time, with work focusing on areas such as nationality, ethnicity and gender. How individuals come to hold strong senses of group identity and differentiation is clearly an important subject for psychological enquiry, especially in multicultural societies. The chapter begins with a discussion of definitions of the key terms 'religion' and 'ethnicity', followed by an overview of research investigating children's awareness of group differences and the theoretical basis for this work, particularly focusing on Piaget's theory of cognitive development. The chapter then presents evidence that children's understanding of social groups develops within a social context, being determined, at least in part, by the social group to which they belong. Takriti goes on to discuss social psychological theories on ethnic and religious identity with a review of some research into the effects of socialization on children's acquisition of a sense of religious group membership and identity, and illustrating the various ways in which work in this area is relevant to our understanding of culture's influence on children's social development. The chapter concludes with a discussion of the importance of work in this area. Takriti points out, for example, that how children come to understand and evaluate other religions is of significance as it has implications for group relations including problems of intercultural contact such as prejudice.

In the last chapter (Chapter 8) we (Dabie Nabuzoka and Janet Empson) discuss the practical and research implications of issues raised in previous chapters and how these may be addressed in developmental psychology applied in different cultures and multicultural societies. The central question is: What are the implications of findings from research on child development in cultural context for the institutions of society? The chapter starts with a discussion on the relevance of theoretical perspectives and models used in various studies. Then their applications are discussed related to children's education, methods of child-rearing and upbringing and children's psychological adjustment. The implications are also discussed of ethnic and socio-economic factors reflected in, for example, child-rearing practices as applied to discipline, education and social adjustment of children; and for policy and practice related to the provision of education, social and mental health services for children. The specific issue of the cognitive development of bilingual children in educational settings is discussed as an example of the relevance of understanding the psychological implications for children growing up in a multicultural society and a global world. Related to this is the issue of the practical implications of the language used as a medium of instruction for children's education. Another focus is on the ways in which cultural and ethnic identity develop in relation to their implications for children's social and emotional adjustment. Finally, a number of practical issues are identified, in applied developmental psychology and research, which have implications for the discipline being attuned to the experiences of the vast majority of the world's children. This includes a discussion of some areas of research, with a focus on evaluation research, for which some examples are outlined. Methodological issues and concerns are then discussed and some guidelines are presented on conducting research that incorporates cultural considerations. The chapter concludes with a brief discussion of the importance of work on cultural influences on the psychological development of children. It is concluded that, if appropriately applied, the outcome of applied research on the role of cultural factors in child development can make a significant contribution to both our understanding child development and how it can be optimized in different cultural contexts.

REFERENCES

Berry, J.W., Poortinga, Y.H., Segall, M.H., and Dasen, P.R. (2002). *Cross-cultural psychology: Research and applications*. Cambridge: Cambridge University Press.

Bronfenbrenner, U. (Ed.) (2005). *Making human beings human: Bioecological perspectives on human development*. London: Sage.

Cole, M. (1992). Culture in development. In M.H. Bornstein and M.E. Lamb (Eds), *Developmental psychology: An advanced textbook* (pp. 731–789). Hillsdale, NJ: Lawrence Erlbaum.

Gauvain, M. (2001). Cultural tools, social interaction and the development of thinking. *Human Development*, **44**, 126–143.

Göncü, A. (Ed.) (1999). *Children's engagement in the world: Sociocultural perspectives*. Cambridge: Cambridge University Press.

Karpov, Y.V. (2005). Psychological tools, internalization, and mediation: The Neo-Vygotskian elaboration of Vygotsky's notions. *International Society for the Study of Behavioural Development Newsletter*, 1(47), 4–7.

Lynch, M. and Cicchetti, D. (1998). An ecological-transactional analysis of children and contexts: The longitudinal interplay among child maltreatment, community violence and children's symptomatology. *Development and Psychopathology*, **10**, 235–257.

Rogoff, B. (2003). *The cultural nature of human development*. Oxford: Oxford University Press.

Sternberg, R.J. (2004). Culture and intelligence. *American Psychologist*, **59**(5), 325–338.

Culture's Influence on Psychological Development

Dabie Nabuzoka

> **OUTLINE**
> 1.1 Introduction
>   1.1.1 Child development in various contexts
>   1.1.2 Understanding human development in cultural context
> 1.2 Socialization of children and developmental outcomes
>   1.2.1 Childrearing as socialization
>   1.2.2 Development of knowledge and understanding of the world
>   1.2.3 Language and social-cognitive development
>   1.2.4 Development of cultural identity
> 1.3 Summary and conclusions
> Further reading
> References

1.1 Introduction

All societies nurture and train their young to become responsible adults who will in turn bring up children of their own. The concern for the welfare of young people is universal in that it applies to all societies irrespective of geographical location. However, the practices involved in nurturing and bringing up children vary in different parts of the world. These practices would have been developed over a long period and become a part of a society's way of life. More significantly, each practice would have developed as a specific way of responding to the particular demands for survival of a given society. So, the experience of childhood is also likely to vary across different societies. But how significant are such differences in the experiences of children across the world? What are their effects on the developing individual? How can we learn about such experiences and their effects on the developing child? Why is it important that we learn more about these experiences? This book addresses these questions from a number of perspectives. In this chapter, I will first outline some of the areas relevant to these questions and some of the efforts made in addressing them. Subsequent chapters illustrate in more depth some of the key issues in the psychological development of children in different cultural contexts.

1.1.1 Child development in various contexts

Let us start with the question of why it is important to learn about the experiences of childhood in various contexts. Over the years, the study of child development that has given rise to dominant theories in psychology has been largely confined to children in North America, Europe and other Western countries who comprise less than 10 per cent of the world's children. The majority of the world's children grow up in Asia, Africa, Latin America and the Pacific where conditions under which they grow up differ dramatically from those that have informed developmental theories. Recognition of the diversity of environments in which children develop all over the world has led us to question what implications there may be for children's psychological development. There are also questions as to whether psychological theories developed in contexts far removed from those of the majority of children can throw any light on the nature of child development in general. It has also been argued that the database for the development of such theories may have even been further limited to the subcultures of middle-class children in Western societies.

It is now generally accepted that the context of child development has a profound effect on developmental outcomes, and that there is a reciprocal relationship between the child and his/her environment. Such effects are perhaps much easier to demonstrate in relation to how variations in physical growth are associated with the child's environment, especially the availability of resources. For example, extreme deprivation of nutrients in early childhood can lead to stunted physical growth. Similarly, in the social domain, lack of social stimulation can lead to limited social responsiveness in infants, which may lead to difficulties in relating to others later on in life. Yet, the particular ways in which such needs for physical and social development are met differ across the world and even between subcultures of the same society. So there has recently been a developing interest in documenting how childhood experiences may differ among peoples of the world, and how variations in child-rearing practices from one population to another may be significant for children's development and our understanding of it. The attitudes, beliefs and other factors which influence the practices are also of significance.

With globalization people all over the world are increasing their contact with members of other cultures and understanding the differences between them is becoming increasingly relevant to governments, international agencies, professionals and businesses. Within a particular society today, there are typically many cultures and subcultures and these are constituted on the basis of income, ethnicity, religion, and so on. Minority groups in multicultural societies may use different childrearing practices to those of the dominant group and their appropriateness may be questioned by those not familiar with that particular culture. It is important for developmental psychologists to understand what gives rise to differing practices and psychological outcomes associated with them. In this chapter, I will outline some of the general areas and issues that have been of particular interest to developmental psychologists. Subsequent chapters provide further discussions of the issues raised with more specific examples and research evidence.

1.1.2 Approaches to understanding human development in cultural context

The initial question is how best to study the influence of culture on psychological development. This has been a subject of some debate in psychology, with various psychological models and theories being generated about the nature of human development, and of the role of cultural factors in such a process (van der Vijver and Poortinga, 2002; see also Chapter 2). These models or theories have guided research efforts in different parts of the world. One approach, known as cross-cultural psychology, has focused on testing the generality of existing psychological knowledge and theories to different societies (Berry, Poortinga, Segall and Dasen, 2002). The aim of this approach has been to try to explore and discover psychological variations in different cultures and to generate a nearly universal psychology valid for a broader range of cultures (Brislin, 1990). Such efforts have focused on comparing whether phenomena observed in one culture exist in another culture and the various ways in which it may be demonstrated.

Another approach emphasizes the view that associations between a society's culture and the psychological development of its members need to be explicable in terms of the mechanisms or processes mediating these. In other words, we need to understand how possibly causal relationships occur over time whereby developmental outcomes differ for children growing up in different cultural contexts. This approach, known as cultural psychology, aims at understanding the significance of certain practices in a given culture (Lamb, Sternberg, Hwang and Broberg (1992). What is of concern in this respect is to address such questions as to why people of a given culture may act in a particular way in given situations. Here interest is on the meanings associated with particular practices, and which provide the context for children's development (Göncü, 1999).

The approach of cultural psychology is also different from that of cross-cultural (comparative) psychology in that it considers culture in terms of the creation of an environment in which children (as young organisms) are provided conditions for optimal growth. Thus, culture is regarded as a medium for development (Cole, 1992). The approach of cross-cultural psychology, however, is more about the relationship between behaviour and elements of culture (e.g., socialization, ecological features, etc.). Thus in this approach, identifying cross-cultural differences can amount to identifying cultural elements behind the differences (Segall, 1984).

The two approaches are however not necessarily mutually exclusive. For example, the study of culture as a medium for child development does not preclude cultural comparisons. However, a discussion of the role of culture in development is essentially concerned with the role of the environment as, for example, represented by Bronfenbrenner's (1979) ecological model. This model regards the developing child as being exposed to a network of influences. Another theoretical framework for studying cultural regulation of the micro-environment of the child is the concept of the developmental niche (Super and Harkness, 1986). This concept tries to describe the environment *'from the point of view of the child in order to understand processes of development and acquisition of culture'* (Super and Harkness, 1986, p. 552). The developmental niche is said to have three components: the physical and social environment in which the child lives; the customs of childcare and childrearing representing the practices that are employed in looking after the young; and the belief systems as to the efficacy of such practices or the nature of child development. These models, as discussed further in Chapter 2, focus on structural components of the environment (social and physical) that define a child's experiences. Arguably, features of these could be amenable to cultural comparisons.

Another approach discussed in some more detail in Chapter 2 focuses on conceptual frameworks that best describe and explain both the child's experiences and the course of their development. Such is the concern of what has been termed 'indigenous psychologies'. This perspective holds that explanations of child development can only make sense with reference to the conditions or society in which they arise. The theories that inform socialization practices that are held intuitively by agents of such practices such as parents can be considered to contribute to an indigenous psychology.

1.2 Socialization of children and developmental outcomes

1.2.1 Childrearing as socialization

The practices of child nurturance and upbringing constitute the socialization of the young for them to acquire those skills and behavioural characteristics that will make them useful members of their society. Socialization has been defined as *'the process by which children acquire the beliefs, values and behaviours deemed significant and appropriate by older members of their society'* (Shaffer, 1999, p. 558). According to Shaffer (1999), socialization of the young serves society in a number of ways: First, it is a means of regulating children's behaviour and controlling undesirable or antisocial impulses; second, it promotes personal growth of the individual as it enables children to acquire the knowledge, skills, motives, and aspirations that enable them to adapt to their environment and function effectively in their communities; and third, it perpetuates the social order in that children become competent, adaptive, pro-social adults who will in turn impart what they have learned to their own children.

There are cultural differences in child-rearing values, beliefs and goals. Thus, parents and other caregivers foster behavioural capacities in their children that maximize their cultural values (LeVine, 1974). Different cultures provide various ways in which child-rearing practices socialize children for adult life (Whiting and Edwards, 1992). Socialization practices in various cultures have been studied from various perspectives. These studies have focused on cultural differences in such areas as infant care, autonomy, discipline and attachment behaviour. Other research, especially within subcultures of a given society, has focused on specific parenting styles and psychological outcomes in the offspring. More recent research has focused broadly on environmental and contextual factors as determinants of parenting goals and practices (Javo, Rønning and Heyerdahl, 2004). One such factor, social class (now more usually termed socio-economic status), has traditionally been identified as a primary social influence on parenting, accounting for significant variance in beliefs and behaviour patterns within a given society (see Chapter 4). Other studies have identified ethnic factors also as important determinants. When social class has been statistically controlled, significant ethnic differences in childrearing can still be identified in cross-cultural studies. Thus, parental child-rearing attitudes may be inculcated through an interaction of ethnic culture, experiences representative of particular socio-economic groups and other environmental factors.

The focus on child-rearing practices and psychological outcomes in the offspring has lead to studies which have sought to explain cultural variations in expressive behaviour in relation to those child-rearing practices. Thus, aspects of childrearing at a given point in the lives of children have been linked to psychological outcomes in adulthood (Harkness and Super, 1983). One dimension of social-psychological functioning with antecedents thought to be in child-rearing practices has been the individualism-collectivism (I-C) construct. This construct is associated with differing values in different societies, which inform social behaviour in different ways and at various levels. Thus, attributes of individualism and collectivism relate to social values and are reflected in social-psychological functioning. For example, a defining difference has been identified as lying in a basic concern for oneself (individualism) in contrast to a concern for the groups to which one belongs (collectivism) (Freeman, 1997).

Various researchers have sought to document evidence that these values are transmitted to children through particular patterns of child-rearing practices. Thus, socialization for interdependence has been documented as one of the most characteristic traits of collectivism. Here values that emphasize strong allegiances to one's cultural group are translated into specific rearing practices such as prolonged body contact between mother and infant, and disciplinary practices that underline empathy with others' feelings. On the other hand, encouragement of child autonomy and independence is supposed to be a dominant trait of childrearing in typical individualist cultures. The links between such psychological attributes and patterns of child-rearing practices are examined fully in a case study by Cecilie Jávo in Chapter 3.

Variations in socialization practices are also apparent in subcultures of a given society, such as in different socio-economic groups where the differences in parenting styles distinguish between subcultures in society and contribute to varying developmental pathways and outcomes for children (Ogbu, 1981; see also Chapter 4). In addition to socialization practices, there are a number of mediating factors for differential pathways and outcomes for children in different social groups. These include differences in lifestyle and access to resources, individual differences between children, particularly in relation to their physical and mental health, and variations in the home environment in both structural and social characteristics (McGlaughlin, 1988). For example, factors associated with social disadvantage such as stress in the parents may be linked with such outcomes as marital discord between parents and/or disturbance of psychological functioning. This can lead to parents being less nurturing and with little involvement in the lives of their children, including the demands of education.

Social circumstances such as stressful life events have been shown to be related not only to difficulties in general functioning of the parents, but also to influence parental beliefs and practices, and to have consequent negative developmental outcomes in children (Conger et al. 1992; 1995). Thus, parent-child relationships have been strongly implicated in the development of, or severity of, externalizing disorders in children (Webster-Stratton and Herbert, 1993). The frequency of such problems has led to difficulties in coping with school for children in social and economically deprived areas, particularly for boys.

In summary, child-rearing practices involve the socialization of the young as a means of regulating their behaviour and helping them acquire the knowledge, skills, motives and aspirations that would enable them to contribute effectively in their communities as adults. Different practices reflect differences in child-rearing values, beliefs and goals. These have been documented between ethnic groups in different societies and also between subcultures defined by such variables as socio-economic status. Such differences have been associated with different psychological outcomes. The question that may arise then is what mechanisms or processes are involved in producing such psychological outcomes. Another question is whether all domains of psychological functioning are affected by cultural variations at all. One area in which such questions have been a central feature of enquiry is in relation to how children come to understand their social and physical worlds.

1.2.2 Development of knowledge and understanding of the world

The development of our understanding of the social and physical world (how we acquire knowledge) is referred to as cognitive development. This has been one of the main concerns in developmental psychology. Various aspects of intellectual development are considered universal. One such ability is logic, which is applied in various contexts. It can be assumed therefore that all children might become logical in the same way. However, it has been pointed out that some aspects of intellectual development may not be universal (Eysenck, 1998). For example, human inventions such as counting systems, written language, scientific methods and so on can vary across cultures but are important aspects of cognitive development. As certain features of these may not be universal, the question is whether cognitive development is entirely a matter of children acquiring those universal aspects of intellectual functioning (e.g., being logical, remembering, etc.) or whether the important part of a child's intellectual development is being taught about these cultural inventions. Debate about culture's influence on cognitive development has historically focused mainly on two theoretical perspectives: Piaget's genetic epistemology and Vygotsky's social constructivism.

The first one, Piaget's theory, has been one of the most influential psychological theories in cross-cultural work on cognition. According to Piaget (1952), the essential element in development is in acquiring logic (a universal), as such, a child's understanding of cultural inventions is merely an offshoot of that fundamental developmental change. Piaget observed children responding to intelligence test questions and noticed that older children adapted their thought processes to deal with questions better than younger ones. He concluded that older children did not simply know more, but thought differently about problems from younger children. He considered this to indicate the flexibility of the brain to adapt to the environment through experience by altering cognitive structures or ways of thinking. This notion of adaptation is a key theme in Piaget's theory.

Piaget's view then was that cognitive development is the combined result of the development of the brain and nervous system and of the experiences that help the individual to adapt to their environment. Because humans are genetically similar, and also share most environmental experiences, they can also be expected to exhibit uniformity in cognitive development. On this basis, Piaget predicted stages of cognitive development the sequence of which would show uniformity across cultures. This latter feature of Piaget's theory became the focus of early cross-cultural work on cognition, as studies sought to demonstrate how children of different ages from different cultures seemed to progress through the qualitative stages identified by the theory (see Serpell, 1976).

Key features of Piaget's theory include that he was more interested in the emergence and sequence of cognitive stages than in the factors that can accelerate, retard or even prevent their appearance. In explaining the construction of necessary knowledge, Piaget emphasized the process of adaptation, not the traditional factors of development, maturation, physical experience and social factors. In addition, the cognitive activities of the human subject were formalized in logicomathematical terms. Such orientations, as noted by Lourenço and Machado (1996), attracted the criticism that Piaget not only fell prey to genetic individualism, but also conceived development in a social vacuum neglecting the role of social factors in development and extending to all domains, subjects, and cultures the forms of thinking found in his studies. Such criticisms have been rebuffed by Piaget's followers whose arguments have included the view that the effects of social factors on development can still be studied within the theory without requiring essential modifications (see Chapman, 1988; and Lourenço and Machado, 1996).

In contrast to Piaget's perspective, the approach of the Soviet psychologist Lev Vygotsky belongs to the contextualist school of thought, which holds that humans are embedded in a social matrix (context). As such, human behaviour cannot be understood independently of this matrix (Wertsch and Tulviste, 1992). According to Vygotsky (1978; 1986), a study of children's development must take a historical account of humankind's intellectual development. He pointed out that over centuries humans have invented cultural tools (e.g., number systems, measurements, computers, etc.) which are an indispensable part of our cognition. Children must master such tools to function effectively in their schools or outside them. However, such skills cannot simply be acquired independently by the children. They have to be passed on from one generation to another. Vygotsky's theory has influenced further development of the view that transmission of cultural tools from generation to generation through social interaction and situated activity is an important part of cognitive development.

As discussed further in Chapter 5, many investigators acknowledge the importance of social and cultural context for the study of cognition, and illustrations of the various interactions between children's cognitive development and such contexts have accumulated over the years.

Central to this has been the view that the mind adapts itself to the circumstances in which growth occurs. Thus, in cognitive development, basic biological capabilities are shaped to fit with the social and cultural context in which they will be used (Gauvain, 2001). This approach to understanding cognitive development is known as the social-contextual approach, which is also referred to as a sociocultural or sociohistorical approach. According to this view, intellectual development can only be fully understood by investigating the role social experiences play in the process either directly through people interacting and supporting each other; indirectly through the tools, symbols and values that influence human action; or both. One such cultural tool with implications for influencing human action is language. Language has been considered as a tool for cognitive as well as social development.

1.2.3 Language and social-cognitive development

Hoff (2006) notes that the fact that all normal children in normal environments learn to talk 'reflects innate capacities of the human species that make language acquisition both possible and virtually inevitable, but it may also reflect universally available environmental supports for language acquisition' (p. 55). Another fact is that children acquiring the specific language of their society and culture is a good example of basic biological capabilities being shaped to fit with the social and cultural context in which they will be used. Thus while all children will typically learn to speak, a child in an English village in Yorkshire is more likely to learn to speak English than, say, Urdu, whereas a child in Bradford, Yorkshire, may learn to speak English and/or Urdu; and a child born in a little village of southern Zambia will most likely learn to speak Tonga or perhaps Ila (Ohannessian and Kashoki, 1978). The ability to speak is a biological outcome whereas the language that is acquired is an outcome of socialization.

However, the second part of the quotation from Hoff (2006) raises a number of questions: what environmental supports are necessary to ensure that children learn to speak? What differences in either environmental supports or socialization account for the differences in the language acquired by the child? What can we learn from children who acquire more than one language? If socialization plays a significant role in language acquisition, and if we accept that socialization accounts for significant cultural differences, what cultural differences should we expect to be associated with different languages? What are the psychological implications of language differences for the developing individual? Such questions are at the centre of efforts examining the interrelationships between culture, language and psychological development.

Language is generally considered a good indicator of cultural differences between different societies. It has also been suggested that there is a link between the acquisition of different languages and aspects of cognitive functioning, as one particular language highlights or segments features of the environment in particular ways different from that of another language (Lemon, 1981). Thus, a link between culture and thought processes specifically suggests that individuals with different linguistic and cultural backgrounds may also think differently. The argument is that children, by being taught a particular language are also taught to think in a particular way about the world, including how they should relate to others. Thus, language is an important tool not only for human interaction but also for socio-cognitive development. Through language, we can shape our worlds as well as communicate with one another. Psychological research into children's language development has therefore explored how language and thinking interrelate, and also how these are linked with the child's social sophistication.

In addition to a general recognition of individual differences in language development, there is also evidence that there may be more than one route to language acquisition. This may be especially true when considering cultures that provide children with different kinds of language learning environments. The study of language acquisition by children who live in other cultures is considered crucial to discovering not only the universal processes of language acquisition, but also how different cultures and circumstances may present children with different tasks for learning language. A particular issue in point concerns bi- and multilingual development and its possible influences on social and cognitive functioning.

Bilingualism or multilingualism has become the norm in the world, and not an exception, as most people learn and speak more than one language. At the beginning of the 1990s it was estimated that about half of the world's children were exposed to more than one language, and that on average between two and five languages were typically known per person (Romaine, 1989). It is expected, with globalization, that the numbers of bilinguals would have increased over the last decade. Circumstances for children vary across families and societies, but a common circumstance is that of immigrant parents. In such cases, one language is spoken at home, while another may be used in the dominant culture and in the schools. Another circumstance is where the community and the country are themselves bilingual environments.

In general, bilingualism is said to flourish in culturally plural societies and also in societies where acculturation is underway. For individuals concerned, the contexts and/or demands for developing proficiency in more than one language can vary. Such circumstances create complex environments for children's language development and experiences. The contexts and process of bilingual development can have some psychological implications for the individuals involved. It is also often the case that while some children learn two languages simultaneously, a second language is often learned later in life for older individuals. Issues of interest regarding bilingual development have often focused on the proficiency of the individual in each of the languages acquired, and the cognitive and social functioning of the bilingual individuals. Language is also important as a marker of cultural identity.

1.2.4 Development of cultural identity

Studying language development in the context of culture is important because, as pointed out above, it is a good indicator of cultural differences between societies or communities, and also one of the ways in which people assert their cultural identity. Cultural identity can however also include such things as ethnicity and religious beliefs. The development of children's cultural identity has been an active area of research for some time. Much of the work in this area has focused on areas such as nationality, ethnicity and gender. Various conceptual frameworks have been associated with work in this area. One approach in particular has been the cognitive-constructivist framework offering a domain-general approach to all social cognition (Aboud, 1988; Elkind, 1970; 1971).

There is evidence that children's understanding of group identity develops within a social context and is influenced by specific features of a culture. One form of group identity is through religious beliefs. Such beliefs have been a powerful focus for group identity throughout history. Most countries across the globe nowadays can be said to be multi-religious. This has mostly resulted from greater personal mobilization. However, relations between divergent religious groups have at times tended to be strained, sometimes leading to direct conflicts. How individuals come to hold such a strong sense of group identity and differentiation is clearly a subject for psychological enquiry. There is also some research into the effects of socialization on religious identity. This examines ways in which children acquire a sense of religious group membership.

Work in this area is relevant to our understanding of culture's influence on children's social development. For example, children born in a number of countries such as the United Kingdom today are entering a society which contains a greater proportion of people from minority groups than ever before. Most of these groups are categorized so by their religion. How children come to understand and evaluate other religions is of importance as it has implications for group relations. Children's understanding of different cultural and ethnic groups and the possible effects of this on group relations may ultimately influence problems of intercultural contact such as prejudice.

1.3 Summary and conclusions

The issues outlined above in relation to the psychological adjustment of children are further discussed and illustrated in the chapters that follow in this book. There are various ways in which culture can be constituted, and also in how it can be defined and studied. To illustrate this, different examples of the constitutions of culture are discussed: traditional, modern, ethnic background, religious affiliation and socio-economic status. A number of outcomes of such cultural factors are identified in social and cognitive functioning, language development, general outcomes in psychological adjustment (including self-esteem and mental health), and the development of cultural and ethnic identity. Each one of these outcomes illustrates culture's influence on the psychological development of children.

In this context, child-rearing practices have been studied as a mechanism for the psychological development of children and their socialization for adult life in different cultures. Such studies have focused on specific parenting practices and styles, and on environmental and contextual factors as determinants of such practices and parenting goals. Other studies have also identified ethnic factors as important determinants of such goals and practices. Psychological outcomes related to such practices have included personality attributes such as individualism or collectivism, the acquisition of the specific language of the community or society, and aspects of the social and cognitive development.

Research evidence illustrates various interactions between children's social-cognitive development and context, and supports the argument that it is important to examine children's thinking and its development in relation to the cultural tools that support the activities in which children engage. A mediator between culture and social as well as cognitive development is language. Research has examined the link between the acquisition of different languages and aspects of socio-cognitive functioning. Specifically, studies have focused on the possible influence of bilingualism, or the ability to speak more than one language, on social and cognitive development. Such studies suggest that language also has wider implications for the development of cultural identity. This and other aspects of cultural identity such as ethnicity and religious beliefs represent a range of psychological attributes for which the developing child is socialized. These issues are discussed fully in chapters that follow in this book.

FURTHER READING

Berry, J.W., Poortinga, Y.H., Segall, M.H., and Dasen, P.R. (2002). *Cross-cultural psychology: Research and applications.* Cambridge: Cambridge University Press.

Bronfenbrenner, U. (Ed.) (2005). *Making human beings human: Bioecological perspectives on human development.* London: Sage.

Göncü, A. (Ed.) (1999). *Children's engagement in the world: Sociocultural perspectives.* Cambridge: Cambridge University Press.

Rogoff, B. (2003). *The cultural nature of human development.* Oxford: Oxford University Press.

Whiting, B.B. and Edwards, C.P. (1992). *Children of different worlds: The formation of social behaviour.* Cambridge, MA: Harvard University Press.

REFERENCES

Aboud, F.E. (1988). *Children and prejudice.* London: Blackwell.

Berry, J.W., Poortinga, Y.H., Segall, M.H., and Dasen, P.R. (2002). *Cross-cultural psychology: Research and applications.* Cambridge: Cambridge University Press.

Brislin, R.W. (1990). Applied cross-cultural psychology: An introduction. In R.W. Brislin (Ed.), *Applied cross-cultural psychology.* Newbury Park, CA: Sage.

Bronfenbrenner, U. (1979). *The ecology of human development: Experiments by nature and by design.* Cambridge, MA: Harvard University Press.

Chapman, M. (1988). *Constructive evolution: Origins and development of Piaget's thought.* Cambridge: Cambridge University Press.

Cole, M. (1992). Culture in development. In M.H. Bornstein and M.E. Lamb (Eds), *Developmental psychology: An advanced textbook.* (pp. 731–789). Hillsdale, NJ: Lawrence Erlbaum.

Conger, R.D., Conger, K.J., Elder, G.J., Jr, Lorenz, F.O., Simons, R.L., and Whitbeck, L.B. (1992). A family process model of economic hardship and adjustment of early adolescent boys. *Child Development,* **63**, 527–541.

Conger, R.D., Patterson, G.R., and Ge, X. (1995). It takes two to replicate: A mediational model for the impact of parents' stress on adolescent adjustment. *Child Development*, **66**, 80–97.
Elkind, D. (1970). The origins of religion in the child. *Review of Religious Research*. **12**, 35–42.
Elkind, D. (1971). The development of religious understanding in children and adolescents. In M.P. Strommen (Ed.), *Research on religious development*. New York: Hawthorn Books.
Eysenck, M. (1998). *Psychology: An integrated approach.* Longman: London.
Freeman, M.A. (1997). Demographic correlates of individualism and collectivism: A study of social values in Sri Lanka. *Journal of Cross-Cultural Psychology*, **28**(3), 321–341.
Gauvain, M. (2001). Cultural tools, social interaction and the development of thinking. *Human Development*, **44**, 126–143.
Göncü, A. (Ed.) (1999). *Children's engagement in the world: Sociocultural perspectives.* Cambridge: Cambridge University Press.
Harkness, S. and Super, C.M. (1983). The cultural construction of child development: A framework for the socialisation of affect. *Ethos*, **11**(4), 221–231.
Hoff, E. (2006). How social contexts support and shape language development. *Developmental Review*, **26**, 55–88.
Javo, C., Rønning, J.A., and Heyerdahl, S. (2004). Child-rearing in an indigenous Sami population in Norway: A cross-cultural comparison of parental attitudes and expectations. *Scandinavian Journal of Psychology*, **45**, 67–78.
Lamb, M.E., Sternberg, K.J., Hwang, C.P., and Broberg, A.G. (1992). *Child care in context: Cross-cultural perspectives.* Hove and London: Lawrence Erlbaum.
Lemon, N. (1981). Language and learning: Some observations on the linguistic determination of cognitive processes. In B. Lloyd, and J. Gay (Eds), *Universals of human thought: Some African evidence.* Cambridge: Cambridge University Press.
LeVine, R.A. (1974). Parental goals: A cross-cultural view. *Teachers College Record*, **76**, 226–239.
Lourenço, O. and Machado, A. (1996). In defense of Piaget's theory: A reply to 10 common criticisms. *Psychological Review*, **103**(1), 143–164.
McGlaughlin, A. (1988). The developmental status of disadvantaged children at 2 1/2 years: The influence of life stress events and interactive experience. In E.J. Anthony and C. Chiland (Eds), *The child in his family. Vol 8: Perilous development: Child raising and identity formation under stress.* Oxford: John Wiley & Sons.

Ogbu, J.U. (1981). Origins of human competence: A cultural ethological perspective. *Child Development*, **52**, 413–429.

Ohannessian, S. and Kashoki, M. (Eds) (1978). *Language in Zambia*. London: International African Institute.

Piaget, J. (1952). *The origin of intelligence in the child.* London: Routledge and Kegan Paul.

Romaine, S. (1989). *Bilingualism*. Oxford: Blackwell.

Segall, M.H. (1984). More than we need to know about culture, but are afraid to ask. *Journal of Cross-Cultural Psychology*, **15**, 153–162.

Serpell, R. (1976). *Culture's influence on behaviour*. London: Methuen.

Shaffer, D.R. (1999). *Developmental psychology: Childhood and adolescence.* Fifth Edition. London: Brooks/Cole.

Super, C.M. and Harkness, S. (1986). The developmental niche: A conceptualisation at the interface of child and culture. *International Journal of Behavioural Development*, **9**, 545–569.

van der Vijver, F.J.R. and Poortinga, Y.H. (2002). On the study of culture in developmental science. *Human Development*, **45**(4), 246–256.

Vygotsky, L.S. (1978). *Mind in society: The development of higher psychological processes.* Cambridge, MA: Harvard University Press.

Vygotsky, L.S. (1986). *Thought and language.* Cambridge, MA: MIT Press.

Webster-Stratton, C. and Herbert, M. (1993). *Troubled families: Problem children.* New York: John Wiley & Sons.

Wertsch, J.V. and Tulviste, P. (1992). L.S. Vygotsky and contemporary developmental psychology. *Developmental Psychology*, **28**(4), 548–557.

Whiting, B.B. and Edwards, C.P. (1992). *Children of different worlds: The formation of social behaviour.* Cambridge, MA: Harvard University Press.

Approaches to Studying Human Development in Diverse Cultures

Dabie Nabuzoka

OUTLINE

2.1 Introduction
    2.1.1 What is culture?
    2.1.2 Summary on the concept of culture
2.2 Cultural perspectives on human development
    2.2.1 Cross-cultural psychology
    2.2.2 Cultural psychology
    2.2.3 Indigenous psychology
    2.2.4 Summary on cultural perspectives
2.3 Models and theories of development
    2.3.1 Ecological model
    2.3.2 Ecological niche model
    2.3.3 Cultural-context model
    2.3.4 Ecological-transactional model
    2.3.5 Summary on models and theories
2.4 Methodological approaches
    2.4.1 Quantitative methods
    2.4.2 Qualitative methods
    2.4.3 Summary on methodological approaches
2.5 Summary and conclusions
Further reading
References

2.1 Introduction

We saw in Chapter 1 that there is now a general recognition that cultural experience is fundamental to the study of psychological functioning. The questions that arise are the following: How can we explain the ways in which such experiences, in their diversity, come to influence development? How can we study these influences? In this chapter, I discuss various theoretical and methodological approaches relevant to the study of culture's influence on human development. I start with a discussion of the concept of culture and how it can be applied to human development. Various ways of conceptualizing culture are first discussed. Different historical traditions of studying culture in developmental psychology are then identified: these include specialized branches of psychology known as cross-cultural psychology and cultural psychology. More recently, there has been a focus on so-called indigenous perspectives in developmental psychology, especially as concerns research in this area. I will outline and discuss the goals of each approach in terms of their theoretical underpinnings and also the implications for methods used in carrying out research. This is followed by an outline and discussion of various theories and models of human development that incorporate a cultural perspective in developmental psychology. In the final part of the chapter, I will focus on discussing methodological approaches to studying culture's influence on development highlighting some of the key issues informing such approaches.

2.1.1 What is culture?

There are various definitions of culture reflecting differing theories for understanding, or criteria for evaluating human activities. One conception of culture as it relates to development is that it can be seen as a way of life for a society, including the behaviours, values, ways of life, arts, beliefs and symbols that people of the society accept, generally without thinking about them, and that are passed along through communication and imitation from one generation to the next. In behavioural terms, culture constitutes the sum of the learned behaviour of a group of people that constitutes their tradition that is passed down generations. For the individual, culture is cultivated behaviour that includes the totality of the person's learned and accumulated experience that is socially transmitted. A key point here is that these attributes of what constitutes culture are passed on to the young of a given society.

Culture thus consists of patterns of behaviour, and for behaviour, which can be explicit or implicit and are acquired and transmitted by symbols that constitute such things as language, counting systems, art and so on. The use of symbols is considered to constitute the distinctive achievement of human groups, including their embodiments in artefacts. At the core of culture are the traditional ideas and especially their attached values. In this sense, culture can be considered as representing ways of thinking that distinguishes members of one group or category of people from another. Implicit in this view of culture is the notion of 'cultural determinism', the view that the ideas, meanings, beliefs and values that people learn as members of society determines human nature. Members of different cultural groups would therefore be expected to think, feel and act differently, amongst other attributes. Children of a given culture are thus seen as being socialized to acquire those attributes. This notion of cultural determinism is discussed further in Chapter 6 in relation to the role of language in the development of thought processes.

Brislin (1990) refers to the term culture as including recurring patterns of behaviour that differ from place to place. These patterns are observable generation after generation within these places, with adults having the responsibility of ensuring that members of new generations adopt those recurring patterns of behaviour that mark people as well socialized individuals. The places within which these patterns of behaviour occur are often countries, or 'a locate with its own norms that exists within a large and highly functionalised country' (Brislin, 1990, p. 10). Brislin (1990) goes on to explain culture as referring 'to widely shared ideals, values, formation and uses of categories, assumptions about life, and goal-directed activities that become unconsciously or subconsciously accepted as "right" and "correct" by people who identify themselves as members of a society' (p. 11). The society in this case can be a country, a more delimited segment of society (such as class or socio-economic status), an ethnic group within a country or other groups with which people can have strong emotional ties.

A number of features of a culture are outlined by Brislin (1990). These include the following:

1. Parts of the environment made by people;
2. Ideas that are transmitted from one generation to another by members of the older generation;
3. Identifiable childhood experiences that lead to the internalization of cultural values;

4. Socialization experiences which, if successful, lead to the children eventually becoming accepted members of adult society;
5. Factors that are not frequently discussed, but rather taken for granted;
6. Concepts and practices that remain despite mistakes of slip-ups; and
7. Characteristics for which attempts at change are likely to be met with some resistance.

Thus, as the part of the environment that people make, culture consists of both visible and physical elements such as houses, and the less visible norms associated with the physical elements. The less visible concepts, values, categories, norms and assumptions about life are subjective and affect behaviour. The transmission of ideas from generation to generation is achieved by such people as parents, teachers, widely respected elders and so on, mostly without explicit instruction. These agents of the transmission of elements of culture, in the context of socialization, are often members of the older generations. Such socialization often leads to the internalization of cultural values, which can be identifiable by specific childhood experiences. Those children who have successfully internalized cultural values, through this process, eventually become accepted members of adult society.

Internalization of values, ideas, concepts and other elements of subjective culture leads to those cultural factors being taken for granted and not being frequently discussed within a society. Associated behaviours are therefore considered natural or normal and thus rarely questioned. There may be exceptions, such as when those behaviours that are strongly influenced by culture meet with or lead to problems, but the acceptance of the associated concepts and practices generally remain even in the face of such 'mistakes or slipups' (Brislin, 1990). The values, ideas and concepts that are strongly associated with a culture therefore exist for long periods, and are unlikely to change quickly even with the most intensive interventions. Attempts at implementing practices that represent cultural change are thus likely to be either ignored at best, or met with stiff resistance.

2.1.2 Summary on the concept of culture

In summary, culture includes all the behaviours, ways of life, arts, beliefs, values, symbols and institutions of a society or population that are passed down from generation to generation. It is a way of life that people of the society accept, generally without thinking about it. Culture includes parts of the environment that people make.

Psychological aspects of these parts include ideas that are transmitted from generation to generation by members of the older generation, as a part of the process of socialization. Such socialization involves identifiable childhood experiences that often lead to the internalization of cultural values. Successful socialization experiences result in the children eventually becoming accepted members of adult society. Internalized cultural values are not frequently discussed, but rather taken for granted. In addition, concepts and practices that are strongly influenced by culture remain despite instances where they may be questioned and as such attempts at cultural change are likely to be met with some resistance.

2.2 Cultural perspectives on human development

The study of the influence of culture on human development in psychology was for some time associated with cross-cultural psychology. Historically, the perspective of cross-cultural psychology tended to dominate research from the early to mid-twentieth century, renewed interest in cultural psychology emerging towards the end of the twentieth century. This development was characterized by a conceptual distinction between cross-cultural and cultural psychology, reflecting contrasting views about the role of culture in psychological theory and the goals of research that focused on culture. While cultural psychology has been a relatively recent development, this is now being followed by the emergence of the so-called indigenous psychology movement. All these perspectives share a common desire to give a greater role to culture in psychological theory and research and to uncover respects in which existing theories may need to be broadened or revised to account for alternative modes of psychological functioning (Berry, 2000; Greenfield, 2000; Shweder, 2000; Yang, 2000). However, each of these approaches has specific goals with particular theoretical underpinnings and implications for methods used in carrying out research. These will be briefly outlined and discussed in the sections below, where key features of each approach are outlined including its goals and the benefits of using that particular approach.

2.2.1 Cross-cultural psychology

According to Berry, Poortinga, Segall and Dasen (2002), 'Cross-cultural psychology is the study of similarities and differences in individual psychological functioning in various cultural and ethnic groups;

of the relationships between psychological variables and sociocultural, ecological and biological variables; and of current changes in these variables' (p. 3). This definition, according to Berry et al. (2002), suggests the following goals of cross-cultural psychology:

1. to test the generality of existing psychological knowledge and theories;
2. to explore and discover psychological variations in different cultures; and
3. to generate a nearly universal psychology valid for a broader range of cultures.

In the first instance, cross-cultural psychology was seen as a means of discovering the degree to which knowledge of behaviour and basic processes obtained in one cultural setting is representative of humanity in general, or whether it is representative only of the cultural setting in which the original work was done. Work towards this 'transport and test' goal (Berry and Dasen, 1974) involved psychologists seeking to transport their present hypotheses and findings, which were often generated in their own culture, to other cultural settings so as to test their applicability. The eventual aim was to find out the extent to which such hypotheses were applicable to all groups of human beings.

There was recognition, however, that such an approach may not be sensitive to other psychological phenomena particularly important in the culture to which findings of the original culture are being tested. It was considered that in pursuing the goal of testing the generality of psychological knowledge and theories, limits to the generality of such existing knowledge may be found. Therefore, the second goal of cross-cultural psychology was to focus on extending the range of observable variables (Whiting, 1968), and finding contrasts in cultural variables not found within the limited experience of the investigator's own culture (Berry and Dasen, 1974; Berry et al., 2002; Strodtbeck, 1964). Thus, cross-cultural research has been seen as also facilitating the discovery and focus on studying novel categories of psychological experience.

The third goal of cross-cultural psychology has been to integrate the information from the first two goals (i.e. involving transporting and testing psychological knowledge and perspectives to other cultures; and exploring with a view to discover new aspects of phenomena in other cultures) into a broader psychology to generate a more nearly universal psychology, 'one that has pan-human validity' (Segall,

Lonner and Berry, 1998). The belief in this subdiscipline of psychology is that eventually the underlying psychological processes that are characteristic of all humans will be discovered. The rationale for such an expectation has been based on the existence of universals in other disciplines such as biology, linguistics, sociology and anthropology. As Berry et al. (2002) put it:

> Our belief is based upon the existence of such universals in related disciplines...in biology there are well-established pan species primary needs (such as eating, drinking, sleeping)...In sociology there are universal sets of relationships (such as dominance); in linguistics there are universal features of language (such as grammatical rules); and in anthropology there are universal customs and institutions (such as tool making and the family). In psychology it is therefore plausible...that we will also discover universals of human behaviour...(p. 4)

Extensive research has been conducted over time in pursuance of these goals in cross-cultural psychology. Contributions to this field have been from such areas as the study of perception, cognition, motivation, interpersonal interaction and group dynamics. Case Study 1 illustrates the type of research that has been conducted within the tradition of cross-cultural psychology and the theoretical perspectives represented.

CASE STUDY 1: CROSS-CULTURAL STUDY OF PERCEPTUAL SKILLS IN CHILDREN

In the late 1960s and early 1970s, psychological theories explained perceptual and attentional changes with age in Western populations solely as indices of central processes in cognitive development. Thus, when evidence accumulated that African respondents performed less well on such tasks as pattern reproduction (involving paper and pencil or block design) than Western respondents of similar age, theoretical explanations were advanced on possible broader differences between African and Western respondents in underlying cognitive structures or processes. These were in turn related to environmental contingencies, such as socialization practices (Vernon, 1967; Witkin and Berry, 1975). Serpell (1971) suggested that such age-related changes and cross-cultural differences arose from *specific perceptual experiences* afforded by Western instructional practices both at home and in school.

> ### CASE STUDY 1 (cont'd)
>
> To test the specific experience explanation, Serpell (1979) designed a study comparing English and Zambian children on tasks containing a number of similar patterns represented in different perceptual media, which the children had to reproduce. Four different categories of tasks were designed such that one drew on a universal pattern of experience (positioning one's own hands), a second drew on experience more readily available to urban English children (drawing with pencil on paper), a third drew on experience more readily available to urban Zambian children (constructing models with strips of pliable wire), and the fourth drawing equally on two similar domains of experiences, one of which was more readily available to the English sample, while the other was more readily available to the Zambian sample (constructing models with plasticine and with clay respectively). It was predicted, on the basis of the specific experience hypothesis, that the samples would not differ in performance on the first and last of these tasks, and that English children would excel on the drawing task while Zambian children would excel on the wire modelling task.
>
> The findings were consistent with the specific experience hypothesis in that when the patterns were reproduced as wire models, the Zambian children excelled the British, and when the patterns were reproduced by drawing, the British children excelled the Zambian. No reliable cross-cultural differences were found when the patterns were reproduced as plasticine models or as configurations of hand positions. Both cultural groups were equally adversely affected when required to perform the modelling tasks or hand-positions task blindfolded.
>
> Serpell (1979) interpreted the findings as suggesting that cross-cultural differences in performance of pattern reproduction tasks reflected different sets of highly specific perceptual skills rather than differences on broader cognitive variables such as practical intelligence. These skills, it was argued, reflected the children's experiences demonstrated in activities in which they were typically frequently involved.

The main concerns of cross-cultural psychology are thus with testing the generality of existing psychological theories and discovering new phenomena in diverse cultural contexts, and with developing a universal model to predict behaviour on a worldwide scale. Within this tradition, culture is conceptualized as an independent variable that impacts on the level of development or on the display of psychological processes considered as a dependent variable. Work within the framework of cross-cultural psychology has focused not only on the validation of the claims to universality of existing psychological theories through subjecting them to cross-cultural testing, but also on using the naturally occurring variation in social environments to assess a wider range of environmental effects.

2.2.2 Cultural psychology

The goal of cultural psychology is the identification of mechanisms or processes that account for particular developmental outcomes. This approach differs from the essentially comparative approach of cross-cultural psychology as it takes a more emic perspective focused on developmental processes. It aims at an understanding of the significance of certain practices in a given culture. Questions of interest in this respect would include why people of a given culture may act in a particular way in given situations. According to this perspective, and in relation to its role in children's development, culture has been 'conceptualised as a system of meanings that provides the context for children's development as one of its constituents rather than a variable that exerts an influence on children's development' (Göncü, 1999, p. 10).

As a field of study, cultural psychology has been growing since the early 1990s (Bruner, 1990; Cole, 1990). It is a multi and interdisciplinary field but essentially occupies the middle ground between psychology and anthropology. Some of its roots can be identified from the earlier work of Luria (1976), Mead (1934) and Vygotsky (1962). Arising also from the growing subdisciplines of psychological and cognitive anthropology, cultural psychology is considered to have developed out of a dissatisfaction with 'psychology's universalistic model of human development' (Shweder, 1990), cross-cultural psychology's treatment of culture as an independent variable rather than as a process (Greenfield, 1997), and what has been considered as psychology's ethnocentric logic. Within psychology, there are a number of fields of investigation which are included in or overlap with cultural psychology.

'Culture', in cultural psychology, is seen, both in focus and definition, to encompass beliefs, traditions and ideologies with respect to such collective categories as age cohort, gender, ethnic identity and so on (Kuper, 1999). The study of meaning is considered central to cultural psychology and leans on the interpretive side of psychology. Thus, it is considered to be of utmost importance to understand meaning from the participant's point of view. The practices that individuals engage in are seen as meaningful to them and with particular reference to the contexts in which they occur. The task therefore, according to this perspective, is to identify the significance attached to particular activities by the people involved, and the rules that they apply in creating those meanings (Bruner, 1990).

Thus, a sociocultural approach to studying behaviour related to child development involves understanding how practices within a community relate to other aspects of the community's functioning such as arrangements for physical space, adult work roles, climate, as well as the values and goals regarding desired characteristics of community members. Included also are beliefs about the significance of practices as they relate to childrearing. Case Study 2 presents an example of a study on sleeping arrangements for infants in two cultural settings as an illustration of how one aspect of childcare practices is related to aspects of community functioning as well as being accompanied by particular beliefs about their significance.

CASE STUDY 2: SOCIOCULTURAL STUDY OF INFANTS' SLEEPING ARRANGEMENTS

In the United States and other Western societies, early night-time separation of infants from their parents has been considered essential for the infant's healthy psychological development. This widespread belief, especially amongst the middle- to upper-class families, has been associated with co-sleeping of infants and their parents not frequently occurring in the US middle class (Mandansky and Edelbrock, 1990). In many non-Western communities however, it is customary for infants to sleep with their mothers for the first few years of life either in the same bed or at least in the same room (Whiting and Edwards, 1992).

Morelli, Rogoff and Oppenheim (1992) were interested in the values expressed by parents from such different cultures regarding the consequences of children co-sleeping or sleeping apart. They examined differences between a US middle-class community and a non-Western (Mayan) community in sleeping arrangements of infants, including where the babies slept, night-time feeding and waking practices, and also parents' rationales for their infants' sleeping arrangements. They also examined practices that could be associated with sleeping arrangements, such as special activities around bedtime.

Morelli et al. (1992) found that all Mayan mothers slept in the same bed with their infants through the first year of life into the second year. Most of the toddlers slept in the same bed with their fathers. The pattern of feeding

> **CASE STUDY 2 (cont'd)**
>
> arrangements in the Mayan families was to nurse the infants on demand. This was achieved with minimal disruption to sleeping patterns of the mothers. There were neither bed time routines in the nightly transition to sleep nor any separate routine to coax the baby to sleep. None of the babies received a bedtime story or any special lullabies. US parents did not usually sleep in the same bed with their infants, instead, co-sleeping involved sharing a room with the newly born often placing their crib near the parent' bed. Almost all the mothers reported having to awake during night feedings. Bedtime events played a significant role in the organization of family evening activities, with most families engaging in routines such as story telling.
>
> When reflecting on the sleeping arrangements, most of the Mayan families considered their arrangements as the only reasonable way for babies and parents to sleep. The idea that toddlers are put to sleep in a separate room by US families was received with shock, disapproval and pity for the toddlers, and implied that such practice was tantamount to child neglect. The Mayans considered their own sleeping arrangements a matter of commitment to a relationship with their young children and not of practical considerations such as number of rooms in the house.
>
> US parents, however, chose to sleep near their newborn infants for reasons that were pragmatic (such as the need to nurse them and the convenience of being nearer), but also developmental and affectionate. The majority of parents sleeping near their babies felt that this helped foster the development of an affectionate tie between them. In all, encouraging independence during infancy seemed to be an important goal for many US families who believed that sleeping apart helped train children to be independent.

Cultural psychology is thus different from cross-cultural (comparative) psychology in terms of approaches to studying influences on development and the predominant methods used. For example, one perspective of cultural psychology considers culture in terms of the creation of an environment to which children (as young organisms) are provided conditions for optimal growth. Thus, in one respect, culture is regarded as a medium for development (Cole, 1992). This represents a molar approach to the study of environmental influences on human development. The approach of cross-cultural psychology, however, is more molecular. Here, the interest is not on culture in its totality as such but on the relationship between behaviour and elements of culture (e.g., socialization, ecological features, etc.). It has been pointed out that, in this approach, identifying cross-cultural differences amounts to identifying cultural elements behind the differences (Segall, 1984; van de Vijver and Poortinga, 2002).

2.2.3 Indigenous psychology

Indigenous psychology has been described as a set of approaches to understanding human behaviour within the cultural contexts in which they have developed and are currently displayed. In addition, they have been described as attempts to root psychological research in the conceptual systems that are indigenous to a culture, including the philosophical, theological and scientific ideas that are part of the historical and contemporary lives of people and their institutions (Allwood and Berry, 2006a; 2006b). According to Miller and Chen (2000), 'indigenous psychological approaches share a concern with understanding developmental processes in terms of concepts, norms, values, practices, and life circumstances found in particular cultural settings' (p. 1).

The rationale for advocating indigenous approaches in developmental psychology has included a number of concerns about the theoretical and empirical bases of existing approaches in the discipline (Nsamenang, 2000; Sinha, 1997). For example, Nsamenang (2000) pointed out that the database and norms regarding human development in mainstream psychology are based largely on limited and unrepresentative samples from highly industrialized nations. As such, the discipline cannot claim to be universal and scientific. In addition, non-Western perspectives are few and are rarely incorporated in the discipline in terms of its paradigms and key concepts. A key argument is therefore that psychology as a discipline has been dominated by the Euro-American image of childhood without any questioning of its relevance to realities and interests in non-Western contexts.

According to Nsamenang (2000), indigenous developmental psychology involves the study of changes in both biological and psychological attributes that define an individual in a particular context, and the processes and principles that are involved. Culture is seen as central to this as humans are biologically disposed to acquire, create and transmit culture, and also because development is mediated by the curricula cultures offer to the young. As such, the emphasis is on the understanding that is rooted in the given ecology and culture, with psychological theory being culturally grounded together with the methods and assessment tools used (Nsamenang, 1994; 2000). In addition, there is emphasis on the need for sensitivity to, and assessment of, contextual conditions (Craik and Feimer, 1987; Nsamenang, 2000). Thus, the conceptual and methodological emphasis of indigenous developmental work is on development-in-context.

Indigenous developmental work is therefore seen as an account of the discourse of how a particular ecoculture imprints onto human psychological development. Such accounts, it is argued, portray a different image of development because a world view, such as that of Sub-Saharan Africa (Nsamenang, 1992), entails a psychological frame different from that of contemporary developmental psychology (Nsamenang, 2000; Serpell, 1994). Case Study 3 illustrates how perspectives on psychological constructs such as 'intelligence' and 'competence' can reflect the cultural context of children's development.

CASE STUDY 3: AN INDIGENOUS PERSPECTIVE ON DEVELOPMENT AND COMPETENCE

One argument for examining the psychology indigenous to non-Western cultures when studying socialization practices is that the behaviour of caregivers is influenced by their ideas (or theories) about the nature of childhood and how they can influence a child's development (Serpell, 1993; Super and Harkness, 1986). While the goal of socialization is the development of competence in the young, there are different notions of what constitutes competence across cultures (Keller, 2003). In this respect, Serpell (1993) saw the task as one requiring specifying an appropriate perspective for interpreting children's development in a given community. In other words, specifying what actually counted as competent behaviour and therefore a successful outcome of socialization.

Serpell (1977; 1993) and other local colleagues focused on a rural eastern Zambian community of the Chewa in an attempt to generate an account of development and competence that made sense in the context of the children's community. They focused on the notion of intelligence, and in order to find out what this entailed in this African community, they asked adults who were familiar with a group of children to select one among them for each of a series of ecologically valid tasks the completion of which could be regarded as displaying competent behaviour. They also examined the terms and expressions used by

> **CASE STUDY 3 (cont'd)**
>
> the adults to describe what would constitute intelligence or intelligent behaviour.
>
> Serpell found that the term *nzeru* had some features in common with the English concept of 'intelligence', but also appeared to have three other dimensions corresponding roughly with the domains covered in English by 'wisdom', 'cleverness' and 'responsibility'. Social harmony was found to be a fundamental dimension of intelligence among the community studied. Thus, while cognitive skills such as observational skills and memory were included in this concept of intelligence, there was also an emphasis on social skills such as obligations and responsibility, honesty, politeness, obedience and respect. Such a conception of intelligence, though with some overlap with that of Western technological societies, was embedded in the culture of the Chewa community.

Developmental psychologists such as Nsamenang (2000) 'acknowledge the contributions of cultural and cross-cultural psychologists to the spirit of indigenous psychology, but regard both as limited and limiting in effectively addressing the emics of non-dominant cultures' (p. 2). It is argued, for example, that a comparative approach such as that applied in cross-cultural psychology contributes little insight into understanding human development in non-Western contexts, when it essentially sets out to validate, extend or expand Western theories or concepts. Such an orientation of the comparative approach is seen as one that trivializes and masks the real nature of the target phenomena in the non-Western context. In this sense, scientific justification for cross-cultural psychological comparison is only seen as feasible when systematic baseline developmental data have been collected, in a way that sensitively draws on indigenous ethnotheories and life-circumstances from diverse cultures and societies. Indigenous researchers are considered essential in efforts at collecting such baseline data as they can contribute to the description of variations in cultural curricula as well as cultural supports for human development (Sta, Maria, 2000).

2.2.4 Summary on cultural perspectives

Traditions of studying culture in developmental psychology include cross-cultural psychology (Berry et al., 2002) and cultural psychology

(Cole, 1992; Göncü, 1999). A more recent theoretical perspective that has gained prominence is that of indigenous psychologies (Sinha, 1997). These approaches to studying cultural influences are not necessarily mutually exclusive but share an emphasis on the role of the context of development in terms of the physical and social environment, and also of the various structures and systems of society. For example, the study of culture as a medium for child development (a perspective of cultural psychology) does not preclude cultural comparisons (a key feature of cross-cultural psychology). In all, a discussion of the role of culture in development is essentially concerned with the role of the environment, both social and physical, in developmental processes.

2.3 Models and theories of development

Various models have been proposed to explain the interrelationships between cultural factors and the developing individual. These include Bronfenbrenner's (1979) ecological model, Super and Harkness's (1986) ecological niche model, Cole's (1992) cultural-context model and the ecological-transactional model proposed by Sameroff and Chandler (1975; Sameroff, 1987). We will outline each one of these in turn.

2.3.1 Ecological model

The ecological model of human development was developed by Bronfenbrenner (1977; 1979; 2005). The approach was defined as,

> ...the scientific study of the progressive, mutual accommodation, throughout the life span, between a growing human organism and the changing immediate environments in which it lives, as this process is affected by relations obtaining within and between these immediate settings, as well as the larger social contexts, both formal and informal, in which the settings are embedded. (Bronfenbrenner, 1977, p. 514)

The ecological environment is seen as a nested arrangement of structures (see Figure 2.1).

The first set of systems is the *microsystem*. This is seen as a complex set of relations between the developing person and environment in an immediate setting containing that person (e.g., parents, friends, etc.). Such a setting is defined as a place with particular physical features in which the participants engage in particular activities and roles (e.g., daughter, parent, teacher, etc.) for particular periods: elements

42 CULTURE AND PSYCHOLOGICAL DEVELOPMENT

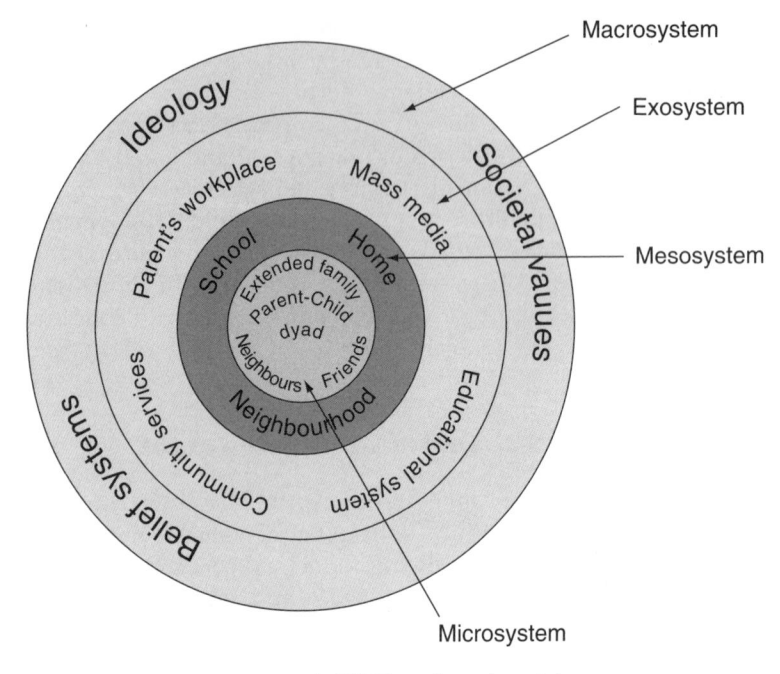

Figure 2.1 Bronfenbrenner's (1979) ecological model

of a setting include the place, time, physical features, activity, participants and role being engaged in. Microsystems are thus made up of the more intimate relationships in the family, but also other significant social contacts of everyday life such as members of the extended family, neighbours and so on. Each microsystem comprises a pattern of activities, roles and relationships which are experienced in a particular setting with specified physical and material characteristics.

The interrelations between two or more of these settings make up the *mesosystems*, such as relations between home, school and neighbourhood. Such interrelations among major settings contain the developing person at a particular point in his/her life. Thus, for a particular child, the mesosystem would encompass interactions among family, school, peer group and so on. In all, a mesosystem is a system of microsystems.

Mesosystems are nested within an *exosystem*, which is an extension of the mesosystem and embraces other specific social structures, both formal and informal. These other social structures do not themselves contain the developing person but impinge upon or encompass the immediate settings in which that person is found, and thereby influence what goes on there. These structures include the major institutions of the society, both deliberately structured and spontaneously evolving, as they operate at a concrete local level. They include, among other structures, the world of work, the neighbourhood, the mass media, agencies of government (local and national), the distribution of goods and services, communication and transportation facilities and informal social networks.

Thus, the exosystem consists of social settings in which the developing child does not participate directly but which, however, influence the child indirectly, often through their influence on the parents. Examples of these are the parents' workplaces, the mass media and the educational system. Thus, as Empson (Chapter 4) points out, parents' working conditions, such as shift work, affect the amount of time they can spend with their children. However, the level of unemployment within a society, which impacts most strongly on the unskilled worker and his family, will also have an influence on family finances and well-being of family members.

The larger structure of these systems is the *macrosystem*. This refers to the overarching institutional patterns of the culture or subculture, which include economic, social, educational, legal and political systems, which are manifested in micro-, meso- and exosystems. According to Bronfenbrenner (1977; 2005), macrosystems can be conceived and examined not only in structural terms but also as carriers of information and ideology that, both explicitly and implicitly, endow meaning and motivation to particular agencies, social networks, roles, activities and their interrelations. The place or priority that children and those responsible for their care have in such macrosystems is seen to be of special importance in determining how a child and his/her caretakers are treated, influenced, and interact with each other in different types of settings (Bronfenbrenner, 1986).

The macrosystem is the most distant from the child, being the belief systems and ideologies of the culture, which constitutes a pervasive set of values around which societal life is organized. Although Bronfenbrenner described one 'macrosystem' as characterizing society with a single culture, it is probably more accurate to think of modern societies as constituting a number of 'macrosystems' representing different subcultures, whether described by political allegiance, religion, region, ethnicity or income (see Chapter 4).

In summary, Bronfenbrenner's (1979) ecological model regards the developing child as being exposed to a network of influences. It emphasizes the reciprocal transactions between the child and different aspects of the environment, thus the importance of studying the child in context, the ecological approach. The child is viewed as a part of a number of systems with differing degrees of involvement of the child and together these comprise the ecological environment. This view of development is a complex and dynamic one with the relationships between the child and the environmental contexts in which s/he participates being multi-dimensional. Children growing up within the same society will be influenced in different ways as personal experiences will be filtered through the different contexts, people and relationships of the other systems. Part of this will be through the different ways in which children are socialized which will vary widely in different locations and families.

2.3.2 Ecological niche model

According to Super and Harkness (2002), one way to examine the processes by which culture affects the course of development is to conceive culture as the organization of the developmental environment. Super and Harkness (1986) introduced the concept of the 'developmental niche' as a theoretical framework for studying cultural regulation of the microenvironment of the child. The conceptual framework tries to describe the environment 'from the point of view of the child in order to understand processes of development and acquisition of culture' (Super and Harkness, 1986, p. 552). The developmental niche has three components, which are seen as operational subsystems: the physical and social settings in which the child lives; the customs of childcare and childrearing which are seen as being historically constituted; and the psychology of the caretakers, particularly parental ethnotheories, which play a directive role and are shared with the community (Super and Harkness, 2002). These components are seen as integrated subsystems of the niche, each with its own set of relations to the larger environment.

According to Super and Harkness (1986; 2002), the most important way in which culture influences child development is by providing the physical and social settings. One feature of these settings is that they are frequented by people who are seen as especially formative of social behaviours as they determine the kind of interactions that children have the opportunity and the need to practice. Thus, in one context of an extended family, these social settings may be exemplified by the immediate availability of a variety of caretakers such as older siblings, aunties, grandparents and so on, who provide the developing infant with a range of nurturant social experiences. Similarly, institutions such as formal schools affect the child in terms of the age and sex of those with whom s/he interacts.

Super and Harkness (1986) point out that features of the physical settings can include the existence of infectious pathogens and parasites, or the physical availability of adequate nutrients. These can be critical and will shape the growing child's experience at the most basic level, slowing, terminating or altering the process of biological growth. Aspects of the physical setting are mediated by cultural adaptations in practices of childcare. For example, the presence of various objects in the immediate vicinity of the child, some of which may be dangerous to the child, will prompt accommodations in techniques of care, which would include closeness of supervision. Thus, parents and other caretakers adapt the customs of childcare to the ecological and cultural settings in which they are situated. Such adaptations are made within the constraints of technological and human resources that are available at a given time.

The customs and practices of childcare and childrearing are therefore behavioural strategies for dealing with children. These practices are moderated by the particular ages of the children, and the environmental constraints. The customs are sequences of behaviour that are commonly used by members of a particular community. Such uses are seen as integrated thoroughly into the larger culture to the extent that they are rarely questioned or given conscious thought by members of the culture, but regarded as normal ways of doing things. In all, the customs and practices of childcare and childrearing are seen as historically constituted ways of coping with developmental issues best regarded as adaptations to the larger environment. Thus, they would have been developed over a period and evolved as acceptable ways of bringing up children.

The final component of the developmental niche is what has been referred to as 'the psychology of the caretakers'. This includes beliefs and values about the significance of the child-rearing customs and practices of the culture. They include parental *ethnotheories* of child behaviour and development. According to Super and Harkness (1986), 'most important among the ethnotheories are beliefs about the nature and needs of children, parental and community goals for rearing, and caretaker beliefs about effective rearing techniques' (p. 556). The psychology of the caretakers, is shared with the community and plays a directive role in organizing parental strategies of childrearing in both the immediate and long term. These strategies are moderated by the physical environment, available technology, customs of childcare and the demands of parents' own activities.

Three organizational aspects of the niche are identified as creating particularly important developmental outcomes (Super and Harkness,

2002): *contemporary redundancy*, which is the mutually reinforcing repetition of similar influences from several parts of the environment during the same period of development; *thematic elaboration*, which is the repetition and cultivation over time of core symbols and systems of meaning; and *chaining*, in which no single element of the environment is sufficient in kind to produce a particular outcome, but the linking of disparate elements creates a qualitatively new phenomenon. Thus, according to Super and Harkness (1986), 'regularities within and among the subsystems, and thematic continuities and progressions across the niches of childhood provides material from which the child abstracts the social, affective and cognitive rules of the culture' (p. 565). In addition, there is a more complex set of second-order effects; sex and temperament, for example, are characteristics whose meaning and consequence are organized by features of the environment.

2.3.3 Cultural-context model

Different approaches to studying human development put different emphasis on the relationships between the developing individual and environment. Cole (1992) identified four such approaches: biological maturation, environmental learning, interactional and cultural-contextual. In the *biological maturation* approach, the environment is only relevant in so far as it provides opportunities for the developing individual to exercise skills that unfold and become available at certain moments in the maturation process. The *environmental learning* approach, in contrast, is characterized by the predominant influence of the environment in shaping development. The third, *interactional*, approach combines input from the child and the environment to produce developmental outcomes. According to Cole (1999), a common feature of these three approaches is that they imply a dualism in which developmental outcome is a function of the contribution of both the child and the environment. This dualism is addressed by the *cultural-contextual* approach. This approach blends the person and the environment, with culture being the meeting point of the two.

Both the interactional and the cultural-contextual approaches are based on the interaction of the organism and the environment. The main difference is the nature of the interaction; whereas in the interactional model the developmental outcome is seen as a mechanistic function of the input from both, the cultural-context model reflects a dynamic interaction where the outcome is not simply related to the input. In this model, environmental factors and biological factors interact indirectly through the medium of culture. According to Cole

(1992), the cultural-context approach offers the best model of the complexities that are found in the study of development in culture.

2.3.4 Ecological-transactional model

Sameroff and Chandler (1975) presented a model of development as a two way process involving reciprocal interactions over time between the active child and an active environment. The model presents a 'transactional' view of development as dynamic and constantly changing, such that discontinuity between developmental stages can also be expected (Sameroff, 1987). Both the child and environment make independent contributions to development and provide the impetus for change. Thus, internal influences (biological and psychological characteristics of the child) and external influences (physical and social aspects of the environment) can provide the impetus for development, including some discontinuities. For example, developmental difficulties may be overcome if the child is brought up in a favourable home environment. On the other hand, children brought up in conditions of socio-economic disadvantage may continue to exhibit developmental difficulties throughout childhood (Empson and Nabuzoka, 2004, see also Chapter 4).

According to the ecological-transactional model, the contributions of individuals and environments to development are determined by a number of factors. For the developing individual, this is determined by their stage of physical and psychological development. The contribution of the environment is such that it is structured and organized so that the rules of the culture and particular social groups prescribe specific behaviours and roles for individuals at different phases of development.

2.3.5 Summary on models and theories

Various theoretical models that have been proposed to explain the interrelationships between cultural factors and the developing individual include Bronfenbrenner's (1979) ecological model, Super and Harkness's (1986) ecological niche model, Cole's (1992) cultural-context model and Sameroff and Chandler's (1975) ecological-transactional model. These models or theoretical perspectives have been refined and further developed over the years, but share a common concern with the influence of contextual factors (physical and social) on the developing individual. The differences lie in the emphasis placed on particular aspects of the child's environment and the interrelationships between them on the one hand, and with the developing child on the other.

2.4 Methodological approaches

The question of how the influence of culture on human development can be studied is related to the ideas that investigators have about the nature of development in general and the specific ways that cultural factors play a role in that development. On the whole, developmental psychology and general psychology have similar debates about methodology which is reflected in such terms as idiographic versus nomothetic, subjective versus objective and qualitative versus quantitative methodology. The contrast between quantitative and qualitative methods has been particularly significant in studies on the role of culture in development. Some polarization of this debate is reflected in the fact that quantitative approaches are prevalent in culture-comparative cross-cultural psychology whereas qualitative methods dominate cultural research. Advocates on indigenous psychologies have opted for a mixture of approaches, though qualitative methods still dominate. We will outline each of these approaches in the subsections below.

2.4.1 Quantitative methods

Quantitative approaches in the study of child development have their origins in methods used in the natural sciences. In following this 'scientific method', researchers have been concerned with the need to obtain 'objective data' and carry out quantitative analyses that will produce accurate descriptions of behaviour that lead to explanations of the phenomena of interest. The researchers are also required to provide precise descriptions of materials and procedures used to enable other researchers to replicate their study should they wish to do so. At each stage of the research process, precautions are taken against bias.

The underlying assumption of the scientific approach is that there is an objective reality in the world that can be observed, measured and categorized. These assumptions reflect what has been referred to as the positivist approach, whereby psychologists adhering to it carry out carefully planned observations of people. The findings of such studies are evaluated according to agreed criteria which include concepts of reliability and validity. Reliability in this sense refers to whether the same results can be obtained if the study was carried out by another person, or on another occasion. Validity has to do with whether the research (especially the instruments used) really assess what they are intended to measure. The overall intention of this approach is to establish the extent to which the findings of a study can be generalized to other populations and other settings. It is easy to see, from this, how this approach fits in with one goal of cross-cultural psychology, which is to work towards a near universal theory of human development (Berry, 1989). However, the issues involved are more complex than that.

One criticism of this approach has been that it imposes the researcher's ideas on the participants about what is to be studied or measured and how that is to be done. An example would be the requirement to summarize one's responses in a questionnaire or, within that, a point on some numerical scale. It is argued that the responses from participants may not be the same in a different and less controlled situation. Such arguments have given rise to the more qualitative approaches favoured by cultural psychologists.

2.4.2 Qualitative methods

Qualitative research methods reflect a different emphasis in the way psychologists conduct research from that of the quantitative approach. It is argued that these methods, through a process that can be both inductive and deductive, allow the understanding of the rules that people have for making sense of their worlds, which are often specific to various domains of enquiry. As we saw earlier, the study of meaning is central to cultural psychology. This perspective leans on the interpretive side of psychology. Thus, it is considered to be of utmost importance to understand meaning from the participant's point of view. According to Bruner (1990), cultural psychology 'seeks out the rules that human beings bring to bear in creating meanings in cultural contexts. These contexts are always *contexts of practice*. It is always necessary to ask what people are *doing* or *trying* to do in that context' (p. 118).

Qualitative methods have been historically prominent in cultural anthropology, whose main method has been ethnography. According to Berry et al. (2002), the goal of anthropology is 'to make sense out of narrations of informants and one's own observations in terms of a system of meanings or values' (p. 288). In psychology, qualitative methods include unstructured interviews, focus groups, non-scheduled observations and interpretative assessment methods where the meaning of the participant's responses is of importance. In qualitative methodology there is a slighting of experiments and measurement; reality is considered subjective, and the values of the researcher are seen as part of the research process. The focus of this approach is on the construction of meaning rather than on explaining behaviour and underlying psychological processes. Thus, authors in cultural psychology (and also in indigenous psychology) favour descriptive and interpretive methods that find their roots in the culture that is being studied. Such methods focus more on the influence of the context on people's behaviour. Examples here would be studies showing how children's performance may differ according to the social setting, the language used and meaningfulness of the situation.

2.4.3 Summary of methodological approaches

Debates about research methodology relevant to studies of the influence of culture on human development have often contrasted qualitative approaches with quantitative approaches; the former is dominant in cultural psychology whereas the latter is much more prevalent in cross-cultural psychology. Differences in choice of research methods largely reflect the goals of research conducted by the psychologists involved. Thus, researchers in cultural psychology and indigenous psychology favour descriptive and interpretive methods that find their roots in the culture that is being studied while those oriented more towards comparative cross-cultural psychology tend to be concerned more with the extent to which generalizations can be made across different populations and settings.

2.5 Summary and conclusions

It is generally recognized that cultural experience is fundamental to the study of psychological functioning. However, there are various ways of defining and conceptualizing culture and how it can be applied to human development. In addition, there are various theoretical and methodological approaches relevant to the study of culture's influence on human development, which reflect different historical traditions in developmental psychology: these have included specialized branches of psychology known as cross-cultural psychology, cultural psychology, and more recently, the so-called indigenous psychologies. Each one of these approaches has specific goals, theoretical underpinnings and implications for carrying out research. In addition to the different branches of psychology concerned with culture's influence on development, there are various models that incorporate a cultural perspective in developmental psychology. These include the ecological model, the ecological niche model, the cultural-context model and the ecological-transactional model. What these models share is an emphasis on the influence of a child's context on his/her development. Debates about methodology in investigating child development mirrors that in general psychology and has contrasted quantitative with qualitative methodology. The emphasis on a particular methodology largely reflects the theoretical underpinnings and goals of research in a particular area. Thus, some advocate for a mixture of approaches, depending on the research questions and focus of the studies (e.g., Nsamenang, 2000; van de Vijver, 2002).

FURTHER READING

Allwood, C.M. and Berry, J.W. (2006). Origins and development of indigenous psychologies: An international analysis. *International Journal of Psychology*, **41**(4), 243–268.

Berry, J.W., Poortinga, Y.H., Segall, M.H., and Dasen, P.R. (2002). *Cross-cultural psychology: Research and applications*. Cambridge: Cambridge University Press.

Cole, M. (1992). Culture in development. In M.H. Bornstein and M.E. Lamb (Eds), *Developmental psychology: An advanced textbook* (pp. 731–789). Hillsdale, NJ: Lawrence Erlbaum.

Greenfield, P.M. (2000). Three approaches to the study of culture: Where do they come from? Where can they go? *Asian Journal of Social Psychology*, **3**, 223–240.

Saraswathi, T.S. (2003). *Cross-cultural perspectives in human development: Theory, research and applications*. London: Sage.

Yang, K.S. (2000). Indigenous, cultural, and cross-cultural psychology: A theoretical, conceptual, and epistemological analysis. *Asian Journal of Social Psychology*, **3**, 265–288.

REFERENCES

Allwood, C.M. and Berry, J.W. (2006a). Special issue on indigenous psychologies. *International Journal of Psychology*, **41**(4), 241–242.

Allwood, C.M. and Berry, J.W. (2006b). Origins and development of indigenous psychologies: An international analysis. *International Journal of Psychology*, **41**(4), 243–268.

Berry, J. (1989). Imposed etics-emics-derived etics: The operationalization of a compelling idea. *International Journal of Psychology*, **24**, 721–735.

Berry, J.W. (2000). Cross-cultural psychology: A symbiosis of cultural and comparative perspectives. *Asian Journal of Social Psychology*, **3**, 207–223.

Berry, J.W. and Dasen, P.R. (1974). Introduction. In J.W. Berry and P.R. Dasen (Eds), *Culture and cognition* (pp. 1–20). London: Methuen.

Berry, J.W., Poortinga, Y.H., Segall, M.H., and Dasen, P.R. (2002). *Cross-cultural psychology: Research and applications*. Cambridge: Cambridge

University Press. (Chapter 1: 'Introduction to cross-cultural psychology').
Brislin, R.W. (1990). Applied cross-cultural psychology: An introduction. In R.W. Brislin (Ed.), *Applied cross-cultural psychology*. Newbury Park, CA: Sage.
Bronfenbrenner, U. (1977). Toward an experimental ecology of human development. *American Psychologist*, **32**, 513–531.
Bronfenbrenner, U. (1979). *The ecology of human development: Experiments by nature and by design*. Cambridge, MA: Harvard University Press.
Bronfennbrenner, U. (1986). Ecology of the family as a context for human development: Research perspectives. *Developmental Psychology*, **22**, 732–742.
Bronfenbrenner, U. (Ed.) (2005). *Making human beings human: Bioecological perspectives on human development*. London: Sage.
Bruner, J. (1990). *Acts of meaning*. Cambridge, MA: Harvard University Press.
Cole, M. (1990). Cultural psychology: A once and future discipline? In J.J. Berman (Ed.), *Nebraska symposium on motivation, 1989: Cross-cultural perspectives*. (Vol. 37, pp. 279–335). Lincoln, NE: University of Nebraska Press.
Cole, M. (1992). Culture in development. In M.H. Bornstein and M.E. Lamb (Eds), *Developmental psychology: An advanced textbook* (pp. 731–789) Hillsdale, NJ: Lawrence Erlbaum.
Craik, K.H. and Feimer, N. (1987). Environmental assessment. In D. Stokols and I. Altman (Eds), *Handbook of environmental psychology*. New York: Wiley.
Empson, J.M. and Nabuzoka, D. (2004). Conceptual and theoretical approaches to atypical development. In J.M. Empson and D. Nabuzoka (Eds), *Atypical child development in context* (pp. 9–38). Basingstoke: Palgrave Macmillan.
Göncü, A. (Ed.) (1999). *Children's engagement in the world: Sociocultural perspectives*. Cambridge: Cambridge University Press.
Greenfield, P.M. (1997). Culture as process: Empirical methods for cultural psychology. In J.W. Berry, Y.H. Poortinga, and J. Pandey (Eds), *Handbook of cross-cultural psychology. Vol. 1: Theory and method* (pp. 301–346). Boston, MA: Allyn & Bacon.
Greenfield, P.M. (2000). Three approaches to the study of culture: Where do they come from? Where can they go? *Asian Journal of Social Psychology*, **3**, 223–240.
Keller, H. (2003). Socialization for competence: Cultural models of infancy. *Human Development*, **46**, 288–311.
Kuper, A. (1999). *Culture: The anthropologists' account*. Cambridge, MA: Harvard University Press.

Luria, A.R. (1976). *Cognitive development: Its cultural and social foundations.* Cambridge, MA: Harvard University Press.

Mandansky, D., and Edelbrock, C. (1990). Cosleeping in a community sample of 2- and 3-year-old children. *Pediatrics,* **86**, 197–280.

Maria, M.S. (2000). On the nature of cultural research. *International Society for the Study of Behavioural Development Newsletter,* 1(37), 4–6.

Mead, G.H. (1934). *Mind, self, and society.* Chicago: University of Chicago Press.

Miller, J.G. and Chen, X. (2000). Indigenous approaches to developmental research: An overview. *ISSBD Newsletter,* 1(37), 1.

Morelli, G.A., Rogoff, B., Oppenheim, D., and Goldsmith, D. (1992). Cultural variation in infants' sleeping arrangements: Questions of independence. *Developmental Psychology,* **28**, 604–613.

Nsamenang, A.B. (1992). *Human development in cultural context: A Third World perspective.* Newbury Park, CA: Sage.

Nsamenang, A.B. (1994). Cross-cultural developmental research. A viewpoint from Africa. *ISSBD Newsletter,* 2(26), 3–4.

Nsamenang, A.B. (2000). Issues in indigenous approaches to developmental research in Sub-Saharan Africa. *International Society for the Study of Behavioural Development Newsletter,* 1(37), 1–4.

Sameroff, A.J. (1987). The social context of development. In N. Eisenberg (Ed.), *Contemporary topics in developmental psychology.* New York: Wiley.

Sameroff, A.J. and Chandler, M.J. (1975). Reproductive risk and the continuum of caretaking casualty. In F.D. Horowitz, M. Hetherington, S. Scarr-Salapatek, and G. Siegal (Eds), *Review of child development research,* Vol. 4. Chicago: University of Chicago Press.

Segall, M.H. (1984). More than we need to know about culture, but are afraid to ask. *Journal of Cross-Cultural Psychology,* **15**, 153–162.

Segall, M.H., Lonner, W.J., and Berry, J.W. (1998). Cross-cultural psychology as a scholarly discipline: On the flowering of culture in behavioural research. *American Psychologist,* **53**(10), 1101–1110.

Serpell, R. (1971). Discrimination of orientation by Zambian children. *Journal of Comparative and Physiological Psychology,* **75**, 312–316.

Serpell, R. (1977). Estimates of intelligence in a rural community of eastern Zambia. In F.M. Okatcha (Ed.), *Modern psychology and cultural adaptation* (pp. 179–216). Nairobi, Kenya: Swahili Language Consultants and Publishers.

Serpell, R. (1979). How specific are perceptual skills? A cross-cultural study of pattern reproduction. *British Journal of Psychology,* **70**, 365–380.

Serpell, R. (1993). *The significance of schooling: Life-journeys in an African society.* Cambridge: Cambridge University Press.

Serpell, R. (1994). African social ontogeny: A review of A. Bame Nsamenang (1992) Human development in cultural context: A Third World perspective. Sage. *Cross-Cultural Psychology Bulletin*, **28**(1), 17–21.

Shweder, R.A. (1990). Cultural psychology: What is it? In J.W. Stigler, R.A. Shweder, and G. Herdt (Eds), *Cultural psychology: Essays on comparative human development* (pp. 1–43). Cambridge: Cambridge University Press.

Shweder, R.A. (2000). The psychology of practice and the practice of the three psychologies. *Asian Journal of Social Psychology*, **3**, 207–222.

Sinha, D. (1997). Indigenizing psychology. In J.W. Berry, Y.H. Poortinga, and J. Pandey (Eds), *Theory and method* (pp. 129–169). Vol. 1 of *Handbook of cross-cultural psychology*. Second Edition. Boston, MA: Allyn & Bacon.

Strodtbeck, F. (1964). Some considerations of meta-method in cross-cultural studies. *American Anthropologist*, **66**, 223–229.

Super, C.M. and Harkness, S. (1986). The developmental niche: A conceptualisation at the interface of child and culture. *International Journal of Behavioural Development*, **9**, 545–569.

Super, C.M. and Harkness, S. (2002). Culture structures the environment for development. *Human Development*, **45**, 270–274.

van der Vijver, F.J.R. and Poortinga, Y.H. (2002). On the study of culture in developmental science. *Human Development*, **45**(4), 246–256.

Vernon, P.E. (1967). Abilities and educational attainment in an East African environment. *Journal of Special Education*, **1**, 335–345.

Vygotsky, L.S. (1962). *Thought and language.* Cambridge, MA: MII Press.

Whiting, B.B. and Edwards, C.P. (1992). *Children of different worlds: The formation of social behaviour.* Cambridge, MA: Harvard University Press.

Whiting, J. (1968). Methods and problems in cross-cultural research. In G. Lindzey and E. Aronson (Eds), *Handbook of social psychology* (Vol. 2, pp. 693–728). Reading, MA: Addison-Wesley.

Witkin, H.A. and Berry, J.W. (1975). Psychological differentiation in cross-cultural perspective. *Journal of Cross-Cultural Psychology*, **6**, 4–87.

Yang, K.S. (2000). Indigenous, cultural, and cross-cultural psychology: A theoretical, conceptual, and epistemological analysis. *Asian Journal of Social Psychology*, **3**, 265–288.

Child-Rearing Goals and Practices

Cecilie Jávo

OUTLINE

3.1 Introduction
3.2 Cultural models and parental ethnotheories
    3.2.1 Individualism/collectivism
3.3 Culture, childrearing and child development
    3.3.1 Parent-child attachment
    3.3.2 Parents' management styles
    3.3.3 Parental discipline
3.4 Acculturation and childrearing
3.5 Childrearing in indigenous Sámi and majority Norwegian cultures: A comparative study
    3.5.1 Sámi and Norwegian cultures
    3.5.2 The study
    3.5.3 The findings
    3.5.4 Discussion of findings
3.6 General conclusions
Further reading
References

3.1 Introduction

Socialization means adapting to the conditions of one's society and culture in order to meet the social necessities of survival. As the ecologies of humans greatly vary around the world, so do the ways children socialize. The people who have the main influence on children's socialization are parents, close and extended families, peers and schoolteachers; social institutions such as schools and day-care centres are also important. Socialization itself should be viewed as a dynamic process in and between different relationships, in which the child in its turn acts as an active agent.

Across cultures, the most important influence on child socialization is parenting. There are parenting universals rooted in human psychology in addition to cultural variations in parenting between societies and within the same society (e.g., by socio-economic status, see Chapter 4). This chapter focuses on the various ways parents' child-rearing goals and practices socialize children for adult life in different cultures. In culturally diverse populations, such knowledge is paramount for professionals dealing with families and children. In particular, a broader cultural perspective is needed when dealing with ethnic minorities whose child-rearing values and practices may be quite different from those of the mainstream culture.

Studies on childrearing have been done from a variety of perspectives. More recent research has focused broadly on environmental and contextual factors as determinants of parenting, for example, the concept of the developmental niche developed by Super and Harkness (1993). One such factor, social class, has traditionally been established as the primary social influence, accounting for most of the variation in parents' beliefs and behaviour patterns (see Chapter 4). However, other studies have identified ethnic factors also as important determinants. When social class has been statistically controlled, significant ethnocultural differences in childrearing could still be identified in early cross-cultural studies (e.g., Bartz and LeVine, 1978). It is now generally accepted that childrearing is inculcated through an interaction of ethnic culture, social-class experience and other environmental factors. As described earlier (Chapter 2), the entire developmental niche is embedded in the larger sociocultural context and mediates the cultural influences onto the child. In order to understand parents' child-rearing goals and practices within a specific cultural context, we have to take into account the relevant cultural characteristics of that culture, as well as its particular ecological conditions.

A growing literature documents the differences between ethnic groups in child-rearing beliefs, values and goals (e.g., Keller, Lamm, Abels et al., 2006; Schwarz, Schäfermeier and Trommsdorff, 2005; Super and Harkness, 1995). The literature indicates that parents and other caregivers foster behavioural capacities in their children that maximize their cultural values, and that these efforts are reflected in cultural differences in such areas as infant care, autonomy, discipline and attachment behaviour (LeVine and Norman, 2001; Mizuta, Zahn-Waxler, Cole and Hiruma, 1996; Trommsdorff and Kornadt, 2003). We should bear in mind that specific child-rearing practices that are considered functional and beneficial to a child's development may well differ from one cultural context to another. Furthermore, practices that are viewed as moral and pragmatic in one cultural context can be viewed as misguided, ineffective and even immoral in others. In particular, parental beliefs about parenting, and the ways in which parents perform parenting functions, differ across Western and non-Western groups. Moreover, Western and other modern urban industrial societies contrast sharply with traditional or indigenous groups in terms of patterns of child development (Greenfield and Cocking, 1994; Javo, Rønning and Heyerdahl, 2004a; Munroe and Munroe, 1975).

However, most of our existing knowledge of child development and socialization comes from studies of middle-class Euro-American families. More longitudinal investigations of the development of children of non-Western, traditional societies are warranted. This lack of research not only undermines a more comprehensive understanding of these children, but also raises questions about the validity of empirical knowledge about child development in general. There is also a need for more research to provide better insight into different patterns of socialization related to culture (Keller et al., 2006) particularly to understand how parents adapt to the challenges they face as ethnic minorities and how these experiences contribute to the socialization goals they hold for their children.

The first part of the chapter is divided into four sections. First, I discuss cultural models and parental ethnotheories. Second, I outline the collectivism-individualism framework to classify cultures and use it as an interpretation of childrearing in different societies. Third, some areas of childrearing that have been a focus of cross-cultural research with respect to their influences on child development are discussed in this broader cultural perspective. Fourth and finally, I introduce another perspective, acculturation, used for studying the ethno-contextual influences on childrearing in ethnic minority groups. The second part of the chapter contains a presentation and discussion of the results from a comparative study of childrearing in a native, minority culture (the Sámi) and a majority Western culture (the Norwegian), thereby illustrating some of the main issues raised earlier in the chapter.

Part I
3.2 Cultural models and parental ethnotheories

It is widely acknowledged that cultural models of the self provide essential frameworks for shaping socialization goals and ethnotheories about what constitutes effective and good parenting (Keller et al., 2006). According to Quinn and Holland (1987), cultural models are shared, presupposed understandings of the world, or interpretative frameworks (cognitive schemas) in a cultural group that 'frame experience, supplying interpretations of that experience and inferences about it, and goals for action' (Quinn and Holland, 1987). Such models involve certain viewpoints about what is right and wrong, and what can or cannot be done to solve problems. A thorough understanding of parental behaviour at the individual level should include the recognition of the interplay between cultural models, parents' individual beliefs and the contribution of the child him/herself. Cultural models, and thus parental goals and ethnotheories, reflect the demands of the ecocultural environment, the socio-economic structure of a society and the type of community (Keller et al., 2006).

Parents' ethnotheories (or parents' 'cultural beliefs'; 'ideas') act as powerful sources of affect (feelings) and motivators of parenting, and thus, they constitute part of the caregiver's psychology which is one of the three independent components in the concept of the developmental niche (Super and Harkness, 1993). Recent studies have validated the significance of parents' ethnotheories on children's socio-emotional development. These include theories about typical child development and developmental milestones, maternal role and influence on the child and the long-term goals for child development. Comparative studies of parenting ethnotheories have been undertaken in many countries within various childrearing and child-developmental domains, such as in the management of sleep, feeding practices, infants' communicative ability and mother-child interaction, infants' motor activity and patterns of rest and state of arousal, development of children's temperament and emotion regulation, and the knowledge acquisition of children; all domains reveal substantial cross-cultural differences (see Harkness and Super, 1996).

The study by LeVine, Dixon, LeVine, et al. (1994) provide an example of the traditional Gusii of western Kenya where the rarity of infant-directed speech might stem from the common parental belief that talking to children less than two years old would be useless, as infants are thought incapable of understanding speech. In some non-Western cultures mothers assume that young children can and should regulate their own feeding. They trust that the children would eat according to their needs, as in Mali where mothers do not feed weaning-age children; rather the children can take food from the family pot when they are ready (Dettwyler, 1986). Ethnotheories about children's sleep practices vary widely; from the belief that co-sleeping is a healthy practice and good for the child (cultures in Africa, Asia and South America) to the opposite belief that it is psychologically damaging and might interfere with the child's independence and autonomous development (Euro-American cultures). Accordingly, children's sleep arrangements differ greatly around the world (Wolf, Lozoff, Latz and Paludetto, 1996).

It is clear from the above examples that we cannot understand children's development or interpret their daily child-rearing experiences adequately without first understanding their parents' culture-specific theories about parenting. However, the study of parenting ethnotheories and how they affect childrearing and child development is a new and most complex field of research, and poses challenging conceptual and methodological issues. For instance, one might ask: To what extent are parents aware of their own beliefs about the complex task of child-rearing, and how can we assess the kind of influence they have on their children? Indeed, more theoretical work is warranted in this area. Besides, more research at the interface of cultural models, socialization goals and parenting ethnotheories is needed in order to refine these different concepts and gain more knowledge about their interrelatedness. Of particular interest is the exploration of parenting ethnotheories linked to the cultural models of independence and interdependence (Keller et al., 2006) which in turn relate to the broader cultural framework of individualism and collectivism.

3.2.1 Individualism/collectivism

Hofstede's pioneering work (Hofstede, 1980; 2001) suggested four dimensions to classify cultures:

(a) power distance,
(b) uncertainty avoidance,

(c) masculinity/femininity, and
(d) individualism/collectivism.

Of these, the 'individualism-collectivism' (I-C) dimension has provided a useful direction and focus in cross-cultural psychology. Several research studies document the existence of a collectivistic cultural pattern in traditional cultures in, for example, Africa and Asia and among migrants to Western societies (e.g., Greenfield, Keller, Fuligni and Maynard, 2003; Keller, 2003). One of the most characteristic traits of collectivism is socialization for interdependence (Kim, 1994). In a collectivistic cultural framework the primary goal of socialization is for the mature person to be embedded in a network of relationships and responsibilities to others; personal achievements are ideally at the service of a collective, usually the family (Georgas, Christakopoulou, Poortinga et al., 1997; Greenfield et al., 2003). The healthy collectivist self is characterized by compliance, nurturance, interdependence and inhibited hedonism (Watson, Sherbak and Morris, 1998). Rearing for interdependence seems to be prevalent in typical rural agrarian societies with low levels of affluence, and in urban low socio-economic status (SES) contexts where intergenerational interdependence is necessary for family livelihood. It is expected that children should contribute to the family upkeep from a very young age, and also act as a 'life insurance' for their parents and extended families as they grow older. To achieve this, an obedience orientation in childrearing is paramount. A child's tendency to develop from interdependence to independence may easily be experienced as a threat, and is therefore discouraged. On the other hand, warm and nurturing relations between family members are strongly encouraged, making the family a harmonic and safe haven. Because of this orientation, the group or family, not the individual, is considered as the important unity. The focus is on the relationship shared by in-group members, which requires the willingness and ability to feel and think what others are feeling and thinking, to absorb this information without being told and to help others satisfy their wishes and realize their goals. In Japanese culture, they use the concept of 'amae' (dependence) and in Korean culture 'chong' (affection) (Kim, 1994). For example, in Japan, cultural values emphasize the group. These values are translated into specific rearing practices such as prolonged body contact between mother and child (i.e., co-sleeping) as well as disciplinary practices, such as stressing empathy with others' feelings about the child's transgressions, or using threats of exclusion from the family (internal or emotional control methods). Child-rearing goals are cooperation, indulgence, thoughtfulness and empathy. The end product is a child who values within-group cooperation over competition and has a high sensitivity to interpersonal cues (Wachs, 1992).

At the other end of the scale, we find the cultural pattern developed in modern, industrial, Western cultures, especially the American middle class, which tends to encourage individualism and independence (e.g., Oyserman, Coon and Kemmelmeier, 2002). In these cultures, the individual person is considered an autonomous entity with distinctive, stable internal attributes influencing behaviour. Because individuals are thought to have autonomous, stable natures, and consistency is considered genuine and valuable, the individual is the important object of focus (Kitayama, 2002; Kitayama, Duffy, Kawamura and Larsen, 2003). Within an individualistic cultural framework, the primary goal of socialization is an autonomous, self-fulfilled individual who enters into social relationships and responsibilities by personal choice. Thus, in typical individualistic cultures, encouragement of child autonomy and independence are dominant traits of childrearing. For example, Chao (1995) found that for European American mothers the most fundamental goal of development was the self-maximization of the child and to have one's child grow up to be an independent and individuated adult. Kagitçibasi (1990) has shown that from a developmental perspective elaborated in Western psychologies, individuation and separation from ascribed relationships are considered necessary for healthy human development, whereas interdependent or 'enmeshed' individuals are considered pathological. Within this individualistic cultural pattern, the adolescents' distancing and disengaging from parents is considered as an important part of healthy development. Thus, good parenting is one that stimulates the child to independence and self-reliance. However, it should be noted that this socialization idea contrasts with recent research demonstrating that close ties and attachment to parents, rather than detachment, is associated with adolescent health and well-being in diverse cultures, including the United States (Chirkov, Kim, Ryan and Kaplan, 2003; Chou, 2000; Ryan and Deci, 2000). In fact, cross-cultural evidence indicates that, even if independence is the ultimate socialization goal for raising children, a complex of constant contact and nurturing behaviours may be the most effective strategy (Greenfield and Suzuki, 1998). Irrespective of such knowledge, the individualistic worldview tends to be seen as the norm and is exported to the rest of the world as the human model to emulate.

It should be noted that individualism and collectivism refer to abstract notions of general cultural beliefs and values, and that their individual representations (e.g., in parents) have to be differentiated conceptually (Harkness, Super and van Tijen, 2000). However, it has been shown that certain general cultural-value orientations predict specific parental goals on the individual level. Triandis (1994) described individualism and collectivism at the individual level as syndromes and named them 'idiocentric' (i.e., selecting mostly individualist solutions) and 'allocentric' (i.e., selecting mostly collectivist solutions). Hence, parents' ways of rearing their children may be either idiocentric, allocentric or both. Such value orientations may lead to different parenting expectations and beliefs, which in turn play an important role in guiding parents' behaviours.

Developmental researchers have recently begun to examine how cultural-value orientations of self-development integrate independent and interdependent psychological functioning at the individual level. Traditionally, the construct of self has been explained in terms of two main components, namely, autonomous entity and interrelational entity with others (Feiring and Taska, 1996; Raeff, 1997). This dichotomous dimension of self-development should be understood as a continuum that exists in the value systems of all cultures. Autonomy and relatedness were viewed as conflicting human needs until recently, but are now debated as compatible.

3.2.1.1 Kagitçibasi's (2005) family change model

Recently, Kagitçibasi (2005) has put forward a cultural model that involves a fourfold combination of the two dimensions, leading to different types of self and the societal and familial contexts in which they develop. The model has two independent dimensions: agency, which varies from autonomy to heteronomy and interpersonal distance, which varies from relatedness to separation and incorporates a family type that has arisen due to the urbanization of developing societies. The previously accepted family types have been:

- Traditional family – material and emotional interdependence between generations (in poor agrarian collectivist societies and low-SES urban contexts)
- Individualistic family – independence of members (in wealthy, industrial, Western societies).

Kagitçibasi identifies a third type of family which comes about with the development of a society and the weakening of material interdependencies between generations. The parental ethnotheories and prevailing cultural ethos are still of psychological interdependency or relatedness so the parenting involves socialization for both relatedness and autonomy as the children grow up. Kagitçibasi argues that with greater access to schooling and the industrial nature of work, the capacity for individual decision-making becomes important and this requires autonomy. For parenting, this means continuing to control the child, but with autonomy also being allowed, the control becomes 'order setting' instead of 'dominating'. Thus, in developing societies the effective self comes to have aspects of both autonomy and relatedness. There is also evidence that this exists to some extent in developed societies: elderly parents are frequently psychologically dependent on, and cared for, by their children; greater well-being is associated with relatedness in adolescents in several countries (Meeus, Oosterwegel and Vollebergh, 2002). Other studies show that autonomy, control and relatedness co-occur in Chinese families (Jose, Huntsinger, Huntsinger and Liaw 2000), more so than in Chinese American, supporting Kagitçibasi's family change model.

As Keller et al. (2006) argue this model needs further theoretical and empirical refinement. As in all typologies, the distinction between the different types is not absolute, and within each type of family there will emerge a range of different kinds of self. Kagitçibasi does however offer a conceptualization of healthy development which incorporates elements of both individualistic and collectivist child-rearing patterns allowing children to thrive in rapidly changing societies.

3.3 Culture, childrearing and child development

Research based on quite different theoretical perspectives has suggested that parenting behaviour may play a major role in child development and child behavioural problems (e.g., Campbell, 1995; Greenberg, Speltz and DeKlyen, 1993; Webster-Stratton, 1990). The emphasis has varied from quality of parent-child attachment to more specific aspects of parents' management styles and discipline. In the following section, some areas of childrearing that have been particularly cross-culturally focused on with respect to their influences on child development are outlined.

3.3.1 Parent-child attachment

There has been a strong and persistent emphasis on the importance of a close and secure relationship with caregivers during infancy and early childhood for healthy personality development. The theoretical links between insecure attachment and behavioural problems in young children are compelling (Campbell, 1995). Partly, there are basic biological predispositions underlying attachment suggesting a strong universality in attachment behaviour. However, attachment theorists acknowledge that there are differences between cultures in the way that attachment behaviour manifests itself. Even as far back as in the 1960s, through the early work of Mary Ainsworth (1967), context and culture-laden factors in understanding attachment-related phenomena were noted. Although a universal repertoire of attachment behaviours may exist among infants across cultures, the selection, shaping and interpretation of these behaviours over time appear to be culturally patterned and transmitted through culture-specific caregiver patterns, parental goals and strategies (van IJzendoorn and Sagi, 1999).

Key constructs in attachment theory, such as 'responsiveness' and 'sensitivity' in caregiving, 'child activity' and 'security base' have been studied in a Western context and mostly by Western measures, and hence do not do justice to their many conceptions and manifestations elsewhere. Thus, we may question the universality of attachment theory, being rooted as it is in Western ideas and values (i.e., autonomy, exploration, self-assertion, low dependence and individuation), and biased by Western samples (Rothbaum, Weisz, Pott et al., 2000).

A core hypothesis of attachment theory is the sensitivity hypothesis, positing that the quality of attachment depends on the caregiver's sensitivity to the child's emotional needs and exploratory behaviours. Differences in sensitivity to infant distress, and to its positive and negative signals, have been found to differ between non-Western and Western mothers (Friedlmeier and Trommsdorff, 1999; LeVine, 2004; Mizuta et al., 1996). Mothers in different cultures may differ in how quickly they respond to their baby's signals, varying from proactive responses (e.g., Japan, Puerto Rico, Cameroon) to responses given after the babies signal a shift in emotional state (e.g., the United States). Such cultural differences may reflect differences in parental cultural values along the independent/individualistic – interdependent/collectivistic dimension, the proactive response promoting accommodative behaviours and the latter response fostering individualistic behaviours (Keller, Papaligoura, Kunsemuller et al., 2003). Furthermore, caregivers' sensitive responsiveness to children's autonomy varies across cultures, depending on the cultural priorities. For instance, recent studies suggest that Anglo-American mothers exhibit greater autonomy in their caregiving than mothers in other cultures (Dennis, Cole, Zahn-Waxler and Mizuta, 2003; Keller et al., 2003).

Observations of infants in different cultures suggest that there may be a biological basis to the link between attachment and child exploration (Rothbaum et al., 2000). However, few studies have examined the concept of 'security base' (i.e., the use of the attachment figure as a secure base from which to explore the environment safely) in different cultures. Its meanings might well differ along the individualistic-collectivistic dimension. Hence, attachment research which includes only the Western concept of security base might be culturally biased. Moreover, in Western, individualistic cultures the notion of 'exploration' as an independent activity aiming at mastery of the environment might differ from that found for collectivistic cultures, which might rather view it as a broadening of social involvement to include other persons and activities (Rothbaum and Morelli, 2005).

The competence hypothesis in attachment theory posits that secure attachment is related to higher competence in dealing with developmental, social and cultural challenges. However, conceptions of competence (as conceptions of intelligence) also vary across cultures. In individualistic cultures competence is independence, autonomy, exploration and personal achievement; whereas, in collectivistic societies it is interdependence, ability to maintain social harmony, acceptance of social roles and respect of elders. Therefore, such differing conceptual meanings must be taken into account when interpreting consequences of attachment in different cultures (Rothbaum and Morelli, 2005).

> **Discussion Point: How Relevant Do You Think Attachment Theory Is To Child Development In Different Cultural Contexts?**

3.3.2 Parents' management styles

Another area of parenting which is associated with different outcomes of child behaviour and social competence is parental management styles. Much of the research in this area has been based on variations in basic dimensions of parenting behaviour as elaborated by Baumrind (1971). Baumrind identified three different styles of parenting:

- Authoritarian parents scored low on measures of warmth and responsiveness, were high in control and demanding of obedience, relying on orders in communicating with their children.
- Authoritative parents are towards the high end of the warmth and responsiveness continuum, are affectionate and supportive of autonomy in the children, using reasoning and discussion in communicating. These parents also score high on control/demand with high expectations of independence and maturity.
- Permissive parents are varied in emotional terms, some being warm and indulgent and others lacking interest in their children, scoring low on control and allowing the children to do what they want.

One fairly constant conclusion has been that the most socially competent children have parents who have received high ratings on both warmth and control, thus endorsing the authoritative parenting style. Authoritarian parents typically tended to have children who were highly dependent with only average social responsibility scores. Children of permissive parents, however, exhibited little social responsibility and were only moderately independent (Baumrind, 1967).

However, we should note that although Baumrind's model of parenting styles have been extensively studied in European American families, it has been less well studied in other cultures. Baumrind's typology is closely tied to the normative goals for child development in North America and to the values of middle-class European American parents. Hence, 'authoritative' parenting is considered the most adaptive style because it is associated with children who are self-reliant, self-controlled, explorative and content, that is, qualities of the independent individual valued in the cultural model of individualism.

In other cultures it has been found that an 'authoritarian' parenting style is prevalent to a much higher degree, for example, in East Asia, Africa and Mexico, as well as among Asian American, African American and Mexican American ethnic groups (Chao, 2001; Greenfield and Suzuki, 1998; Schwarz et al., 2005). 'Authoritarian' parenting behaviour may be quite different where the culture has an interdependence-oriented developmental script. Whereas 'authoritarian' parenting was associated with negative effects, such as hostile, rejecting parental behaviours, in the United States, the Chinese version of authoritarianism was perceived in a more positive light from within the culture, emphasizing harmonious, respectful relations, and parental concern and care for children (Chao, 1994). Contrary to Western cultures, like Germany, in Japanese culture parental control and positive child development were found to be positively related (Trommsdorff and Friedlmeier, 1993).

It seems that different parental ideas, values and goals give different meanings and a different emotional context to similar styles of parental behaviour, indicating qualitatively different cultural patterning of parenting (Greenfield and Suzuki, 1998; Querido, Warner and Eyberg, 2002). From this, we may conclude that the influence of control and authoritarian parenting on children's development differs with culture. More studies that examine cultural differences in the developmental consequences of various parenting styles are warranted in order to examine the cross-cultural validity of Baumrind's parenting styles on a more extensive scale.

A final point to be made is that in contrast to white, middle-class populations, the use of physical punishment in other cultural groups may not simply indicate authoritarian parenting, but instead may be a behavioural practice under the influence of other factors (Kelley, Power and Wimbush, 1992). In addition to authoritarian parents, physical punishment is also used by parents with other parenting styles. It is therefore important to separate these constructs in order to understand their unique contributions on child outcomes (Benjet and Kazdin, 2003).

3.3.3 Parental discipline

Patterson (1980) and Webster-Stratton (1990) have found that parental control techniques employed in disciplinary situations exert significant influences on child outcomes in their own right. However, contrasts appear across cultures in the relative emphasis that parents place on external as compared with internal or emotional control (Greenfield and Suzuki, 1998; Javo et al., 2004a). It has been accepted for a long time that emotional techniques of discipline, utilizing feeling-oriented appeals and relying on affective ties inhibit the outward expression of child aggression (Alliensmith, 1960; Hackett and Hackett, 1993; Lester, 1967), as does a lower parental tolerance of aggressive behaviour (Hackett and Hackett, 1994; Munroe and Munroe, 1975). On the other hand, punitive types of discipline and power-assertive techniques to control the child have been found to relate to defiant, aggressive and oppositional behaviour (Becker, 1964; Lytton, 1990; Webster-Stratton, 1990). However, recent reviews of physical punishment have come to rather different and sometimes opposite conclusions as to child outcomes (Benjet and Kazdin, 2003). The only consistent finding in the literature, as documented in a meta-analysis by Gershoff (2002), was that the frequency of physical punishment was positively related to aggression, misconduct and related constructs. Whether physical punishment is an antecedent of subsequent increases in child aggressive behaviour has not been firmly established. It is also quite possible that physical punishment is associated with a host of other child, parent, family and contextual factors that might, alone or in combination with physical punishment, better account for the outcomes. Thus, it has been argued that the effects of harsh treatment are not necessarily negative or positive, but may be either or both depending on these other conditions. Conclusive findings are still warranted (Benjet and Kazdin, 2003; Javo, Rønning, Heyerdahl and Rudmin, 2004b). Furthermore, due to methodological limitations, no conclusions regarding causality can be drawn. More longitudinal prospective studies are clearly needed to rule out potential confounding variables and any long-term effects on behaviour (Benjet and Kazdin, 2003).

An interesting aspect of parental discipline is that the effects of it may be moderated by the meaning the child ascribes to it, and that this meaning may be influenced by factors such as parenting context, gender and ethnic culture. In cultures where physical discipline is used more frequently and is not perceived by children as rejection, such as among African Americans, it was found that, unlike for white Americans, punitive and directive parental disciplinary strategies were not associated with negative behavioural outcomes, that is, hostility, resistance, aggression and antisocial behaviour (Deater-Deckard, Dodge, Bates and Pettit, 1996; McLeod, Kruttschnitt and Dornfield, 1994; Stormshak, Bierman, McMahon and Lengua, 2000). In fact, in a review by Larzelere (1994), low to moderate physical punishment was found to have benign and, in one study, beneficial outcomes in African Americans. In a study by Carlson and Harwood (2003), mothers' physical control was related to insecure attachment in Anglo-American families, but not in Puerto Rican families. So it seems that stricter parental control and directiveness are more valued and emphasized in other ethnocultural groups (including African American, Korean, Chinese and Iranian) than they are among Euro-Americans (Carlson and Harwood, 2003). As non-Euro-Americans' socialization goals favour attentive, calm and well-behaved children, parenting would demand a higher degree of physical prompting and control for socialization than in typical individualistic societies where teaching children to be assertive and self-confident is more valued. Thus, what might be a risk factor for disruptive behaviour in white Euro-American cultures may not be so in other cultures with different cultural orientations and child-rearing techniques. However, it should be stressed that ethnocultural differences do not hold when physical punishment rises to an abusive level (Deater-Deckard et al., 1996).

In order to predict the soundness and effectiveness of a specific parenting method within a specific culture, it is essential to understand the place of the method within the broader child-rearing structure. For instance, in some cultures harsh disciplinary methods and toughening the child seem to be balanced by a high degree of physical closeness and love (Javo, Alapack, Rønning and Heyerdahl, 2003). Other research suggests that a positive maternal attitude and positive active involvement are capable of neutralizing the effects of harsh discipline, and otherwise disruptive types of parental behaviour (Pettit, Bates and Dodge, 1997).

Generally, it seems that the influence of specific child-rearing practices should be minimized, while the importance of caregivers' emotional attitudes towards their children, and the interpersonal context in which particular forms of behaviour occur, should be given more weight (e.g., Bowlby, 1989).

> **Discussion point:** What factors do you think influence the effects of different kinds of discipline on children?

3.4 Acculturation and childrearing

In addition to viewing childrearing from the individualism-collectivism perspective, another angle might be needed for studying the ethnocontextual influences on childrearing in ethnic minority groups living in close and continuous contact with a superordinate majority culture. Often, these minorities are originally collectivistic cultures from Africa, South America or Asia seeking a new future in the more urban and industrialized societies of the West. Or they might be indigenous or minority cultures living within non-Western countries. Such a sociopolitical context gives rise to the process called *acculturation*, which may substantially affect the course of childrearing, often in interaction with ecological influences.

An acculturation process might be defined as a cultural and psychological change which involves the selective adoption, by members of the minority group, of the values, beliefs and traditions of one or both of the cultures involved. It is a complex, dynamic process with potentially diverse choices and outcomes as to child socialization. The cultural struggle to survive in such a minority position, and the constant threat presented by the majority culture to traditional values, language and epistemology may complicate the child's socialization process. In such a predicament, it would be important to identify which values and traditions are so closely linked to the minority's own identity that they should be kept and nourished in contemporary childrearing, and which values have become less important, due to changes in the wider social context. Greater consciousness of the core values of one's own culture may reinforce ethnic identity in minority children and prevent confusion of norms and rootlessness.

An important effect of acculturation is the interruption of the normal continuity of cultural transmission across generations (Kwak, 2003). Faced with new values in a different kind of society, parents try to alter their own value orientation, and adapt their children to the future by adopting new ways of bringing up their children, often by borrowing sets of rules and ideas from the majority culture. It has been shown that minority or immigrant cultures' length of exposure to majority culture is associated with predictable shifts in parental child-rearing practices and child behaviour (e.g., Dalgety-Gaitan, 1994; Kobayashi-Winata and Power, 1989).

However, parents may act as agents of their own ethnic heritage culture, raising their children according to the procedures they have learned earlier in their own childhood, even though these values and techniques may have lost some of their relevance. Many aspects of traditional child-rearing practices and attitudes appear to be continued among minority cultures over generations in spite of acculturation (Chao, 2000; Javo et al., 2003; 2004a; Kelley and Tseng, 1992).

It appears that ethnic groups with higher levels of social integrity and a stronger sense of identity tend to maintain certain core values of their own culture in childrearing. On the contrary, a group undergoing greater trauma of acculturation might not do so, and become disoriented, ambiguous and normless (Lefley, 1976). International studies of minorities have demonstrated that some aspects of childrearing might be more resistant to change than others (e.g., Dosanjh and Ghuman, 1996). However, few studies have explored why some cultural traditions in childrearing have proven to be resilient, while others have been abandoned more easily. Any answer would have to include explanatory factors relevant both to the dynamics of environmental change/adaptation and to the forces that preserve and sustain psychological identity.

Parents' acculturation level has been found to have an impact on parenting by influencing (a) developmental expectations (b) mother-infant interactions (c) feeding and caregiving practices and (d) the role of the extended family (Garcìa Coll et al., 1995). It should be noted that within immigrant or minority families, the degree to which individual family members carry on cultural continuity in the dominant society can vary substantially (Kwak and Berry, 2001). This may account for significant sources of intergenerational discrepancies and conflicts in the child-rearing area (Berry and Sam, 1997; Rosenthal, Ranieri and Klimidis, 1996).

Recent studies have found that for immigrant groups that are experiencing a differential rate of acculturation, the cultural distance between their culture of origin and that of the new society is crucial to their adaptation (e.g., Szapocznik and Kurtines, 1993). Earlier studies (Berry and Annis, 1974) suggested that hunter-gatherers had greater cultural dissimilarity with the demands of the new ecology (urban, close-group living) than agriculturalist groups, and that the native peoples in Canada who came from 'traditional' migratory communities had enormous difficulties acculturating into 'modern' Canadian society. Difficulties of cultural dissimilarity sometimes manifest themselves in acculturative stress and lead to psychological and social pathologies, such as anxiety, depression, suicide, family violence and substance abuse (Berry, 1994). For immigrant children, an increased risk of psychological problems might stem from pre-migration factors, migration experiences and resettlement (i.e., minority status, discrimination, and lack of cultural competence).

On the other hand, several studies have reported that acculturation is generally not stressful. Perhaps immigrant families develop resources to cope with the various challenges. According to the summary report of the International Comparative Study of Ethnocultural Youth (ICSEY) which included 42 samples of immigrant adolescents in 13 nations found that immigrant youth were equal to, or better than, their non-immigrant peers in psychological well-being (life satisfaction, self-esteem, mental health) and school well-being (school adjustment, school behaviour) (Berry, Phinney, Sam and Vedder, 2006). These findings should remind us that acculturation is embedded in a social-cultural context, and that this context is the focus of concern. Although acculturation in itself might not be a risk factor, contextual factors related to integration in the new country might. Lack of achievement in cultural competence leading to reduced social support would be an important risk factor. Parental values and attitudes would be particularly important for gaining integration knowledge and skills. A supportive parenting attitude would influence the child's achievement values which in turn might promote a healthy integration process. However, research in this field is still scarce, and further investigation on the role of acculturation on childrearing and family relations is needed in different ethnic groups, including the impact of ethnocultural network and cultural distance to the majority society (Kwak, 2003; Phinney, Ong and Madden, 2000).

> Discussion point: In what circumstances would you expect the experience of acculturation to be stressful and why?

Part 2

3.5 Childrearing in indigenous Sámi and majority Norwegian cultures: A comparative study

Comparative studies of childrearing in native/indigenous peoples are scant. In the following sections, some of the results obtained from an empirical, cross-cultural study on Sámi and Norwegian childrearing in northern Norway are summarized and discussed. The study amply demonstrates differences in parenting attitudes and practices between two contrasting cultures. The discussion highlights the phenomenon of cultural transition in minority groups and its impact on child socialization. The results are compared with findings from studies of other native peoples, and are further discussed in the individualism-collectivism perspective.

3.5.1 Sámi and Norwegian cultures

The Sámi are a small, indigenous, arctic people who inhabit the northern part of Scandinavia, Finland and Russia. The exact number of

Sámi (also called Laps or Laplanders) is unknown, but is estimated to approximately 50,000–100,000. At least 70 per cent live in Norway. Traditionally, their society was a hunting and gathering society. Since the seventeenth century and until recent times, a nomadic lifestyle was prevalent, reindeer-herding being one of their main ways of living. Today, this lifestyle is vanishing. Due to a long-standing history of forced assimilation, a large proportion of the Sámi have lost their ethnic identity and native language. However, within the Sámi highlands or 'core area' in the northernmost county of Norway, the institutional and practical support for Sámi culture is stronger, and the process of assimilation has not been as strong as in other areas. It was within this specific area that our study was conducted.

The Norwegians are a Scandinavian ethnic group, and primary descendants of the Norse (along with the Swedes, Danes, Icelanders and Faroese). There is a noticeable genetic affinity between Norwegians and central Europeans, especially Germans. The total population in Norway is 4.3 million. The Norwegian language is a North Germanic language, highly different from the Sámi language which belongs to the Uralic language family. The Norwegian society is a modern, industrial, highly egalitarian and secularized Western society. It is top-ranked in the United Nations Human Development Index, an index made up by literacy rate, educational level and per capita income.

3.5.2 The study

The participants in the project were parents of 191 four-year-olds living within the Sámi core area. It is a sparsely populated, rural area, and the population is multi-ethnic, comprising indigenous Sámi, majority Norwegians, people of mixed heritage and historically immigrant Finns. The target sample comprised all four-year-old children within this area who were listed in the population register of 1991–1994, and whose parents were called in for the obligatory health assessment of their child at the age of four. Parents were invited to participate in the project when they visited the 'well-baby clinics'. The sample which was used in this referred study encompasses mothers of 76 monoethnic Sámi children and mothers of 86 monoethnic Norwegian children. Semi-structured interviews covering various child-rearing domains were conducted in the subjects' homes using their own language. The main aims of the study were to examine current Sámi child-rearing attitudes and practices and to compare these with those of the Norwegians living within the same geographic area.

3.5.3 The findings

3.5.3.1 Family background data

The Sámi and Norwegian groups did not differ in terms of birth order of child, number of siblings, size of household or employment status of parents. Most were nuclear families, with both parents employed outside the home and were not different socio-economically. However, in 28 per cent of the Sámi families, one or both of the parents were reindeer herders compared with none of the Norwegian parents.

In both groups, the majority lived within walking distance of their relatives, such as grandparents and aunts/uncles (Sámi: 74 per cent/ Norwegians: 61 per cent). However, the two groups differed in how often the child had contact with his/her grandparents and as to whether grandparents participated in childrearing. Of the Sámi mothers, 70 per cent reported daily or weekly grandparent contact, compared with 54 per cent of the Norwegian mothers. Of the Sámi grandparents, 46 per cent participated actively in childrearing, while only 22 per cent of the Norwegian grandparents did. The father's participation in childcare and decision-making in childrearing did not differ significantly between the groups. In both groups, most of the fathers participated actively. No differences in the degree of parental disagreement in childrearing were found, nor in the physical or mental health of parents or their offspring.

3.5.3.2 Child independence

A *Physical independence (Self-care ability)* Physical independence was assessed in terms of what the child was able to do on his/her own. Self-care items covered children's ability to dress and undress themselves, their need for assistance during meals and their ability to use the toilet unaided. Parental expectations of child self-care were inferred by asking at what age a child should be able to dress alone. No differences in children's self-care ability, or in parental expectations, were found between the groups. However, across ethnic groups, gender differences emerged. Physical independence was found to be higher among girls than in boys in their ability to dress and undress themselves, their need of assistance during meals and their unaided use of the toilet. Similarly, mothers' expectations of child self-care ability were higher for girls than for boys (girls: 59 months; boys: 66 months).

B *Social independence* Social independence covered items pertaining to parental attitudes to children's demands for attention, the ability to play alone and to the degree of clinging behaviour. Sámi children were able to play for a significantly longer period before demanding their parents' attention, and wanted less to be babied by their parents than did the Norwegian children. Parents' tolerance of dependent behaviour was inferred by asking whether they would mind a clinging behaviour in children at this age. The Sámi mothers tended to have less tolerance of clinging behaviour than did Norwegian mothers. No gender differences in social independence were found.

3.5.3.3 Toilet training

A significant difference between ethnic groups was found as to mothers' expectation of the child's ability to keep dry at night. The Sámi mothers reported a stricter norm with regard to developmental achievement in keeping dry than did Norwegian mothers (Sámi children: 43 months; Norwegian children: 49 months). However, toilet training started at about the same mean age for both groups (Sámi: 24 months; Norwegian: 23 months). Significant gender differences were found both as to when mothers expected their child to be dry at night and in the age at which they started toilet training. Across ethnic groups, girls were expected to be dry significantly earlier than boys, and toilet training of girls started earlier than for boys. Similarly, girls were found to wet their bed significantly less often than boys, both across and within ethnic groups. While 73 per cent of the girls never wet their bed, only 53 per cent of the boys were dry.

3.5.3.4 Mealtime and feeding practices

When parents were asked about infant feeding practices and the age of weaning, no significant differences between the ethnic groups appeared. In both groups, the preferable mean age of weaning in the opinion of the mothers was 14 months. The norm was stricter for girls than for boys. When asked for how long they had actually breastfed their child, the Sámi mothers reported a mean age of 11 months; whereas, the Norwegian mothers reported 9 months.

In contrast to the answers on infant feeding, significant ethnic differences were found in mothers' attitudes regarding current feeding and mealtime rules. The Sámi mothers reported a generally more permissive attitude than did the Norwegian mothers. This was true for the following items: allowing children to leave food on the plate, talking during meals, bringing toys to table, leaving the table during meals and parental efforts to teach children good table manners. The groups also differed as to the importance they placed on regularity of meals, the Sámi mothers being more indulgent. Self-regulation of food was practised more often by the Sámi than by the Norwegian mothers. Of the Sámi mothers, 40 per cent practised self-regulation of food during the week, compared with 5 per cent of the Norwegian mothers. During weekends, 70 per cent of the Sámi mothers and 24 per cent of the Norwegian mothers had this practice.

3.5.3.5 Bedtime and sleeping arrangements

The Sámi mothers were generally more lenient about sleeping arrangements and bedtime rules than the Norwegian mothers. Significantly more Sámi than Norwegian children slept with their parents, and more Sámi children shared a bedroom. The two groups also differed with respect to when children began to sleep alone. The Sámi children slept with their parents considerably longer than did the Norwegian children (Sámi children: 26.1 months; Norwegian children: 10.7 months).

The Sámi mothers were more permissive than the Norwegian mothers in letting children stay up late if they wanted to, and accepted it more if the child returned to join its parents after being put to bed. Bedtime was later for the Sámi than for the Norwegian children (Sámi children: 9.00 PM; Norwegian children: 8.00 PM).

The two ethnic groups also differed as to the importance they placed on regularity of sleep. More Sámi mothers practised self-regulation of sleep than did the Norwegian mothers (Sámi: 26 per cent, Norwegian: 6 per cent). Similarly, more Sámi than Norwegian mothers regulated bedtimes according to the season, letting the child stay up much longer during the summer period. Sámi mothers imposed significantly stricter norms for girls than for boys in this area, while Norwegian mothers imposed similar norms on boys and girls.

3.5.3.6 Freedom in play

Parental tolerance of disruptive play in the home was assessed by asking whether they would allow the children to use furniture in play, make loud noises, or make a mess with paint or water. The Sámi mothers tended to be more tolerant in their attitudes than the Norwegian mothers, but differences between groups were significant for only one of the single items: 'Do you allow the child to jump on the sofa/bed and to use furniture in play?' No gender differences emerged.

3.5.3.7 Discipline

In both groups, the most common methods were sending the child to bed, or telling the child that misbehaviour made the parent unhappy. The Sámi mothers reported that they slapped their child more often than did the Norwegian mothers. Threats of physical punishment were also used more often by the Sámi mothers. However, in both groups, the frequency of physical punishment was low. Three times as many Sámi as Norwegian mothers would say they would not love the child or would threaten to go away or send the child away if it did not behave. Half of the Sámi mothers used to threaten the child with supernatural beings, a method not used by any of the Norwegians. Tricking the child into doing things, such as going errands, was more common among the Sámi than among the Norwegian mothers.

Sámi and Norwegian mothers also differed as to whether parents should actively train their children to be hardy in order to be able to endure hardships. The Sámi mothers were almost twice as likely to train their children for hardiness, than were Norwegian mothers (Sámi: 65 per cent; Norwegian: 35 per cent). Teasing was the main method of training for mental hardiness and self-control, and was significantly more common in Sámi than in Norwegian families.

No gender differences were found for any of the specific items.

3.5.3.8 Attitudes to child aggression

Parental attitudes to child aggression revealed significant ethnic differences. Compared with Norwegian parents, more Sámi parents tended to be less tolerant towards fights between peers in general; 50 per cent of the Sámi mothers said fights were unacceptable, compared with 36 per cent of the Norwegian mothers. The Sámi mothers were less tolerant of temper tantrums, thinking that they should be stopped as early as possible (Sámi: 30 per cent; Norwegian: 13 per cent). Also, displays of jealousy among children were less tolerated by the Sámi parents: Significantly more of the Sámi parents (37 per cent) would stop such displays, compared with the Norwegian parents (16 per cent).

3.5.4 Discussion of findings

3.5.4.1 Historical and environmental perspectives

As described above, significant ethnic differences in various aspects of childrearing were found between the Sámi and Norwegian ethnic groups. Our findings were similar to those reported in previous studies of Sámi childrearing (Balto, 1997; Pelto, 1962; Seitamo, 1991), as well as consistent with traditional Sámi childrearing which has been characterized by great freedom and permissiveness, encouragement of independence and self-reliance, and indirect types of disciplinary control (Bruhn, 1935; Demant-Hatt, 1913). Our study demonstrates that in spite of a strong assimilation policy during several decades, the child-rearing attitudes and practices of Sámi parents are remarkably well preserved. It shows that unscheduled feeding and sleeping are still practised in Sámi families, in spite of a modern, more clock-bound and structured way of living. This practice relates to the common cultural belief about innate regularity of food and sleep, which contrasts the Western idea of regularity held by the Norwegian parents. Moreover, their traditional types of disciplinary control, which differ greatly from those of the Norwegians, such as threatening the child with supernatural beings, and teasing it in order to teach it self-control and make it hardy, were still practised by the Sámi parents. A new contribution provided by the present research was the demonstration of prolonged co-sleeping being so dominant in Sámi families. This practice was fairly uncommon in the Norwegian families, and is, as previously mentioned, generally rare in Western European societies.

However, traditional and modern ideas of childrearing live side by side in contemporary Sámi society. Expert advice from the 'well-baby clinics' compete with advice transmitted from their mothers and grandmothers, thus creating maternal uncertainty and frustrations. In their childrearing, the Sámi mothers face a struggle on two separate fronts: maintaining and nourishing the traditional native ways of being a Sámi, and psychologically adapting to the modern ways of the Western world. In present-day Sámi society, the relevance of the traditional way of living is diminishing, and the modern ways of Western society are taking over. However, our research suggests that in spite of strong pressure from the outside world to conform, Sámi parents still try to preserve the old values and ways of their own culture. This strong persistence in maintaining their own cultural practices and values might not be possible without the Sámi hardiness and independence, and without the autonomy inculcated by the childrearing of previous generations. That is perhaps why these traditional values have proven so resilient to change.

There is, however, no turning back the clock. It seems that the old techniques of teasing children ('narrideapmi') and threatening them with supernatural beings are less practised today, and that unscheduled eating and sleeping are not as common as in earlier generations. More young parents put their children in their own beds in a separate room as advised by the 'well-baby clinic'. The crucial question is how to adapt to the new conditions without losing one's cultural identity and connectedness. Recent political, social and economic changes in Sámi society have created a different environmental context. The language used and the traditions and lifestyle practised within the extended family have formed necessary contextual constituents for the support of specific child-rearing practices, but are now weakened by modern ways of living (Javo et al., 2003). The old enclave community is losing its cohesion and social control as it is replaced by another, more complex and less concrete social structure governed by a multitude of different values. This move from a 'simple' community into a more 'complex' community fundamentally influences the socialization process (Hoem, 1978). Without the original structure of their society that made extensive autonomy possible, freedom in this new context might easily deteriorate into laissez-faire and even parental neglect. The juxtaposition of traditional values and new values favouring external rules and control could also lead to ambivalence and inconsistency in childrearing, making genuine autonomy even more difficult to accomplish. The eventual outcome of this predicament is yet to be seen. Hopefully, more effective styles of parenting will develop in the wake of this cultural shift.

3.5.4.2 Comparisons with other indigenous studies

The findings from our study are consistent with other studies done on indigenous populations, such as the Inuit in Canadian Arctic and Greenland, Alaskan Natives and American Indians. In her qualitative study on the Canadian Inuit, Briggs (1970; 1998) described Inuit childrearing as permissive, promoting independence and self-control. According to Chance (1966), characteristics of Inuit childrearing in North Alaska were permissiveness, flexibility of routines, a minimum of rules and early responsibilities. Threats (of supernatural beings, e.g., 'little people'), as well as teasing or mild humiliation were used to control the child. The misbehaving child was treated more severely, although physical punishment was relatively rare. In his study on American Indians, Locke (1992) found that, like the Inuit children, American Indian children were given considerable autonomy, and were allowed to explore and be independent quite early in their lives. No fixed schedules for eating or sleeping were imposed. The value placed on child autonomy and child self-control among American Indians has also been described by Sue and Sue (1990).

These findings suggest that native or indigenous cultures living within the circumpolar region have certain common basic traits in their childrearing, such as granting the child great freedom and autonomy, the encouragement of independence and self-control, and non-confrontational, more indirect types of discipline. It may be speculated that these similar patterns of child socialization might stem from the similar environments and ways of living that these peoples have shared.

3.5.4.3 Individualism-collectivism in indigenous cultures

The patterns of Sámi childrearing may provide a useful commentary on the general cultural issue of individualism-collectivism. It seems to be a widespread opinion that indigenous peoples generally favour the value of the community over that of the individual, and hence are seen as collectivist cultures. However, this may be misleading, at least for the Sámi culture (Oskal, 1999). Anthropological literature on the Sámi, especially Sámi reindeer herders, has demonstrated that individual autonomy has been the core value, and that their nomadic, pastoral lifestyle is highly individualistic (Anderson, 1978; Paine, 1970; Pelto, 1962). Interestingly, as early as in the 1950s, Barry, Child and Bacon (1959) found that in migratory tribes (hunting and gathering societies with low levels of food accumulation), child-rearing practices emphasized assertiveness, autonomy, achievement and self-reliance. As a result, adults in these communities tended to be self-assured, independent and venturesome, consonant with a more individualist orientation. In contrast, they found that in sedentary communities (societies that have relatively high food accumulation through agriculture and animal husbandry), child-rearing practices emphasized compliance, obedience and responsibility. As a result, adults in these communities tended to be conscientious, compliant and conservative, consonant with a more collectivist orientation.

In today's Sámi society, reindeer-herding remains as a source of employment on a relatively small scale, but it still maintains a strong influence on Sámi identity, values and way of living. In our study, some of the main features in Sámi childrearing were the parents' emphasis on individual autonomy, on freedom with few external rules and regulations imposed. Their children's independence was higher than that of the Norwegian children. Teaching the children internal self-control and training them to be hardy through methods such as teasing were commonly practised by the Sámi parents. In this way, the child was encouraged to decide for itself how to act, and to possess the individual initiative to act on those decisions These patterns of childrearing, which were confirmed by our qualitative, in-depth study on parental values (Jávo et al., 2003), are congruent with traits found in individualist cultures.

However, values found in rural, collectivist cultures, such as in-group harmony and cooperation based upon close relationships with a high sensitivity to interpersonal cues, could also be traced in Sámi culture and were moulded into their child-rearing practices. In our study, the Sámi families' more stringent attitude towards child's outbursts of aggression or jealousy, and their use of non-confrontational, indirect methods of control, minimizing frustrations and direct conflicts, indicate that in-group harmony was important. The specific traits of child-rearing practices found in collectivist cultures, such as indirect communication, prolonged bodily contact between mother and child, disciplinary practices that stress empathy with others' feelings about the child's transgressions, and use of threats such as exclusion from the family, could also be seen in Sámi childrearing: prolonged co-sleeping was commonly practised, and indirect or emotional techniques of control, such as threatening to send the child away, or not to love the child any more were used to socially condition the child. Such collectivist traits are congruent with the traditional Sámi society of small, migrant, tightly knit social entities, highly dependent on mutual responsibilities and contributions among its members for survival.

Recent literature confirms that individualism and collectivism do not always exist as opposites across cultures or are not necessarily opposed, either within individuals, or as individuals and societies change from one way of living to another (Brewer and Chen, 2007; Freeman, 1997). The study discussed above supports this position. One plausible explanation to our findings is that for societies struggling to survive in harsh environments, individualism and collectivism would be two essential cultural survival strategies. In such environments, it would seem sensible to use both.

An aspect to reconsider is that the meaning of the I-C constructs may differ dependent on culture and social class (Kagitçibasi, 1997; Kusserow, 2004). The constructs are complex and not simply a matter of either/or. More refinement of the concepts is needed, as well as a re-examination of the overall characteristics of I-C in different societies such as native, indigenous cultures. The current construct needs to be revised or modified for groups differing largely from mainstream cultures.

3.5.4.4 Closing remarks

In conclusion, our study shows that indigenous Sámi childrearing, in spite of a long period of assimilation, differs from that of the majority Norwegian culture in many important aspects. The patterns were found to be similar to those reported from studies of native Inuit and American-Indians. Similar findings might be found among yet other minority groups. This leads us to speculate about how cultural norms and values in times of transition influence family dynamics as well as child development and child psychopathology. Such knowledge might be particularly relevant to professionals in understanding the predicament of various ethnic groups that are trying to come to terms with living permanently under the influence of modern, Western values. Moreover, an understanding of culturally specific value systems is needed in order to develop and implement effective health interventions among minority child populations.

> Discussion point: What does the study of Sámi and Norwegian families described above show about the relationship between lifestyle and child-rearing behaviours?

3.6 General conclusions

As we have seen in this chapter, child-rearing goals and practices largely differ across cultures. Cultural differences in parenting and child socialization pertain largely to how individuals define themselves and their relationships with others, in particular the group to which they belong. In most Western cultures, the core of self-definition is based on individual autonomy and separation from others and labelled 'independent self-construal' or 'idiocentrism'. In contrast, in most non-Western cultures the self-concept is defined as primarily based on social embeddedness and interdependence with others comprising their in-groups ('interdependent self-construal' or 'allocentrism'). However, there are many different ways of being 'separate individuals', and many ways of being 'embedded' in social relations or groups. It should be noted that recently, many investigations of the construct of individualism-collectivism acknowledge such cultural variations in meanings, and have further pointed to the multidimensionality of the attitudes, values and practices that compose the construct.

Childrearing viewed from a cultural perspective should take into account the nuances of such multidimensionality. Further, as demonstrated in this chapter, a multi-level approach in the conceptualization of childrearing is needed, including the broader cultural dimensions, cultural models, socialization goals, and parenting ethnotheories, as well as parents' individual child-rearing practices and behaviours. Hopefully, future research in non-Western societies may facilitate an understanding of the complexities of cultural influences on child-rearing, both through more elaborated and nuanced cultural concepts, and through studies at the interface of such concepts, socialization goals and childrearing.

FURTHER READING

Bornstein, M.H. (1995). *Handbook of parenting, Vol. 2*. Hillsdale, NJ: Lawrence Erlbaum.
Friedlmeier, W., Chakkarath, P., and Schwarz, B. (2005). *Culture and human development*. Sussex: Psychological Press.
Javo, C., Ronning, J. A., and Heyerdahl, S. (2004). Child-rearing in an indigenous Sami population in Norway: A cross-cultural comparison of parental attitudes and expectations. *Scandinavian Journal of Psychology*, **45**, 67–78.
Kim, U., Triandis, C., Kagitçibasi, C., Choi, S.-C., and Yoon, G. (1994). *Individualism and collectivism. Theory, methods and applications*. Thousand Oaks, CA: Sage.

REFERENCES

Ainsworth, M.D.S. (1967). *Infancy in Uganda: Infant care and the growth of love*. Baltimore, MD: Johns Hopkins University Press.
Alliensmith, B.B. (1960). Expressive styles: II Directness with which anger is expressed. In D.R. Miller and G.S. Swanson (Eds), *Inner conflict and defence* (pp. 315–336). New York: Holt.
Anderson, M. (1978). Saami ethnoecology: Resource management in Norwegian Lapland. Doctoral dissertation. Yale University: USA.
Balto, A. (1997). *Sámi child-rearing in transition*. Oslo: Ad Notam, Gyldendal AS.
Barry, H., Child, I.L., and Bacon, M.K. (1959). Relations of child training to subsistence economy. *American Anthropologist*, **61**, 51–63.
Bartz, K.W. and LeVine, E.S. (1978). Child-rearing by black parents: A description and comparison to Anglo and Chicano parents. *Journal of Marriage and the Family*, **40**, 709–719.
Baumrind, D. (1967). Child-care practices anteceding three patterns of preschool behaviour. *Genetic Psychology Monographs*, **75**, 43–88.
Baumrind, D. (1971). *Current patterns of parental authority*. Berkeley, CA: Developmental Psychology Monograph, 4(1 part 2).
Becker, W.C. (1964). Consequences of different kinds of parental discipline. In M.L. Hoffman and L.W. Hoffman (Eds), *Review of child*

development research Vol.1 (pp. 169–208). New York: Russel Sage Foundation.

Benjet, C. and Kazdin, A.E. (2003). Spanking children: The controversies, findings, and new directions. *Clinical Psychology Review*, **23**, 197–224.

Berry, J.W. (1994). Ecology of individualism and collectivism. In U. Kim, H.C. Triandis, C. Kagitçibasi, S.-C. Choi, and G. Yoon (Eds), *Individualism and collectivism. Theory, method and applications* (pp. 77–84). Thousand Oaks, CA: Sage.

Berry, J.W. and Annis, R.C. (1974). Acculturative stress: The role of ecology, culture and differentiation. *Journal of Cross-Cultural Psychology*, **5**, 382–406.

Berry, J.W. and Sam, D. (1997). Acculturation and adaption. In J.W. Berry, M.H. Segall, and C. Kagitçibasi (Eds), *Handbook of cross-cultural psychology: Vol. 3. Social behavior and applications.* Second Edition (pp. 291–326). Boston, MA: Allyn & Bacon.

Berry, J.W., Phinney, J.S., Sam, D.L., and Vedder, P. (2006). *Immigrant youth in cultural transition: Acculturation, identity, and adaptation across national contexts.* London: Lawrence Erlbaum.

Bowlby, J. (1989). *The making and breaking of affectional bonds.* Routledge, London.

Brewer, M.B. and Chen, Y. (2007). Where (who) are collectives in collectivism? Toward conceptual clarification of individualism and collectivism. *Psychological Review*, **114**, 133–151.

Briggs, J.L. (1970). *Never in anger. Portrait of an Eskimo family.* Cambridge, MA: Harvard University Press.

Briggs, J.L. (1998). *Inuit morality play: The emotional education of a three-year-old.* New Haven, CT: Yale University Press.

Bruhn, K. (1935). *Child-rearing of the Nordic nomads.* Helsingfors, Finland: Söderstrøm.

Campbell, S.B. (1995). Behavior problems in preschool children: A review of recent research. *Journal of Child Psychology and Psychiatry*, **36**, 113–149.

Carlson, V. and Harwood, R. (2003). Attachment, culture, and the caregiving system: The cultural patterning of everyday experiences among Anglo and Puerto Rican mother-infant pairs. *Infant Mental Health Journal*, **24**, 53–73.

Chance, N.A. (1966). *The Eskimo of North Alaska.* Holt, Rinehart & Winston, Inc: Fort Worth, Texas.

Chao, R. (1994). Beyond parental control and authoritarian parenting style: Understanding Chinese parenting through the cultural notion of training. *Child Development*, **65**, 1111–1119.

Chao, R.K. (1995). Chinese and European American cultural models of the self, reflected in mothers' childrearing beliefs. *Ethos*, **23**, 328–354.

Chao, R.K. (2000). Cultural explanations for the role of parenting in the school success of Asian-American children. In R.D. Taylor and M.C. Wang (Eds), *Resilience across contexts: Family, work, culture, and community* (pp. 333–363). Mahwah, NJ: Lawrence Erlbaum.

Chao, R. (2001). Integrating culture and attachment. *American Psychologist*, **56**, 822–823.

Chirkov, V., Kim, Y., Ryan, R., and Kaplan, U. (2003). Differentiating autonomy from individualism and independence: A self-determination theory perspective on internalization of cultural orientations and well-being. *Journal of Personality and Social Psychology*, **84**, 97–110.

Chou, K.-L. (2000). Emotional autonomy and depression among Chinese adolescents. *Journal of Genetic Psychology*, **161**, 161–169.

Dalgety-Gaitan, C. (1994). Socializing young children in Mexican-American families: An intergenerational perspective. In P.M. Greenfield and R.R. Cocking (Eds), *Cross-cultural roots of minority child development* (pp. 55–86). Hillsdale, NJ: Lawrence Erlbaum.

Deater-Deckard, K., Dodge, K.A., Bates, J.E., and Pettit, G.S. (1996). Physical discipline among African-American and European-American mothers: Links to children's externalizing behaviors. *Developmental Psychology*, **32**, 1065–1072.

Demant-Hatt, E. (1913). *With the Lapps in the highlands. The Lapps and their land.* Stockholm, Sweden: H.Lundbohm II.

Dennis, T.A., Cole, P.M., Zahn-Waxler, C., and Mizuta, I. (2003). Self in context: Autonomy and relatedness in Japanese and U.S. mother-preschool dyads. *Child Development*, **73**, 1803–1817.

Dettwyler, K.A. (1986). Infant feeding in Mali, West Africa: Variations in belief and practice. *Social Science and Medicine*, **23**, 651–664.

Dosanjh, J.S. and Ghuman, P.A.S. (1996). *Child-rearing in ethnic minorities.* Clevedon: Multilingual Matters Ltd.

Feiring, C. and Taska, L.S. (1996). Family self-concept: Ideas on its meaning. In B.A. Bracken (Ed.), *Handbook of self-concept: Developmental, social, and clinical considerations* (pp. 317–373). New York: John Wiley & Sons.

Freeman, M.A. (1997). Demographic correlates of individualism and collectivism. A study of social values in Sri Lanka. *Journal of Cross-Cultural Psychology*, **28**, 321–341.

Friedlmeier, W. and Trommsdorff, G. (1999). Emotion regulation in early childhood. A cross-cultural comparison between German and Japanese toddlers. *Journal of Cross-Cultural Psychology*, **30**, 684–711.

Garcìa Coll, C., Meyer, E.C., and Brillion, L. (1995). Ethnic and minority parenting. In M.H. Bornstein (Ed.), *Handbook of parenting, Vol. 2* (pp. 189–209). Hillsdale, NJ: Lawrence Erlbaum.

Georgas, J., Christakopoulou, S., Poortinga, Y.H., Angleitner, A., Goodwin, R., and Charalambous, N. (1997). The relationship of family bonds to family structure and function across cultures. *Journal of Cross-Cultural Psychology*, **28**, 303–320.

Gershoff, E.T. (2002). Parental corporal punishment and associated child behaviors and experiences: A meta-analytic and theoretical review. *Psychological Bulletin*, **128**, 539–579.

Greenberg, M.T., Speltz, M.L., and De Klyen, M. (1993). The role of attachment in the early development of disruptive behavior problems. *Development and Psychopathology*, **5**, 191–213.

Greenfield, P.M. and Suzuki, L.K. (1998). Culture and human development: Implications for parenting, education, pediatrics, and mental health. In W. Damon, I.E. Sigel, and K. A. Renninger (Eds), *Handbook of child psychology, child psychology in practice, Vol. IV* (pp. 1059–1109). New York: John Wiley & Sons.

Greenfield, P.M., Keller, H., Fuligni, A., and Maynard, A. (2003). Cultural pathways through universal development. *Annual Review of Psychology*, **54**, 461–490.

Greenfield, P.M. and Cocking, R.R. (Eds) (1994). *Cross-cultural roots of minority child development*. Hillsdale, NJ: Lawrence Erlbaum.

Hackett, L. and Hackett, R. (1993). Parental ideas of normal and deviant child behavior. A comparison of two ethnic groups. *British Journal of Psychiatry*, **162**, 353–357.

Hackett, L. and Hackett, R. (1994). Child-rearing practices and psychiatric disorder in Gujarati and British children. *British Journal of Social Work*, **24**, 191–202.

Harkness, S. and Super, C.M. (1996). *Parents' cultural belief systems. Their origins, expressions, and consequences*. New York: The Guilford Press.

Harkness, S., Super, C.M., and van Tijen, N. (2000). Individualism and the 'Western mind' reconsidered: American and Dutch parents' ethnotheories of the child. In W. Damon (Series Ed.), S. Harkness, C. Raeff, and C.M. Super (Vol. Eds), *New directions for child and adolescent development, 87. Variability in the social construction of the child* (pp. 23–39). San Francisco, CA: Jossey Bass.

Hoem, A. (1978). *Socialization*, Universitetsforlaget: Oslo.

Hofstede, G. (1980). *Culture's consequences: International differences in work-related values*. Beverly Hills, CA: Sage.

Hofstede, G. (2001). *Culture's consequences: Comparing values, behaviors, institutions and organizations across nations.* Second Edition. Thousand Oaks, CA: Sage.

Javo, C., Alapack, R., Rønning, J.A., and Heyerdahl, S. (2003). Parental values and ethnic identity in indigenous Sami families: A qualitative study. *Family Process*, 42, 151–164.

Javo, C., Rønning, J.A., and Heyerdahl, S. (2004a). Child-rearing in an indigenous Sámi population in Norway: A cross-cultural comparison of parental attitudes and expectations. *Scandinavian Journal of Psychology*, 45, 67–78.

Javo, C., Rønning, J.A., Heyerdahl, S., and Rudmin, F.W. (2004b). Parenting correlates of child behavior problems in a multiethnic community sample of preschool children in northern Norway. *European Child & Adolescent Psychiatry*, 13, 8–18.

Jose, P.E., Huntsinger, C.S., Huntsinger, P.R., and Liaw, F.-R. (2000). Parental values and practices relevant to young children's social development in Taiwan and the United States. *Journal of Cross-Cultural Psychology*, 31, 677–702.

Kagitçibasi, C. (1990). Family and socialization in cross-cultural perspective: A model of change. In J. Berman (Ed.), *Nebraska symposium on motivation* (pp. 135–200). Lincoln, NE: University of Nebraska Press.

Kagitçibasi, C. (1997). Individualism and collectivism. In J.W. Berry, M.H. Segall, and C. Kagitçibasi (Eds), *Handbook of cross-cultural Psychology* (Vol. 3) (pp. 1–47). Boston, MA: Allyn & Bacon.

Kagitçibasi, C. (2005). Autonomy and relatedness in cultural context. Implications for self and family. *Journal of Cross-Cultural Psychology*, 20, 1–20.

Keller, H. (2003). Socialization for competence: Cultural models of infancy. *Human Development*, 46, 288–311.

Keller, H., Lamm, B., Abels, M., Yovsi, R., Borke, J., Jensen, H., et al. (2006). Cultural models, socialization goals, and parenting ethnotheories. A multicultural analysis. *Journal of Cross-Cultural Psychology*, 37, 155–172.

Keller, H., Papaligoura, Z., Kunsemuller, P., Voelker, S., Papaliou, C., Lohaus, A., et al. (2003). Concepts of mother-infant interaction in Greece and Germany. *Journal of Cross-Cultural Psychology*, 34, 677–689.

Kelley, M.L., Power, T.G., and Wimbush, D.D. (1992). Determinants of disciplinary practices in low-income Black mothers. *Child Development*, 63, 573–582.

Kelley, M. and Tseng, H.-M. (1992). Cultural differences in child rearing: A comparison of immigrant Chinese and Caucasian American mothers. *Journal of Cross-Cultural Psychology*, 23, 444–455.

Kim, U. (1994). Individualism and collectivism. Conceptual clarification and elaboration. In U. Kim, H.C. Triandis, C. Kagitçibasi, S.-C. Choi, and G. Yoon (Eds), *Individualism and collectivism: Theory, method and applications* (pp. 19–40). Thousand Oaks, CA: Sage.

Kitayama, S. (2002). Culture and basic psychological processes – toward a system view of culture: Comment on Oyserman et al. (2002). *Psychological Bulletin*, **128**, 89–96.

Kitayama, S., Duffy, S., Kawamura, T., and Larsen, J.T. (2003). Perceiving an object and its context in different cultures: A cultural look at new look. *Psychological Science*, **14**, 201–206.

Kobayashi-Winata, H. and Power, T.G. (1989). Child-rearing and compliance – Japanese and American families in Houston. *Journal of Cross-Cultural Psychology*, **20**, 333–356.

Kusserow, A. (2004). *American individualisms: Childrearing and social class in three neighbourhoods*. New York: Palgrave Macmillan.

Kwak, K. (2003). Adolescents and their parents: A review of intergenerational family relations for immigrant and non-immigrant families. *Human Development*, **46**, 115–136.

Kwak, K. and Berry, J.W. (2001). Generational differences in acculturation among Asian families in Canada: A comparison of Vietnamese, Korean, and East-Indian groups. *International Journal of Psychology*, **36**, 152–162.

Larzelere, R.E. (1994). Should the use of corporal punishment by parents be considered child abuse? No. In M.A. Mason and E. Gambrill (Eds), *Debating children's lives* (pp. 204–206, 217–218). Thousand Oaks, CA: Sage.

Lefley, H.P. (1976). Acculturation, child-rearing and self-esteem in two North American Indian tribes. *Ethos*, **4**, 385–401.

Lester, D. (1967). The relationship between discipline experiences and the expression of aggression. *American Anthropologist*, **69**, 734–737.

LeVine, R.A. (2004). Challenging expert knowledge: Findings from an African study of infant care and development. In U.P. Gielen and J.L. Roopnarine (Eds), *Childhood and adolescence: Cross-cultural perspectives and applications*. Westport, CT: Praeger.

LeVine, R.A. and Norman, K. (2001). The infant's acquisition of culture: Early attachment re-examined in anthropological perspective. In C.C. Moore and H.F. Mathews (Eds), *The psychology of cultural experience* (pp. 83–104). Cambridge: Cambridge University Press.

LeVine, R., Dixon, S., LeVine S., Richman, A., Keefer, C., Leiderman, P.H., and Brazelton, T.B. (1994). *Child care and culture: Lessons from Africa*. New York: Cambridge University Press.

Locke, D.C. (1992). *Increasing multicultural understanding. A comprehensive model.* Multicultural aspects of counseling, series 1. Newbury Park, CA: Sage.

Lytton, H. (1990). Child and parent effects in boys' conduct disorder: A reinterpretation. *Developmental Psychology,* **26**, 683–697.

McLeod, J.D., Kruttschnitt, C., and Dornfield, M. (1994). Does parenting explain the effects of structural conditions on children's antisocial behavior? A comparison of Blacks and Whites. *Social Forces,* **73**, 575–604.

Meeus, W., Oosterwegel, A., and Vollebergh, W. (2002). Parental and peer attachment and identity development in adolescence. *Journal of Adolescence,* **25**, 93–106.

Mizuta, I., Zahn-Waxler, C., Cole, P.M., and Hiruma, N. (1996). A cross-cultural study of preschoolers' attachment: Security and sensitivity in Japanese and U.S. dyads. *International Journal of Behavioral Development,* **19**, 141–159.

Munroe, R.L. and Munroe, R.H. (1975). *Cross-cultural human development.* Belmont, CA: Wadsworth.

Oskal, N. (1999). Culture and rights. In H. Eidheim (Ed.), *Sami and Norwegians: Themes in law, history and social anthropology* (pp. 141–166). Oslo: Cappelen Akademisk Forlag.

Oyserman, D., Coon, H.M., and Kemmelmeier, M. (2002). Rethinking individualism and collectivism: Evaluation of theoretical assumptions and meta-analysis. *Psychological Bulletin,* **128**, 3–72.

Paine, R. (1970). Lappish decisions, partnerships, information management and sanctions – a nomadic pastoral adaptation. *Ethnology,* **9**, 52–67.

Patterson, G.R. (1980). Mothers: The unacknowledged victims. *Monographs of the Society for Research in Child Development,* **45**, 1–54.

Pelto, P.J. (1962). *Individualism in Skolt Lapp Society.* Helsinki: Finnish Antiquities Society.

Pettit, G.S., Bates, J.E., and Dodge, K.A. (1997). Supportive parenting, ecological context, and children's adjustment: A seven-year longitudinal study. *Child Development,* **68**, 908–923.

Phinney, J.S., Ong, A., and Madden, T. (2000). Cultural values and intergenerational value discrepancies in immigrant and non-immigrant families. *Child Development,* **71**, 528–539.

Querido, J.G., Warner, T.D., and Eyberg, S.M. (2002). Parenting styles and child behavior in African American families of preschool children. *Journal of Clinical Child Psychology,* **32**, 272–277.

Quinn, N. and Holland, D. (1987). Culture and cognition. In D. Holland and N. Quinn (Eds), *Cultural models in language and thought* (pp. 3–40). New York: Cambridge University Press.

Raeff, C. (1997). Individuals in relationships: Cultural values, children's social interactions, and the development of an American individualistic self. *Developmental Review*, 17, 205–238.

Rosenthal, D., Ranieri, N., and Klimidis, S. (1996). Vietnamese adolescents in Australia: Relationships between perceptions of self and parental values, intergenerational conflict, and gender dissatisfaction. *International Journal of Psychology*, 31, 81–91.

Rothbaum, F. and Morelli, G. (2005). Attachment and culture: Bridging relativism and universalism. In W. Friedlmeier, P. Chakkarath, and B. Schwarz (Eds), *Culture and human development* (pp. 99–121). Sussex: Psychology Press.

Rothbaum, F., Weisz, J., Pott, M., Miyake, K., and Morelli, G. (2000). Attachment and culture. Security in the United States and Japan. *American Psychologist*, 55, 1093–1104.

Ryan, R.M. and Deci, E.L. (2000). Self-determination theory and the facilitation of intrinsic motivation, social development, and well-being. *American Psychologist*, 55, 68–78.

Schwarz, B., Schäfermeier, E., and Trommsdorff, G. (2005). Relations between value orientations, child-rearing goals, and parenting: A comparison of German and South Korean mothers. In W. Friedlmeier, P. Chakkarath, and B. Schwarz (Eds), *Culture and human development* (pp. 203–230). Sussex: Psychological Press.

Seitamo, L. (1991). *Psychological development in arctic cultures. A comparative study of Skolt Sami and Finnish children in the north of Finland within the frame of reference of ecological psychology*. Doctoral dissertation. Oulo, Finland: Department of Behavioral Sciences, University of Oulu.

Stormshak, E.A., Bierman, K.L., McMahon, R.J., and Lengua, L.J. (2000). Parenting practices and child disruptive behavior problems in early elementary school. *Journal of Clinical Child Psychology*, 29, 17–29.

Sue, D.W. and Sue, D. (1990). *Counseling the culturally different. Theory & practice*. New York: John Wiley & Sons.

Super, C.M. and Harkness, S. (1993). The developmental niche: A conceptualization at the interface of child and culture. In R.A. Pierce and M.A. Black (Eds), *Life-span development: A diversity reader* (pp. 61–77). Dubuque, IA: Kendall/Hunt Publishing Co.

Super, C.M. and Harkness, S. (1995). Culture and parenting. In M. Bornstein (Ed.), *Handbook of parenting, Vol. 2* (pp. 211–234). Hillsdale, NJ: Lawrence Erlbaum.

Szapocznik, J. and Kurtines, W. (1993). Family psychology and cultural diversity. *American Psychologist*, 48, 400–407.

Triandis, H.C. (1994). Theoretical and methodological approaches to the study of collectivism and individualism. In U. Kim, H.C. Triandis, C. Kagitçibasi, S.-C. Choi, and G. Yoon (Eds), *Individualism and collectivism: Theory, method and applications* (pp. 41–51). Thousand Oaks, CA: Sage.

Trommsdorff, G. and Friedlmeier, W. (1993). Control and responsiveness in Japanese and German mother-child interactions. *Early Development and Parenting*, **2**, 65–78.

Trommsdorff, G. and Kornadt H.-J. (2003). Parent-child relations in cross-cultural perspective. In L. Kuczynski (Ed.), *Handbook of dynamics in parent-child relations* (pp. 271–306). Thousand Oaks, CA: Sage.

Van IJzendoorn, M.H. and Sagi, A. (1999). Cross-cultural patterns of attachment: Universal and contextual determinants. In J. Cassidy and P.R. Shaver (Eds), *Handbook of attachment theory and research* (pp. 713–734). New York: The Guildford Press.

Wachs, T.D. (1992). *The nature of nurture.* Newbury Park, CA: Sage.

Watson, P.J., Sherbak, J., and Morris, R.J. (1998). Irrational beliefs, individualism – collectivism, and adjustment. *Personality and Individual Differences*, **24**, 173–179.

Webster-Stratton, C. (1990). Stress: A potential disruptor of parent perceptions and family interactions. *Journal of Clinical Child Psychology*, **4**, 302–312.

Wolf, A.W., Lozoff, B., Latz, S., and Paludetto, R. (1996). Parental theories in the management of young children's sleep in Japan, Italy, and the United States. In S. Harkness and C.M. Super (Eds), *Parents' cultural belief systems. Their origins, expressions, and consequences* (pp. 364–385). New York: The Guilford Press.

Social Disadvantage and Child Development

Janet M. Empson

OUTLINE

4.1 Introduction
4.2 Subcultures of social disadvantage
    4.2.1 What are subcultures in society?
    4.2.2 Poverty as a subculture
4.3 Poverty and social disadvantage
    4.3.1 Poverty in developed and developing countries
    4.3.2 Poverty and ethnic minority status
4.4 Effects of poverty on children
    4.4.1 Lifestyle
    4.4.2 Physical development
    4.4.3 Cognitive development and educational attainment
    4.4.4 Emotional and behavioural development
4.5 Individual differences in susceptibility to effects of social disadvantage
    4.5.1 What is resilience?
    4.5.2 Resilience in parents
    4.5.3 Resilience in children
    4.5.4 Summary
4.6 A theoretical framework for child development in conditions of poverty

> **OUTLINE (cont'd)**
> 4.7 Conclusions
> Further reading
> References

4.1 Introduction

Social disadvantage has often been associated with poverty and low socio-economic status. For centuries, poets and others have written of poverty as a condition scorned (Shakespeare, 1592), shameful (Farquhar, 1707), associated with stealing (Defoe, 1721), 'a great evil' (Johnson, 1763) or 'The greatest of evils' (Shaw, 1907) and as the poor finding it difficult to maintain their worth, experiencing great suffering and having no hope of a better life:

> O Death! The poor man's dearest friend,
> The kindest and the best.
> (Robert Burns, 1786, *Man was made to Mourn* st 11)

Today, in Western countries many think that poverty has been tackled politically and economically to reduce in particular the number of children living in poverty. One of the central aims of the Labour government in the United Kingdom has been to provide employment, childcare and improve educational opportunity thereby reducing social disadvantage. But the reality is, as we shall see in this chapter, that even now many children are growing up in poverty in the richest countries of the world. What are the implications of this in terms of children's health and unfulfilled potential? Damage in the early stages of development often persists affecting individuals throughout their lives. In this chapter, we will consider the evidence relating to the possible effects of low socio-economic status of families and child poverty on child development, parenting and relationships in the family and with the neighbourhood. As most of the empirical evidence is from studies in Western industrialized societies, this will be the main focus for discussion. Within each culture there is a wide range of individual differences and most children growing up in poverty are developmentally normal (Bowman, 1994).

In this chapter, I develop some of the issues explored in the previous chapter on cultural variations in socialization, focusing in particular on childrearing in impoverished circumstances. The chapter begins with a discussion of the differences between absolute and relative poverty in different countries across the globe and then concentrates on the relative poverty of Western society about which a considerable body of research has been established. The substantial group of people living in poverty in the United States and the United Kingdom have been referred to as a particular subculture in society which has common ways of behaving, motivations and aspirations, is related to ethnicity, and is associated *in some families* with various forms of social disadvantage. Such views of those living in poverty are critically discussed. The lives of children growing up in poverty are discussed in relation to Bronfenbrenner's (1979) ecological view of development and as a particular developmental niche. A critical review of empirical evidence is presented which demonstrates a possible relationship of poverty with various outcomes including cognitive, educational, social and emotional development, as well as with physical and mental health. A number of reasons are suggested for differential achievement in different social groups whilst acknowledging wide variations in outcome for children *within* a particular social group. For example, variations both within and between social groups in children's developmental progress may result from differences on a number of factors including lifestyle and access to resources, resilience of individual children, and the structure and social characteristics of home environments. In addition, factors such as stress in the parents which is more likely in disadvantaged circumstances may be associated with such outcomes as marital discord and/or disturbance of psychological functioning and little involvement in helping children with the demands of education. Stressful life circumstances have been shown to be related to difficulties in general functioning of the parents and could also influence parental beliefs and practices and have consequent negative effects on the rest of the family (Empson and McGlaughlin, 1979). However, some parents cope well with similar adverse conditions and their children develop well. The processes involved in resilience and vulnerability to adversity in both children and parents are discussed.

4.2 Subcultures of social disadvantage

4.2.1 What are subcultures in society?

Culture can be briefly defined as 'the shared way of life of a group of people' (Berry, Poortinga, Segall and Dasen, 2002, p. 2). The groups that form the focus of this chapter are socially and economically disadvantaged compared with the rest of the society, in the context of Western countries. Lewis (1966) described such groups as forming subcultures within the larger society; they may contain further subgroupings, for example, different ethnicities. In Western countries it is now common to find various ethnocultural groups living in close proximity, especially within the poorer strata of society, and these groups will interact and change their attitudes, values, beliefs and behaviours as they adapt to living together. The different forms of cultural transmission – *enculturation* and *acculturation* – were described in previous chapters. The reciprocal nature of these processes is one whereby the individual can influence the nature of the acquisition as well as being influenced by the culture(s) s/he encounters. There is a vertical transmission component, from adult to child, and this works in the opposite direction as well, in that the child also influences the adult, usually the parent (Sameroff and Chandler, 1975). Case Study 1 provides an example of how children's school attendance may have an effect on the parents' reading skills.

CASE STUDY I: PARENTAL INVOLVEMENT IN CHILDREN'S EDUCATION

Examples of children influencing parents come from attendance at school where young children reading with parents at home is very much emphasized as desirable in the UK educational system. Through spending time on this activity on a regular basis, parents whose first language is not English may improve their English language skills and be encouraged to read more in English. Parents who are unable to read may be motivated to learn as adults in order to assist their children with their schoolwork.

There is also a horizontal component involving mutual influences with peers and siblings (see Berry et al., 2002). Again, many examples are available in everyday life of how children acquire the social and behavioural norms of their friendship group, such as clothes worn, leisure activities, football team supported, gang membership and carrying knives. The conditions of socialization, the socialization practices and the success or otherwise of outcomes for the children of families in poverty and social disadvantage are the focus of the research presented here. The main theoretical model which is used to integrate the research findings is that of Bronfenbrenner (1979 and subsequently). In relation to different subgroups in society, Bronfenbrenner's systems analysis can explain how children growing up within the same society will be influenced in different ways by multiple influences being filtered through the different contexts, people and relationships of the other systems.

Thus, socialization of children will vary widely in different locations and families. Many societies nowadays are termed culturally plural, in which 'a number of different cultural groups reside together within a shared social and political framework (Skelton and Allen, 1999)' (Berry et al., 2002, p. 346). Usually the different groups within plural societies are considered to be defined by ethnicity or religion, but there are also subgroups defined by their social status and way of life or subculture. A subculture characterizes a group within a society which has its own shared set of customs, attitudes and values: it is a distinctive group within a larger cultural group, which may accept or reject the values of the larger group (Harris and Hodges, 1983). Such a group can be organized around a common activity, occupation, age, status, ethnic background, race, religion or any other unifying social condition. The characteristic feature of members of a particular subculture is that they have distinct behaviours and beliefs from those within the mainstream culture.

4.2.2 Poverty as a subculture

By classifying people on the basis of their socio-economic status, social classes can be identified in which groups of people are 'labelled' by their education, occupation and wealth or income. Members of the lowest social class mainly live in conditions of poverty which has been described as having its own culture, 'the culture of poverty', by Lewis (1966). This is characterized by particular behaviours, attitudes and beliefs which are common to the developmental niche of poverty, and this culture may occur in a range of different settings across different societies and countries. This culture may also have variations because it overlaps with other subcultures, such as those of different ethnic groups. Indeed, in the United Kingdom, those living in long-term poverty are more likely to come from non-indigenous racial groups than

Caucasian and indigenous. Of course, there are also varied behaviours, attitudes and beliefs displayed by individuals and families *within* each social group, including those with the lowest incomes and living in poverty. Also, there will be much overlap between the conceptions and way of life of poor people and those who are better off, in a particular society. Thus, the concept of a 'culture of poverty' is more limited in its application now than in Lewis's day although the concept persists, especially in education (Pather, 2006).

> **Discussion point: Do you think that the concept of a 'culture of poverty' has any validity and use today?**

People living in poverty often have similar needs, desires, aims and aspirations to those living in more comfortable circumstances, albeit to a different level, and they have an attachment to, or identification with, the mainstream society. For example, Shropshire and Middleton (1999) found that poor children held lower career aspirations and asked for less expensive presents for birthdays and Christmas as they had a realistic understanding of the likelihood that their goals or desires would be realized. This means that they have adapted psychologically to the circumstances of their lives and the way these influence their likely outcomes as adults. However, given that individuals in poverty are inevitably aware, through the media and through personal contact with other people, of the material goods and personal and social opportunities that others have, this discrepancy between their own and others' opportunities and resources is likely to be stressful. The stress experienced by those in poverty will derive also from other sources – negative life events, chronic strain and daily hassles – but the particular dissonance arising from the difference between their way of life and expectations for the future and those of other social groups generates a stress similar to that described by Al-Issa and Tousignant (1997) as *'acculturative stress'*. Acculturative stress is associated with personal problems, such as anxiety, hopelessness, depression and psychopathology, and social difficulties, such as not being able to join in social activities or to benefit from services. Multiple stresses feature in the lives of people living in poverty as discussed next.

4.3 Poverty and social disadvantage

4.3.1 Poverty in developed and developing countries

Poverty has been defined in both absolute and relative terms. Those living in absolute poverty have such limited resources (material, and social) that they are excluded from the minimum acceptable way of life in the society to which they belong (EEC, 1985). They are living below the poverty line which specifies a minimum income level below which an individual is officially considered to lack adequate subsistence. Over a third of all children in 'developing' countries (37% or 674 million) are living in absolute poverty. Different countries set their own poverty line usually in relation to international conventions. For the poorest countries, which are in the southern hemisphere, living on less than one or two US dollars a day is considered to constitute absolute poverty. The poverty line for middle-income countries is US$4. On many indicators of child poverty, the poorest region is Sub-Saharan Africa (Gordon, Nandy, Pantazis et al., 2003) where 65 per cent of children live in absolute poverty so it is a normative state to be in. Such children do not have access to safe water, adequate housing or education and are likely to be malnourished, 48.5 per cent have stunted growth and there is a life expectancy of just 48 years (Save the Children, 2000). Case Study 2 illustrates what might be notable to a visitor from a more affluent industrialized country.

CASE STUDY 2: POVERTY IN AN AFRICAN CITY

Visitors to most Sub-Saharan African countries are often struck by the many indicators of poverty characteristic of the majority of the region. On a recent visit to Zambia, I came across many poor people, both rural and urban, the latter living in large shanty communities on the outskirts of the capital Lusaka. The dilapidated houses of sacking and corrugated iron were very inadequate in keeping out the rain and there was no running water or electricity. The area was lacking formal employment opportunities or amenities such as schools, clinics and shops. The children played in the dirt spaces between the shacks which constituted their homes.

> **CASE STUDY 2 (cont'd)**
>
> Younger children (mostly less than ten years old) made creative use of available materials – such as cardboard boxes and pliable wire – to play with in a range of games. At the same time, the people who lived in such conditions were hard at work – mostly in informal occupations such as making things, selling goods, salvaging – to support their families and themselves. Such work activities included both adults and some older children who displayed impressive mastery of their crafts.

Zambia is representative of countries in Sub-Saharan Africa in many respects, one of which is having the highest rates of severe deprivation with respect to lack of shelter and sanitation (more than half of children [Gordon et al., 2003]). The other human needs that are used as indicators of deprivation are information, water, food, health and education.

In the United Kingdom and other Western countries, the experience of poverty for children is much more likely to be that of relative poverty. Relative poverty refers to relative deprivation 'when they lack the resources to obtain the types of diet, participate in the activities and have the living conditions and amenities which are customary... in the society to which they belong' (Townsend, 1979, p. 31). As the United Nations (UN) also points out, low income is important but the definition of poverty also includes denial of access to services (UN, 1995). The UK Department of Social Security (1999) lists the opportunities in life which are denied to those living in poverty, as follows:

- to work
- to learn
- to live healthy and fulfilling lives
- to live out retirement years in security
- an adequate income (and material resources)
- access to quality health services, education and housing
- quality of local environment.

All of these affect quality of life and well-being for many families, and children are over-represented in populations living in poverty.

> **CASE STUDY 3: POVERTY IN A CITY OF THE UNITED KINGDOM**
>
> In the 1970s, I participated in a research project in a northern city in England which investigated mother-child interaction and child development in disadvantaged families, at least half of whom were experiencing relative poverty on the basis of their income. Although for many of these families the conditions of their homes were inadequate in that they were overcrowded, poorly heated, ventilated and damp, they all had access to running water, a bath and a source of hot water even if they could not afford to use hot water much. Some homeless families were placed in temporary accommodation. All families could afford basic foods but were denied by their income a varied and interesting diet and many of the adults were overweight. All the families had access to education for their older children but the schools they attended had poor reputations and again there was no choice available to them. Many of the children suffered chronic health conditions, such as bronchitis, which could be related to their living circumstances, and many of the parents for whom unemployment was a reality or a threat had anxiety, depression or other stress-related conditions. The material and psychological conditions of the neighbourhoods in which these families lived have not changed substantially over the 30 years between then and now.

The example of Britain (United Kingdom) as one of the wealthiest countries in the world demonstrates that poverty rates are not related directly to the stage of economic development of a country, but depends also upon other factors such as the values of society. It is impossible to compare directly what poverty means in the developed and developing countries. In the developing world, poverty is described in terms of severe deprivation of basic human need for shelter, sanitation, information, water, food, health and education. In developed countries, poverty is estimated with reference to the United States poverty line, a certain income deemed necessary to pay for the basic essentials in life, which in 2007 amounts to about £15,000 in the United Kingdom for a family of 4 people. In the richest countries the percentage of children living in absolute poverty varied between nearly 15 per cent (in 1997) in the United States to just more than 2 per cent in Luxembourg (in 1994) (Smeeding, Rainwater and Burtless, 2000). In the developed world, it is more customary for researchers to consider children living in relative poverty than absolute poverty. On this basis, there are many more children living in relative than absolute poverty such that the total number of children living in poverty in the United Kingdom in 1998/99 was one in three (Harper and Marcus, 1999). This chapter focuses on children growing up in conditions of relative poverty and so is based mainly on empirical evidence from Western countries.

4.3.2 Poverty and ethnic minority status

In most Western countries, ethnic minority status tends to be associated with high rates of poverty, for example, Britain (Ridge, 2002). For example, ethnic minority children in Britain suffer from very high rates of poverty (Ridge, 2002). Pakistani and Bangladeshi children in particular have much higher chances of living in poverty. The Family Resources Survey (Adelman and Bradshaw, 1998) found that 80 per cent of these children lived below 50 per cent of median income poverty line after housing costs. Black Caribbean and Pakistani children were found to be three times as likely to be living in conditions of severe deprivation as white children, and Bangladeshi children five times as likely (Census analysis using Sample of Anonymised Records, Moore, 2000). Platt (2000) found that the depth of poverty in which ethnic minority children lived was greater than that of white UK children. On the other hand, white children tended to experience poverty for longer durations.

So, for children in ethnic minority families in the United Kingdom any risks to development associated with poverty are more likely than in white UK families. A number of factors work together to make this so:

- unemployment and low income when employed (Ridge, 2002)
- large family size (Department for Work and Pensions, 2001)
- lone-parent family status.

The first two factors are the main contributors to a life in poverty for these families. If families are first generation immigrants to this country, they are also less likely to receive any financial support from the extended family who are living in the country of origin. It is also possible that the residents in the United Kingdom, as in other Western European countries, will be sending what money they can to help the family back in their country of origin. Figures from the Office of Population Censuses and Surveys (OPCS) covering the period from 1987 to 1989 (OPCS, 1991) show that the third factor, lone-parent status, is much less frequent in Asian groups than white, but much higher in West Indian (49%) and African (30%) than in white (15%) families. Not only are the children of West Indian and African families more likely to live with a lone parent, but also that parent is more likely to be a single mother than separated or divorced and so she is less likely to be able to access an income additional to benefits in the form of maintenance. As the age profile of ethnic minority groups is younger than that of whites, benefit restrictions for younger people will disproportionately hit the ethnic minority groups on benefit. West Indian families, like Asian families, are also likely to have large numbers of children which will increase the likelihood of poverty for these large families in ethnic minority groups (Amin and Oppenheim, 1992). *Overall, then it is apparent that the difficulties faced in society by those on low incomes will be more a part of the lives of ethnic minority groups than of indigenous white people in Britain.*

Members of ethnic minority groups also experience more health problems, which may or may not be associated with poverty. These include more stillbirths and infant mortality (OPCS, 1992) and greater rates of mortality for certain infectious diseases, heart disease and cirrhosis of the liver (Marmot, Adelstein and Bulusu, 1984). These figures are, however, based on immigrants who were not born in Britain. Further, health care is compromised in these groups by low priority of screening and health promotion in health centres, poor availability of translation services and ignorance of factors influencing health such as diet or health beliefs (Fenton, 1989). In addition, retaining behaviours traditional to the country of origin, for example, the diet in Asian families, can lead to a lack of Vitamin D in the United Kingdom (which has less sunshine than India, Bangladesh and Pakistan) and this is associated with ischaemic heart disease, diabetes, TB and rickets (Shaw and Pal, 2002).

4.4 Effects of poverty on children

Poverty has harmful effects on many children, both directly and indirectly as mediated by the effects on their parents. The direct effects may be on children's health, through inadequate diet, housing and clothing, or their education, as perhaps through having time off through illness and no quiet place to do homework. Parents may be affected through the constant stress of trying to make ends meet which may have damaging effects on family relationships and their own mental health. Their physical health may also be affected as parents deprive themselves of material and other resources to spare their children from going without. Also, long-standing illness and disability are more frequently occurring in poor families than in the population as a whole (Gordon, Parker and Loughran, 2000). Other factors which are associated with children's experience of living in poor families (as discussed above) are unemployment, lone parent, a large number of children and being of ethnic minority status (Lloyd, 2006). Whether this is because such conditions lead to poverty or result due to conditions of poverty is debatable.

When parents are functioning poorly there will inevitably be an impact on the rest of the family. Belsky, Steinberg and Draper (1991) used the concept of a 'culture of poverty' to explain intergenerational continuities in personal and social circumstances. Factors in the early life of the child relate to differences in later sexual and reproductive behaviour in different families. Belsky et al. contrasted two different types of family. The first family type was characterized by stressful living circumstances, limited resources and insecure attachment patterns. Sexual maturity was reached by girls at an earlier age and boys and girls engaged in earlier sexual activity. The second family type comprised families characterized by warmth and security of attachment, stability and positive interactions. Later in life, behaviour patterns regarding relationships were continued in both groups: in the impoverished group it led to less stable heterosexual relationships, a higher rate of divorce and less parental involvement. This led to an insecure social environment for the children of the next generation.

The 'culture of poverty' (Lewis, 1966) describes the ideas and behaviours adopted by poor people in industrialized societies to enable them to adapt to their circumstances. Thus, poor people are more likely to commit criminal acts, come before the courts and be sentenced to a prison term; they claim financial benefits from the state more frequently. Their financial circumstances are generally characterized by shortages, no savings, living on credit and pawning goods. They are more likely than other groups to have inadequate education and to distrust the institutions of society such as the government. Their social experience is characterized by temporary and discordant relationships, disruptive family life, absent fathers and illegitimacy being common.

Lewis's original research took place in Costa Rica about 40 years ago and it may be unworkable as a concept in understanding the experience of families in industrialized societies since then. For example, in the 1970s and 1980s, the findings of McGlaughlin and Empson (1979) questioned the lack of attention paid to individual differences (Empson and McGlaughlin, 1979; McGlaughlin and Empson, 1979).

They found that while the attitudes and behaviours described by Lewis (1966) were present in some families living in poverty, others showed a determination to provide their children with opportunities to make a better life for themselves. The families studied had widely differing relationships with, and expectations for their children. Two contrasting illustrations are given in Case Study 4.

> **CASE STUDY 4: POVERTY AND ATTITUDES TO PARENTING**
>
> Mrs Bunting ran a highly organized, clean and tidy home in a new council house to which the family had recently moved from a poor-quality maisonette. She had long periods of lone parenting while her husband was away at sea and was devoted to her two daughters, one of whom was at school so Mrs Bunting had plenty of time to spend with the younger one. She saw the future as very rosy for her children, believing them to be very bright, doing well at school and that her own involvement with them was important to their later success.
>
> Ms Wark was a single mother of two children. The elder, a daughter, suffered from obesity and behaviour problems, having poor relationships with other children at school. The younger, a boy, was vicious towards other children, and relatives suspected Ms Wark of beating both children. She lived in damp, dirty and overcrowded conditions with her parents and none of the adults paid more than minimal attention to the children. The mother's view was that children learnt from each other, teaching by adults was unimportant and she did not think about her children's future.

All members of the family are affected in various ways by the experience of living in poverty. For children, as well as having immediate and short-term effects, poverty also has implications for their longer-term development and well-being. This can be examined through four main aspects:

- general standard of living and family life
- physical outcomes, for example, health
- cognitive outcomes including educational attainment
- emotional and behavioural development.

In the next four sections of this chapter, I discuss the above aspects of children's lives.

4.4.1 Lifestyle

The standard of living and way of life among children in families at the bottom of the income distribution is extremely low. This was illustrated in Bradshaw and Holmes's (1989) study in Tyne and Wear, England, of families on supplementary benefit whose lifestyle was a long struggle to cope with the lack of resources and who economized with a basic, unvarying diet of small portions, poor clothing and little leisure outside the home.

However, parents did differ from each other considerably in their competence in protecting their children against the worst effects of poverty. Kempson (1996) gives the example of how some mothers achieve healthier diets for their children than others. Attitudes towards eating, cooking and shopping are influential, and the mothers interviewed differed in the importance they attached to the quality and quantity of food they provided for their families. Some used cheaper, lower quality food but there was plenty of it while others kept the quality good but smaller meals were produced. The mothers who provided the most nutritionally healthy meals saw managing the family diet on a low income as a challenge and shopped around to find fresh, healthy food at more reasonable prices. They prepared a more varied diet than other mothers. There were difficulties though, in that the locality in which many families lived did not have shops where fresh food was available, and mothers on low incomes, even those who produced the more healthy diets, gave their families poorer diets than better-off mothers. Of course, mothers also differ in their expertise at planning, cooking and baking. Since the 1970s when domestic science became a non-compulsory part of the school curriculum in the United Kingdom, there has been a serious loss of skill in the country in this regard, with an increased reliance on processed and pre-packed foods. The greater availability of take-away meals has also influenced people's nutrition for the worse. So, by the late 1970s, in a study of poor families in a northern city in England (McGlaughlin and Empson, 1979), many mothers were found to have very limited culinary skills and dietary knowledge and some fed their children on a shared packet of biscuits at lunchtime or scrapings from the local fish and chip shop.

Poor children have an increased likelihood of an unhealthy diet which is low in fresh food, fruit and vegetables, and high in fats. The intake levels of vitamin C, iron, fibre and folate are likely to be too low, and these are associated with poor health and low energy levels (Kempson, 1996).

Kempson found that families also differed in their ability to manage their consumption of fuel and water without either being cut off from these amenities or going into debt to pay for them. Many of those taking part in Kempson's study felt a particular stigma attached to being in debt.

> You feel degraded. You think other people know that you are in debt. You think you have done something wrong. (p. 56)

Similarly, many felt badly about borrowing from other members of the family. It would mean burying their pride and accepting the feelings of stigma and degradation.

> Even when I had nothing, I wouldn't go to my family. I wouldn't degrade myself. (p. 60)

Kempson (1996) found that, in general, families on Income Support managed their inadequate income either by going without essentials or by juggling bills and living on credit.

Children growing up in these circumstances on the whole have a pretty realistic view of their family's financial circumstances (Shropshire and Middleton, 1999). For example, Shropshire and Middleton asked children if they thought that their families had enough money or not and found that children of lone parents and those on Income Support were four or five times as likely to say that their family income was too low than other children. This accurate perception is related to the frequency of interactions between parents and children about the family budget and the frequency with which they are denied items. Children from lone-parent families are also aware that their family income is lower than that of two-parent families. As the children grow older, they are more likely to think that their family income is inadequate, whether or not their parents inform them about the real state of affairs, so children from the poorest families all seem to learn that they are poor. Besides having lower expectations as to how much money their families have, children from the poorer families also have more limited aspirations regarding their future careers. They are more likely to expect to gain employment in low-SES occupations and less likely to want to go into higher education before obtaining paid employment. Thus, the experience of living in poverty at a young age may be restricting children's aspirations for educational qualifications and a rewarding career. Also, the reasons why parents talk to their children about the family budget differ in low-income families from higher: the former use such discussions to inform the children of their low income and reduce their demands for things and the latter, to teach their children money management and budgeting skills. So, the better-off children are likely to acquire more useful and effective financial skills than the children from poor families (Shropshire and Middleton, 1999).

In summary, parents on low incomes are found to do their best for their children, often going without themselves in order to provide for the children, but parents use different ways of adding quality to their children's lives as in the case of food and diet. The children have realistic views of the family finances which appears to limit their aspirations and subsequent achievements.

4.4.2 Physical development

Evidence of physical effects of living in poverty shows that damage to a child's prospects begins before birth and continues through childhood. Differences in both mortality and morbidity between the poor and the better-off appear to be growing. Those in the lowest social classes are more likely to experience birth complications, stillbirths and neonatal deaths as well as deaths in early childhood. Large population surveys show that the death rate increases from Social Class I through to Social Class V (where Class I is higher than Class V) and that this differential increases with age (Quilgars, 2001). To be born into poverty is one of the best predictors of poor child health, as shown by measures of prematurity, low birthweight and infant mortality (Botting and Crawley, 1995), infant mortality being approximately twice as high in Social Class V as in Social Class I.

Similar findings are obtained for infant and child death rates, where environmental influences on cause of death become stronger as the child grows up. Factors which have been implicated are area deprivation and ethnicity (which is associated with a higher incidence of poverty). In the United States, black infants are more likely to die than white ones. This could be due to biological or socio-demographic factors, as different studies show contradictory findings. Two major studies show that when income is controlled for there are still higher rates of infant mortality in black babies compared to white babies (Singh and Yu, 1995; Schoendorf, Hogue, Kleinman and Rowley, 1992). Also relevant are maternal age, births outside marriage and low birthweight and these are all associated with social class. A number of studies have examined the wider relationship between early childhood mortality and socio-economic conditions. Robinson and Pinch (1987) looked at different geographical areas and found that those characterized by measures of deprivation – high levels of unemployment, lone-parent density and poor housing – had significantly higher levels of early child mortality. Elbourne, Pritchard and Dauncey (1986) found similar outcomes for perinatal deaths in their study. Similar relationships have been found between social class and/or levels of area deprivation and childhood non-fatal accident rates, in some studies (Quilgars, 2001). Other studies have failed to find such relationships but *no* studies have found poverty to be associated with fewer accidents. With regard to fatal accidents in children, these also show considerable differences associated with social class and, in particular, exposure to risk, especially in relation to road accidents.

For all of these links between social class and morbidity and mortality more research is needed to see how the different factors interact; in particular to show *how* childhood accidents are related to poverty. One way in which accidents involving children may be related to poverty is through the processes of child neglect or physical abuse, the risk of which seems to be elevated in families living in chronically stressful conditions as discussed below.

Between them *child neglect* and *child physical abuse* accounted for 69 per cent of children on the United Kingdom (England) Register in 1995 (Quilgars, 2001). This figure comprised 37 per cent of children who had physical injury and 32 per cent with physical neglect. There is another category (9%) of more than one type of abuse. The latter is probably a gross underestimate as most studies (e.g., Belsky, 1991) have found co-occurrence of different types of abuse to be very frequent. When considering links between social class and frequency of occurrence of abuse, it is useful to bear in mind the findings of O'Toole (1983) who gave doctors in the United States a hypothetical case study of child abuse. Where the parents of the child were described as 'low social status', 70 per cent of doctors judged it to be child abuse, but where the parents were described as of 'high social status' only 51 per cent thought that it was abuse.

These findings illustrate the greater likelihood of families from lower social classes being identified as abusive compared with other families, thus introducing considerable bias into the system. Of the different types of abuse, physical neglect, and to a lesser extent physical injury, occur more frequently in families characterized by low incomes and high levels of insecurity and disorder. Other types of abuse, such as sexual abuse and emotional abuse, have an equal distribution across all socio-economic groups (Quilgars, 2001). In the United Kingdom, unemployment was much higher in parents whose children were on the National Society for the Prevention of Cruelty to Children (NSPCC) register of abuse (Creighton, 1992). Parents of low occupational status were also over-represented. Stress factors were also recorded, of which the most frequently occurring were marital problems (in 35% of families), an inability to respond to the 'maturational needs' of the children (24%) and marital violence (22%). Other frequently occurring factors were debts (23%) and unemployment (22%).

Gordon and Gibbons (1998) analysed the poverty indicators of children referred for physical abuse or neglect. For neglect, 69 per cent of families were on Social Security with no wage earner, 37 per cent had debts and 33 per cent had other financial problems, 19 per cent had four or more children and 18 per cent were homeless. The figures for physical abuse closely mirrored these data but the indicators were much lower in cases of sexual abuse. *There seem, therefore, to be different processes involved in incidents of different kinds of abuse with the strongest link with poverty being with physical neglect and failure to thrive.* Associations between different kinds of abuse and indicators of poverty were studied by Gillham, Tanner, Cheyne et al., (1998) across a particular area (not in individual families). All measures were found to be correlated with some forms of abuse and the strongest associations were between male unemployment and physical abuse, accounting for two-thirds of the variance of total abuse rates. Other studies have focused on the characteristics of neighbourhoods and incidence of child abuse. In Australia, Vinson, Baldry and Hargreaves (1996) studied two economically depressed areas with different rates of abuse and found that a higher rate of abuse was associated with lower rates of interaction with family, friends and neighbours. Thus, good social networks are associated with lower rates of abuse (Quilgars, 2001).

In all, there is sufficient evidence to conclude that low income, particularly associated with male unemployment, is a major associate of abuse. In addition, characteristics of the parents and their relationships are also relevant. For example, marital discord and domestic violence are associated with child abuse cases, as is single-parent density. Parental characteristics such as psychopathology, depression, drug use, immaturity and low intelligence have all been identified in abusive families. These multiple influences led Baldwin and Spencer (1993) to state that 'material deprivation, though often treated as such, is not a one-dimensional variable but a complex web of circumstances acting and reacting upon each other' (p. 363) (Quilgars, 2001).

Physical abuse and neglect are linked with adverse physical and mental health consequences for children who have been abused in these ways – and the frequency of such abuse is associated with poor socio-economic conditions. Poor health is also linked with poverty in non-abusive families and where parents are doing the best they can for their children. The problems lie in other circumstances of their children's lives, such as poor diet, clothing, housing conditions and stress. Reading (1997) states, 'The links between poverty and child health are extensive, strong, and pervasive' (cited in Shaw, Dorling, Gordon and Davey Smith, 1999. p. 463). Low birthweight occurs more frequently in the lowest social classes and is also associated with increased morbidity in both early life and in adulthood. Malnutrition early in life may give rise to impaired brain development and poor nutrition through childhood leads to an increased likelihood of having a low birthweight baby. Later in childhood, children growing up in poverty also have poorer health; iron-deficiency anaemia is associated with poor diet; asthma, TB, other respiratory infections and gastro-enteritis are associated with poor living conditions (Harding, 2001).

It is important to note that *social inequality* per se as distinct from absolute levels of living conditions is associated with poor physical health. Thus, low social status and being treated without respect causes social stress which brings about greater insecurity, low self-esteem and more conflict and aggression. Such patterns of daily life are not only associated with poor physical health, but also elevated levels of emotional and behavioural problems in children living in poverty (Beiser, Hou, Hyman and Tousignant, 2002). Beiser's study also showed that the adverse effect of poverty on children's mental health in Canadian children, and long-term immigrant families, was stable and probably an indirect effect, mediated by lone-parent status, ineffective parenting, parental depression and family dysfunction. In contrast, foreign-born children, who had not lived long in Canada, were twice as likely to live in poor families, but had lower levels of emotional and behavioural difficulties. Beiser et al. explained that for these families poverty is a temporary state, a transient part of the resettlement process and hence the family process variables were different. The relationship between disadvantage and mental health in children is discussed later in this chapter.

4.4.2.1 Summary

Both higher mortality and poor health in children is related to low family income. The relationship is accentuated in black children and in societies where there is high social inequality. Accidents to children and non-accidental injuries are also higher in deprived areas which may be related to chronically stressful living conditions, lack of good social networks in communities and poor relationships within families. The effects of poverty are greater if it is long lasting.

4.4.3 Cognitive development and educational attainment

As described above in relation to physical outcomes, there are many adverse effects on child development of the lived experience of poverty. Other effects are in the behavioural, emotional and cognitive domains (McLloyd, 1998). When genetically transmitted influences are controlled for, there is evidence from a range of studies using different methods that children's cognitive, academic and socio-emotional functioning are influenced by living in poverty. The relationships between the influences are complicated. Family income and poverty status are significant predictors of IQ scores in five-year-olds, even when accounting for the influences of maternal education, family structure, ethnicity and other variables previously found related to intelligence in children (Duncan, Brooks-Gunn and Klebanov, 1994). *Poverty was a more powerful predictor of IQ than was maternal education.* However, low levels of maternal education are associated with poverty and with less cognitive (academic and language) stimulation in the home environment, and levels of cognitive stimulation have been related to child IQ (Bradley, Whiteside, Mundfrom et al., 1994). Furthermore, preschool children's IQs decline in association with the number of stresses in the home, and an increase in stressful life events (Brooks-Gunn, Klebanov and Liaw, 1995). Other factors in the home related to children's cognitive development are the material resources that provide stimulation for learning, such as educational toys and books (Smith, Brooks-Gunn and Klebanov, 1997).

> **Discussion point:** Consider the factors discussed above relating to children's IQ in poor socio-economic conditions and how they fit into Bronfenbrenner's systems.

Persistent poverty has greater effects on preschool children's development than transitory poverty, although children experiencing either type score lower than children who have never been poor (Duncan et al., 1994). Duncan also found that neighbourhood characteristics were typically long-standing.

Looking at the wider society, disturbing findings from recent studies such as that by the Sutton Trust (Blanden, Gregg and Machin, 2005) showed that social mobility in Britain has not improved in the past 30 years and is worse than any other comparable European industrialized country. The gap between rich and poor is on a par in Britain and the United States, but is widening in Britain, so the outlook for the poor in this country appears to be worse than in any of the other countries in the study. The main reasons given for lack of social mobility were the disparity of educational opportunity and the increasing link between family income and educational achievement.

A very recent United Kingdom government report (Cabinet Office, 2008) cites rather different evidence to suggest that the tide is now turning and social mobility is rising. The key evidence is from the General Certificate of Secondary Education (GCSE) results of 16-year-olds in 2006 which suggest that family background is less important for the achievement of today's young people than for a comparison cohort born in 1970. While the government argues that this finding reflects the positive effects of their interventions, others maintain that the findings do not negate the fact that in Britain social mobility is the lowest of industrialized countries and poverty is rising steadily (Watt, 2008). The complexity of the influences, possible measures and other methodological factors makes it very difficult to produce unequivocal findings in this area and more research is needed.

4.4.3.1 Academic achievement

Intellectual development is, of course, related to academic achievement, and poor children have been found to perform significantly less well than other children on numerous measures of achievement including test scores, grade retention and completed years of schooling. The highest correlate of academic achievement is income, which has a stronger association than parental occupation and parental education which are also linked to academic performance. Considering duration of poverty, Korenman, Miller and Sjaastad (1995) found that long-term poverty had a much stronger association with deficits in verbal, reading and mathematical skills than current financial status when other relevant variables were controlled for. It has been suggested that the preschool years are a period of heightened vulnerability to the effects of poverty (Bronfenbrenner, McClelland, Wethington et al., 1996) and this is also the most likely period when the child may experience poverty.

The mediators of these links between poverty and academic achievement are found in both the home and the school. Studies indicate that the parenting characteristics of lack of emotional support and cognitive stimulation account for one-third to one-half of the disadvantages in verbal, reading and mathematical skills among persistently poor children (Korenman et al., 1995). Where there is similarity of progress for poor and better-off children during school, this is lost in summer when the poor children do not have access to home resources such as computers, books and outings (Entwistle, Alexander and Olson, 1997), whereas other children continue to make gains.

Ethnic differences in literacy practices were identified by Goldenberg, Reese and Gallimore (1992) in that Hispanic parents did not focus on comprehension or motivational factors but saw reading as decoding and rote learning. This could result in their children viewing reading as an inherently dull activity. The congruence between home and school practices and aspirations for children's education are of importance in relation to children continuing academically related activities during the long summer holidays (Serpell, Baker and Sonnenschein, 2005).

4.4.3.2 Parental aspirations

As described earlier, the aspirations of children from the lowest socio-economic groups are lower than those of children from better-off circumstances, and realistically so. Children from disadvantaged social-class origins have to show more 'merit' than children from the higher groups in order to achieve similar 'class positions' (Flouri, 2006). However, the finding that aspirations for their children's educational progress are not uniformly low in parents living in deprived circumstances is of significance. Schoon, Parsons and Sacker (2004), in a longitudinal study in the United Kingdom comparing socio-economically advantaged and socio-economically disadvantaged adolescents, showed that high parental aspirations, as measured by when parents hoped their child would leave school, could act as a protective factor against educational failure, poor adjustment in work and poor health-related outcomes in socio-economically deprived youth.

In a study in the United States by Hill, Castellino, Lansford et al. (2004), different findings were obtained. Here, parental aspirations functioned differently in different social ethnic and socio-economic groups. Parental aspirations were more strongly related to achievement for African American than for European American children, possibly because there are more sources of encouragement to achieve in the latter group, so parents are more important in the former group. Hill (2001) also found less involvement with school in African American as compared with European American parents. Black parents who had high involvement with school had children with better performance at mathematics. So, *ethnicity moderated the relationship between parental involvement, including the value they place on education, and children's performance at mathematics.* Brody and Flor (1998) found that rural African American children's self-regulation and social competence at school was higher when the parenting style to which they were exposed was characterized by high levels of control, but also warmth. This parenting style has been shown in other contexts to be related to adaptation to the environment by poor black children.

Hill et al. (2004) also showed that in low socio-economic status (SES) families, high parental aspirations operated to make their offspring want to be more upwardly mobile, but did not have an effect on their school behaviour or achievement. This could be because even the high aspiring parents had no better resources to help their children achieve educationally than the less aspiring parents. Another possibility is the 'sleeper effect'; the effect on achievement could appear in the long term. In the high SES groups, the parents' aspirations for their children worked indirectly, reducing children's behaviour problems and improving attainment.

The difference between the findings for the United Kingdom and the United States may be related to different definitions being used to define socio-economic disadvantage. Although the terms poverty, deprivation/disadvantage and social exclusion are often used interchangeably (Flouri, 2006), definitions need to bear in mind the distinctions between low income, poor quality of life and the social processes acting in these circumstances. The study of DeGarmo, Forgatch and Martinez (1999) showed that social class and poverty have a differential relationship with academic achievement. Parents' low social class (defined by employment and parental education) predicted children's academic achievement, after adjustment for controls, whereas income poverty did not. Definition is also important with respect to aspirations which are often confused with expectations in the literature (Flouri, 2006).

Parental aspirations may influence children's educational attainment by various routes such as child aspirations, and/or adjustment. High parental aspirations may also be related to their sound mental health, or their involvement and investment in their children. Alternatively, children who do well educationally (they may have a high IQ) may inspire high aspirations in their parents so the effect is from child to parent (Ritchie, Flouri and Buchanan, 2005). It is also likely that high parental aspirations for their children will be associated with the warm and stimulating parenting activities that promote good adjustment and create resilience in children from socio-economically disadvantaged circumstances (Kim-Cohen, Moffitt, Caspi and Taylor, 2004).

This recent research is consistent with the findings of a short, longitudinal study in the 1970s of mothers and children living in disadvantaged circumstances (McGlaughlin and Empson, 1979) which highlighted the importance of individual differences (see Case Study 5) in a number of maternal characteristics.

CASE STUDY 5: PARENTAL ASPIRATIONS AND CHILDREN'S DEVELOPMENT

McGlaughlin and Empson (1979) investigated the development of preschool children and the mothers were asked about their hopes and aspirations for their children's future. It was found that mothers had clear ideas about what they desired for their children even when the children were aged 12 to 30 months, but the ideas were different even for mothers from very similar socio-economic circumstances. This difference in ideas was complemented by a wide range of developmental progress in the children. Pairs of sisters took part in this study to examine intergenerational family similarities. Interestingly, it was found that, overall, pairs of sisters were no more similar to each other than were unrelated mothers, and the progress of their children who were cousins also was *not* found to be similar. A few pairs of sisters were very similar, a few very dissimilar and the rest had no particular relationship in terms of their parenting, aspirations and play techniques with their child. The most significant variables relating to the children's development were the level of stress in the family and the degree of malaise (anxiety) in the mother. Thus, of more significance than being members of the same family of origin, or the level of deprivation was the state of well-being of the family and, in particular, the mother.

The findings by McGlaughlin and Empson (1979) were replicated by Ritchie et al. (2005) some 30 years later and indicate the great importance of paying attention to *individual differences in the cognitions and behaviour of the mother* when investigating child development. This will be discussed further later in this chapter in relation to resilience.

4.4.3.3 Teacher influences

Another factor that may influence the academic performance of poor children is the attitudes of teachers. Teachers were found to affect their students by viewing the poor children less positively and having lower expectations for their achievement than other children (Alexander, Entwistle and Thompson, 1987). The teachers also treated poor children less favourably, providing them with less positive attention and reinforcement and fewer learning opportunities. Because children of low SES are more likely to have externalizing problems, they are less likely to pay attention in class, regulate their emotions and relate well to peers, all of which contribute to poor school performance (McLelland, Morrison and Holmes, 2000). Teachers paying attention to their misdemeanours but not providing better learning opportunities can contribute further to their academic failure (Carr, Taylor and Robinson, 1991). Other studies show that children with behaviour problems receive less academic instruction from teachers (Arnold, 1997).

4.4.3.4 Influence of the home environment

The home environment also contributes to academic success or failure. There is a relationship between children's early home environment and success in learning literacy. For example, a child's interest in picture books at 20 months predicts later literacy achievement (Crain-Thoreson and Dale, 1992). Also, shared reading between parent and child in the early years predicts literacy and later achievement (Whitehurst and Lonigan, 1998). This may often not occur in low-SES homes as such homes are less likely to have suitable books. In the United States, only half of preschool children on public assistance were found to have access to alphabet books in their homes compared with 97 per cent of children of professional parents (McCormick and Mason, 1986).

The relationship between SES and academic skills develops earlier than that between SES and academic interest or motivation (Arnold and Doctoroff, 2003) and both have important influences on achievement. Indeed, the relation between interest and achievement grows stronger with time (Wingfield, Eccles, Yoon et al., 1997) and is stronger for low-SES children than their higher SES peers. This finding suggests that core skills need to be taught in ways which foster interest (in all social and ethnic groups), including active learning. Thus, interventions need to be flexible in their methods, and understanding of the most favourable methods for boys or girls and different ethnic groups is necessary to enable all to perform at the best level possible.

The effect of poverty on development in the early years may be mediated by ineffective parenting, and an inadequate home environment, which results in the children not being ready for school at the appropriate age, and then they are less helped by the teachers (Alexander et al., 1987). This would leave them lagging further and further behind their peers. The effect of poverty experienced during the first five years of a child's life in reducing completed years of schooling is greater for African Americans than whites and may operate by hindering the development of school-readiness skills (McLloyd, 1998).

Absence from school due to periods of physical illness would also have adverse effects on learning and ability to keep up in school, and the children of poverty experience poorer health status than other children (Crooks, 1995). Other risk factors discussed previously such as prematurity, low birthweight and birth complications are also more frequently occurring in the histories of poor children and such factors interact with conditions in the home environment to have greater or lesser effects on development in middle childhood (Empson, 2004; Sameroff and Chandler, 1975). There are racial differences in vulnerability to these risk factors associated with higher infant mortality rates in black infants than white ones as discussed previously. Thus, poor health in poor children is related to less success educationally through various direct and indirect pathways.

4.4.3.5 Summary

Poverty has a stronger relationship with IQ in young children than SES, and persistent poverty has the strongest effect. This is also true for academic performance which is related to lack of cognitive stimulation and emotional support from parents as well as lack of material resources. However, the attainment is not uniformly low. High parental aspirations and their provision of a warm and stimulating environment for their children act as protective factors, particularly in African American children. The optimal parenting style differs between black and white families as higher levels of control are more favourable for child achievement in African American families. Teacher behaviour is also relevant. Relevant variables involve all levels of Bronfenbrenner's ecological-systems model of child development.

4.4.4 Emotional and behavioural development

As I indicated earlier, mental health in children is also affected by growing up experiencing the stresses and strains of poverty. A number of studies have shown a higher prevalence of emotional and behavioural problems among poor and low-SES children than in middle-class children of similar ages (e.g., Adams, Hillman and Gaydos, 1994). It is only in studies of very young children that no significant differences were found. The differences are greater for externalizing than internalizing problems. So, externalizing behaviours such as fighting, negativity, disobedience and impulsivity are more frequently occurring among poor children and these social-class differences increase as children grow older so there are relatively more externalizing problems in poor older children (McLloyd, 1998). A larger percentage of poor children become chronically delinquent in the lowest social classes; such children are also at greater risk of early onset conduct disorder. SES is correlated with other risk factors for such problems, including family discord, parental psychopathology and family size (Arnold and Doctoroff, 2003).

The longer the duration of poverty experienced by children, the greater the prevalence of both internalizing and externalizing problems (McLloyd, 1998). The most commonly occurring internalizing problems are anxiety, sadness, depression and withdrawal. The frequency of a child's problems also appears to be related to the neighbourhood. In a study of preschool children it was found that there were higher levels of externalizing problems in children with more low-income neighbours when family variables were accounted for (Jencks and Mayer, 1990). One explanation given is that parents do not discourage aggression in their children so much in poor neighbourhoods as the children need to be able to defend themselves in contexts where there is more violence. Peer group influences may also work to increase levels of delinquency and late onset conduct disorder.

4.4.4.1 Family influences

It is also possible that more externalizing problems occur in poor families because of the negative nature of many of the interpersonal interactions within many of these families. There is evidence of an increased likelihood of parents using discipline techniques which are punitive and inconsistent, and that they also ignore their children's dependency needs (Dodge, Pettit and Bates, 1994). McLeod and Shanahan (1993) found in their study of four- to eight-year-old children that their mothers used physical punishment frequently and, at the same time, had generally low levels of involvement with their children. Frequent smacking in some contexts brings about poor relationships between parent and child and may lead to behaviour problems in the children. Thus, *many of the adverse emotional and behavioural effects on children of living in poverty are indirect effects mediated by the behaviours and mental states of their parents.*

For adults living in conditions of chronic stress with more than usual negative stressful life events it is a constant struggle to cope, and many parents demonstrate this with irritability, intolerance, a low threshold for losing their temper and engaging in arguments and worse. For the children being parented by highly stressed adults there are similar difficulties, lack of control, lack of opportunity, lack of positive things to look forward to and eventually this leads to emotional problems in many of them. The negative effects of stress on children's mental health was demonstrated by Shaw and Emery (1988) who found that low-income school children who experienced a large number of family stressors had low self-worth, more internalizing difficulties and more behaviour problems at clinical levels.

4.4.4.2 Neighbourhood influences

In Shaw and Emery's study, children were also influenced by the stressors in the environment outside the home – such factors as violence in the neighbourhood, run-down housing, graffiti and rubbish in the streets – and these contributed to their mental health difficulties. High levels of post-traumatic stress symptoms are associated with contact with neighbourhood violence, especially in female adolescents (Fitzpatrick and Boldizar, 1993).

The mechanisms whereby neighbourhoods influence the families living in them are important for understanding the effects of urban poverty (Klebanov, Brooks-Gunn and Duncan, 1994). Klebanov et al. found that neighbourhood poverty was associated with a poorer home physical environment and with less maternal warmth. Klebanov et al. speculates that less maternal warmth may be adaptive in teaching their children to adjust to a harsh and dangerous environment as was suggested by ethnographic studies of poor urban families (Jarrett, 1992). The mothers may have been less warm overall, rather than explicitly in the socialization of their children. *The poverty of the neighbourhood had an additional effect over and above family poverty and other family variables.* Klebanov proposed that this could have been due to a kind of *'collective socialization'* in which neighbours influence mothers by communicating norms and values. There were, however, no neighbourhood effects of provision of learning experiences for children, which was related to family resources such as, income, parental education, smaller household size, better coping skills and greater social support.

Klebanov et al.'s (1994) findings support the mechanisms of contagion – strength of peer influences on individuals' behaviour – and socialization whereby neighbourhoods may influence children, which had also been found by earlier studies (e.g., Brooks-Gunn, Duncan, Klebanov and Sealand, 1993). However, poor neighbourhoods did not influence maternal depression in Klebanov et al.'s study, and, overall, they found that maternal characteristics and behaviour were influenced more by proximal factors – resources available to the mother in the family.

4.4.4.3 Interactions between ethnicity, neighbourhood and home environments

Children from particular ethnic groups – African American and Hispanic – in the United States were found to have the most stressful life events in the most disadvantaged neighbourhoods (Attar, Guerra and Tolan, 1994). Stressful life events were related to higher concurrent and later levels of aggression, but interacted with neighbourhood disadvantage, so that the effects were only significant for children living in the most disadvantaged neighbourhoods. Research conducted on African American children growing up in such neighbourhoods, aged 10–12 years, found that these conditions were related to higher levels of *'deviant peer affiliation'* (Brody, Ge, Conger et al., 2001) which is associated with delinquency. But the most important variables for such peer affiliation were related to parental behaviour, involved and nurturant parenting being *inversely* related, and harsh, inconsistent parenting being *positively* related to deviant peer association. The effects of good parenting were greatest for those children from the worst backgrounds.

The relationship between characteristics of the home environment and child development is stronger for poverty than ethnicity (Bradley, Corwyn, McAdoo and Coll, 2001). The differences are a direct function of insufficient money to access goods and services which affects all ethnic groups, and an indirect function of how parents cope with the stress of economic hardship.

Different ethnic groups vary in what parents do, how time is spent in the family and exchanges between family members. For every culture, there is a cultural frame of reference that 'refers to the correct or ideal way to behave within the culture' (Ogbu, 1994, p. 375) which guides, for example, parenting practices. In all ethnic groups, the poor mothers were less likely to communicate effectively, and to show affection and discipline by talking or ignoring. African

American mothers reported more spanking, except in the younger age groups of nine years or less. But when likelihood of using spanking was separated from frequency of use, the African Americans were more likely to use spanking but less frequently. Also, poor African American mothers were less socially isolated than poor European American or Hispanic mothers. All groups were similar in spending much leisure time watching TV and discussing programmes and having few outings. Bradley et al. (2001) suggested that parenting practices in the home may be influenced by coping with discrimination and oppression.

In some ways, African American culture may operate to protect children against many urban risk factors as this culture emphasizes strong family bonds, flexible family roles, high achievement orientation, positive self-esteem and religious beliefs (Littlejohn-Blake and Darling, 1993). So, for example, the association between depressive symptoms and scholastic achievement is not as great for African American children as Caucasian children. Arnold and Doctoroff (2003) suggest that the relationship between resilience and culture should be explored further as there has been little research in this area.

4.4.4.4 Summary

Emotional and behavioural problems are related to poverty, in many instances mediated through stress in the home and negative, punitive interactions between parent and child. Violence in the neighbourhood also has a negative impact on children's socio-emotional functioning. Good parenting acts as a protective factor, especially for children in the worst environments and strong family bonds and other aspects of African culture are beneficial for children in these families.

> **Discussion point:** By focusing on the characteristics of groups, has research paid too little attention to possible personal and interpersonal mechanisms whereby the impact of poverty on children's development may be mediated? Consider what mechanisms may be involved with respect to the different aspects of development discussed above.

4.5 Individual differences in susceptibility to effects of social disadvantage

4.5.1 What is resilience?

Despite the difficulties for good development imposed on children by social disadvantage, there are children who do well despite the adverse circumstances in which they live (Rutter, 1979; Werner and Smith, 1982). These children show *resilience*, or the ability to overcome risk for poor development generated by their circumstances. Resilience may result from characteristics of the child him/herself, or from influences in the family or wider environment which are protective. Resilience is demonstrated as competence in adapting effectively to the challenges of an adverse environment and to developmental difficulties. To identify resilience in a child s/he must have been exposed to severe adversity or threat to the individual. The developmental tasks which a child needs to display competence in achieving will differ from one cultural group to another, and in different subcultures, creating difficulties in making judgements of competence for all children. For example, Ogbu (1981, Ogbu and Fordham 1986) suggested that African American ghetto youth who have few opportunities in mainstream society therefore create alternative ways of achieving their goals, which may be illegal, and their goals may be different, for example, to be a gang leader rather than the captain of the school chess team. This may be highly adaptive for success in the environment in which these young people live.

Successful adaptation requires mastery over the environment, and White (1959) argued that there is a mastery motivational system inbuilt in our species which is exhibited by pleasure in achievements in different activities from infancy onwards. There are many factors which will aid achievement of mastery, two of the most important being *attachment* and *self-regulation*. There is much evidence that secure attachment early in life is predictive of mastery at tasks later on in both social-emotional and cognitive domains (Carlson and Sroufe, 1995). The ability to self-regulate behaviour and emotions is associated with less reactivity to stress, higher self-control of attention and behaviour and greater social competence (Eisenberg, Fabes, Shepard et al., 1997). Social competence is linked with good relationships with peers. All of these, if well developed, will enable a child to cope better with the stresses and difficulties of life in poverty. Ultimately, such abilities develop through the efforts of competent and caring parents who are crucial in protecting their children from poor development.

4.5.2 Resilience in parents

Competence in parents in protecting their children against the worst effects of poverty has been discussed earlier in relation to Kempson's (1996) investigation of parents' approaches to money management, shopping, provision of food and other practical activities. In addition to such activities being important in safeguarding children's health and to minimize the likelihood of them being scapegoated by their peers for their poor clothes and lack of money to spend, they are also a demonstration of parental love and care of their children. Although some parents were more competent than others in making the best provision for their children on a low income, economies in the use of heating and lighting were practised in nearly every poor home. The resulting cold conditions affected people's feelings of self-worth, mood and ability to fight off infection. Respiratory diseases, in particular, result from inadequate living conditions (Braback et al., 1995; Sprangers et al., 2000).

Poor housing (or homelessness), poor health and poor diet all contribute to mental health problems. The constant worry of trying to make ends meet, to pay the bills and feed the family lead to stress, depression and despair at above average rates of occurrence. Feelings of hopelessness and depression are understandable when there is no realistic way of escaping from the poverty trap. Such parental feelings also affect the rest of the family. Those in poverty are also unable to escape by going out and enjoying themselves at social functions; they are on the fringes of society and its institutions because all of these cost money. The lives of both adults and children are ones of social isolation and bare existence (Morrow, 2001).

As Kempson (1996) found, the stigma of being poor in an affluent society possibly has a greater impact on the experiences of the children and their relationships with other children, in part because other children can be so cruel in teasing and bullying anyone whom they perceive as being different, or inferior, to themselves. So, many parents make efforts to protect their children from negative experiences with other children. When Kempson interviewed poor children, she found that many had experienced teasing and taunting from other children; when asked what happened if they were not dressed like their friends, they said:

> You'd feel left out
> They hassle you. They say nasty things like 'You get your shoes from the tip', and stuff like that. (p. 67)

Many parents would go without goods for themselves, or even food, in order to buy the right kind of jeans for their child, in order that they did not suffer the stigma of being different.

So, most parents do their best to protect their children from the worst of the negative effects of living in poverty, but they differ in the degree to which they are able to do this. This is due in part to the parents' own abilities, as developed through their experiences, education and employment, and their own relationships with other people, and, in part, to their child-rearing beliefs and practices. If parents have a good marital relationship and supportive relationships with other family members, friends and neighbours, they build self-regard, self-belief and a positive attitude that they can help their children to develop resilience and be successful despite the adverse circumstances of their lives. Such factors are effective for all ethnic groups.

4.5.3 Resilience in children

The nature of the relationship between parent and child is one of the best predictors of children's resilience to stressful life circumstances. Wyman, Cowen, Work et al., (1999) found in their low-income sample that, what they termed *nurturant involvement* – emotional closeness and time spent together – by a primary caregiver was effective in enabling children to cope. Such parenting is likely to be the outcome of a secure attachment between carer and child in infancy in which the infant will have developed experience of mastery in securing satisfaction of his/her needs by engaging the attention of a responsive carer. The attachment relationship helps self-regulation of emotion in the child and cognitive development by providing a safe base from which the infant can explore the environment. Such good relationships are predictive of success in later developmental tasks in toddlers and older children.

Masten's (1994) longitudinal studies of successful adaptation in competent children and adolescents showed the importance of caregiver-child relationships. Early compliance to the requests of the caregiver and prosocial behaviour, which would be expected in securely attached children, pave the way for later successful social functioning. Compliance with social rules is associated with sensitive and consistent caregiving and warm but firm parenting, whereas power-assertive methods, especially when combined with hostility, are associated with more negative and deviant behaviour (Schaffer, 1996). Relationships with peers depend on the social functioning of the child, and these not only influence feelings of well-being, but also later adjustment or maladjustment and educational outcome. As self-regulation seems to be intimately related to the early parent-child relationship, intervention to assist these early relationships where necessary could help to develop skills of importance to successful functioning in various aspects of life.

Additional protective factors for the child are family-related. Parental social support predicts resilience in children brought up in socio-economically disadvantaged circumstances (Runyan, Hunter, Socolar et al., 1998). The effect may be mediated via parental behaviour, such as expressions of warmth and affection (Mason, Cauce, Gonzales et al., 1994) and learning experiences being provided (Klebanov et al., 1994). Also, social support may act to reduce the effect of the stresses in their environment on the parents, and to maintain their confidence in their own parenting abilities (Cutrona and Troutman, 1986). Lack of social support is associated with an increase in risk of child abuse in vulnerable families.

Child factors related to resilience and successful adjustment in adverse circumstances include child personality characteristics and child intellect. The child who is good-natured and sociable tends to be resilient to the adversity associated with low socio-economic status (Werner and Smith, 1992) and children who approach life in a positive way, are intellectually curious and confident also tend to be competent (Caspi, Henry, McGee et al., 1995). Cognitive outcomes are related to mothers' engagement in cognitively stimulating activities with their children (Cowen, Wyman, Work and Parker, 1990) and these children are later found to be more resilient to the stresses of the socially and economically disadvantaged circumstances in which they live. Such children from cognitively stimulating homes are also likely to be protected from emotional and behavioural problems (Linver, Brooks-Gunn and Kohen, 2002). Children who are easy to relate to and are adaptive to circumstances early in life are easier to parent and to form warm and loving relationships with. They are then more likely to benefit from the style of parenting most likely to engender successful adaptation to life circumstances.

Thus, the three main adaptive systems which promote the development of competence, even in unfavourable environments (Masten and Coatsworth, 1998) arise from a healthy, warm and structured parent-child relationship, good cognitive development and intellectual functioning and self-regulation of attention, emotion and behaviour.

Behavioural genetic research shows a substantial genetic influence in children's successful adaptation to socio-economic deprivation. This is because child characteristics, such as temperament and intelligent behaviour are influenced by the genes (e.g., Plomin and Bergeman, 1991). There is also the suggestion that likelihood of living in socio-economic disadvantage is in part determined via the parents' genes (Plomin, DeFries, McClearn and McGuffin, 2001). It could be expected, then, that children's resilience to socio-economic disadvantage is also influenced in part by the action of the genes. Good cognitive development helps children's resilience to adversity. Braungart, Fulker and Plomin (1992) found that genetic factors mediate the association between the home environment and young children's cognitive development.

It has also been shown, in relation to genetic and environmental influences on most domains of development, that non-shared environmental influences are the salient environmental influences, accounting for up to 60 per cent of the variance. This means that 'environmental influences that affect development operate to make children growing up in the same family no more similar than children growing up in different families' (Plomin et al., 2001, p. 298). It follows from this that it cannot be assumed that that all the children in a family will be resilient to the negative effects of poverty. Part of the non-shared environmental effects may be due to measurement error. Sibling reports of parental treatment of themselves being very different, compared with parental reports that they treat all their children similarly (Reiss, Neiderhiser, Hetherington and Plomin, 2000) shows that measurement variables are of considerable importance.

Interactions between genetic and environmental influences are of significance in the processes involved in resilience. There is much evidence (Kim-Cohen et al., 2004) that environmental processes work to produce relationships between environmental factors and resilience; also, environmental interventions produce environmental change and thus influence resilience in children. Kim-Cohen et al.'s study of children growing up in conditions of socio-economic deprivation demonstrated both genetic and environmental factors operating in protective processes, and genetic factors added to environmental processes in resilience.

Overall, resilient children are likely to have a resilient parent with whom they have a secure attachment and a warm and nurturant relationship. Such children will have good self-regulation, social skills and good relationships with peers. Resilient children are protected from emotional and behavioural problems by the cognitive stimulation of their home environment which fosters good cognitive and educational development. The positive and harmonious personality of these children makes them easy to relate to so they will benefit from supportive relationships in all their social networks. In addition to the environmental influences, the child's genetic makeup will predispose some children to develop the characteristics of resilience.

4.5.4 Summary

The development of competence, even in unfavourable environments, is facilitated by a healthy, warm and structured parent-child relationship, good cognitive development and intellectual functioning, and self-regulation of attention, emotion and behaviour. There is a strong genetic component to successful adaptation in adverse circumstances. Social support for parents is also important. It has been found that different ethnic groups may require different child characteristics for children to become resilient so cultural context also influences the development of resilience in children.

4.6 A theoretical framework for child development in conditions of poverty

Bronfenbrenner's (1979) ecological approach has become increasingly utilized as an integrating theoretical framework for understanding variations in child development in a range of contexts, usually within developed countries. Figure 4.1 shows how Bronfenbrenner's systems model links a number of factors (discussed earlier in this chapter), at the different ecological levels, which have been empirically demonstrated to be of significance for child development in disadvantaged socio-economic conditions.

A clear distinction needs to be held in mind between poverty per se and social disadvantage, which are often but not necessarily co-existent in families living in such conditions.

The importance of differences between individuals has been stressed earlier, and some individuals and families have been shown to be remarkably resilient to the likely negative effects of a life in poverty, whether it be relative or absolute. The concept of resilience is addressed in the theoretical approach of Lynch and Cicchetti (1998) which combines Bronfenbrenner's ecological approach with the transactional approach of Sameroff and Chandler (Sameroff, 1991; Sameroff and Chandler, 1975), the latter having been described earlier in this chapter. This 'ecological-transactional' (ET) approach has been used to provide an explanation of variations in child development in a range of circumstances, particularly in relation to child maltreatment and violence in the community (Lynch and Cicchetti, 1998) (see also Chapter 2).

Figure 4.2 illustrates a possible application of the ET approach to the particular cultural context of poverty, where many of the potentiating

128 CULTURE AND PSYCHOLOGICAL DEVELOPMENT

Macrosystems
Ideology
- Individualism or collectivism
- Autonomy or interconnectedness
- Personal or shared achievement

Societal values
- How materialistic
- How much waste
- How altruistic

Belief systems
- Association between beauty and good
- Cult of celebrity and success
- About different groups for example, the deserving poor

Exosystems
Community services
- E.g. youth clubs, affordable sports facilities, family centres

Educational system
- Lack of choice of schools
- Low achieving schools
- Travelling long distances to school

Mass media
- Portrayal of lives very different from children's own experience
- Much violence
- Advertising of unattainable goods
- Dysfunctional relationships the norm

Macrosystems
Exosystems
Mesosystems
Microsystems
CHILD

Mesosystems relationships between
Home and school
- Cultural differences
- Gender expectations
- Different goals

Home and neighbourhood
- Violence in neighbourhood and home
- Neighbourhood violence and mental health
- Presence or lack of social support
- Lack of amenities for example, shops, clinics
- Lack of play areas for outdoor pursuits

Nuclear and extended family
- Supportive or otherwise for example, money, services

Microsystems
Child in family
- Large family size/lone parent
- Unemployment/low income
- Parental education minimal
- Father absent for example, in prison
- Ethnicity
- Relationships – negative, neglecting
- Expectations low (of parents for children or children for self)

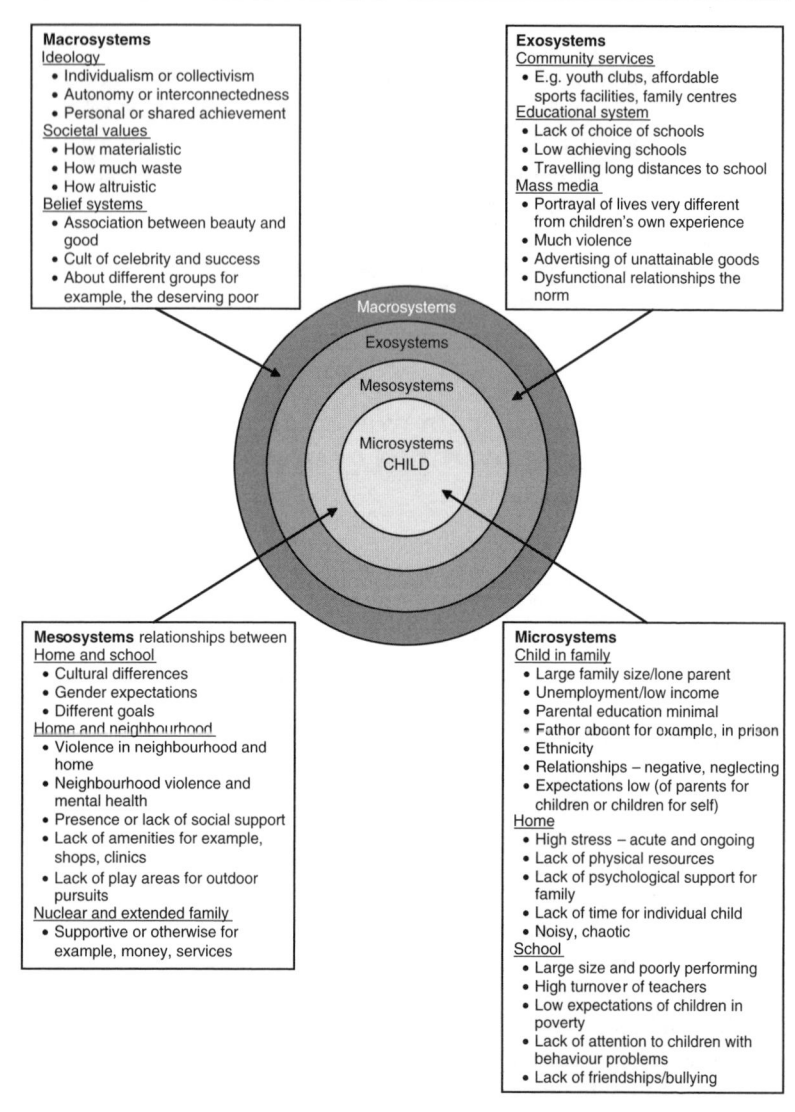

Home
- High stress – acute and ongoing
- Lack of physical resources
- Lack of psychological support for family
- Lack of time for individual child
- Noisy, chaotic

School
- Large size and poorly performing
- High turnover of teachers
- Low expectations of children in poverty
- Lack of attention to children with behaviour problems
- Lack of friendships/bullying

Figure 4.1 Bronfenbrenner's (1979) model applied to cultural variables and SES

and compensatory factors identified reflect individual differences in resilience to the vicissitudes of poverty.

Bronfenbrenner (2005) wrote of the increasing neglect of children in American families perhaps due to the separation of the generations

Figure 4.2

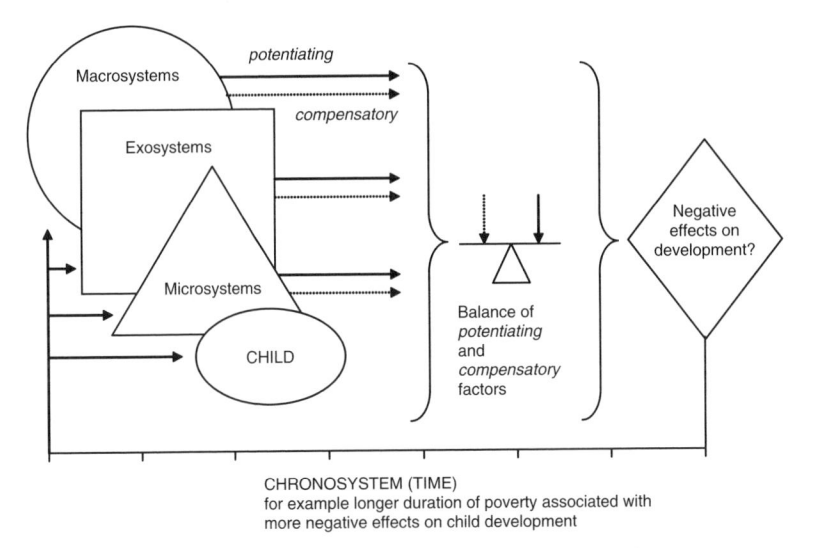

[Diagram showing Macrosystems, Exosystems, Microsystems, Child, with potentiating and compensatory arrows leading to a balance with "Negative effects on development?"]

CHRONOSYSTEM (TIME)
for example longer duration of poverty associated with more negative effects on child development

Factors influencing likelihood of negative child outcomes of poverty

Potentiating factors
- stress in parents/acculturative stress
- parental benefits and practices (ethnic and variations)
- neighbourhood with high deprivation index
- male unemployment
- low maternal education
- punitive, hostile parenting
- low resilience in child for example, low self-regulation

Compensatory factors
- high parental aspirations for child
- secure attachment
- positive family interactions
- positive harmonious relationship between parent and child
- social support
- high resilience in child eg high self-regulation, positive personality

Figure 4.2 Ecological-transactional (ET) model of possible effects of social disadvantage on child development

so that children and young people become increasingly 'peer-oriented'. Such children, who experienced lack of attention and care at home tended to be as follows:

- pessimistic about the future
- less responsible and lacking in leadership
- more likely to engage in antisocial behaviour and delinquent acts.

Bronfenbrenner (1985; 2005) stated that the main stresses of childhood were financial (poverty), parents working long hours and neighbourhood violence and distrust. The way to provide a better future for children living in such conditions, Bronfenbrenner proposed, was for government to introduce reduced working hours, increase the number of women in positions of power and change the ethos of society from a deficit model into 'new structures that emphasize empowerment, initiative and self-respect' (Bronfenbrenner, 2005, p. 257). In 2009, it seems possible that the first African American President of the United States, Barack Obama, has such an agenda for reform in mind.

4.7 Conclusions

Currently, child development is viewed as involving an active child in an active environment. The particular cultural context in which development takes place has been termed the 'developmental niche' by Super and Harkness (1986) and described as involving psychological, social and physical components. A specific developmental niche involves children who are disadvantaged by living in a culture of poverty and social disadvantage. These children, in the context of Western societies have been the focus of this chapter. Empirical research demonstrates that, as a group, socially deprived children are disadvantaged in their educational achievements, and have more social, emotional and behavioural problems than children from other social groups. The processes involved in creating these differences between different social groups may be personal, for example, motivations and aspirations; interpersonal, as, for example, in harsh parenting; social, perhaps where families are isolated and lacking social support; or material, in that the child is lacking cognitive stimulation, safe places to play and may be living in an unhealthy environment. The implications of research are that the potential of many children is not being realized. However, there is also evidence that there is wide variation in strategies and adaptations employed by different families who are all living in socially disadvantaged conditions, and that these are more or less adaptive.

Thus, the outcomes for children growing up in poverty are not uniformly poor. Werner (1989) in a longitudinal study in Hawaii found that one-third of children born at risk had successful outcomes in the long term. These parents and children showed more resilience to the impact of poverty on their cognitive and social-emotional functioning. A wide range of outcomes has also been shown in other studies. The mechanisms through which resilience operates may be genetic; the functioning of psychological characteristics of the child, such as intelligence, self-regulation or sociability; a parent-child relationship characterized by 'nurturant involvement' and parental social support.

The pattern of care received in infancy sets the pattern for the kind of care given in adulthood through the internalization of social and cultural processes. The most valid and successful methods of childrearing used by the middle classes may not be those most appropriate for rearing the deprived child or for those in different ethnic groups (Woodhead, 1991). A child brought up in conditions of poverty may be subject to more constraints on his/her behaviour because of unsafe conditions at home or in the neighbourhood. Thus, the successful modes of childrearing are those appropriate to the 'cultural niche' in which the child is growing up. In addition, child characteristics are viewed differently in different cultures and subcultures, so the likelihood of a successful pathway to adulthood will be influenced by the interaction between these factors. Again, 'goodness of fit' is of great importance. So, to 'understand children's development in a given culture we need to understand that culture's particular definitions and goals of development for its children' (Goncu, 1999, p. 4). When, because of income inequality and associated social disadvantage for some, childrens' development is being compromised, social change is needed to offer better developmental opportunities for these disadvantaged children of different social and ethnic groups.

FURTHER READING

Bradshaw, J.J. (Ed.) (2001). *Poverty: The outcomes for children.* London: Family Policy Studies Centre.

Lloyd, E. (2006). Children, poverty and social exclusion. In C. Pantazis, D. Gordon, and C. Levitas (Eds), *Poverty and social exclusion in Britain. The millennium survey.* Bristol: The Policy Press.

Lynch, M. and Cicchetti, D. (1998). An ecological-transactional analysis of children and contexts: The longitudinal interplay among child maltreatment, community violence and children's symptomatology. *Development and Psychopathology,* **10**, 235–257.

McLloyd, V.C. (1998). Socioeconomic disadvantage and child development. *American Psychologist,* **53**, 185–204.

Masten, A.S. and Coatsworth, J.D. (1998). The development of competence in favorable and unfavorable environments. Lessons from research on successful children. *American Psychologist,* **53**(2), 205–220.

REFERENCES

Adams, C., Hillman, N., and Gaydos, G. (1994). Behavioural difficulties in toddlers: Impact of socio-cultural and biological risk factors. *Journal of Clinical Child Psychology,* **23**, 373–381.

Adelman, A. and Bradshaw, J. (1998). *Children in poverty in Britain: An analysis of the Family Resources Survey 1994/95.* Social Policy Research Unit: University of York.

Alexander, K., Entwistle, D., and Thompson, M. (1987). School performance, status relations, and the structure of sentiment: Bringing the teacher back in. *American Sociological Review,* **52**, 665–682.

Al-Issa, I. and Tousignant, M. (Eds) (1997). *Ethnicity, immigration and psychopathology.* New York: Plenum.

Amin, K. and Oppenheim, C. (1992). *Poverty in black and white. Deprivation and ethnic minorities.* London: Child Poverty Action Group.

Arnold, D.H. (1997). Co-occurrence of externalizing behaviour problems and emergent academic difficulties in high-risk boys: A preliminary evaluation of patterns and mechanisms. *Applied Developmental Psychology,* **18**, 317–330.

Arnold, D.H. and Doctoroff, G.L. (2003). The early education of socioeconomically disadvantaged children. *Annual Review of Psychology,* **54**, 517–545.

Attar, B.K., Guerra, N.G., and Tolan, P.H. (1994). Neighbourhood disadvantage, stressful life events and adjustments in urban elementary-school children. *Journal of Clinical Child Psychology,* **23**(4), 391–400.

Baldwin, N. and Spencer, N. (1993). Deprivation and child abuse: Implications for strategic planning in children's services. *Children and Society,* **7**(4), 357–375.

Beiser, M., Hou, F., Hyman, I., and Tousignant, M. (2002). Poverty, family process and the mental health of immigrant children in Canada. *American Journal of Public Health,* **92**(2), 220–227.

Belsky, J. (1991). Psychological maltreatment: Definitional limitations and unstated assumptions. *Development and Psychopathology,* **3**, 31–36.

Belsky, J., Steinberg, L., and Draper, P. (1991). Childhood experience, interpersonal development and reproductive strategy: An evolutionary theory of socialization. *Child Development,* **62**, 647–670.

Berry, J.W., Poortinga, Y.H., Segall, M.H., and Dasen, P.R. (2002). *Cross-cultural psychology. Research and applications.* Cambridge: Cambridge University Press.

Blanden, J., Gregg, P., and Machin, S. (2005). *Intergenerational mobility in Europe and North America.* London: The Sutton Trust.

Botting, B. and Crawley, R. (1995). Trends and patterns in childhood mortality and morbidity. In B. Botting (Ed.), *The health of our children. Decennial Supplement.* Office of Population Censuses and Surveys. Series DS no. 11. London: HMSO, pp. 61–81.

Bowman, B.T. (1994). Cultural diversity and academic achievement. *Urban education monograph.* North Central Regional Educational Laboratory http://www.ncrel.org/sdrs/areas/issues/educatrs/leadrshp/le0bow. htm#author. Accessed 31/08/09.

Bråbäck, L., Breborowicz, A., Julge, K., Knutsson, A., Riikjärv, M.A., Vasar, M., and Björksten, B. (1995). Risk factors for respiratory symptoms and atopic sensitization in the Baltic area. *Archives of Disease in Childhood*, **72**(6), 487–493.

Bradley, R.H., Corwyn, R.F., McAdoo, H.P., and Coll, C.G. (2001). The home environments of children in the US. Part 1: Variations by age, ethnicity and poverty status. *Child Development*, **72**(6), 1844–1867.

Bradley, R., Whiteside, L., Mundfrom, D., Casey, P., Kelleher, K., and Pope, S. (1994). Early indications of resilience and their relation to experiences in the home environments of low birth-weight, premature children living in poverty. *Child Development*, **65**, 346–360.

Bradshaw, J. and Holmes, H. (1989). *Living on the edge. A study of the living standards of families on benefit in Tyne and Wear*. London: Tyneside Poverty Action Group.

Braungart, J.M., Fulker, D.W., and Plomin, R. (1992). Genetic mediation of the home environment during infancy: A sibling adoption study of the HOME. *Developmental Psychology*, **28**, 1048–1055.

Brody, G. and Flor, D. (1998). Maternal resources, parenting practices, and child competence in rural, single-parent African American families. *Child Development*, **69**, 803–816.

Brody, G.H., Ge, X., Conger, R., Gibbons, F.X., Murry, M., Gerrard, M., and Simons, R.L. (2001). The influence of neighbourhood disadvantage, collective socialization and parenting on African American children's affiliation with deviant peers. *Child Development*, **72**(4), 1231–1246.

Bronfenbrenner, U. (1979). *The ecology of human development*. Cambridge, MA: Harvard University Press.

Bronfenbrenner, U. (1985). The future of childhood. In V. Greaney (Ed.), *Children: Needs and rights* (pp. 167–186). New York: Irvington Publishers, Inc.

Bronfenbrenner, U. (Ed.) (2005). *Making human beings human. Bioecological perspectives on human development*. London: Sage.

Bronfenbrenner, U., McClelland, P., Wethington, E., Moen, P., and Ceci, S. (1996). *The state of Americans: This generation and the next*. New York: Free Press.

Brooks-Gunn, J., Duncan, G.J., Klebanov, P., and Sealand, N. (1993). Do neighbourhoods influence child and adolescent development? *American Journal of Sociology*, **99**, 353–395.

Brooks-Gunn, J., Klebanov, P., and Liaw, F. (1995). The learning, physical and emotional environment of the home in the context of poverty: The

Infant Health and Development program. *Children and Youth Services Review*, **17**, 231–250.

Burns, R. (1786). *Man was made to Mourn* st 11. In C.W. Eliot (Ed.), *The Havard classics* (Vol. 6, *The poems and songs of Robert Burns*). New York: P.F. Collier and Son.

Cabinet Office (2008). Getting on, getting ahead. http://www.cabinetoffice.gov.uk/media/66447/gettingon.pdf. Accessed 31/08/09.

Carlson, E.A. and Sroufe, L.A. (1995). Contribution of attachment theory to developmental psychology. In D. Cicchetti and D. Cohen (Eds), *Developmental psychopathology, Vol 1: Theory and methods* (pp. 581–617). New York: John Wiley & Sons.

Carr, E.G., Taylor, J.G., and Robinson, S. (1991). The effects of severe behavior problems in children on the teaching behavior of adults. *Journal of Applied Behavior Analysis*, **24**, 523–535.

Caspi, A., Henry, B., McGee, R.O., Moffitt, T.E., and Silva, P.A. (1995). Temperamental origins of child and adolescent behaviour problems: From age three to age fifteen. *Child Development*, **66**, 55–68.

Cowen, E. L., Wyman, P. A., Work, W. C., and Parker, G. R. (1990). The Rochester Child Resilience Project (RCRP): Overview and summary of first year findings. *Development and Psychopathology*, 2, 193-212.

Crain-Thoreson, C. and Dale, P.S. (1992). Do early talkers become early readers? Linguistic precocity, preschool language and emergent literacy. *Developmental Psychology*, **28**, 421–429.

Creighton, S.J. (1992). *Child abuse trends in England and Wales, 1988–1990*. London: NSPCC.

Crooks, D. (1995). American children at risk: Poverty and its consequences for children's health, growth, and school achievement. *Yearbook of Physical Anthropology*, **38**, 57–86.

Cutrona, C.E. and Troutman, B.R. (1986). Social support, infant temperament and parenting efficacy: A mediational model of postpartum depression. *Child Development*, **57**, 1507–1518.

Defoe, D. (1722). *Moll Flanders*. London: Penguin.

DeGarmo, D.S., Forgatch, M.S., and Martinez, C.R. (1999). Parenting of divorced mothers as a link between social status and boys academic outcomes: Unpacking the effects of socio-economic status. *Child Development*, **70**, 1231–1245.

Department of Social Security-UK (1999). *Opportunity for all: Tackling poverty and social exclusion*. London: The Stationery Office.

Dodge, K., Pettit, G., and Bates, J. (1994). Socialization mediators of the relation between socioeconomic status and child conduct problems. *Child Development*, **65**, 649–665.

DSS (Department of Social Security) (1999). *Opportunity for all: Tackling poverty and social exclusion.* London: The Stationery Office.

Duncan, G., Brooks-Gunn, J., and Klebanov, P. (1994). Economic deprivation and early childhood development. *Child Development,* **65**, 296–318.

DWP (Department for Work and Pensions) (2001). *Households below average income: A statistical analysis 1999/2000.* Leeds: Corporate Document Services.

EEC (1985). *On Specific Community Action to Combat Poverty* (Council Decision of 19 December 1984) 85/8/EEC, Official Journal of the EEC, 2/24.

Eisenberg, N., Fabes, R.A., Shepard, S.A. et al. (1997). Contemporaneous and longitudinal prediction of children's social functioning from regulation and emotionality. *Child Development,* **68**, 642–664.

Elbourne, D., Pritchard, C., and Dauncey, M. (1986). Perinatal outcomes and related factors: Social class differences within and between geographical areas. *Journal of Epidemiology and Community Health,* **40**(4), 301–308.

Empson, J.M. (2004). Risk Factors in Child Development. In J.M. Empson and D. Nabuzoka (Eds), *Atypical child development in context* (pp. 39–72). Basingstoke: Palgrave Macmillan.

Empson, J.M. and McGlaughlin, A. (1979). *Stress in the lives of disadvantaged children.* Paper given to the Annual Conference of the BPS Developmental Psychology Division, Nottingham University.

Empson, J.M. and Nabuzoka, D. (2004). Understanding atypical development in context. In J.M. Empson and D. Nabuzoka (Eds), *Atypical child development in context.* (pp. 209–238). Basingstoke: Palgrave Macmillan.

Entwistle, D., Alexander, K., and Olson, L. (1997). *Children, schools and inequality.* Boulder, CO: Westview Press.

Farquhar, G. (1707). *The Beaux' Stratagem.* Act 1, scene 1.

Fenton, S. (1989). Racism is harmful to your health. In J. Cox and S. Bostock (Eds), *Racial discrimination and the health service.* Newcastle-under-Lyme: Penrhos Publications.

Fitzpatrick, K. and Boldizar, J. (1993). The prevalence and consequences of exposure to violence among African-American youth. *Journal of the American Academy of Child and Adolescent Psychiatry,* **32**, 424–430.

Flouri, E. (2006). Raising expectations. *The Psychologist,* **19**(11), 664–666.

Gillham, B., Tanner, G., Cheyne, B., Freeman, I., Rooney, M., and Lambie, A. (1998). Unemployment rates, single parent density and indices of child poverty: Their relationship to different categories of child abuse and neglect. *Child Abuse and Neglect,* **22**(2), 79–90.

Goldenberg, C., Reese, L., and Gallimore, R. (1992). Effects of literacy materials from school on Latino children's home experiences and early reading achievement. *American Journal of Education*, **100**, 497–536.

Göncü, A. (Ed) (1999). *Children's engagement in the world: Sociocultural perspectives*. Cambridge: Cambridge University Press.

Gordon, D. and Gibbons, J. (1998). Placing children on child protection registers: Risk indicators and local authority differences. *British Journal of Social Work*, **28**, 423–436.

Gordon, D., Nandy, S., Pantazis, C., Pemberton, S., and Townsend, P. (2003). *Child poverty in the developing world*. Bristol: The Policy Press.

Gordon, D., Parker, R., and Loughran, F., with Heslop, P. (2000). *Disabled children in Britain: A reanalysis of the OPCS Disability Surveys*. London: The Stationery Office.

Harding, L.M. (2001). *Child poverty*. Sheffield: Sheffield Hallam University Press.

Harper, C. and Marcus, R. (1999). Mortgaging Africa's future: The long-term cost of child poverty. *Development*, **43**(1), 1–24.

Harris, T.L. and Hodges, R.E. (Eds) (1983). *A dictionary of reading and related terms*. London: International Reading Association/Heinemann Educational Books.

Hill, N.E. (2001). Parenting and academic socialization as they relate to school readiness: The roles of ethnicity and family income. *Journal of Educational Psychology*, **93**(4), 686–697.

Hill, N.E., Castellino, D.R., Lansford, J.E., Nowlin, P., Dodge, K.A., Bates, J.E., and Pettit, G.S. (2004). Parent academic involvement as related to school behavior, achievement and aspirations: Demographic variations across adolescence. *Child Development*, **75**, 1491–1509.

Ho, D. Y. F. (1986). Chinese patterns of socialization: A critical review. In M. H. Bond (ed.) *The psychology of Chinese people*. New York: Oxford University Press.

Jarrett, R.L. (1992). Adolescent development in low-income African American neighbourhoods. The Ethnographic Evidence. *Northwestern University Centre for Urban Affairs and Policy Research Working Paper*. Evanston, IL: Center for Urban Affairs and Policy research.

Jencks, C. and Mayer, S. (1990). The social consequences of growing up in a poor neighbourhood: A review. In M. McGeary and L. Lynn (Eds), *Inner city poverty in the United States*. Washington, DC: National Academy Press.

Johnson, S. (1763). in Boswell *Life*, vol. 1 p. 441.

Kempson, E. (1996). *Life on a low income*. York: Joseph Rowntree Foundation.

Kim-Cohen, J., Moffitt, T.E., Caspi, A., and Taylor, A. (2004). Genetic and environmental processes in young children's resilience and vulnerability to socioeconomic deprivation. *Child Development*, **75**, 651–668.

Klebanov, P.K., Brooks-Gunn, J., and Duncan, G.J. (1994). Does neighborhood and family poverty affect mothers' parenting, mental health, and social support? *Journal of Marriage and the Family*, **56**, 441–455.

Korenman, S., Miller, J., and Sjaastad, J. (1995). Long-term poverty and child development in the United States: Results from the NLSY. *Children and Youth Services Review*, **17**, 127–155.

Lewis, O. (1966). *La Vida*. London: Secker and Warburg.

Linver, M.R., Brooks-Gunn, J., and Kohen, D.E. (2002). Family processes as pathways from income to young children's development. *Developmental Psychology*, **38**, 719–734.

Littlejohn-Blake, S.M. and Darling, C.A. (1993). Understanding the strengths of African American families. *Journal of Black Studies*, **23**, 460–471.

Lloyd, E. (2006). Children, poverty and social exclusion. In C. Pantazis, D. Gordon, and C. Levitas (Eds), *Poverty and social exclusion in Britain. The millennium survey*. Bristol: The Policy Press.

Lynch, M. and Cicchetti, D. (1998). An ecological-transactional analysis of children and contexts: the longitudinal interplay among child maltreatment, community violence and children's symptomatology. *Development and Psychopathology*, **10**, 235–257.

McCormick, C.E. and Mason, J.M. (1986). Intervention procedures for increasing preschool children's interest in and knowledge about reading. In W.H. Teale and E. Sulzby (In *Emergent literacy: Writing and reading*, (pp. 90–115). Norwood, NJ: Ablex.

McGlaughlin, A. and Empson, J. (1979). Early child development and the home environment. Paper given to the BPS Developmental Conference, *Bulletin BPS*, **32**, 148.

McLelland, M. M., Morrison, F. J. and Holmes, D. L. (2000). Children at risk for early academic problems: the role of learning-related social skills. *Early Child Research Quarterly*, 15, 307-329.

McLeod, J. and Shanahan, M. (1993). Poverty, parenting and children's mental health. *American Sociological Review*, **58**, 351–366.

McLloyd, V.C. (1998). Socioeconomic disadvantage and child development. *American Psychologist*, **53**, 185–204.

Marmot, M.G., Adelstein, A.M., and Bulusu, L. (1984). *Immigrant mortality in England and Wales 1970–75: Causes of death by country of birth*, Studies on Medical and Population Subjects, No. 47. London: HMSO.

Mason, C.A., Cauce, A.M., Gonzales, N., Hiraga, Y., and Grove, K. (1994). An ecological model of externalizing behaviors in African-American adolescents: No family is an island. *Journal of Research on Adolescence*, 4, 639–655.

Masten, A.S. (1994). Resilience in individual development: Successful adaptation despite risk and adversity. In M. Wang and E. Gordon (Eds), *Risk and resilience in inner city America: Challenges and Prospects* (pp. 3–25). Hillsdale, NJ: Erlbaum.

Masten, A.S. and Coatsworth, J.D. (1998). The development of competence in favorable and unfavorable environments. Lessons from research on successful children. *American Psychologist*, 53(2), 205–220.

Moore, R. (2000). Material deprivation amongst ethnic minority and white children: The evidence of the sample of anonymised records. In J. Bradshaw and R. Sainsbury (Eds), *Experiencing poverty*. Hampshire: Ashgate Publishing.

Morrow, V. (2001). *Networks and neighbourhoods: Children's and young people's perspectives*. London: Health Development Agency.

Office of Population Censuses and Surveys (OPCS) (1991). *1989-based national population projections*. London: OPCS.

Ogbu, J.U. (1981). Origins of human competence: A cultural-ethological perspective. *Child Development*, 52, 413–429.

Ogbu, J.U. (1994). From cultural differences to differences in cultural frame of reference. In P.M. Greenfield and R.R. Locking (Eds), *Cross-cultural roots of minority child development* (pp. 365–392). Hillsdale, NJ: Lawrence Erlbaum.

Ogbu, J. and Fordham, S. (1986). African American students' school success: Coping with the burden of 'acting white'. *Urban Review*, 18, 176–206.

OPCS series DH3 No 23 (1992). *1989 Mortality Statistics, Perinatal and Infant: Social and biological factors*. London: HMSO.

O'Toole, R., (1983) in S.J. Creighton (1992) *Child abuse trends in England and Wales, 1988–1990*. London: NSPCC.

Pather, E.U. (2006). A cultural mismatch between school and home: Home culture versus school culture. *Fourth international conference on new directions in the humanities*. University of Carthage, Tunis, Tunisia, July.

Platt, L. (2000). The experience of poverty: Welfare dynamics among children of different ethnic groups. Unpublished thesis, Cambridge: Cambridge University.

Plomin, R. and Bergeman, C.S. (1991). The nature of nurture: Genetic influence on 'environmental' measures. *Behavioral and Brain Sciences*, 14, 373–427.

Plomin, R., DeFries, J.C., McClearn, G.E., and McGuffin, P. (2001). *Behavioural Genetics*. Fourth Edition. New York: Worth Publishers.

Quilgars, D. (2001) Child Mortality Ch 2, Child Abuse Chapter 5. In *Poverty: The Outcomes for Children*. Ed J. Bradshaw. London: Family Policy Studies Centre.

Reading, R. (1997). Poverty and the health of children and adolescents. *Archives of Disease in Childhood*, **76**, 463–467.

Reiss, D., Neiderhiser, J.M., Hetherington, E.M., and Plomin, R. (2000). *The relationship code: Deciphering genetic and social patterns in adolescent development.* Cambridge, MA: Harvard University Press.

Ridge, T. (2002). *Childhood poverty and social exclusion. From a child's perspective.* Bristol: The Policy Press.

Ritchie, C., Flouri, E., and Buchanan, A. (2005). *Aspirations and expectations. Policy discussion paper.* National Family and Parenting Institute.

Robinson, D. and Pinch, S. (1987). A geographical analysis of the relationship between early childhood death and socio-economic environment in an English city. *Social Science and Medicine*, **25**(1), 9–18.

Runyan, D.K., Hunter, W.M., Socolar, R.R.S., Amaya-Jackson, L., English, D., Landsverk, J. et al. (1998). Children who prosper in unfavorable environments: The relationship to social capital. *Pediatrics*, **101**, 12–18.

Rutter, M. (1979). Protective factors in children's responses to stress and disadvantage. In M.W. Kent and J.E. Rolf (Eds), *Family prevention of psychopathology*, Vol. 3, *Social competence in children.* Hanover, NH: University Press of New England.

Sameroff, A.J. (1991). The social context of development. In M. Woodhead, R. Carr, and P. Light (Eds), *Becoming a person.* London: Routledge/Open University.

Sameroff, A.J. and Chandler, M.J. (1975). Reproductive risk and the continuum of caretaking casualty. In F.D. Horowitz, M. Hetherington, S. Scarr-Salapetek, and G. Siegal (Eds), *Review of child development research*, Vol. 4. Chicago: University of Chicago Press.

Save the Children (2000). *What is child poverty? Facts, measurements and conclusions.* London: Save the Children, UK.

Schaffer, H.R. (1996). *Social development.* Oxford: Blackwell.

Schoendorf, K.C., Hogue, C.J.R., Kleinman, J.C., and Rowley, D. (1992). Mortality among infants of black as compared with white college-educated parents. *New England Journal of Medicine*, **326**, 1522–1526.

Schoon, I., Parsons, S., and Sacker, A. (2004). Socioeconomic adversity, educational resilience, and subsequent levels of adult adaptation. *Journal of Adolescent Research*, **19**, 383–404.

Serpell, R., Baker, L., and Sonnenschein, S. (2005). *Becoming literate in the city.* Cambridge: Cambridge University Press.

Shakespeare, W. (1592). *Henry VI*, Part 2, act 1, scene 3, 1.

Shaw, D. and Emery, R. (1988). Chronic family adversity and school-age children's adjustment. *Journal of the American Academy of Child and Adolescent Psychiatry*, **27**, 200–206.

Shaw, G.B. (1907). *Major Barbara*. Preface. New York: Brentano's.

Shaw, M., Dorling, D., Gordon, D., and Davey Smith, G. (1999). *The widening gap: Health inequalities and policy in Britain*. Bristol: The Policy Press.

Shaw, N.J. and Pal, B.R. (2002). Vitamin D deficiency in UK Asian families: Activating a new concern. *Archives of Diseases in Childhood*, **86**, 147–149.

Shropshire, J. and Middleton, S. (1999). *Small expectations: Learning to be poor*. York: Joseph Rowntree Foundation.

Singh, G.K. and Yu, S.M. (1995). Infant mortality in the United States: Trends, differentials and projections, 1950 through 2010. *American Journal of Public Health*, **85**, 957–964.

Skelton, T. and Allen, T. (Eds) (1999). *Culture and global change*. London: Routledge.

Smeeding, T.M., Rainwater, L., and Burtless, G. (2000). United States poverty in a cross-national context. Luxembourg Income Study Working Paper No. 244. Prepared for IRP Conference Volume, *Understanding poverty in America: Progress and problems*.

Smith, J., Brooks-Gunn, J., and Klebanov, P. (1997). Consequences of living in poverty for young children's cognitive and verbal ability and early school achievement. In G. Duncan and J. Brooks-Gunn (Eds), *Consequences of growing up poor* (pp. 132–189). New York: Russell Sage Foundation.

Sprangers, M.A.G., de Regt, E.B., Andries, F., van Agt, H.M.E., Bijl, R.V., de Boer, J.B., Foets, M., Hoeymans, N., Jacobs, A.E., Kempen, G.I.J.M., Miedema, H.S., Tijhuis, M.A.R., Hanneke C.J.M., and de Haes, H.C.J.M., (2000). Which chronic conditions are associated with better or poorer quality of life? *Journal of Clinical Epidemiology*, **53**(9), 895–907.

Super, C.M. and Harkness, S. (1986). The developmental niche: A conceptualization at the interface of child and culture. *International Journal of Behavioural Development*, **9**, 545–569.

Townsend, P. (1979). *Poverty in the United Kingdom*. London: Allen Lane and Penguin Books.

UN (1995). *The Copenhagen declaration and programme of action: World Summit for Social Development 6–12 March 1995*. New York: United Nations Department of Publications.

Vinson, T., Baldry, E., and Hargreaves, J. (1996). Neighbourhoods, networks and child abuse. *British Journal of Social Work*, **26**, 523–543.

Watt, N. (2008). Social mobility on the rise at last, says report. *The Guardian*, 4 November.

Werner, E. (1989). High-risk children in young adulthood: A longitudinal study from birth to 32 years. *American Journal of Orthopsychiatry*, **59**, 72–81.

Werner, E.E. and Smith, R.S. (1982). *Vulnerable but invincible: A study of resilient children.* New York: McGraw-Hill.

Werner, E.E. and Smith, R.S. (1992). *Overcoming the odds: High risk children from birth to adulthood.* Ithaca, NY: Cornell University Press.

White, R.W. (1959). Motivation reconsidered: The concept of competence. *Psychological Review*, **66**, 297–333.

Whitehurst, G.J. and Lonigan, C.J. (1998). Child development and emergent literacy. *Child Development*, **69**, 848–872.

Wingfield, A., Eccles, J., Yoon, K., Harold, R., Arbreton, C. et al. (1997). Change in children's competence beliefs and subjective task values across the elementary school years: A three-year study. *Journal of Educational Psychology*, **89**, 451–469.

Woodhead, M. (1991). Psychology and the cultural construction of 'children's needs'. In M. Woodhead, P. Light, and R. Carr (Eds), *Growing up in a changing society.* London: Routledge and Open University Press. www.statistics.gov.uk/nugget.asp?id=1003. Accessed 26/9/2006.

Wyman, P.A., Cowen, E.L., Work, W.C., Hoyt-Meyer, L., Magnus, K.B., and Fagen, D.B. (1999). Caregiving and developmental factors differentiating young at-risk urban children showing resilient versus stress-affected outcomes: A replication and extension. *Child Development*, **70**, 645–659.

Culture and Cognitive Development

Janet M. Empson and Dabie Nabuzoka

OUTLINE
5.1 Introduction
5.2 Models of the relationship between culture and intellectual functioning
5.3 Theoretical perspectives
    5.3.1 Piagetian constructivist theory
    5.3.2 Neo-Piagetian theory
    5.3.3 Sociocultural perspectives
5.4 Relationship between cognitive and social development
    5.4.1 Socialization of cognition
    5.4.2 Relationships and feelings driving cognitive change
5.5 Implications of the cultural context on cognitive development
5.6 Summary and conclusions
Further reading
References

5.1 Introduction

The term cognition refers to the mental processes which enable us to understand the world in which we live. These include perception, attention, learning, memory, reasoning and problem-solving. So, cognitive development refers to the development of our understanding of the social and physical world (how we acquire knowledge). This has been one of the main concerns in developmental psychology. Various aspects of intellectual development are considered universal. One such ability is logic, which is applied in various contexts. It can be assumed therefore that all typically developing children might become logical in the same way. However, it has been pointed out that some aspects of intellectual development may not be universal (Eysenck, 1998). For example, human inventions such as counting systems, written language, scientific methods, and so on, can vary across cultures but are important aspects of cognitive development. As certain features of these may not be universal, the question is whether cognitive development is entirely a matter of children acquiring those universal aspects of intellectual functioning (e.g., being logical, remembering and so on) or whether the important part of a child's intellectual development is being taught about these cultural inventions.

Cognitive development has been viewed in the past as the development of intellectual functioning and, therefore, describes the development of intelligence. The concept of intelligence is a very controversial one and it has been argued that it has little value in explaining individual differences between children in their performance at various tasks involving cognitive activity. However, intelligence remains a notable research area in psychology, and no discussion of cognitive development would be complete without reference to intelligence. Intelligence tests are still widely used as measures of performance in the sphere of education and so are of relevance here to a discussion of cognitive development in cultural context.

Over the years, there has been increased recognition of the importance of cultural context for intellectual development. For example, there has been an increased interest in studying the impact of rapid cultural change on aspects of cognitive development and functioning (e.g., Beach, 1995; Saxe and Esmonde, 2005) following the early work by Luria (1976). Other work has been on the impact of culturally organized activity, including cognitive consequences of literacy (Scribner and Cole, 1981), organization of instructional activity (Hedegaard, 1996; Rogoff, 2003), and the socialization of cognitive development and functioning (Correa-Chávez and Rogoff, 2005; Nunes, 2005). Such work has taken a cultural or cross-cultural perspective.

In general, different approaches and theoretical perspectives have underpinned work on the role of culture in cognitive development and functioning. This chapter introduces some of these approaches and highlights some of their key features. First, some of the general models of the relationship between culture and intellectual functioning are outlined and discussed. Second, key features of some theories of cognitive development are presented as they relate to the influence of culture or the context of development. These theories include two main perspectives that have generated much of the research in children's cognitive development: the constructivist theory of Piaget and the social constructivist theory of Vygotsky. These are discussed in turn, including a more specific focus on key features of sociocultural perspectives, following Vygotsky, as they place great emphasis on the assumption that cognitive processes depend fundamentally on and cannot be meaningfully understood independently of sociocultural and historical processes. Third, the social aspects of cognitive development are discussed, including the socialization of cognition and how relationships and feelings drive cognitive change in children. The chapter concludes with a focus on the implications of the wider cultural context on children's cognitive development.

> **Discussion point:** Before you continue reading this chapter, you might first want to reflect on the various ways in which your view of the world might differ from that of someone from another culture. How might this come about?

5.2 Models of the relationship between culture and intellectual functioning

The relationship between culture and intellectual functioning has been well discussed by Sternberg (2004) in the context of the study of intelligence. Sternberg identified four models of the relationship of culture to intellectual functioning, and specifically intelligence. The models are said to differ in two key respects: whether or not there are cultural differences in the nature of the mental processes and representations involved in adaptation that constitute intelligence, and whether there are differences in the instruments needed to measure such processes and representations as a result of cultural differences in the content required for adaptation. The differences in the instruments needed to measure such functioning would be those that go beyond simple translation and adaptation of those developed in one culture for use in another.

In the first model, the nature of intellectual functioning is considered the same across cultures. Similarly, the tests used to measure such functioning should be the same. The model is reflected in theoretical positions such as those of Jensen (1998) and Eysenck (1986). According to Sternberg (2004), for example, Jensen (1998) was of the view that general intelligence or g (Spearman, 1927) is the same across time and space and that what varies are its levels. The main argument is that the nature of intellectual functioning is the same across various cultures and that this can be assessed the same way without regard to culture. What may be required would simply be appropriate translations of text. The view that similar processes characterized cognitive functioning across cultures was also reflected in early studies examining aspects of Piaget's theory (see Serpell, 1976).

The second model proposed by Sternberg (2004) represents a difference in the nature of intelligence without any difference in the instruments used to measure it. The measures used to assess intelligence are the same across cultures, but the outcomes obtained from using those measures are structurally different as a function of the culture being investigated. This approach is compared with that taken by Nisbett (2003), who found that the same tests given in different cultures suggested that people think about problems in different ways across cultures. Thus, in the application of this model essentially the same tests are used to elicit different ways of thinking across cultural groups.

The third model, favoured by Sternberg (2004), considers the dimensions of intelligence to be the same, but the instruments of measurement are different. From this perspective, it is argued that measurement processes for a given attribute must be derived from within the context of the culture being studied rather than from outside it. While it is acknowledged that the same instruments may be used across cultures, it is pointed out that when they are, the psychological meanings that should be assigned to the scores will differ from one culture to another.

This model is consistent with Sternberg's theory of successful intelligence (Sternberg, 1997; 1999). According to this theory, the components of intelligence and the mental representations on which they act are universal, in the sense that they are required for mental functioning in all cultures. Thus, people in all cultures need to execute various components of information processing including the following (Sternberg, 2004): (a) recognizing the existence of problems (b) defining the nature of the problem (c) representing the problems mentally (d) formulating one or more strategies for solving the problems (e) allocating resources to solving the problems (f) monitor solution of the problems and (g) evaluating problem-solving after it is done. The mental contents (i.e., types and items of knowledge) to which such processes are applied and the judgements as to what are considered 'intelligent' applications of the processes are what vary across cultures.

Sternberg (2004) argues that a wholly relativistic view of intelligence and culture would be inadequate, as some things are constant across cultures (mental representations and processes), whereas others are not (the contents to which they are applied and how their application is judged). As such, he argues that tests must be modified if they are to measure the same basic processes as they apply from one culture to another. So, one can translate a particular test of intelligence, but it will not necessarily measure the same thing in one culture as in another (Valsiner, 2000):

> For example, a test that is highly novel in one culture or subculture may be quite familiar in the next. Even if the components of information processing are the same, the experiential novelty to which they are applied may be different. Moreover, the extent to which the given task is practically relevant to adaptation, shaping, and selection may differ. Hence, the components may be universal, but not necessarily the relative novelty or adaptive practicality of the components as applied to particular contents. (Sternberg, 2004, p. 327)

The fourth model proposed by Sternberg (2004) presents both the instruments and the ensuing dimensions of intelligence as being different in relation to the culture under investigation. This position embraces the radical cultural-relativist position that intelligence, or any other mental processes can be understood and measured only as an indigenous construct within a given cultural context (see Kagitçibasi, 2000; and earlier discussion of indigenous psychologies in Chapter 2). At one extreme end is the view that intelligence is largely a cultural invention, and as such, nothing about it is necessarily common across cultures.

The relativity of intelligence and other hypothetical constructs is illustrated by considering the cultural context in which these constructs reside as consisting of different nested levels (Berry and Irvine, 1986, cited by Sternberg, 2004). The ecological level is the broadest and comprises the permanent or almost permanent characteristics that provide the backdrop for human action. The pattern of recurrent experiences within the ecological context constitutes another level, the experiential context that provides a basis for learning and development. The performance context comprises the limited set of environmental circumstances that account for particular behaviours at specific points in space and time. What psychologists and others manipulate to elicit particular responses or test scores are the environmental characteristics within the narrowest, experimental context.

> **Discussion point:** Do you agree with Sternberg's model of the relationship between culture and intellectual functioning? Can you think of examples to support your view?

5.3 Theoretical perspectives

The two main theoretical perspectives that have informed much of the research on children's cognitive development are those of Piaget and Vygotsky. Over the years, these perspectives have generated some debate about culture's influence on cognitive development. The first one of these, Piaget's theory, has been one of the most influential psychological theories in early cross-cultural work on cognition (Maynard, 2008; Serpell, 1976). According to Piaget (1952), the essential element in development is in acquiring the ability to think systematically about logical relations within a problem. This development is universal, being applicable to all humans. A child's understanding of cultural inventions is merely an offshoot of that fundamental developmental change. In contrast to Piaget's perspective, the approach of the Soviet psychologist Lev Vygotsky belongs to the contextualist school of thought. Vygotsky's approach holds that humans are embedded in a social matrix (context). Hence, human behaviour cannot be understood independently of this matrix. According to Vygotsky (1978; 1986), a study of children's development must take a historical account of humankind's intellectual development. He pointed out that over centuries humans have invented cultural tools (e.g., number systems, measurements, computers and so on) which are an indispensable part of our cognition. Children must master such tools to function effectively in their schools or outside them. However, these skills cannot simply be acquired independently by the children. They have to be passed on from one generation to another. According to Vygotsky and his followers, such transmission of cultural tools from generation to generation is an important part of cognitive development (Gauvain, 2001a).

On balance, there has been increasing recognition of the role of contextual and cultural factors in children's acquisition of knowledge about their social and physical world. In the following sections, we outline the particular ways in which each of these theoretical approaches has accounted for such factors. We first outline key features of each approach including some of the refinements and clarifications that have been made over the years since their original formulations.

5.3.1 Piagetian constructivist theory

Constructivist theory of cognitive development is associated with Jean Piaget. Piaget thought that all knowledge is constructed in fundamentally the same way in all human cultures by the active selection and interpretation of environmental information by the child. Therefore, the child actively constructs his/her knowledge of the world from their experience. Piaget's main assumptions were as follows: knowledge aids adaptation to the world, and cognition serves action; children are cognitively active and inventive; knowledge is acquired through active interaction with the world; maturing cognitive abilities interact with the context of people and objects to produce new abilities; and stages in development do not just follow a maturational sequence, reaching them depends upon the individual child's activities and opportunities.

Piaget identified a series of stages of cognitive development which he considered universal. Essentially, the characteristics of these were that in the course of development the modes by which knowledge or understanding was acquired changed from linking perception to action in babies and toddlers (using imagery of the different sensory modalities – vision, audition, touch, taste, smell and kinaesthesis), through acquiring the ability to use successively more abstract ways of thinking (using the symbols and concepts of words, mathematics and so on) as the child grows to reach approximately the age of puberty. Around the age of seven, key changes occur in the child's thinking reflecting the increasing use of logic and the ability to classify objects according to several features at the same time.

One of the most important developments described by Piaget as occurring at this time was that of *conservation,* the ability of the child to understand that certain essential features of an object remain the same even if the appearance of it changes. Another of Piaget's important concepts is that of *egocentricity*. This describes the way in which young children view the world from their own perspective and their inability to understand that other people can have a different perspective on the same situation. Egocentricity was first demonstrated by Piaget and Inhelder (1956) in the 'three-mountains experiment' in which children were unable to describe a model from different points of view but was considered by Piaget to apply widely across different domains of development. For example, as Schaffer (2004) relates, a young child when asked if he has a brother will answer 'yes', but when asked if his brother has a brother may not be able to answer correctly.

Since the 1960s, the validity of Piaget's work has been investigated empirically, and some of the key ideas in Piaget's theory have stood the test of time. There is empirical evidence to support the qualitative shifts in cognitive development as described in Piaget's stages (Goswami, 1998) although Pascual-Leone has commented that the neo-Piagetians agree that stages do not really exist in that they are 'only found in suitable situations!'(2000, p. 843). Piagetian ideas continue to influence educational practice but a considerable body of research has suggested modifications of Piaget's concepts. The studies of Margaret Donaldson (1978) and her team in Edinburgh showed the importance of the context in which problems were presented for children to solve. For example, the essential features of the three-mountains situation cited earlier were replicated in a different situation more relevant to the lives of the children taking part. In Martin Hughes's study (in Donaldson 1978), the problem presented to the child required positioning a doll representing a boy hiding from a policeman behind intersecting walls. In this study, the children were able to take the perspective of the policeman in relation to the doll representing the boy.

This investigation demonstrated the importance of the child's understanding of the problem to be solved, the language used in explaining the task and 'a situation...which *makes sense to the child*' (Donaldson, 1978, p. 23). This finding is of relevance to children's differing cultural experiences (such as whether they are familiar with mountains and/or policemen) and highlights the importance of the ecological validity of the situation when assessing children's capabilities.

The significance of the language, communication and instruction used by adults in investigations of children's cognition was emphasized by the work of David Wood and others (Wood, 1988). Wood (1988) argued that Piaget attached insufficient importance to the role of adults' language and interaction in children's cognitive development. Bruner's view, based on many years of his own empirical work (e.g., Wood, Bruner and Ross, 1976) was that the child's active construction of his/her own knowledge was the product of the 'joint construction' of understanding by the child and more expert members of the culture. This view very much reflects that of Vygotsky (1978), which is further discussed below. Bruner also emphasized the importance of the cultural symbols of language, pictures and so on in forming the child's intelligence. While Piaget saw the mature system of thinking as being the operations of logic by the child, this was questioned by Wood as his studies with Bruner had pointed to the significant role of *strategies and processes* in reasoning and problem-solving rather than Piagetian structures.

For Bruner the importance of processes of thinking were that they explained individual differences between children and the situation-dependent nature of children's reasoning and problem-solving. In children's learning, they searched for patterns, regularity and predictability in situations and creative thought that goes beyond these and creates new rules and codes. Thus, Bruner stressed the importance of interpersonal and cultural influences on learning, but also acknowledged the influence of biology and evolution. The latter were, of course, the basis of Piaget's theory of cognitive development.

While Bruner argued against the existence of stages of cognitive development, Crain's (2000) evaluation of Piaget's legacy is that there is strong empirical support for the *sequence* of stages although Piaget (1966) himself found in cross-cultural studies that there could be delays of several years in developmental level. In addition, some individuals and, normatively, in some societies, usually small village and tribal communities, the use of formal operational thinking seemed to occur rarely (Cole and Cole, 2001). It was suggested (Buck-Moss, 1975) that abstract formal cognition reflects a particular social structure characterized by exchange value and alienation which govern production and exchange in the industrialized West. There was also little support for the notion of generality of thinking within stages in that low correlations were found between performances on different tasks.

Another much criticized aspect of Piaget's work is that he underestimated children's abilities. For example 'object permanence' has been shown to be acquired earlier than Piaget's studies suggested. In addition, 'egocentrism' – the child's inability to view things from the point of view of another – does not universally last as long as was thought by Piaget, a point demonstrated by the work of Hughes and Donaldson discussed earlier.

Lourenço and Machado (1996) also have discussed the substantial criticisms of Piaget's work, of which it is important to note that Piaget's description of child development at the early stages was in terms of deficits rather than strengths; he overemphasized competence at the expense of performance; and he failed to explain, rather than simply describe, developmental progress. The most significant criticism of Piaget in relation to accounting for cultural factors has been his alleged relative neglect of the role of social factors in development. Since the early 1980s, Piaget has been attacked on the basis that he assumes that individual cognitive development is largely genetically determined, that it occurs in a social vacuum, and that his description of cognitive development holds for all children across cultures. Tomasello (2000), for example, suggests that Piaget's theory was 'detailed, elaborate, comprehensive, and in many important respects, wrong' (p. 207). Other critics claim that Piaget's work ignores the child's gender, temperament and social context.

Although much of Piaget's work focuses on the individual child and the physical environment, he was of the view that 'The human being is immersed right from birth in a social environment which affects him just as much as his physical environment. Society, even more, in a sense, than the physical environment, changes the very structure of the individual' (Piaget, 1973, p. 156). In addition, Piaget's methods of investigation acknowledged the significance of the social aspects of the research situation. Burman (1994) pointed out that in 1929 Piaget was interpreting the child's development in terms of what s/he said and did to 'take account of the whole mental context' (p. 19) and Vygotsky (although strongly criticizing Piaget for his neglect of attention to language and culture) also acknowledged Piaget's method as his most important contribution. Both Piaget and Vygotsky agreed on the active participation of the researcher in their studies of cognitive development.

In providing a comprehensive rebuttal of these criticisms, Lourenço and Machado (1996) note that although criticisms of Piaget seem reasonable on the surface, they are based on a selective reading and misinterpretation of Piaget's work. They also suggest that although Piaget never pursued empirical investigations of the impact of culture on child development, he nevertheless made frequent reference to the importance of social interaction in the acquisition of cognitive skills. They quote Piaget discussing, for example, the importance of social exchanges in assisting the individual to organize cognitive structures into a coherent system, the role of social interaction in the transition from egocentric to socialized thought processes, and the need for the individual to have contact with significant others in order to achieve conservation and reversibility and to advance his/her moral development. It must be said that during the later periods of his work, Piaget gave increasing emphasis to self-regulation in the construction of knowledge, particularly in coordinating the influences of maturation, physical experience and social factors, but he never abandoned the idea that social factors are indeed an important influence.

5.3.2 Neo-Piagetian theory

In the 1970s, the Geneva School of developmental psychologists (Doise, Mugny and others, 1975; 1984) investigated the social context of children's problem-solving, initially using modifications of Piagetian tasks. Like Piaget they were constructivists, but emphasized the constructive nature of social interaction. Social psychology had demonstrated that group performance tended to be better than that of individuals due to cognitive and motivational gains. So the Genevans investigated whether children's problem-solving in a social context and through collaboration with peers would encourage developmental gain. They hypothesized that developments in thinking are not the result of imitation or of accepting someone else's authority or instruction, but from the resolution of *'socio-cognitive conflict'*. New ways of thinking about problems arise from exposure to contradictory perspectives on the same problem (e.g., Doise and Mugny, 1984) which create 'disequilibrium' and movement to a higher cognitive level. Interestingly, the concept of socio-cognitive conflict has not been found to be applicable to children in collectivist societies (see later in this chapter). In addition, Light et al. (1994) argued that socio-cognitive conflict was not necessary to improve performance. In a study in the United Kingdom, they found that the mere presence of another child working on the same task improved performance as much as peer interaction.

Such cognitive developments were first demonstrated by Doise et al. (1975) using a conservation task: Six- to seven-year-olds were pretested individually. They then worked together on the task in groups of two or three. A post-test showed that initially non-conserving children learned to conserve after working with children who could conserve. The explanation Doise et al. gave for this was that through exposure to another with a different point of view, cognitive conflict was created within the individual, and this was resolved through new insights (shown by the children's explanations for the choices they made) such as reversibility and compensation of height for width.

Other studies showed developmental gain of correct solutions to conservation tasks in pairs of children where neither of them could conserve. Ames and Murray (1982) studied children divided into three groups as follows: In Group 1 (social interaction) children were paired with others who gave a different response; In Group 2 (modelling) the correct answers were demonstrated; and in Group 3 (instruction) the children had to pretend the opposite answer was correct, or were given corrective feedback. Findings indicated that the social interaction group (Group 1) showed marked cognitive gains while the other groups did not. Moreover, Ames and Murray found a generalization of progress to other tasks. This suggested, therefore, that through social interaction knowledge which was not previously possessed can be constructed.

Doise and Mugny's (1984) investigation highlighted the importance of social marking. They gave children conservation tasks which were set in the context of social rules such as giving equal quantities of orange juice to different children because they both worked equally hard. Juice initially in same-shaped containers was then poured into differently shaped vessels (a test of conservation). It was observed that non-conserving, four- to six-year-old children who initially thought that the two differently shaped containers held different quantities of liquid, but who then discussed the problem in the context of social rights, made more cognitive progress than control children. Doise and Mugny explained this as resulting from the mental effort required to achieve social harmony (a fair outcome for each), which instigated cognitive processes leading to better scores on the conservation task. Others however argue that imitation is more important than Doise and his colleagues believed, and that understanding advances from a better representation of the situation and the acceptance of the correct answer during social interaction (Durkin, 1995).

Further studies of social interaction between peers in problem-solving situations were carried out by Paul Light and colleagues using the Tower of Hanoi task (Glachan and Light, 1982; Light and Glachan, 1985). Improvement between pre- and post-tests on the Tower of Hanoi problem in eight-year-olds was greater for pairs of children who worked together during the intervening practice period, compared with those who practised alone. Even those who were paired with a less able peer improved more than a child who had the same initial performance but then worked alone.

Another experiment investigated the effects of different kinds of communication in eight-year-old children's ability to solve a modification of the Tower of Hanoi problem. The children were divided into three groups: Group 1 (structured interaction) – moved the tile together in that they had to resolve their differences and agree on a solution to the problem; Group 2 (unstructured interaction) – could move tiles independently; and Group 3 (instruction) – had an adult coach. Group 1 was found to have most improvement in their performance in generalizing their learning; Group 2 was less effective because one child carried out most of the moves; and Group 3 did not improve through instruction. Light and colleagues argued that this was because this group of children had no opportunity to resolve cognitive conflicts between their own original strategy and what they were being told. The benefits of collaborative learning were found in other situations also, such as in a computer-based code-breaking context. Not only did the social interaction pairs improve more but the nature and extent of talk between the children was also correlated with post-test scores. In a second study, children were allocated to high-argument and low-argument pairs on the basis of videotaped recordings of their behaviour in the first study and it was found that the pairs of children who argued more improved more.

Fitzpatrick (1996) investigated the effects of gender on performance of different tasks. Pairs of children of different sexes showed more assertiveness in discussion than same sex pairs. Girls were more assertive in non-computer-based language tasks and boys were more assertive in a computer-based language task. Light and Littleton (1999) pointed out that most computer software for classroom use is male-oriented and their studies showed that boys' performance was initially superior to that of girls in typical computer games, but that the superiority was reversed in the context of a specially written, girl-oriented 'honeybears picnic' puzzle. Light and Littleton (1999) also emphasized that much work on peer facilitation of learning shows no gender differences.

Recent work by a team of neo-Piagetian psychologists in Montreal (Larivée, Normandeau and Parent, 2000) has extended Piaget's ideas and produced a model integrating inter- and intra-individual differences within the context of a general theory of cognitive development. Cognitive development is shown to be multidimensional involving various modes of information processing, which can be interchangeably activated during problem-solving (Reuchlin, 1978). Although all children possess the same modes, they are hierarchically organized in different ways in terms of efficacy and personal preference and their use will vary in different situations. An empirical demonstration of this is in class-inclusion tasks where children may use two different kinds of argument, and training on the kind of argument not previously used leads to greater gains in performance than training the one spontaneously used. Two widely used modes of processing, propositional and analogical, co-exist and are differentially useful in logicomathematical and infralogical tasks (Lautrey, 1991). Larivée et al. (2000) point out that these have similarities to the two types of knowledge, everyday and scientific concepts, proposed by Vygotsky (1978; 1987). We suggest here that different cultures will differentially favour the use of particular modes of processing to aid the child's adaptation and cognitive progress in his/her specific developmental niche and this could be tested empirically.

5.3.2.1 Conclusion

The works of the neo-Piagetian researchers discussed above investigates the processes, both intra-individual and inter-individual, underlying cognitive development. They have increasingly emphasized the importance of contextual factors (physical and social) which can be likened to the 'developmental niche' of cultural psychology. The interpersonal dynamics of the learning situation in particular have assumed more priority in this research path which also makes it more complementary to the sociocultural theorists following the theoretical perspective of Vygotsky.

5.3.3 Sociocultural perspectives

The group of work under the label of 'sociocultural perspectives' has intellectual roots in Vygotsky's theory. Vygotsky was born in 1896, the same year as Piaget. However, Piaget lived until 1980 and hence was able to modify and develop his views, while Vygotsky died at the age of 38. Much of Vygotsky's work was discovered and published in the West some time after his death. Vygotsky can be described as one of the fathers of cultural psychology. He was one of the first to stress the importance of sociocultural context for cognitive development and influenced the thinking of many other psychologists, such as Bronfenbrenner. While Piaget was a 'constructivist', Vygotsky was a 'social constructivist'. He acknowledged the role of both biological and environmental factors in cognitive development but argued that the same factors may have very different effects depending upon the people among whom the child grows up – both cultural and personal characteristics are important (see Das Gupta, 1994). Vygotsky thought that cognitive development was dominated by biological influences until the age of two years – the *natural line* – and after that was heavily influenced by the *cultural line* – cultural sign systems such as language. So, the course of development is determined by the integration of cultural, interpersonal *(intermental)* and individual *(intramental)* influences.

Essentially, Vygotsky saw children as learning and developing cognitively through the engagement with adults in shared activities on a day-to-day basis, a very different view from Piaget's. Piaget saw children's learning as being due mainly to personal exploration of the environment. For Vygotsky, cognitive development was guided and encouraged by social interaction; it was a cooperative enterprise. Partners who were more skilled influenced the child's learning in significant ways. Vygotsky was particularly interested in the development of the 'higher mental functions' – thinking, reasoning and understanding – and his basic premises regarding how these develop were as follows:

- Complex forms of thinking have their origins in internalizing social interactions. The key processes involved are the language used by the adult and the way the task is structured by the adult.
- Adults are important in providing effective assistance, the relevant factors being characteristics of the adult, of the child and of the adult-child relationship. New steps in learning are achieved in the 'Zone of Proximal Development'.

Although work with intellectual roots in Vygotsky's theory can be grouped under the label of 'sociocultural perspectives', much of this has developed in some distinctive ways and is known by what may sometimes be contrasting theoretical labels. What these perspectives share is a monistic view of culture and cognition. According to Miller and Chen (2005), 'rather than treating cognition as a purely internal psychological activity that can be understood independently from sociocultural and historical processes, approaches within this broad and somewhat eclectic tradition assume that cognitive processes depend fundamentally on and cannot be meaningfully understood independently of such influences' (p. 1). In the following sections, we outline some of the key theoretical positions and concepts that reflect these perspectives.

5.3.3.1 Sociocultural theory

The notions of psychological tools, internalization and mediation are considered to be cornerstones of both Vygotsky's *sociocultural theory* and *activity theory* developed by his followers (Karpov, 2005). According to Vygotsky, the major characteristic of human mental processes is that they are mediated by tools, just like human labour. But these are special, psychological tools. Just as tools are invented by human society, and children acquire and master them, the same is true of psychological tools, and these reflect the accumulated experience of humankind. Children are not born with such tools, they acquire and master them. When psychological tools have been mastered by children, they come to mediate their mental processes. Vygotsky specifically referred to human mental processes, which are mediated by tools, as 'higher mental processes'. This was to distinguish them from lower mental processes, with which children are born and which are possessed by both young children and animals.

Vygotsky referred to language, concepts, signs and symbols as examples of psychological tools. However, it is argued that a child's learning of a new word, concept, sign or symbol does not automatically make this word, concept, sign or symbol a psychological tool. As pointed out by Karpov (2005), in considering scientific concepts as psychological tools that come to mediate mental processes of school-age children, Vygotsky (1986) noted that 'the difficulty with scientific concepts lies in their *verbalism*' (p. 148, also cited by Karpov, 2005, p. 5). He also pointed out that 'scientific concepts...just start their development, rather than finish it, at a moment when the child learns the term or word meaning denoting the new concept' (Vygotsky, 1986, p. 159). Karpov (2005) notes that Vygotsky never elaborated these reservations, and as a result, his theory is traditionally associated with the notion of semiotic tools as mediators of human mental processes (Kozulin, 1986; See also Chapter 6 on role of Language).

The question that arises is whether words, concepts, signs or symbols by themselves serve as psychological tools mediating human mental processes. Vygotsky's (1981) perspective was that a sign 'alters the entire flow and structure of mental functions. It does this by determining the structure of a new instrumental act, just as a technical tool alters the process of a natural adaptation by determining the form of labor operations' (p. 137). According to neo-Vygotskians, a practical (or technical) tool by itself does not determine the form or structure of a human operation, since the possession of a tool does not lead automatically to the mastery of the procedure for its use.

Similarly with psychological tools, students' memorization of scientific conceptual knowledge (rules, concepts, definitions or theorems) that is not supported by their mastery of relevant procedural knowledge does not lead to the students' use of this knowledge for solving subject-domain problems. Karpov (2005) cites an example of elementary school students who, having memorized the concepts of mammals, birds, and fish when classifying animals, were shown to proceed from surface characteristics of the animals rather than from the concepts that they had memorized (e.g., they associated the whale with the class of fish). The argument is that the mastery of a psychological tool requires that the child has mastered the procedure for the use of this tool (Karpov, 2005). Scientific concepts are seen as mediators of students' thinking and problem-solving in different subject domains only if they are supported by students' mastery of relevant procedures that underlie these concepts. In this sense, a child can only fully develop generalization of a concept if they have developed the system of psychological operations or procedures that are relevant to such generalization. The students' mastery of concepts implies that not only are they able to repeat them, but they have also mastered the procedures for identifying those attributes that are necessary and sufficient for associating different objects.

According to Vygotsky, a major aspect of the mastery of psychological tools by children is *internalization* of the tools. When memorizing a set of words, for example, children are able to use external memory aids, such as cards with different pictures, which they can then use to recall the words proceeding from the association between a word and a picture that they have developed. Adults, in contrast, do not need such external memory aids to memorize and recall since they possess internal psychological tools (mnemonics). Thus, a process of internalization takes place between childhood and adulthood, such that the external signs required by children (e.g., cards) are transformed into internal signs that adults produce as means of remembering.

As the Vygotskian perspective holds that the mastery of a psychological tool requires that the child has mastered the *procedure* for the use of this tool, the primary difference between the performance of the school children and the adults in the above example was not that the children were using external signs and adults were using internal signs in order to memorize and recall but was rather in the level of internalization of their mnemonic procedures: school children were partially exteriorized and therefore could not perform without a visual support (e.g., cards), whereas the adults were internalized and did not require a visual support. In this sense, internalization is of procedures rather than the internalization of signs (Karpov, 2005).

To Vygotsky and the neo-Vygotskians, mediation is considered to be the determinant of mental development. This is a process with two aspects. The first aspect relates to children's mastery of new psychological tools, which become internalized and come to mediate the child's mental processes. The second component is the role of adults as mediators of children's acquisition and mastery of new psychological tools. According to Vygotsky and his followers, psychological tools, being products of human culture, should be taught to children by representatives of this culture. Just as nobody would expect a new generation to reinvent tools of labour, the same is true of psychological tools that serve as mediators of human mental processes. However, Karpov (2005) points out that there is a difference between Vygotsky and neo-Vygotskians in their understanding of the nature of psychological tools, resulting in differences of understanding the process of adults' mediation of the acquisition and mastery by children of new psychological tools.

Karpov (2005) argues that Vygotsky, who defined psychological tools as words, concepts, signs or symbols, held that a natural context for a child's acquisition of such tools is the situation of child-adult verbal communication. Although he did not view children as passive recipients of semiotic tools presented by adults in the course of interpersonal communication, Vygotsky's discussion from general theoretical issues to children's development at different stages is seen as often limited to the analysis of children's acquisition of semiotic tools in the course of interpersonal communication with adults. The neo-Vygotskians, in contrast, emphasize the importance of procedures for the use of psychological tools as mediators of human mental processes. They hold that only in the context of their joint activity with adults aimed at performing a task, rather than in context of their verbal communication, can children master these procedures. Thus,

> mediation starts with the adult's 'exteriorizing' (modeling and explaining) the procedure for the use of the new psychological tool, which is necessary to perform the task. Then, the adult involves the child into joint performance of this procedure, creating in this way the zone of proximal development of a new mental process, and guides the child's mastery and internalization of this procedure. As the child becomes more and more proficient in the use of the procedure, the adult withdraws himself or herself from the situation of joint performance, passing more and more responsibility for performing the task to the child. As a result, the mastered and internalized procedure comes to mediate the child's mental processes. (Karpov, 2005, p. 6)

This notion of mediation has been especially important for the development of innovative instructional procedures, and has been the basis of activity theory (Cole, 2005).

5.3.3.2 Activity theory

The *Zone of Proximal Development* (ZPD) (Vygotsky, 1978) was probably Vygotsky's most important theoretical concept. The ZPD describes the range of tasks the child cannot do alone but can do with help from a more experienced partner. The ZPD shifts upwards as the child learns through changes in the way the adult structures and communicates guidance to him/her. To be effective teachers, adults need to be sensitive to each child's abilities and potential and to be able to perceive the child's goal in the activity.

Vygotsky also viewed play as important in cognitive development, creating its own ZPD. According to Vygotsky (1978), 'in play a child is always above his average age, above his daily behaviour; in play it is as though he were a head taller than himself' (p. 102). Through play, peers also can be seen as important influences on the individual child's learning, and play is acknowledged to be one of the cultural universals of children's development (Bruner, Jolly and Sylva, 1976). Bruner argues that play has the function of facilitating the acquisition of tool use in the young, frequently through symbolism as when a child uses sticks to represent swords. The tools of the culture are used in both physical skills and language skills and both are in part developed through play. Playing games also teaches the rules and conventions of society such as sharing, cooperating and turn-taking. In essence, play is essential for optimal cognitive and social development in all cultures.

Wood et al. (1976) developed the concept of 'scaffolding' to describe the process of modelling and structuring of the situation whereby the more knowledgeable person facilitates the child's progress through the ZPD. This involves the following stages:

1. 'Structuring of learning', by the more experienced person, which includes suggestions, reminders, demonstrations and encouragement. Here the adult has the dominant role.
2. The learner takes over the role of the scaffolder and talks him/herself through the task; the child acquires control of the task.
3. Falling away of self-guidance as the learning becomes automatic and smooth (characteristics of all skilled performance).
4. The recognition that the learning can be thrown back to earlier stages if the child is tired or there are changes to the conditions for task solution.

Much research (e.g., Wood et al., 1976) has demonstrated 'scaffolding' in use in everyday learning situations. Wood and colleagues studied mothers showing their children how to do a 3-D puzzle. Mothers who were flexible in their approach showed a 'contingency strategy' in which their behaviour varied depending on how well the child was doing. Joint engagement or shared attention on activities is an essential feature of successful facilitation of children's learning or problem-solving in both informal and formal teaching situations. The concept of 'scaffolding' is now widely adopted in formal education and forms part of the teacher-training curriculum in the United Kingdom.

Vygotsky's ideas have been elaborated into a theory of *teaching as assisted performance*. Learning is seen as a process of guided reinvention whereby social guidance enables the learner to achieve a constructive 'reinvention' of culturally elaborated knowledge. Interpersonal processes are of central importance and the necessary information has to be available in the culture (Tharp and Gallimore, 1988). In making progress through the ZPD, the focus changes from intermental to intramental; the child becomes skilled, self-directed and self-controlling.

Barbara Rogoff (1990) has extended Vygotsky's work by developing his original concepts (e.g., ZPD) and subjecting his ideas to empirical test in different social and cultural contexts. Rogoff described the overall process whereby children learn the skills approved by their culture as *guided participation*. In the processes of guided participation, adults provide direction and organization for children's cognitive development in widely differing cultures by building bridges between what children know and new information to be learned. Adults arrange children's activities and provide opportunities for them to take responsibility as they gain skills and knowledge. Adults adjust their provision to facilitate children's extension of their existing knowledge to encompass new situations. Children participate in cultural activities with the guidance of others and so are socialized into their sociocultural environment. There are many commonalities across different social environments which facilitate the development of universal skills such as talking, singing and dancing, but the different technologies, such as books or computers, in different societies contribute to differences between them.

There are clearly many similarities between Rogoff's 'guided participation' and Bruner's 'scaffolding', but Rogoff (1990; 2003) takes a broader view, specifying that the cognitive performance of children needs to be considered in the light of the goal of the activity and its interpersonal and sociocultural context. The cross-cultural studies of Rogoff and others illustrate how cultural factors influence what is taught to children, when and how, within the broad universal goals of socialization. For example, Rogoff and Mosier (1993) compared parenting styles in Guatemala and the United States. In interaction with their children, parents in the United States saw themselves as playmates whereas in Guatemala they viewed themselves as supervisors and instructors. Rogoff's (1990) framework for learning includes the following:

- the child has an active role in the way s/he uses social guidance
- this process-oriented approach also stresses action
- the central importance given to problem-solving emphasizes the dynamic nature of thinking – that it is flexible, goal-directed and varied according to context
- there is cultural variation in the goals of cognitive development and the shared understandings of these between the child and others. These are developed through the processes of guided participation
- guided participation is a collaborative activity involving *intersubjectivity*, the sharing of focus and purpose between child and more skilled others involving *cognitive, social and emotional exchange*.

Rogoff's work has been highly influential within the sociocultural approach to development and learning. Within this framework, aspects of development such as collaborative learning, peer tutoring and joint problem-solving which involve cultural tools such as language or computers have been investigated. For Wertsch (1997; 1998), the focus is on '*mediated action*' which involves a relationship between an agent and a mediational means or '*cultural tool*'. Both of these are intrinsic to the task. The socioculturalists see the child's competence in the use of such tools as essential for intellectual development and to becoming an effective member of society (a key component of socialization). Schaffer (2004) describes the cultural tools in a particular society as '... *the objects and skills which each society has perfected to carry on its traditions and which therefore must be handed down from one generation to the next*' (p. 198). They become a part of how we construe the world, approach problems and even how we relate to each other. To possess and use in a skilled or expert way the cultural tools of one's society confers power and influence within the culture. For example, educational success in Western society has become inextricably linked to the effective use of computers, not least in researching and presenting student essays!

As discussed earlier, there are both psychological and technological (such as those of labour) cultural tools, and these work together. Schaffer gives the example of time (a concept that is stressed in industrialized societies) which is a particular way of organizing events and thinking about the world, and tools such as watches and calendars that have been developed to facilitate its use. Schaffer cites language as the most essential cultural tool because of its social and internal regulatory functions as follows:

- The communicative role of language is the principal vehicle for social exchange, for the reciprocal relationship of teaching and learning, and enabling the young to benefit from society's experience.
- It helps children to regulate their own activities – the use of monologues show that children have become capable of using language as a tool for thought.
- It becomes internalized and transformed into thought so the social function becomes the main tool for cognition.

> **Discussion points:** Can you identify ways in which Piaget's theory might be similar to that of Vygotsky?
>
> Do you agree with the arguments by people like Lourenço and Machado (1996) that criticisms of Piaget are wholly unjustified?
>
> How might activities in which adults and children are regularly jointly engaged differ between Western and non-Western societies?

5.4 Relationship between cognitive and social development

One key idea of sociocultural theory is that cognition cannot simply be thought of in terms of mental faculties related to memory, attention, perception, plans, logic and so on, given that cognitive development greatly depends on social engagement with other people (Correa-Chávez and Rogoff, 2005). Such mental processes are seen as being 'closely tied with social goals and with individuals learning to function as participants in cultural communities, which means that social engagement and communication are a key aspect of cognitive development' (p. 8). According to Rogoff (1998; 2003), social interaction, particularly communication, is an integral part of the cognitive process. Thus, 'understanding cognitive development requires attention to how people's thinking occurs as they participate in socially, culturally, and historically shaped events' (Correa-Chávez and Rogoff, 2005, p. 8). Of particular interest therefore should be the investigation of how people think in ways that serve their functioning in the world. The question of specific interest to developmental psychologists would then be: How do children come to remember, attend, perceive, plan, reason and so on, in particular ways and how does that prepare them for functioning in the world?

Sessions designed to examine mental processes are also events rooted in social, cultural and historical contexts. The performance of participants in such sessions can reflect their interpretation of the demands of the immediate situation as much as, or to a greater degree than, possession of the cognitive skills being assessed. This is partly illustrated in the description of the frustrations of Western psychologists on encountering African children who showed little responsiveness during psychological tests with adults, yet would seemingly be active amongst peers (Harkness and Super, 2008, see also discussion on social context of language development in Chapter 6). The acquisition of specific cognitive skills can also be a function of the sociocultural and historical context of functioning in a particular domain. The processes involved in both the acquisition and demonstration of those skills have been referred to as the 'socialization of cognition' (Goodnow, 1990; Nunes, 2005).

5.4.1 Socialization of cognition

5.4.1.1 *The context of cognitive development and functioning*

The notion of cognition being a function of socialization relates to how skills develop in different social contexts, the values attached to the subsequently different developmental pathways and the impact they may have on children as learners. In this respect, it has been suggested that socialization of cognition does not only involve learning how to solve problems, but it also involves learning what counts as a successful solution to the task at hand (Goodnow, 1990; Hatano and Inagaki, 1998). This was demonstrated by Terezinha Nunes and her colleagues in their studies of the development of mathematical skills amongst Brazilian children in school compared with contexts out of school (Nunes, 2005).

Nunes and her colleagues (Nunes-Carraher, Carraher and Schliemann, 1985) initially set out to explain the failure of poor Brazilian children in mathematics in school in terms of cognitive disadvantage as characteristic of the children. Evidence contrary to such cognitive disadvantage soon emerged when they observed that children who worked in the informal economy of selling commodities in the streets were able to solve correctly arithmetic problems similar to those they could not solve in school. The significance of this was that the context for solving arithmetic problems in the street was more relevant to the daily functioning of the children's communities. The school on the other hand, emphasized abstract computational concepts removed from such functioning. In addition, and although the tasks demanded the same logicomathematical principles, the difference in performance seemed to lie in the cultural form of the same knowledge: oral versus written arithmetic, with the former characteristic of street trading and the latter of school learning. The children who engaged in both of these different cultural practices of the street and school found themselves torn between the two when it came to performance on school mathematics.

Of additional interest to Nunes and her colleagues then was the basis on which the children made their choice of which skill to use in solving the problems (Nunes, Schliemann and Carraher, 1993). They observed that the children chose written arithmetic when solving computational problems of the type encountered in school tasks, even though they were more proficient at 'mental arithmetic' based on oral skills. The latter strategy seemed to be reserved largely to problems that resembled those encountered in the markets. The question then was as to why these children would choose written arithmetic when they were more competent in oral arithmetic.

One explanation as to which choice of approach was made by the Brazilian children was that it reflected implicitly learned values as to what counted as a competent solution (Abreu, Bishop and Pompeu, 1997). In other words, and as Nunes (2005) observed, 'what teachers and children count as mathematics in school settings includes written but not oral arithmetic'. Similar observations regarding conceptualization of intelligence as being context specific have been made by Nunes Carraher (1988) regarding illiterate Brazilian adults, and also by Serpell (1993) amongst members of a community in Eastern Zambia.

5.4.1.2 *Social cognition: Understanding others*

The dependence of cognitive development on social engagement with other people makes the processes by which people relate to each other a suitable candidate for psychological investigation. Social engagement requires understanding of others in relation to the self, and is seen as a key problem-solving task, particularly in social interaction and communication. When communicating, people try to make sense of the communicative efforts of others, and to address their own goals in the process through their own communicative efforts. This involves coordinating ideas and actions together, including perceiving and attending to the others' contributions as well as other ongoing events; it involves reasoning about and taking the perspective of others; remembering the course of events at hand; and planning one's contributions to the exchange while predicting the possible effects on others and ongoing activities. In this sense, communication as a process of social engagement is seen as both a social and cognitive process (Correa-Chávez and Rogoff, 2005). Social engagement also involves understanding of the self, including one's emotions, in relation to others. Such understanding is part of the self-concept and develops in parallel with other aspects of cognitive development.

There is much evidence that social-emotional and cognitive development are inextricably related. The relationships between cognitive, social and emotional aspects of development now comprise an ever-expanding area of research, as demonstrated for example by the plethora of publications on 'theory of mind' and 'mind-mindedness'. Universally, children develop the capacity to interpret their own feelings, intentions and actions and their effects on others; also, to understand others states of minds, intentions and actions. Greenfield et al. (2003a) discuss how these underlie two different cultural emphases in the development of understanding of people which correspond to those of so-called individualistic and collectivistic societies. 'Some cultures emphasize the individual psyche, individual traits, and the individual intentions behind action ... ; other cultures emphasize the social effects and social context of a person's action' (p. 472).

Research into 'theory of mind' or the ability to think about the mental states of others has usually taken the approach of individual minds whereas Greenfield et al. view 'theory of mind' as a construct of particular cultures. When the traditional 'theory of mind' research paradigm (Perner, 1991) used in Western societies was applied to Quechua children aged four to eight in a non-literate, subsistence community in Africa they performed at only chance levels. The situation used was decontextualized, included only one person and was asked about the mind rather than the heart. In another instance, a situation was presented to children from similar ecologies, Baka children in southeast Cameroon, and embedded the task in social action and used the term heart rather than mind. In this case, children aged between two and four showed similar understanding to those in the United States.

Wellman, Cross and Watson (2001) in a meta-analysis of 'theory of mind' tasks showed that children from subsistence cultures perform better when they are presented in context, that is, they are ecologically valid. Studies such as that reported by Vinden (1999), which used the word 'think', found a lag in age in performance especially for children in the most isolated communities. Such cultures interpret mental states as an integration of heart and mind whereas the school-based Western cultures emphasize the latter. Greenfield et al. (2003b) view lags in development as indicating that the culture does not view as important the ability being investigated. It shows the necessity of incorporating cultural values into research and providing explanations of cognitive development in different societies.

5.4.2 Relationships and feelings driving cognitive change

The cognitive developmental perspective holds that it is only when cognitive development has reached a certain level that social developments can occur, whereas an alternative view (e.g., Dunn 1988 and subsequently) is that social-emotional experiences drive cognition and cognitive change. The latter view is more compatible with the work of Vygotsky than that of Piaget. It is also consistent with the approach of more collectivist societies which emphasize the importance of the relationship between heart and mind. The early research of Dunn and colleagues resulted in a model of the development of the self which links cognitive developmental changes with everyday experiences and these lead to the development of the self and social understanding, as shown in Figure 5.1.

Dunn's (1988; 1995) work emphasized the importance of the ecological validity of the research environment by taking place in the everyday contexts of home, play and school. Her studies have shown the central importance of the emotional contexts of interpersonal interactions in the development of relationships and have led to a model of the development of social understanding which emphasizes the

```
┌─────────────────────────┐
│ Cognitive Developmental │
│ Changes (including      │
│ maturational change)    │
└─────────────────────────┘                ┌──────────────────────────────────┐
                                           │ Development of the self and social│
            +                 ⟶            │ understanding (an emergent property│
                                           │ of relationships)                 │
┌─────────────────────────┐                └──────────────────────────────────┘
│ Cognitive and Affective │
│ Experiences (especially │
│ with other people)      │
└─────────────────────────┘
```

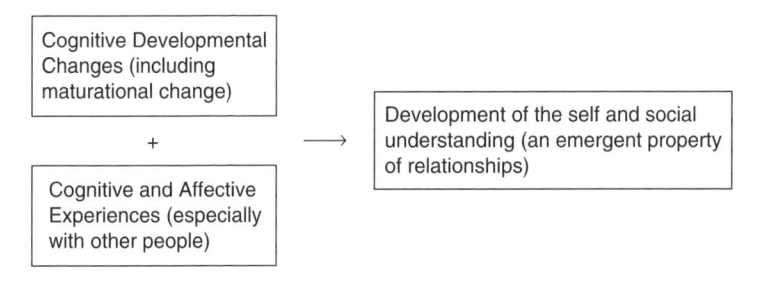

Figure 5.1 Influence of cognitive changes and affective experiences on development of the self and social understanding

importance of the contribution of the different familial roles, parent and sibling within a particular cultural context.

As discussed in Chapter 3, similar to the difference in ethnotheories about parenting, contribution of siblings to the child's developing social cognitive understanding also differs between societies. In smaller, more communal developing societies such as the Zinacantec Mayan people (Maynard, 2002), highly sophisticated understanding of the mental states of others was demonstrated by 3- to 11-year-olds by their behaviour in teaching younger siblings. By the age of eight, these children were skilled at interpreting the relative lack of knowledge of the younger child compared to themselves, obtaining relevant materials for the task in hand, simplifying it and using suitable verbal instructions to scaffold the task. Other studies have demonstrated how sibling caregivers demonstrate tutoring skills in a variety of social situations. Such abilities also develop in Western societies, especially in play situations, but typically, there is less social imperative to do so. For example, Dunn, Creps and Brown (1996) demonstrate that siblings in the United Kingdom appear to play a highly significant role in the early development of comprehension of distressing social situations. This is shown by the finding that young children place siblings in a negative light more frequently than they do others. Such references to sibling negativity decline with age.

The intensity of the negative aspects of sibling relationships may well be linked to the nuclear family societal structure in which siblings compete for parental love and attention. Cicirelli (1995) describes sibling relationships as having three dimensions: affectional closeness, rivalry and involvement. It is likely that the specification of the role of sibling as caregiver in other cultures leads to less competition among siblings, unlike societies such as the United Kingdom. However, research is needed to further document the nature of such cultural differences, if any, and the implications for children's social cognitive functioning. The psychological processes of the sibling relationship are in many ways similar to those of the parental attachment relationship and in the absence of parents, the sibling can take the part of protector/comforter. The younger sibling learns much about his/her mental states and that of others from their intense involvement with siblings with whom, especially in the early years, they spend much of their time.

In summary, the development of person knowledge has been demonstrated to involve the integration of social-emotional and cognitive components to achieve culturally relevant goals. One current view

(Dunn and others) is that everyday social situations involving close interpersonal relationships and the emotions, particularly negative ones, aroused by these, drive cognitive change. These social situations and the role-specifications for key players vary between cultures, independent or interdependent, influencing diversity in development between individualistic and collective societies within the common developmental pathway (Greenfield et al., 2003b).

> **Discussion points:**
>
> In what ways would you consider social factors to influence cognitive development? Can you cite specific examples to support your view?
>
> To what extent would you consider the influence of relationships and feelings on cognitive development be mediated by culture?

5.5 Implications of the cultural context of cognitive development

As children develop their ability to function effectively broadens in many domains, including solving problems and influencing their Social and Physical environments. Of importance in this process is the child's acquisition of knowledge and skills relevant to the culture in which s/he is functioning. Therefore, the task for the child is to acquire and master the cultural tools of their society. As Greenfield et al. (2003b) state, the 'developmental tasks and modes of cultural learning have evolved in response to selection pressures from the environment' (p. 462). These selection pressures are historical and cultural, and influence both process and content of cultural learning and teaching, stimulated by and adapted to the cultural niche.

So, the psychological tools (modes of cognitive functioning) of importance for the child to master depend on historical and cultural factors. The contexts for acquiring these are informal, as in the daily activities of a family or community, or formalized in institutions such as schools. These contexts can have implications for modes of children's cognitive functioning. For example, Greenfield and Bruner's (1966) early research in Senegal showed how the Western institution of formal schooling was related to greater metacognitive self-awareness – the separation of self and world. This reflected the view of intellectual functioning promoted in Western-style formal schooling, which has to do with individual attainment and the ability to think systematically about logical relations within a problem, and is consistent with Piaget's notion of cognitive development. It emphasizes the type of intelligence described as 'technological intelligence' by Mundy-Castle (1974), who showed that it tended to be more developed in the independent-minded people of 'individualistic societies' like those of Europe and the United States. 'Social intelligence', on the other hand, is more developed in the 'interdependent' peoples of Africa and other parts of the majority world. These observations are consonant with the later work on different intelligence concepts in different cultures (e.g., Serpell, 1994; Sternberg, 2004), which also showed the validity of different developmental pathways and achievements across cultures.

The specific consequences of formal schooling in various cultures have been a subject of some theoretical discussion and debate (see Cole, 2005; Serpell, 2005; Wertsch; 2005). As Serpell (2005) observed, the rationale for promoting schooling in various cultures is that it 'reliably affords students beneficial developmental opportunities, like growth of intellectual competencies, orientation towards society's expectations, and preparation to focus their energies in ways that will be beneficial to the whole society' (p. 217). However, the extent to which these outcomes are attained, especially in Third World countries, has been debatable. The arguments focus on the relevance of categories of cognitive functioning promoted by schooling for the children's current and later functioning in their communities (Cole, 2005; Nsamenang, 2003; Serpell, 2005). Thus, the knowledge and associated skills acquired in formal settings of the school may be divorced from the contexts of application. In contrast, the informal setting such as that of indigenous African education is seen as one aimed at socializing children for socially responsible cognitive functioning and participation in acceptable and valued social and economic activities (Nsamenang, 2003).

In multicultural societies of the industrialized countries the differing conceptions of knowledge and intelligence and the aims of different ethnocultural groups in socialization can create more immediate problems for children in school. For example, Okagaki and Sternberg

(1993) studied immigrants to the United States from southeast Asian countries whose primary concept of education was not academic learning but the acquisition of respectful social behaviour. Parents were asked questions about what teachers should teach their children and what characterized an intelligent child. The immigrant parents rated conformity to external standards as being more important to develop in their children than developing autonomous behaviours. American-born parents, in contrast, favoured autonomy over conformity. In addition, all parents other than the Anglo-Americans considered non-cognitive characteristics (such as motivation, social skills and practical skills in school) important or more important than cognitive characteristics (such as problem-solving skills, verbal ability, creative ability) to their conceptions of an intelligent child. These findings suggest that different behaviours would be promoted in the homes of the immigrant children than those emphasized in school contexts. Also, there are some cultural differences in approaches to children's acquisition of relevant skills. For example, in Native American children, learning is appropriately acquired through observation which conflicts with the expectation of participation by the dominant white American culture. Such findings could help teachers vary their teaching methods and expectations for different groups of children. They also point at social factors that may account for differences between children from different cultural groups in performance on measures of cognitive functioning (Greenfield, 1997).

5.6 Summary and conclusions

The two main theoretical perspectives that have inspired much of the research on children's cognitive development are those of Piaget and Vygotsky. Over the years, these perspectives have generated some debate about culture's influence on cognitive development. Piaget's theory has been one of the most influential psychological theories in early cross-cultural work on cognition (Maynard, 2008). According to Piaget (1952), the essential element in development is in acquiring logic (a universal) so, a child's understanding of cultural inventions is merely an offshoot of that fundamental developmental change. Over the years, Piaget's theory has become radically altered, primarily to include the social context, but also to substantiate and refine Piagetian concepts. In contrast to Piaget's original position, Vygotsky's view was that humans are embedded in a social matrix (context) and their behaviour cannot be understood independently of this matrix. According to Vygotsky (1978; 1986), a study of children's development must take a historical account of humankind's intellectual development. He pointed out that over centuries, humans have invented cultural tools which are an indispensable part of our cognition. Children must master such tools to function effectively, either in their schools or outside them. However, such skills cannot simply be acquired independently by the children, rather, they have to be passed on from one generation to another. According to Vygotsky and his followers, this transmission of cultural tools from generation to generation is an important part of cognitive development (Gauvain, 2001a; 2001b). The contexts in which such transmission of cultural tools occurs in most cultures tend to be in joint activity with more knowledgeable others, and involve some form of guided participation, by children, in the day-to-day activities of their society.

So, there has been increasing rapprochement of post-Piagetian and post-Vygotskyan views of cognitive development so that today the primary importance of the sociocultural context of learning is generally accepted. Because cognitive development depends on social engagement with other people (Correa-Chávez and Rogoff, 2005), it is increasingly being seen as closely tied with children learning how to engage and communicate with others as participants in social interaction. Of significance also have been the roles of relationships and feelings in driving cognitive change. The relationship between emotional and cognitive development in different contexts has been little explored but is a promising avenue for further research, as is the relationship between physical and cognitive development.

FURTHER READING

Carpendale, J. and Lewis, C. (2006). *How children develop social understanding.* Oxford: Blackwell.

Gauvain, M. (2001). *The social context of cognitive development.* New York: Guilford.

International Society for the Study of Behavioural Development (ISSBD) (2005) Newsletter, (Special Section: Sociocultural perspectives on cognitive development). 1(47) 1–20.

Rogoff, B. (2003). *The cultural nature of human development.* Oxford: Oxford University Press.

Sternberg, R.J. (1997). *Successful intelligence.* New York: Plume.

Vygotsky, L.S. (1978). *Mind in society: The development of higher psychological processes.* Cambridge, MA: Harvard University Press.

REFERENCES

Abreu, G. de, Bishop, A., and Pompeu Jr, G. (1997). What children and teachers count as mathematics. In T. Nunes and P. Bryant (Eds), *Learning and teaching mathematics. An international perspective* (pp. 233–264). Hove: Psychology Press.

Ames, G.J. and Murray, F.B. (1982). When two wrongs make a right: Promoting cognitive change by social conflict. *Developmental Psychology*, 18, 894–897.

Beach, K. (1995). Activity as a mediator of sociocultural change and individual development: The case of school-work transition in Nepal. *Mind, Culture and Activity*, 2(4), 285–302.

Berry, J.W. and Irvine, S.H. (1986). Bricolage: Savages do it daily. In R.J. Sternberg and R.K. Wagner (Eds), *Practical intelligence: Nature and origins of competence in the everyday world* (pp. 271–306). New York: Cambridge University Press.

Bruner, J.S., Jolly, A., and Sylva, K. (Eds) (1976). *Play. Its role in development and evolution.* Harmondsworth: Penguin.

Buck-Moss, S. (1975). Socio-economic bias in Piaget's theory and its implications for cross-cultural studies. *Human Development*, 18, 35–49.

Burman, E. (1994). *Deconstructing developmental psychology.* London: Routledge.

Cicirelli, V.G. (1995). *Sibling relationships across the lifespan.* New York: Plenum Press.

Cole, M. (2005). Cultural-historical activity theory in the family of sociocultural approaches. *International Society for the Study of Behavioural Development Newsletter*, 1(47), 1–4.

Cole, M. (2005). Cross-cultural and historical perspectives on the developmental consequences of education. *Human Development*, 48, 195–216.

Cole, M. and Cole, S.R. (2001). *The development of children.* Fourth Edition. New York: W.H. Freeman.

Correa-Chávez, M. and Rogoff, B. (2005). Cultural research has transformed our ideas of cognitive development. *International Society for the Study of Behavioural Development Newsletter*, 1(47), 7–10.

Crain, W. (2000). *Theories of development. Concepts and applications.* Fourth Edition. Upper Saddle River, NJ: Prentice Hall.

Das Gupta, P. (1994). Images of childhood and theories of development. Chapter 1. In J. Oates (Ed.), *The foundations of child development* (pp. 2–43). Oxford: Blackwell/The Open University.

Doise, W. and Mugny, G. (1984). *The social development of the intellect.* Oxford: Pergamon Press.

Doise, W., Mugny, G., and Perret-Clermont, A.-N. (1975). Social interaction and the development of cognitive operations. *European Journal of Social Psychology*, 5, 367–383.

Donaldson, M. (1978). *Children's minds.* Glasgow: Fontana Press.

Dunn, J. (1988). *The beginnings of social understanding.* Oxford: Blackwell.

Dunn, J. (1995). Studying relationships and social understanding. In P. Barnes (Ed.), *Personal, social and emotional development of children.* Oxford: Open University/Blackwell.

Dunn, J., Creps, C., and Brown, J. (1996). Children's family relationships between two and five: Developmental changes and individual differences. *Social Development,* **5,** 230–250.

Durkin, K. (1995). *Developmental social psychology.* Oxford: Blackwell.

Eysenck, H.J. (1986). A theory of intelligence and the psychophysiology of cognition. In R.J. Sternberg (Ed.), *Advances in the psychology of human intelligence* (Vol. 3, pp. 1–34). Hillsdale, NJ: Lawrence Erlbaum.

Eysenck, M. (1998). *Psychology: An integrated approach.* London: Longman.

Fitzpatrick, H. (1996). *Peer collaboration and the computer.* Unpublished PhD thesis, University of Manchester.

Gauvain, M. (2001a). Cultural tools, social interaction, and the development of thinking. *Human Development,* **44,** 126–143.

Gauvain, M. (2001b). *The social context of cognitive development.* New York: Guilford.

Glachan, M. and Light, P. (1982). Peer interaction and learning: Can two wrongs make a right? In G. Butterworth and P. Light (Eds), *Social cognition: Studies of the development of understanding.* Chicago: University of Chicago Press.

Goodnow, J.J. (1990). The socialization of cognition: What's involved? In J.W. Stigler, R.A. Shweder, and G. Herdt (Eds), *Cultural psychology. Essays on comparative human development* (pp. 259–286). Cambridge: Cambridge University Press.

Goswami, U. (1998). *Cognition in Children.* Hove: Psychology Press Ltd., Publishers.

Greenfield, P.M. and Bruner, J.S. (1966). Culture and cognitive growth. *International Journal of Psychology,* **1,** 89–107.

Greenfield, P.M. (1997). You can't take it with you: Why ability assessments don't cross cultures. *American Psychologist,* **52,** 1115–1124.

Greenfield, P.M., Keller, H., Fuligni, A., and Maynard, A. (2003a). Cultural pathways through universal development. *Annual Review of Psychology,* **54,** 461–491.

Greenfield, P.M., Maynard, A.E., and Childs, C.P. (2003b). Historical change, cultural learning, and cognitive representation in Zinacantec Maya Children. *Cognitive Development,* **18,** 455–491.

Harkness, S. and Super, C.M. (2008). Why African children are so hard to test. In R.A LeVine and R.S. New (Eds), *Anthropology and child development: A cross-cultural reader.* (pp. 182–186). Oxford: Blackwell Publishing.

Hatano, G. and Inagaki, K. (1998). Cultural contexts of schooling revisited: A review of the learning gap from a cultural psychology perspective. In S.G. Paris and H.M. Wellman (Eds), *Global prospects for education. Development, culture and schooling* (pp. 79–104). Washington, DC: American Psychological Association.

Hedegaard, M. (1996). How instruction influences children's concepts of evolution. *Mind, Culture, and Activity,* **3**(1), 11–24.

Jensen, A.R. (1998). *The g factor.* Westport, CT: Praeger-Greenwood.

Kagitçibasi, C. (2000). Indigenous psychology and indigenous approaches to developmental research. *International Society for the Study of Behavioural Development Newsletter*, 1(37), 46–49.

Karpov, Y.V. (2005). Psychological tools, internalization, and mediation: The Neo-Vygotskian elaboration of Vygotsky's notions. *International Society for the Study of Behavioural Development Newsletter*, 1(47), 4–7.

Kozulin, A. (1986). The concept of activity in Soviet psychology: Vygotsky, his disciples and critics. *American Psychologist*, 41(3), 264–274.

Larivée, S., Normandeau, S., and Parent, S. (2000). The French connection: Some contributions of French-language research in the post-Piagetian era. *Child Development*, 71, 823–839.

Lautrey, J. (1991). Les chemins de la connaissance. *Revue Franciase de Pedagogie*, 96, 55–65.

Light, P. and Glachan, M. (1985). Facilitation of individual problem solving through peer interaction. *Educational Psychology*, 5, 217–225.

Light, P. and Littleton, K. (1999). *Social processes in children's learning*. Cambridge: Cambridge University Press.

Light, P., Littleton, K., Messer, D., and Joiner, R. (1994). Social and communicative processes in computer-based problem solving. *European Journal of Psychology of Education*, 9, 93–109.

Lourenço, O. and Machado, A. (1996). In defense of Piaget's theory: A reply to 10 common criticisms. *Psychological Review*, 103, 143–164.

Luria, A.R. (1976). *Cognitive development*. Cambridge, MA: Harvard University Press.

Maynard, A.E. (2002). Cultural teaching: The development of teaching skills in Zinacantec Maya sibling interactions. *Child Development*, 73, 969–982.

Maynard, A.E. (2008). What we thought we knew and how we came to know it: Four decades of cross-cultural research from a Piagetian point of view. *Human Development*, 51, 56–65.

Miller, J.G. and Chen, X. (2005). Sociocultural perspectives on cognitive development. *International Society for the Study of Behavioural Development Newsletter*, 1(47), 1.

Mundy-Castle, A.C. (1974). Social and technological intelligence in Western and non-Western cultures. *Universitas*, 4, 46–52.

Nisbett, R.E. (2003). *The geography of thought: Why we think the way we do*. New York: Free Press.

Nsamenang, A.B. (2003). Conceptualizing human development and education in Sub-Saharan Africa at the interface of indigenous and exogenous influences. In T.S. Saraswathi (Ed.), *Cross-cultural perspectives in human development: Theory, research and applications*. New Delhi: Sage.

Nunes Carraher, T. (1988). Illiteracy in a literate society: Understanding reading failure. In D. Wagner (Ed.), *The future of literacy in a changing world* (pp. 95–110). Oxford: Pergamon Press.

Nunes, T. (2005). What we learn in school: The socialization of cognition. *International Society for the Study of Behavioural Development Newsletter*, 1(47), 10–12.

Nunes Carraher, T., Carraher, D.W., and Schliemann, A.D. (1985). Mathematics in the streets and in school. *British Journal of Developmental Psychology*, **3**, 21–29.

Nunes, T., Schliemann, A.D., and Carraher, D.W. (1993). *Street mathematics and school mathematics*. New York: Cambridge University Press.

Okagaki, L. and Sternberg, R.J. (1993). Parental beliefs and children's school performance. *Child Development*, **64**, 36–56.

Pascual-Leone, J. (2000). Is the French connection neo-Piagetian? Nor nearly enough? *Child Development*, **71**, 843–845.

Perner, J. (1991). *Understanding the representational mind*. London: MIT Press.

Piaget, J. (1952). *The origin of intelligence in the child*. London: Routledge and Kegan Paul.

Piaget, J. (1966). Nécessité et signification des recherches comparatives en psychologie génétique. *Journal International de Psychologie*, **1**, 3–13.

Piaget, J. (1973). *The psychology of intelligence*. Totowa, NJ: Littlefield & Adams

Piaget, J. and Inhelder, B. (1956). *The child's conception of space*. London: Routledge & Kegan Paul

Reuchlin, M. (1978). Processus vicariants et differences individuelles. *Journal de Psychologie*, **2**, 133.

Rogoff, B. (1990). *Apprenticeship in thinking: Cognitive development in social context*. New York: Oxford.

Rogoff, B. (1998). Cognition as a collaborative process. In D. Kuhn and R.S. Siegler (Eds), *Cognition, perception and language* (Vol. 2, *Handbook of child psychology* [Fifth Edition], W. Damon [Ed.]) (pp. 679–744). New York: John Wiley & Sons.

Rogoff, B. (2003). *The cultural nature of human development*. Oxford: Oxford University Press.

Rogoff, B., and Mosier, C. (1993). Guided participation in San Pedro and Salt Lake. In B. Rogoff, J. Mistry, A. Göncü, and C. Mosier, Guided participation in cultural activity by toddlers and caregivers. *Monographs of the Society for Research in Child Development*, **58** (7, Serial No. 236, pp. 59–101).

Saxe, G.B. and Esmonde, I. (2005). Studying cognition in flux: A historical treatment of 'fu' in the shifting structure of Oksapmin mathematics. *Mind, Culture, and Activity*, **12**(3&4), 171–225.

Schaffer, H.R. (2004). *Introducing child psychology*. Oxford: Blackwell.

Scribner, S. and Cole, M. (1981). *The psychology of literacy*. Cambridge, MA: Harvard University Press.

Serpell, R. (1976). *Culture's influence on behaviour*. London: Methuen.

Serpell, R. (1993). *The significance of schooling: Life-journeys in an African society*. Cambridge: Cambridge University Press.

Serpell, R. (1994). The cultural construction of intelligence. In W.L. Lonner and R.S. Malpass (Eds), *Psychology and culture* (pp. 157–163). Boston, MA: Allyn & Bacon.

Serpell, R. (2005). Optimizing the developmental consequences of education: Reflections on issues raised by Michael Cole. *Human Development*, **48**, 216–222.

Spearman, C. (1927). *The abilities of man*. London: Macmillan.

Sternberg, R.J. (1997). *Successful intelligence.* New York: Plume.
Sternberg, R.J. (1999).The theory of successful intelligence. *Review of General Psychology,* **3**, 292–316.
Sternberg, R.J. (2004). Culture and intelligence. *American Psychologist,* **59**(5), 325–338.
Tharp, R. and Gallimore, R. (1988) *Rousing minds to life: Teaching, learning and schooling in social context.* Cambridge: Cambridge University Press.
Tomasello, M. (2000). Culture and cognitive development. *Current Directions in Psychological Science,* **9**, 37–40.
Valsiner, J. (2000). *Culture and human development.* Thousand Oaks, CA: Sage.
Vinden, P. (1999). Children's understanding of mind and emotion: A multi-culture study. *Cognition and Emotion,* **13**, 19–48.
Vygotsky, L.S. (1978). *Mind in society: The development of higher psychological processes.* Cambridge, MA: Harvard University Press.
Vygotsky, L.S. (1981). The genesis of higher psychological functions. In J.V. Wertsch (Ed.), *The concept of activity in Soviet psychology* (pp. 144–188). Armonk, NY: Sharpe.
Vygotsky, L.S. (1986). *Thought and language.* Cambridge, MA: MIT Press.
Vygotsky, L.S. (1987). *The collected work of L. S. Vygotsky: Vol 1. Problems of general psychology.* New York: Plenum Press.
Wellman, H.M., Cross, D., and Watson, J. (2001). Meta-analysis of theory-of-mind development: The truth about false belief. *Child Development,* **72**, 655–684.
Wertsch, J.V. (1997). Narrative tools of history and identity. *Culture and Psychology,* **3**, 5–20.
Wertsch, J.V. (1998). *Mind as action.* Oxford: Oxford University Press.
Wertsch, J.V. (2005). Cole's 'cross-cultural and historical perspectives on the developmental consequences of education'. *Human Development,* **48**, 223–226.
Wood, D. (1988). *How children think and learn. The social contexts of cognitive development.* Oxford: Blackwell.
Wood, D., Bruner, J.S., and Ross, G. (1976). The role of tutoring in problem-solving. *Journal of Child Psychology and Psychiatry,* **17**(2), 89–100.

Language and Psychological Development

Dabie Nabuzoka

OUTLINE

6.1 Introduction
    6.1.1 Significance of language
6.2 Universal features and cultural variations across languages
    6.2.1 Structure of language
    6.2.2 Development of a language
    6.2.3 Language acquisition
6.3 The role of language
    6.3.1 Relationship between language and thought processes
    6.3.2 Language socialization and behaviour
    6.3.3 Summary and conclusions
6.4 Bilingualism
    6.4.1 Bilingual development in children
    6.4.2 Second-language acquisition in adolescents and adults
    6.4.3 Cognitive and social outcomes of bilingualism
    6.4.4 Summary on bilingualism
6.5 Summary and conclusions
Further reading
References

6.1 Introduction

6.1.1 Significance of language

Language is a widely recognized distinguishing characteristic of humans amongst other species, and for different cultures. In addition to serving as a means of communication, language is considered to mediate between culture and behaviour (Serpell, 1976). It is a means by which the young are socialized regarding appropriate behaviours and skills. Thus, language is not only a good indicator of cultural differences between social groups and societies, but is also an important aspect of the social and psychological development of individuals. There is a general recognition of individual differences in language development and that there may be more than one route to language acquisition. This may be especially true when considering cultures that provide children with different kinds of language learning environments. Studies of language acquisition by children who live in different cultures, and the study of the acquisition of other languages, are considered crucial to discovering the universal processes of language acquisition as well as culture-specific differences. Therefore, as a means of socialization, language is a suitable subject for studying effects on some aspects of social and psychological functioning of individuals from different cultures.

This chapter discusses the evidence for the link between the acquisition of different languages in various cultural contexts and aspects of psychological development and functioning. The chapter is divided into three main sections. The first section provides an outline of some universal features and cultural variations in languages. The section outlines aspects of the structure of different languages, the particular ways in which they develop and how children come to acquire language as a part of their socialization. The second section looks at the role of language in terms of how its transmission is considered to be a means of socialization and, in particular, how it has been linked with psychological outcomes such as thought processes. Another focus is on the role of language socialization as a mediator between culture and the transmission of aspects of behavioural attributes in the young. The final section discusses the fact that most people in the world learn and speak more than one language, increasingly making bilingualism or multilingualism the norm and not an exception. The section first outlines some aspects of the acquisition of more than one language in children, adolescents and adults. Then the consequences of bilingualism are discussed in terms of cognitive functioning and psychosocial adjustment. The chapter concludes with an overview of the relationship between language, culture and psychological development of individuals.

6.2 Universal features and cultural variations across languages

6.2.1 Structure of language

On the whole, there has been no scientific evidence to support the existence of any simple continuum from primitive to sophisticated, or from simple to complex languages amongst humans. All languages studied have been shown to possess similar properties, which linguists have tended to consider as subsystems (Carroll, 1999). Three major subsystems into which linguists have commonly subdivided language are in terms of *semantics, syntax* and *phonology*. Semantics is the relation between words and the world to which they refer. It is the main system governing meaning. Syntax is the set of rules by which words are ordered into sentences. Phonology refers to the sound system which specifies what elementary sounds can be combined to make words and also certain restrictions on how they can be combined. All languages studied have been shown to posses these abstract, formal properties and do not vary greatly in degree of complexity (Gerrig and Banaji, 1994; Greenberg, 1963).

There are, however, some considerable qualitative differences across languages within these subsystems. At the semantic level the contrasts may be between how the world is segmented by the meanings of single words. In English, for example, a word can mean various things in different contexts: 'Book' can mean the bound article from which you may be reading this text. It could also mean to reserve (a seat on the train, plane and so on), whereas, if you said 'brought to book' that actually means being made accountable. At the phonological level, contrasts may parallel semantic ones. An example of two sounds which can be used to signal a difference in meaning (i.e., phonemes) and to distinguish between the two words are 'l' and 'r' in Liver and River. Some languages do not distinguish such letters in sound. Contrasts in syntax, however, can be more subtle. For example, in highly inflected languages additions to the meaning of a verb can be achieved by tacking on various prefixes and suffixes in a way different to English. In terms of syntactical structures, nearly all languages permit some way to communicate actions, agents of actions and objects of actions (Carroll,

1999). The difference across languages is the range of grammatical inflections and other markers that speakers include as key elements of a sentence. Thus, different languages comprise different lexicons and use different syntactical structures.

How do these differences come about? In particular, how do the specific meanings associated with certain words develop in relation to a particular culture?

6.2.2 Development of a language

The development of a language is linked to a given culture in that it is those concepts which play an important part in the life of a community that are coded into the language to facilitate communication among adults and transmission of the culture to the young. An example is the growth of vocabulary reflecting modern technology, such that as a new artefact or process comes within the scope of a culture's need for communication, the language adapts accordingly. For example, the growth of Information and Communication Technology (ICT) in particular has been accompanied by specific concepts and terminology such as a 'mouse', 'e-mail' 'web page' and so on, while the widespread use of the mobile phone has led to the development of a shorthand 'text language', which would have been incomprehensible only a few decades ago. Such developments reflect accompanying changes in the technological, social and cultural environments in which the language arose and developed. Differences in these areas would also be reflected in the languages used. A question that arises then is: How do children come to master such language with apparent ease?

6.2.3 Language acquisition

The fact that all normal human infants eventually acquire the language of their society is an attribute shared by all cultures. Initially, interest in studying and understanding child language development was inspired by the linguistic theory of Noam Chomsky (1965). Chomsky proposed that children universally and innately mastered grammatical speech in their first language without being taught. In this sense, the child's early environment was irrelevant except for specifying the particular grammar to be acquired. The age of 18–36 months was identified by psychologists as the period of language acquisition (Brown, 1973). An alternative view of language development was formulated by some linguistic anthropologists and socially orientated psycholinguists, a school of thought collectively known as sociolinguistics (Gumperz and Hymes, 1972). The view held by sociolinguists was that the child acquires not only grammar but also communicative competence based on culture-specific social interactions during the 18–36-month period (Hymes, 1974).

Sociolinguistics focused on the functions of speech or rather simply its formal structure. In this way, sociolinguists were able to show that young children are heavily influenced by the culture-specific language environment of their social surroundings. The emphasis was not necessarily on the children's basic cognitive ability to encode and decode sentences 'but in the ways they use speech, together with gestures and facial expressions, to get what they want, behave appropriately, and express themselves' (LeVine and New, 2008, p. 160). Cross-cultural studies of language socialization with this orientation can be traced from the 1960s and 1970s (Bates, 1976; Blount, 1971; 1975; Ervin-Tripp and Slobin, 1967) through the 1980s (Ochs, 1988; Ochs and Schieffelin, 1984) into 1990s and to this day (Hoff, 2006; Miller, Wiley, Fung and Liang 1997).

Psychological research has focused on examining how particular child-rearing practices may be related to children's language development and social sophistication (Carpendale and Lewis, 2006), and whether language socialization (an aspect of child-rearing) is different across cultures. For example, in the Western context, it has been documented that speech used to address very young children is different from that used among adults (Oates, 1994). Specifically, adults are said to modify the tone of their speech to young children in ways designed to help them develop their language skills. However, as Case Study 1 below shows, studies of other cultures put into question the contention that such speech modifications play an essential role in language acquisition in all cultures.

CASE STUDY 1: PATHWAYS TO LANGUAGE LEARNING

Clifton Pye (1986) reported a study of children learning the Mayan language Quiche' in South America. He was interested in the idea that characteristics of adult speech to children contribute to language learning. He therefore studied the language addressed to children in this particular Mayan linguistic group. For example, it is widely reported that in Western cultures speech to young children is delivered at a relatively slow rate, is at a higher pitch and has exaggerated intonational contours. Pye used a

> ### CASE STUDY 1 (cont'd)
>
> frequency-intensity analyser to investigate changes in Quiche' maternal speech to infants. Contrary to extensive data previously reported, Pye observed that Quiche mothers:
>
> - did not exhibit significant prosodic adjustments when speaking to their children; and
> - did not use exaggerated intonation, but confined its use to infrequent exclamations to both children and adults.
>
> According to Pye, the idea that maternal speech modifications play an essential role in language acquisition could not be supported, since this evidence showed that there are cultures in which language development occurs without the benefit of these modifications. Pye further observes that the feature of caretaker's speech to children is limited by the structural characteristics of each language and also depends crucially upon cultural concepts about children and conventions for interacting with them. These conclusions have been generally supported over the years since Pye's study. Hoff (2006), for example, provides evidence from various studies on how various social contexts support language development.

There are differing circumstances under which children acquire language, and of the amount, nature and content of the speech to which they are exposed from infancy (Harkness, 1990; Hoff, 2006; Soderstrom, 2007). Thus, various contexts all provide enough support for language acquisition, while variations in communicative interactions may reflect the cultural uses to which a particular language is applied. Thus, cross-cultural studies on language acquisition have been concerned with documenting how socialization practices may explain the ability of children from different cultures to learn not just the language but also the specific cultural meanings associated with it. In addition, these studies have demonstrated that language may also be associated with the child's acquisition of other aspects of a culture. In this way, language plays a wider role in the acculturation and psychological development of individuals in addition to being a communicative tool. Some of the ways in which this may be achieved are discussed in the next section.

> Discussion point: Outline some universal and culture-specific features of language. What would you consider most significant in the development of children who are learning to speak different languages?

6.3 The role of language

Cross-cultural research on language socialization has greatly contributed to our understanding of not only how children of different cultures learn language but also the specific cultural meanings associated with the language. In addition, such studies have provided an insight into the particular ways in which language may be associated with the child's acquisition of other aspects of a culture. In the next section, I will discuss some views on how language plays a wider role in the acculturation and psychological development of individuals. I will focus specifically on two areas that have been of particular interest to psychologists: the links between language and thought, and between language socialization and behaviour.

6.3.1 Relationship between language and thought processes

The concern initially was whether language differences influence or even constrain the users to think about things differently because of the language they use while thinking. A theoretical link between culture and thought processes specifically suggests that individuals with different linguistic and cultural backgrounds may also think differently (Carroll, 1999; Sapir, 1929; 1949; Whorf, 1956). It has been suggested that by being taught a particular language children are also taught to think in a particular way about the world. Thus, in the transmission of language from one generation to the next, there occurs a very fundamental kind of socialization. In this process, the child was not considered as merely being taught to express his/her ideas but also how to think. Sapir (1929; 1949, cited by Serpell, 1976) had suggested that individuals see, hear and experience the way they do because language habits of their community predisposed them to certain choices of interpretation. This suggestion, as commented by Serpell (1976), was a very radical assertion because philosophically it undermined the possibility that humans have access to the real world. While the latter view would, in more recent times, be consistent with some features of social constructivism, Sapir's assertion drew attention to the significance of language in cognitive processes.

This assertion of the link between language and thought processes became known as the *linguistic relativity hypothesis* or the *Sapir-Whorf hypothesis* as it is sometimes referred to. Edward Sapir and Benjamin Lee Whorf were the two men most forceful in propagating this assertion or hypothesis. Whorf (1956), in particular, was impressed by the fact that different languages emphasize in their structure rather different aspects of the world. He believed that these emphases must have great influence on the way language speakers think about the world. An example of this was the variety of terms used by different cultural groups to describe features of the world: Eskimos (Inuits) having different words for snow; Hanunoo people in Philippines having different words for rice varieties; Arabic having different ways of naming Camels and so on. Whorf believed that such variety of terms could cause the speaker of the language to perceive the world differently from a person who had only a single word for a particular category.

Linguistic relativity, then, is the assertion that speakers of different languages have different cognitive systems that influence the ways in which they think about the world. In this sense, language would shape thought. The linguistic relativity hypothesis was therefore that language determines or strongly influences the way a person thinks or perceives the world. Thus, language may be an important tool used by humans not only to interact with one another but also for sociocognitive development. In this sense, we can shape our worlds as well as communicate with one another through language.

The view that language determines or strongly influences the way a person thinks or perceives the world represents a 'strong' version of the linguistic relativity hypothesis. A 'weak' version is that there are no differences in what is actually perceived by native speakers of different languages. Instead, languages serve to draw attention to differences in the environment and act as a label to help store these differences in memory (Lucy, 1992). In this way, language determines how easily we recognize an object or situation, how much attention is paid to it, how *codable* certain concepts are to speakers of a language? Language therefore merely predisposes people to think or perceive in certain ways, or about certain things. It does not determine these thoughts and perceptions (Gumperz and Levinson, 1996).

At the psychological level, the theory of linguistic relativity suggests a very intimate connection between language on the one hand and perception and thought on the other. Such a connection has been made by psychologists on other grounds. For example, the fact that the human infant develops into an intelligent adult has been attributed to the role of language in the regulation of behaviour (Luria, 1961). Other researchers discussed the development of verbal mediating processes in children (Kendler and Kendler, 1962). On the other hand, people like Furth (1966) argued that intelligence is a prerequisite for symbolic use of language and that perception and thought processes themselves may have separate origins.

An alternative question is whether language depends on thought, such that thinking processes determine language. An argument by Aristotle over 2500 years ago was that categories of thought determined the categories of language. The evidence for this would be the earlier evolution and development of cognitive ability (remembering, problem-solving) than language. For example, children give clear evidence of relatively complex cognition before they are effective at using language. If thought occurred before language, we can suppose that language is a tool whose function is to communicate thought (Tomasello, Kruger and Ratner, 1993). As tools are shaped to fit objects on which they must operate, it seems reasonable to suppose that language would be shaped to fit the thoughts it must communicate. This view is related to that held by Vygotsky (1986), who considered language important in the cognitive development of children. According to Vygotsky, language and thought are interdependent but have separate origins in childhood; initially thought is non-verbal in early childhood with speech emerging for self-direction (speech to the self) and communicative purposes. At about two years of age, children start using speech, and therefore language, in their thoughts. Thought processes, as indicated in Chapter 5, are considered to have social origins, in that it is the interactions and communications between the child and others at the *inter-mental* level that later become internalized as thought (at the *intra-mental* level).

6.3.2 Language socialization and behaviour

So far, we have considered how the process of development and the structure of language may be related to psychological attributes in perceptual and cognitive domains. It would seem reasonable to expect that links between language and these psychological attributes would be reflected in behavioural characteristics of people socialized in different languages. This would be consistent with the observation made earlier that those features central to the functioning of a given community or society would be highly salient in the language of that community. It would follow then that highly valued behavioural attributes would be well articulated in the language of that society. The transmission of a language to the young should therefore reflect the significance of particular behaviours in a given culture. There are, however, some indications that the context for transmission of a language may be as significant as the language being transmitted, especially as regards behaviour deemed appropriate in facilitating this process. Various studies have examined the contexts for language socialization and development in children, but few have examined outcomes in expressive verbal behaviour associated with particular socialization practices.

One study of such a link between language socialization and behaviour of children was by Harkness and Super (2008), who compared sociolinguistic training of children in Kokwet, a rural community of western Kenya, with that of American middle-class children. The initial interest of Harkness and Super was to identify explanations for the difficulties that psychologists encountered in trying to administer tests to African children. Harkness and Super had observed that on tests that required verbal responses, only 10 per cent of three-year-olds said anything, and the proportion of children answering did not reach 50 per cent until they were six or seven years of age. Even by the age of ten, a full third of the children did not give any replies that could be scored. Such children would be generally healthy and well nourished; they could be active and vocal as children anywhere; and they engaged in all sorts of boisterous play with peers. Yet the testing situation seemed to produce inhibition of responses relevant for psychological testing.

One rationale identified by Harkness and Super (2008) for studying child-language socialization was that the structure of verbal interactions between young children and others should indicate how much practice children received in the type of talking necessary for responding to psychological tests. Another reason was that the acquisition of communicative competence reflects the child's learning of more general norms of social behaviour from different classes of people. The study included 20 children aged between two and three-and-a-half years in the Kenyan community of Kokwet. These children were tape-recorded and observed at home in naturally occurring situations. The children's mothers were also interviewed about beliefs and values related to child-language development.

Harkness and Super found that socialization of communicative competence differed between the Kokwet community and America. In comparison with mother-child verbal interaction in middle-class American families, the norms of verbal interaction for Kenyan families indicated a profound change in the relationship between children and important adult figures during the second and third year of life. It was observed that during this period, there developed a social distance between the child and adults discouraging verbal expressiveness in children. Children were thus socialized to maintain silence in the presence of older or higher-status people, accounting for little verbal responsiveness during psychological testing. In terms of language development, the traditional view was that children will learn to talk on their own but must be taught to understand requests and commands, and to respond appropriately to them (see Case Study 1 earlier about parental approaches to stimulating language development in young children).

These observations indicated an intimate link between the process of language socialization and valued behavioural outcomes in children. They suggested that for the people of Kokwet (Kipsigis), comprehension, and not production, was the important linguistic skill by traditional criteria. The emphasis on language comprehension, rather than production, seemed to fit within the larger cultural values of obedience and respect as they were realized in many African societies. Such attributes as obedience and respect were required in many relationships between people of differing status: children and parents; women and men; younger people and older people; apprentices and masters; clients and patrons and so on. The expression of obedience and respect was seen to characteristically entail a quiet, even impassive, demeanour which could be encoded as a requirement for avoidance between certain classes. Thus, behavioural characteristics associated with language socialization in childhood were carried over to adulthood and thereafter would be difficult to alter. These patterns of interaction are consistent with categorizations of collectivist societies and the socialization of allocentric individuals (see Chapter 3). In this sense, the expression of language was itself a vehicle for the transmission of cultural values of society.

6.3.3 Summary and conclusions on the role of language

In addition to serving as a means of communication, language is considered to mediate between culture and behaviour. Interest in the mediating role of language has focused on possible links between language transmission and the shaping of particular types of thought processes.

Research evidence indicates that there are many cross-cultural similarities in properties of language as an instrument for thinking. However, there does not seem to be conclusive evidence that different languages predestine individuals to different kinds of thinking. Other studies have demonstrated how language socialization is the means by which the young are socialized regarding appropriate culture-specific behaviours and skills. Thus, language is an important aspect of the social and psychological development of individuals. What about individuals who acquire more than one language? What individual, social and cultural processes are involved in such acquisition of the languages? If language is an important aspect of the social and psychological development of individuals, are children who learn more than one language advantaged or disadvantaged in this respect? Such questions have been of interest to those studying bilingualism and will be discussed in the next section.

> **Discussion point:** What are the key features of the linguistic relativity hypothesis? Do you think there is adequate support for either the stronger or weaker version of this hypothesis?

6.4 Bilingualism

Bilingualism has been defined as 'the ability of persons or communities to meet...the communicative demands of the self or society in two or more languages in interaction with speakers of any or all of these languages' (Mohanty and Perregaux, 1997, cited in Berry et al. 2002, p. 169). It has been observed that bilingualism or multilingualism has become the norm in the world, and not an exception, as most people learn and speak more than one language. Estimates by the early 1990s were that about half of the world's children were exposed to more than one language, and that on average between two and five languages were typically known per person (De Houwer, 1995; Romaine, 1989). In Africa, for example, it is estimated that 50 per cent of the population is multilingual (Wolff, 2000). These figures are set to be higher as people all over the world continue to increase contact with other cultures. The term 'bilingualism' in this chapter is used broadly to sometimes also include multilingualism (where more than two languages may be involved).

Circumstances for bilingual development of children vary across families and societies, but a common circumstance is that of immigrant parents. In such cases, one language is spoken at home, while another may be used in the dominant culture and in the schools. Another circumstance is whereby the community and the country are themselves bilingual environments. In general, bilingualism is said to flourish in culturally plural societies and also in societies where acculturation is underway. For individuals concerned, the contexts and/or demands for developing proficiency in more than one language can vary. Such circumstances create complex environments for children's language development and experiences. The contexts and process of bilingual development can have some psychological implications for the individuals involved. It is also often the case that while some children learn two languages simultaneously, older individuals often learn a second language later in life.

Issues of concern regarding bilingual development have often focused on the proficiency of the individual in each of the languages acquired, and their cognitive and social functioning. Research on bilingual development has therefore focused on whether children exposed to more than one language can successfully acquire two languages at the same time without confusion or delay in the syntactic realm; and whether the vocabulary of such children may be limited in each language being learned. Other questions of interest have been on the difference between the particular ways of learning a second language later in life and the simultaneous acquisition of two languages in childhood, and the social and psychological implications associated with this. Concerns regarding the cognitive functioning of bilingual children have focused on whether there are some disadvantages or benefits associated with bilingualism, and what are the implications for functioning in other domains such as those central to educational attainment. Finally, questions on social psychological consequences of bilingualism have focused on wider cultural implications that go beyond mere knowledge and usage of two or more linguistic systems, especially for children from ethnic minority populations. In the sections that follow, the evidence for each of these developmental and psychological implications of bilingualism are examined and discussed further.

6.4.1 Bilingual development in children

Many studies on bilingual development have been based on diary records of single children, often the child of a linguist. An example is

Werner Leopold's study (1939–1949) of his daughter's bilingual development of English and German. Other studies have been larger-scale studies of children in immigrant families. These latter studies have typically focused on documenting the children's skill in the majority language, and not on the children's development of both languages. But what are the processes involved in children's acquisition of more than one language, and how do they differentiate one from the other? What are the effects of one language on the other? Answers to such questions have implications for the communicative competence of bilingual children, which may be of concern to both parents and teachers. Issues raised by each of these questions are considered in turn below.

6.4.1.1 Language differentiation

It was proposed by Volterra and Taeschner (1978) that bilingual children start by constructing a single system in which one lexicon contains the words in both languages and one system of rules. Later they distinguish two lexicons but apply the same syntactic rules to both languages. In the third stage at about three years of age, the children have two fully differentiated systems. Eckman and Hoff-Ginsberg (1997) identify two types of evidence for arguments over an initial single system. One involves children's knowledge of different words in each language rather than two sets of words for a single set of meanings. The lack of overlap would suggest a single undifferentiated lexicon. Other evidence relates to language mixing, where utterances of words from both languages are used. This would suggest a failure to differentiate the two systems. But does this necessarily mean that children fail to differentiate the two languages?

There is some evidence showing that children have enough cross-language synonyms in their vocabulary, by 30 months of age, to suggest that they are building two systems (Eckman and Hoff-Ginsberg, 1997; Pearson, Fernández and Oller, 1995). It is also argued that children simply learn different words because they tend to hear their two languages from different people in different contexts (Pearson and Fernández, 1994). Regarding language mixing, one argument is that if children reach into one language for a word that they do not know in the other language when speaking to someone who knows both languages, such language mixing could be a communicative strategy, and therefore evidence of sociolinguistic skill (Eckman and Hoff-Ginsberg, 1997). The term 'code switching' is applied when language mixing is not seen as a sign of confusion between two systems. Studies on code switching by bilingual children indicate that children as young as two years of age can use their two languages in contextually sensitive ways (e.g., Lanza, 1992). In addition, children may also learn to code switch by observing parents doing so, often for communicative effect (Goodz, 1989).

6.4.1.2 Effects of development of one language on another

If children learn two languages at the same time, do they learn each language more slowly, and does one language interfere with the other? There has been considerable debate on the idea that a person's ability to learn additional languages is impaired by the languages already known (Hakuta, 1986). Early work on bilingualism suggested that learning two languages was detrimental to a child's cognitive abilities (Hakuta, 1986; Thompson, 1952). This was based on the idea that the two languages were learned independently and that the knowledge of learning one did not transfer into the other. It was also held that as more was learned in one language, less could be learned in the other. This suggests that there is a limit to the amount of language acquisition and the simultaneous learning of multiple languages will lead to saturation. A consequence of this was that parents and teachers were encouraged to force children to learn only one language instead of cultivating the ability to learn both.

The literature indicates that both in the course and the rate of development, bilingual and monolingual development are highly similar (de Houwer, 1995). However, studies of vocabulary development provide mixed data. Studies of five-year-olds and older children have found that bilingual children have smaller vocabularies in each of their languages than monolingual children of the same age (Umbel, Pearson, Fernández and Oller, 1992). In contrast, studies on children who were followed from the age of 8 to 30 months found that bilingual children had comprehension vocabularies in each language that were comparable to monolinguals' vocabularies. However, in spontaneous speech production, these same children had smaller vocabularies in each of their languages than did their monolingual age-mates. Their total vocabularies in the two languages were comparable to monolinguals' vocabularies (Pearson, Fernández and Oller, 1993).

In reviewing these findings, Eckman and Hoff-Ginsberg (1997) identified two opposing, though somewhat extreme, possibilities: either children can learn two languages as easily as one, or learning two languages is so difficult that simultaneous exposure to two languages in infancy should be avoided. According to Eckman and Hoff-Ginsberg, simultaneous acquisition of two languages was possible, but the notion that learning two languages is as easy as learning one may be an overstatement. Input probably plays a role in language acquisition such that it is easier to learn a language one is more exposed to. The consensus among linguists, as well as the public today, is leaning away from the idea that knowledge in the two languages would be kept separate instead of influencing each other.

6.4.2 Second-language acquisition in adolescents and adults

While the process of acquisition of more than one language can occur simultaneously in childhood, this is often as a second or even third language in adolescence or adulthood. The literature on second-language acquisition indicates a number of well-established facts, albeit with some disagreement about how to explain them, including the following general observations by Eckman and Hoff-Ginsberg (1997):

- Children are more successful than adults at acquiring a second language;
- Second language learning is generally less successful than first language acquisition; and
- Difficulties second-language learners encounter are somewhat consistent and predictable.

These features of second-language learning have been a focus of research that seeks to explain bilingual development. Such research has focused on the following: the role of age; the role of the native language; and whether an underlying mechanism for acquiring a second language exists in a manner similar to that involved in first language learning. Most of this research has tended to focus on the processes involved in second-language acquisition in relation to the individual involved or the structure of the languages concerned. Some of these issues are discussed later in the context of cognitive effects of bilingualism. However, research on the effect of age on second-language learning has also highlighted the role of social factors. It has been indicated, for example, that although initially older adolescents and adults learn a new language more rapidly than young children, younger children ultimately achieve more native-like proficiency in the phonology and syntax of the target language than adult learners. While these findings suggest that there might be a critical period for language acquisition, another explanation has been provided by the 'acculturation model' (Eckman and Hoff-Ginsberg, 1997; Schumann, 1987; 1993).

6.4.2.1 The acculturation model

The acculturation model holds that second-language proficiency is a function of certain social and psychological variables related to contact between members of different cultures. It is held that as learning a second language involves coming into contact with people who are members of another culture and speak another language, the process of learning the second language is not just a process of acquiring a new vocabulary, phonological and grammatical rules. Rather, it is also a process of *acculturation*: a social and psychological process that involves making contact with and, to some extent, joining another social group (Eckman and Hoff-Ginsberg, 1997).

The acculturation model for second-language acquisition was proposed by Schumann (1987; 1993). According to the model, second-language learning is one aspect of acculturation controlled by the degree to which the learner acculturates to the target-language group: their social and psychological integration into the group. Thus, the degree to which learners acquire the target language depends on their social and psychological proximity to the speakers of the target language. The process of acculturation, according to Schumann, involves several social and affective variables. Social variables include social dominance patterns, that is, the political, cultural, economical or technological superiority of one group over the other, leading to social distance between them and resulting in impediment of second-language acquisition. In such a situation, the two groups are socially distant and second-language acquisition would be impeded.

Affective variables relate to individuals, and one factor associated with second-language acquisition in this regard is motivation. Gardner and Lambert (1972) had identified two kinds of motivational orientation associated with second-language proficiency: *integrative motivation* and *instrumental motivation*. Individuals with integrative motivation were interested in learning the language in order to associate with members of the target culture. Those with instrumental motivation were less interested in integrating with the target culture and more interested in learning the language for utilitarian reasons, such as professional advancement. Individuals with integrative motivation were generally more successful learners, with an integrative orientation being better at sustaining the long-term effort needed to gain proficiency in a second language. Similarly, Schumann considered learners with an integrative motivation as being more acculturated. In this regard, instrumentally motivated learners would integrate with the target culture only to the extent of satisfying their instrumental goals.

In summary, the acculturation model attempts to explain why language acquisition is different in children and adults in terms of differences in attitudes towards the target language and culture. The motivation for learning the target language is also considered a factor; it has generally been shown that an integrative motivation in which the learner seeks to associate with the target-language culture correlates most strongly with second-language proficiency (Gardner and Lambert, 1972). The acculturation model thus addresses different end states in first- and second-language acquisition, and hypothesizes that children and adults are subject to different social and psychological variables in learning a language. Another important factor may be the context in which the language is learned. For example, one major difference between first- and second-language acquisition is the fact that second languages may be learned in a classroom situation as opposed to the first language acquired in the home context. The social and affective variables associated with the two contexts are therefore likely to be different.

> **Discussion point:** How useful would you consider the acculturation to be in explaining second-language acquisition in adolescents? Are there any other explanations why young children may be more adept at acquiring a second language?

6.4.3 Cognitive and social outcomes of bilingualism

So far we have looked at the process of acquisition of more than one language, either simultaneously in childhood, or in adolescence or adulthood as a second language. But could being bilingual itself have an effect on aspects of psychological functioning, and if so, what domains may specifically be affected? Research addressing this question has focused a great deal on cognitive and social functioning of bilingual individuals. The following questions have been of particular fascination to psycholinguists: Does a person who can speak and think in two languages think differently in each language? Do bilinguals think differently from monolinguals? What differences, if any, emanate from the availability of two languages compared with just one? and

Does being bilingual affect intelligence, positively or negatively? These questions have essentially been concerned with the cognitive and social functioning of bilingual individuals.

6.4.3.1 Cognitive effects of bilingualism

Several studies on cognitive development during the 1930s and 1940s compared immigrant bilingual children with non-immigrant monolingual children and found consistently poorer performance among the immigrant children. Explanations were either that the immigrant children were genetically inferior, or that their bilingualism accounted for the poorer performance. At the time, the consensus leaned more towards the latter view, which represented an environmental argument. Thus, the bilingualism of the children was seen as a mental burden causing lower levels of intellectual functioning.

Evidence to the contrary was provided by the findings of a study of French-English bilingual children in Canada by Peal and Lambert (1962). This study corrected what were perceived to be major flaws of previous work: first, the children were balanced bilinguals in the sense that they were relatively equal in their mastery of both languages, unlike the immigrant children who tended to be more competent in their parents' language; second, the children were also from the same social class as the monolinguals to whom they were compared. It was found, for the balanced middle-class sample studied, that bilinguals performed better than monolinguals on a set of cognitive tests. The conclusion by Peal and Lambert was that the wider experiences of the bilingual children had given them advantages over monolingual children. In particular, experience in the two languages was considered to have enhanced the intellectual functioning of the bilingual children as regards mental flexibility, concept formation and a range of mental abilities. These findings and conclusions were in stark contrast to earlier conclusions.

Some cognitive advantages were also found to be associated with bilingualism in subsequent studies (Ben-Zeev, 1977; Diaz, 1983). Ben-Zeev compared middle-class bilingual speakers of Hebrew and English with middle-class monolingual speakers of Hebrew and of English on several non-verbal and verbal tests. Again, the findings showed that bilingual children performed better than monolingual children. However, not all later studies found such positive effects of bilingualism. Hakuta (1986) reviewed a number of studies in this field and found the data to be equivocal, again reflecting some of the methodological problems identified earlier (Palij and Homel, 1987). For example, differences in subject populations, methodologies, language groups, and also experimenter biases could have contributed to the inconsistencies in the literature. Hakuta concluded that the answer was not simple. He suggested that when bilinguals are balanced, roughly equally fluent in both languages, and came from middle-class backgrounds, positive effects of bilingualism tend to be found, but negative effects may result under other circumstances.

One explanation for some of the equivocal findings was provided by Cummins (1976, cited by Sternberg, 1996), who suggested a distinction between what may be called additive compared with subtractive bilingualism. In additive bilingualism, a second language is acquired in addition to a relatively well-developed first language. In subtractive bilingualism, elements of a second language replace elements of the first language. Cummins's hypothesis was that the additive form results in increased cognitive functioning, whereas the subtractive form results in decreased functioning. In particular, there may be some kind of threshold effect, such that individuals may need to be at a certain relatively high level of competence in both languages for a positive effect of bilingualism to be found. Children from lower socio-economic backgrounds may be more likely to be subtractive bilinguals than children from higher socio-economic backgrounds. In this case, their background may be the cause of the negative rather than the positive effects of bilingualism (see Chapter 4 for a discussion of other effects of social disadvantage).

More recent studies further suggest that when all these other factors are controlled for, higher degrees of bilingualism are associated with higher levels of cognitive attainment (Collier, 1992). Such outcomes have included cognitive flexibility, metalinguistic awareness, inhibitory control, concept formation, creativity and generally better academic performance than monolingual children (Collier, 1992). It has been pointed out for example, that when a child is fluent in two languages, they know more than one word for the same object or concept. This, it is believed, can add to the cognitive flexibility of the child. The explanation for this is that the child's knowledge of the different connotations and ideas around a word in different languages allows him/her to build a more complex understanding of the word at a younger age (Hakuta and Bialystok, 1994).

In discussing the benefits of bilingualism, Hakuta and Bialystok (1994) argue that 'the knowledge of two languages is greater than the sum of its parts'. Their view is that the benefits from being bilingual go much further than simply knowing two languages. The fact that the structures and ideas of the two languages are so different force children to think in more complicated ways than if they were learning only one language. Thus, one benefit of language acquisition for bilingual children is the increase of metalinguistic awareness, that is, a greater sensitivity to language in general and a greater awareness of meaning and structure in language (Bialystok, 1988). One reason suggested for this is that multilingual children receive more linguistic input, requiring a greater amount of language analysis on the part of the child.

Other effects of bilingualism have been observed in perceptual abilities. A study by Bialystok and Martin (2004) showed that bilingual children have better inhibitory control for ignoring perceptual information. The explanation for this is that bilingual children are constantly sorting out extra perceptual information. For every object and action they have two words, one in each language, they could use. Because such children need to choose which word to use based on the context they are in and the rules that apply to that context, this enhances their ability to selectively pay attention to appropriate information and inhibit focusing on other more irrelevant information. The research, using a card sort task, showed that this does seem to be the case.

This ability lends itself to application in other areas of education also. For example, in mathematical problem-solving, the first part of the problem is often to do with understanding what the question is asking and figuring out what information helps in answering that question and finding what other information is needed. Bilingualism has also been shown to have an impact on learning to read. For example, a study by Bialystok, Luk and Kwan (2005) showed the impact of knowing one language and its writing system on learning another. Bialystok et al. compared a group of monolinguals and three groups of bilinguals with different relationships between English and the second language: for Spanish-English bilinguals the languages are similar and they are both written alphabetically in the same script, for Hebrew-English bilinguals the languages are different but they are both written alphabetically (phonetic Hebrew) in different scripts, for Chinese-English bilinguals both the language and the writing system are different.

Bialystok et al. (2005) found that Spanish-English and Hebrew-English biliterates had the highest levels of literacy. Their interpretation of the results is that bilingualism has two effects on early acquisition of literacy: (1) a general understanding of reading and its basis in a print system and (2) the potential for transfer of reading principles across languages. All bilinguals showed an advantage in these areas over monolinguals, but the more similar the two languages the larger the advantage. In all, it is probably all these enhanced abilities demonstrated in bilingual children account for better academic attainments found amongst them. More recently, Bialystok (2007) presented a range of empirical evidence showing that bilingualism has cognitive advantages across the entire lifespan, from children to ageing adults.

6.4.3.1.1 Summary on cognitive effects of bilingualism

One central question has been whether bilingualism makes thinking in any one language more difficult, or whether it enhances thought processes. Early studies tended to be equivocal, probably reflecting the use of different subject populations, methodologies and language groups. In addition, experimenter biases could have also contributed to the inconsistencies in the literature. Overall, however, research suggests that when bilinguals are balanced, roughly equally fluent in both languages, and came from middle-class backgrounds, positive effects of bilingualism tend to be found. Such outcomes would account for better academic achievement amongst bilingual children compared with their monolingual peers. However, negative effects may result under other circumstances. Cummins (1976) suggested a distinction between additive and subtractive bilingualism. The additive form is said to result in increased cognitive functioning, whereas the subtractive form results in decreased functioning. In addition, it has been suggested that there may be a threshold of competence in both languages, below which positive effect of bilingualism may not be found. Children from lower socio-economic backgrounds may be more likely to be subtractive bilinguals than children from more advantaged backgrounds, and this could be the cause of the negative rather than the positive effects of bilingualism for such children (see Chapter 4 for a discussion on effects of social disadvantage).

6.4.3.2 Psychosocial aspects of bilingualism

Hakuta and Garcia (1989) argued that the debate over the merits of bilingualism has been characterized by confusion over whether bilingualism should be considered as simply knowledge and usage of two linguistic systems, or whether it involves the social dimensions encompassed by the languages. According to Hakuta and Garcia (1989), a focus on either the linguistic or the social aspects of bilingualism has implications for conceptions about the development of bilingual children. They point out that bilingualism has been defined predominantly in linguistic dimensions even though it is correlated with a number of *non-linguistic* social dimensions. It is suggested that this view of bilingualism as simply a bivariate function of linguistic proficiency in two languages under-represents the intricacies of the social setting.

Although Hakuta and Garcia (1989) acknowledge that language provides an important empirical handle on some of the problems associated with bilingualism, they advocate caution to avoid overattributing the causes of those problems to linguistic parameters. For example, the symbolism contained in language and its correlation with cultural or ethnic group membership may be of particular importance (see Case Study 2 below). The extent to which problems associated with bilingualism may reflect larger issues of social and cultural adjustment in bicultural or multicultural environments has been a focus of a number of studies (e.g., Romero and Roberts, 2003).

CASE STUDY 2: LANGUAGE AND CULTURAL IDENTITY

A colleague from Kenya who had been living in England for 15 years was at pains to get her daughter, aged 3 years, to develop a sense of African identity. She thought one way of doing this would be to get the girl to one day carry some specifically African food to preschool. She decided to discuss this with the young girl:

'No, I don't want to!' said the girl.
'Why not?' asked the mother.
'I don't want to!' repeated the girl.
'Don't you like the food?' enquired the mother, surprised at the intensity of the girl's reaction.
'I like the food...very much'.
'So why won't you take it to school?'
'Because I don't want everybody to think I am a second language girl!' Clearly, even for this girl at that age, being seen as different from everybody else (by eating different food) had negative connotations that were also associated with having a different (second) language. She would perhaps have noticed that other children who ate food different from that eaten by the majority of children also had a label of having a second language and, for some reason, that this was undesirable.

Research on acculturation of ethnic groups in bicultural or multicultural communities in the United States provides an illustration of language as a complex interaction of linguistic, psychological and social domains. Of particular interest in these studies has been the focus on the concept of acculturation to assess cultural influences on mental health, as specifically related to stress and coping (Lazarus, 1997; Sanchez and Fernandez, 1993). In this context, language stress has been identified as a culture-specific stressor in addition to discrimination and minority status (Cervantes, Padilla and Salgado de Snyder, 1991; Hovey, 1998). For example, Hovey (1998) examined the bilingual environment of Latino adolescents as a bicultural environment, and found an association between depressive symptoms and cultural-specific stress such as intergenerational stress, peer group racism, school discrimination, gang influence on ethnicity and monolingualism.

Romero and Roberts (2003) commented that such research suggests that Latino youths live in a dual cultural world that is reflective of a family environment that may include individuals of different generations, language preferences and acculturation levels. They argued that being monolingual (only speaking one language fluently) may be specifically stressful for youths who live in a bilingual world; they may experience stress not only from being a Spanish-dominant speaker but also from being an English dominant speaker. Latino youths who speak only English may feel stress from the need to speak better Spanish for communication with other family members. In such situations, bilingual youths are better adapted to live in bilingual environments. Thus, the extent to which bilingualism may or may not account for psychological problems would depend on the specific context and dynamics of the community.

Romero and Roberts (2003) examined differences between immigrant and US-born Latino adolescents with regard to perceptions of stressors and depressive symptoms by focusing on cultural aspects of bilingual and bicultural environments. The participants were divided into three categories of language preference: English only, bilingual preference and Spanish only. Measures of self-esteem, depressive symptoms and bicultural stressors were also obtained. The results indicated that US-born youths reported experiencing fewer total number of stressors than immigrant students. However, US-born youths reported significantly more perceived stress than immigrants as a result of needing better Spanish and feeling that their parents' culture kept them from being like other American kids. Immigrant youths reported more perceived stress than US-born adolescents from problems at school because of poor English. It was suggested that US-born youths may have been speaking or exposed to English for a longer period than immigrant children. Overall, more stress was significantly associated with speaking less English, lower socio-economic status, older students, more depressive symptoms and lower self-esteem. These findings indicate that bilingual contexts of the youths of Mexican descent provided stressors unique to the situation of being in dual cultural and linguistic contexts.

6.4.3.2.1 Summary on psychosocial aspects of bilingualism

Acculturation theory suggests that there is a link between changes in culture, acculturation and mental health. The findings from the study by Romero and Roberts (2003) indicate that stress can be experienced from stressors unique to dual cultural and linguistic contexts. This and other factors discussed earlier indicate that there are more issues faced by the bilingual individual than can be simply represented by language proficiency in one or two languages. As noted by Hakuta and Garcia (1989), 'the linguistic aspects of bilingualism provide only a window into a complex set of psychological and social processes in the development of bilingual children' (p. 378).

6.4.4 Summary on bilingualism

A significant number of children are exposed to more than one language during the course of their development. The contexts and specific circumstances differ, but this and the process of bilingual development can have some psychological implications for the individuals involved. Concerns have often focused on the proficiency of the individual in each of the languages acquired, and the cognitive and social functioning of the bilingual individual. While a second language is often learned later in life, some children learn two languages simultaneously. Research on bilingual children suggests that they can successfully acquire two languages at the same time with minimal confusion or delay in the syntactic realm. The evidence regarding vocabulary development is rather mixed: some data suggest that bilingual children have smaller vocabularies in each of their languages than monolingual children do, even though they have equivalent-size total vocabularies. Research on cognitive functioning suggests that there are some advantages associated with bilingualism on certain measures of cognitive ability and in metalinguistic awareness. Finally, research on social psychological functioning of bilingual and monolingual children from ethnic minority populations suggests that bilingualism has much wider cultural and psychological implications than the mere knowledge and usage of two or more linguistic systems.

> **Discussion point:** What would you consider to be the most significant effects of bilingualism on non-linguistic aspects of children's development? What are the implications of such effects?

6.5 Summary and conclusions

Language is considered an important aspect of psychological development and a good indicator of cultural differences between different societies. It has been considered a mediator between culture and behaviour, making language an important tool used by humans not only to interact with one another, but also of socio-cognitive development. Psychological research into children's language development has explored how language and thinking interrelate, and also how these are linked with the child's social sophistication. There is overall, some recognition that there may be more than one route to language acquisition and socialization, and that different cultures provide children with different kinds of language learning environments. The study of language acquisition by children who live in other cultures and the study of the acquisition of other languages have contributed to understanding both the universal processes of language acquisition, and also some culture-specific outcomes of such development. Of particular interest in this regard has been the mediating role of language between culture and behaviour, and possible links between language transmission and the shaping of particular types of thought processes. Research evidence indicates that there are many cross-cultural similarities in properties of language as an instrument for thinking. However, there is no conclusive evidence that different languages predestine individuals to different kinds of thinking. On the other hand, some studies have demonstrated how the process of language transmission in various cultures is a means of socialization for culture-specific behaviours and skills. Thus, language is an important aspect of the social and psychological development of individuals.

As most people in the world learn and speak more than one language, bilingualism or multilingualism has increasingly become the norm rather than an exception. Attention has therefore been on the processes involved in multiple- or second-language acquisition, and outcomes of such acquisition of different languages in terms of psychological functioning. Some children learn two languages simultaneously, while a second language is often learned later in life. Research indicates that children can successfully acquire two languages at the same time with minimal confusion or delay in the syntactic realm. As regards second-language learning, questions have focused on why children are more successful than adults at acquiring a second language. While there are various explanations for these, there is little agreement among them. There is some evidence, however, that other aspects of the cultural orientation of the individuals concerned may be implicated. As regards the outcomes of bilingualism, the focus of interest has been on cognitive and social functioning. There is some evidence of advantages associated with bilingualism on certain measures of cognitive ability and in metalinguistic awareness. Psychosocial outcomes of bilingualism in multicultural contexts mostly relate to levels of acculturation to the dominant culture.

FURTHER READING

Eckman, F. and Hoff Ginsberg, E. (1997). Learning more than one language. Second language learning and bilingual development. In E. Hoff-Ginsberg (Ed.), *Language Development*. Pacific Grove, CA: Brooks/Cole.

Hoff, E. (2006). How social contexts support and shape language development. *Developmental Review*, **26**, 55–88.

Levine, R.A. and New, R.S. (2008). Early childhood: Language acquisition, socialization, and enculturation. In R.A. LeVine and R.S. New (Eds), *Anthropology and child development: A cross-cultural reader*. Oxford: Blackwell.

Mohanty, A., and Perregaux, C. (1997). Language acquisition and bilingualism. In J.W. Berry, P.R. Dasen, and T.S. Saraswathi (Eds), *Basic processes and human development* (pp. 217–253). Vol II of *Handbook of cross-cultural psychology*. Second Edition. Boston, MA: Allyn & Bacon.

Romaine, S. (1989). *Bilingualism*. Oxford: Blackwell.

REFERENCES

Bates, E. (1976). *Language and context: The acquisition of pragmatics*. New York: Academic Press.

Ben-Zeev, S. (1977). The influence of bilingualism on cognitive strategy and cognitive development. *Child Development*, **48**, 1009–1018.

Berry, J.W., Poortinga, Y.H., Segall, M.H., and Dasen, P.R. (2002). *Cross-cultural psychology: Research and applications*. Second Edition. Cambridge: Cambridge University Press.

Bialystok, E. (1988). Levels of bilingualism and levels of linguistic awareness. *Developmental Psychology*, **24**, 560–567.

Bialystok E. and Martin, M.M. (2004). Attention and inhibition in bilingual children: Evidence from the dimensional change card sort task. *Developmental Science*, **7** *(3)*: 325–339.

Bialystok, E., Luk, G., and Kwan, E. (2005). Bilingualism, biliteracy, and learning to read: Interactions among languages and writing systems. *Scientific Studies of Reading*, **9***(1)*: 43–61.

Bialystok, E. (2007). Cognitive effects of bilingualism: How linguistic experience leads to cognitive change. *The International Journal of Bilingual Education and Bilingualism*, **10***(3), 210–223*.

Blount, B.G. (1971). Socialization and pre-linguistic development among the Luo of Kenya. *South-Western Journal of Anthropology*, **27**, 41–50.

Blount, B.G. (1975). Studies in child language: An anthropological view. *American Anthropologist*, **77**, 580–600.

Brown, R. (1973). *A first language: The early stages*. Cambridge, MA: Harvard University Press.

Carpendale, J. and Lewis, C. (2006). *How children develop social understanding*. Oxford: Blackwell.

Carroll, D.W. (1999). *Psychology of language*. 3rd Edition. Pacific Grove, CA: Brooks/Cole.

Cervantes, R.C., Padilla, A.M., and Salgado de Snyder, N. (1991). The Hispanic stress inventory: A culturally relevant approach to psychosocial assessment. *Psychological Assessment*, **3**, 438–447.

Chomsky, N. (1965). *Aspects of the theory of syntax*. Cambridge, MA: MIT Press.

Collier, V.P. (1992). A synthesis of studies examining long-term language-minority student data on academic achievement. *Bilingual Research Journal*, **16**, 187–212.

Cummins, J. (1976). The influence of bilingualism on cognitive growth: A synthesis of research findings and explanatory hypothesis. *Working Papers on Bilingualism*, **9**, 1–43.

De Houwer, A. (1995). Bilingual language acquisition. In P. Fletcher and B. MacWhinney (Eds), *The handbook of child language* (pp. 219–250). Oxford: Blackwell.

Diaz, R.M. (1983). Thought and two languages: The impact of bilingualism on cognitive development. *Review of Research in Education*, **10**, 23–54.

Eckman, F. and Hoff-Ginsberg, E. (1997). Learning more than one language: Second language learning and bilingual development. In E. Hoff-Ginsberg (Ed.), *Language development*. Pacific Grove, CA: Brooks/Cole.

Ervin-Tripp, S. and Slobin, D. (1967). *A field manual for cross-cultural study of the acquisition of communicative competence*. Berkeley: University of California Press.

Furth, H.G. (1966). *Thinking about language: Psychological implications of deafness*. New York: Free Press.

Gardner, R.C. and Lambert, W.E. (1972). *Attitudes and motivation in second language learning.* Rowley, MA: Newbury House.

Gerrig, R. and Banaji, M.R. (1994). Language and thought. In R.J. Sternberg (Ed.), *Handbook of perception and cognition* (Vol. 12). New York: Academic Press.

Goodz, N. (1989). Parental language mixing in bilingual families. *Infant Mental Health Journal,* **10**, 25–44.

Greenberg, J.M. (Ed.) (1963). *Universals of language.* Cambridge, MA: MIT Press.

Gumperz, J. and Hymes, D. (1972). *Directions in sociolinguistics: The ethnography of communication.* New York: Holt, Rinehart & Winston.

Gumperz, J.J. and Levinson, S.C. (1996). Introduction: Linguistic relativity re-examined. In J.J. Gumperz and S.C. Levinson (Eds), *Rethinking linguistic relativity* (pp. 1–18). Cambridge: Cambridge University Press.

Hakuta, K. (1986). *Mirror of language: The debate on bilingualism.* New York: Basic Books.

Hakuta, K. and Bialystok, E. (1994). *In other words: The science and psychology of second-language acquisition.* New York: Basic Books.

Hakuta, K. and Garcia, E.E. (1989). Bilingualism and education. *American Psychologist,* **44**(2), 374–379.

Harkness, S. (1990). A cultural model for the acquisition of language: Implications for the innateness debate. *Developmental Psychobiology,* **23**, 727–740.

Harkness, S. and Super, C.M. (2008). Why African children are so hard to test. In R.A LeVine and R.S. New (Eds), *Anthropology and child development: A cross-cultural reader.* Oxford: Blackwell.

Hoff, E. (2006). How social contexts support and shape language development. *Developmental Review,* **26**, 55–88.

Hovey, J.D. (1998). Acculturative stress, depression, and suicidal ideation among Mexican adolescents: Implications for the development of suicide prevention programs in schools. *Psychological Reports,* **83**, 249–250.

Hymes, D. (1974). *Foundations in sociolinguistics: An ethnographic approach.* Philadelphia: University of Pennsylvania Press.

Kendler, H.H. and Kendler, T.S. (1962). Vertical and horizontal processes in problem solving. *Psychological Review,* **69**, 1–16.

Lanza, E. (1992). Can bilingual two-year-olds code switch? *Journal of Child Language,* **19**, 633–658.

Lazarus, R.S. (1997). Acculturation isn't everything. *Applied Psychology,* **46**, 39–43.

Leopold, W.F. (1939–1949). *Speech development of a bilingual child: A linguist's record* (Vols 1–4). Evanston, IL: Northwestern University Press.

LeVine, R.A. and New, R.S. (2008). Early childhood: Language acquisition, socialization, and enculturation. In R.A. LeVine and R.S. New (Eds), *Anthropology and child development: A cross-cultural reader.* Oxford: Blackwell.

Lucy, J.A. (1992). *Language diversity and thought: A reformulation of the linguistic relativity hypothesis.* Cambridge: Cambridge University Press.

Luria, A.R. (1961). *The role of speech in the regulation of normal and abnormal behaviour.* London: Pergamon Press.

Miller, P.J., Wiley, A.R., Fung, H., and Liang, C.-H. (1997). Personal story telling as a medium of socialization in American and Chinese families. *Child Development*, **68**, 557–568.

Mohanty, A. and Perregaux, C. (1997). Language acquisition and bilingualism. In J.W. Berry, P.R. Dasen, and T.S. Saraswathi (Eds), *Basic processes and human development* (pp. 217–253). Vol II of *Handbook of cross-cultural psychology*. Second Edition. Boston, MA: Allyn & Bacon.

Oates, J. (1994). First relationships. In J. Oates (Ed.), *The foundations of child development*. Oxford: Blackwell/The Open University.

Ochs, E. (1988). *Culture and language development: Language acquisition and language socialization in a Samoan village*. New York: Cambridge University Press.

Ochs, E. and Schieffelin, B. (1984). Language acquisition and socialization: Three developmental stories and their implications. In R.A. Shweder and R.A. LeVine (Eds), *Culture theory: Essays on mind, self and emotion* (pp. 276–320). New York: Cambridge University Press.

Palij, M. and Homel, P. (1987). The relationship of bilingualism to cognitive development: Historical, methodological and theoretical considerations. In P. Homel, M. Plij, and D. Aaronson (Eds), *Childhood bilingualism: Aspects of linguistic, cognitive and social development* (pp. 131–148). Hillsdale, NJ: Lawrence Erlbaum.

Peal, E. and Lambert, W.E. (1962). The relation of bilingualism to intelligence. *Psychological Monographs*, **76**(76, No. 546).

Pearson, B.Z. and Fernández, S.C.(1994). Patterns of interaction in the lexical growth in two languages of bilingual infants and toddlers. *Language Learning*, **44**, 617–653.

Pearson, B.Z., Fernández, S.C., and Oller, D.K. (1993). Lexical development in bilingual infants and toddlers: Comparison to monolingual norms. *Language Learning*, **43**, 93–120.

Pearson, B.Z., Fernández, S.C., and Oller, D.K. (1995). Cross-language synonyms in lexicons of bilingual infants: One language or two? *Journal of Child Language*, **22**, 345–368.

Pye, C. (1986). Quiche' Mayan speech to children. *Journal of Child Language*, **13**, 85–100.

Romaine, S. (1989). *Bilingualism*. Oxford: Blackwell.

Romero, A.J. and Roberts, R.E. (2003). Stress within a bicultural context for adolescents of Mexican descent. *Cultural Diversity and Ethnic Minority Psychology*, **9**(2), 171–184.

Sanchez, J.I. and Fernandez, D.M. (1993). Acculturative stress among Hispanics: A bidimensional model of ethnic identification. *Journal of Applied Social Psychology*, **23**, 654–668.

Sapir, E. (1929). The status of linguistics as a science. *Language*, **5**, 207–214.

Sapir, E. (1949). *Culture, language and personality*. Berkeley: University of California.

Schumann, J. (1987). The expression of temporality in basilang speech. *Studies in Second Language Acquisition*, **9**, 21–41.

Schumann, J. (1993). Some problems with falsification: An illustration from SLA research. *Applied Linguistics*, **14**, 295–306.
Serpell, R. (1976). *Culture's influence on behaviour* (Chapter 4: The roles of language, pp. 55–68). London: Methuen.
Soderstrom, M. (2007). Beyond babytalk: Re-evaluating the nature and content of speech input to preverbal infants. *Developmental Review*, **27**, 501–532.
Sternberg, R.J. (1996). *Cognitive psychology.* Fort Worth, TX: Harcourt Brace.
Thompson, G.G. (1952). *Child psychology.* Boston, MA: Houghton Mifflin.
Tomasello, M., Kruger, A.C., and Ratner, H.H. (1993). Cultural learning. *Behavioral and Brain Sciences*, **16**, 495–552.
Umbel, V.M., Pearson, B.Z., Fernández, S.C., and Oller, D.K. (1992). Measuring bilingual children's receptive vocabularies. *Child Development*, **63**, 1012–1020.
Volterra, V. and Taeschner, T. (1978). The acquisition and development of language by bilingual children. *Journal of Child Language*, **5**, 311–326.
Vygotsky, L.S. (1986). *Thought and language.* (Translated by A. Kozulin). Cambridge, MA: MIT Press.
Whorf, B.L. (1956). *Language, thought and reality: Selected writings of Benjamin Lee Whorf* (Edited by J.B. Carroll). New York: John Wiley & Sons.
Wolff, E.H. (2000). Language in society. In B. Heine and D. Nurse (Eds), *African languages: An introduction.* (pp. 298–347). Cambridge: Cambridge University Press.

The Development of Cultural and Ethnic Identity

Rachel Takriti

OUTLINE

7.1 Introduction
7.2 Religion and ethnicity
    7.2.1 What is religion?
    7.2.2 The interaction between religion and ethnicity
7.3 Prejudice and children's understanding of ethnic groups
    7.3.1 Theories of children's development of prejudice
7.4 Children's ethnic attitudes
    7.4.1 White children's attitudes to other groups
    7.4.2 White children's attitudes to whites
    7.4.3 Black children's attitudes to own and other groups
    7.4.4 Attitudes held by other minority groups
    7.4.5 Implications of empirical work relating to ethnicity
7.5 Religious identity
7.6 Social-psychological theories
    7.6.1 Social Identity Theory (SIT)
    7.6.2 Self-Categorization Theory (SCT)
    7.6.3 Social categorization, in-group and out-group relations
7.7 Summary and conclusions
Further reading
References

7.1 Introduction

The development of children's cultural identity was actively researched in the 1960s and 1970s focusing on areas such as nationality, ethnicity, religion and gender; recently, there has been a re-emergence of this as an active area of research. Two of these areas, ethnicity and religion, have been the main defining and consolidating features of social groups with particular cultural identities. These have also been associated with various tensions and conflicts. Religion and ethnicity can be implicated in many violent clashes over the course of history, from the Crusades and the Reformation to recent clashes in the former Yugoslavia, Northern Ireland, northern states of India, Sri Lanka, Rwanda, Darfur in the Sudan and the ever-present disputes in the Middle East between Jews and Muslims in Israel and Palestine. It follows, therefore, that religion and ethnicity are likely to be highly emotive components of identity, if not for indigenous majority people of any society, certainly for minorities who have their origins in countries where religion or ethnicity is of significant importance. This chapter examines and discusses how children come to understand and evaluate ethnic and religious groups and their own group membership. Such development is of vital importance as it has implications for the shape and future of countries such as the United Kingdom and other multicultural societies in terms of group relations.

It can be said that most countries across the globe nowadays are composed of people from various ethnic and religious groups. The UK Office for National Statistics (ONS) estimates that 7 per cent of the UK population are from non-white ethnic origins and a majority of this being from the Indian subcontinent, with approximately one million of Indian origin and approximately nine hundred thousand of Pakistani and Bangladeshi origin (ONS, Labour Force Survey, 2000). In certain areas of the United Kingdom, such as West Yorkshire, the proportion of ethnic minorities in particular towns is estimated to be as high as 70 per cent (ONS, Social Trends, 2000). In one city of West Yorkshire, Bradford, Asians and British Asians make up 52 per cent of the population. Such demographic patterns have been associated with inter-ethnic tensions. For example, during 2000 and 2001, Bradford was the scene of racially motivated riots and violence. Similar examples can be cited from across the United Kingdom in recent years, with the murder of, and violent attacks on, asylum seekers in Glasgow and London and racially motivated riots in Oldham, Greater Manchester. The rise in immigration and a marked increase in asylum seekers entering the United Kingdom (Bennett, Heath and Jeffries, 2007), coupled with the Home Office's policy of dispersion of asylum seekers, is likely to significantly affect the population distribution of ethnic minorities leading to doubts on its impact on race relations. It is clear, however, that children being born in the United Kingdom today are entering a society which contains a greater diversity of ethnic groups than ever before.

This chapter aims to describe the development of children's cultural and ethnic identity, with particular reference to religious identity development. The chapter begins with a discussion of definitions of the key terms 'religion' and 'ethnicity' followed by an overview of research investigating children's awareness of group differences and the theoretical basis for this work, particularly focusing on Piaget's theory of cognitive development. The chapter then presents evidence that children's understanding of social groups develops within a social context, being determined, at least in part, by the social group to which they belong.

7.2 Religion and ethnicity

7.2.1 What is religion?

The six main world religions are Buddhism, Christianity, Hinduism, Islam, Judaism and Sikhism (Beit-Hallahmi and Argyle, 1997). These religious groups are extensively varied, and the beliefs and practices which define them vary significantly. However, it is necessary to stipulate what religious groups have in common, in order to reach a definition of religion.

In his analysis of religion, Wallace (1966) states,

> It is the premise of every religion – and this premise is religion's defining characteristic – that souls, supernatural beings, and supernatural forces exist. Furthermore, there are certain minimal categories of behaviour, which in the context of the supernatural premise, are always found in association with one another and which are the substance of religion itself. (Wallace, 1966, p. 52)

A distinction can be drawn between two interrelated concepts in religion: belief in the supernatural and behaviour in relation to the supernatural. It can be seen that all religions believe in an invisible world and see the purpose of life as increasing harmony in the world through doing good and avoiding evil (Loewenthal, 1994). The majority of religions believe that this invisible world is inhabited by various types of supernatural beings such as Angels, Djinn, Devils and God(s) who are believed to impact on the behaviour, reasoning and emotional reactions of the individual (Thouless, 1971). The behaviour which is preordained through organized religion acts as a mediator between the individual and the supernatural (Beit-Hallahmi and Argyle, 1997). This definition of religion is, by necessity, broad and somewhat generalized, to account for the wide variety in religions.

Verbit (1970), however, specified the content of religiosity: that is, what makes one individual more religious than another. He defined six dimensions of religiosity:

Ritual – involvement in behaviours associated with the religion;
Doctrine – religious beliefs held by the individual;
Emotion – emotional reactions experienced in relation to the religion;
Knowledge – level of knowledge held by the individual of the ritual and doctrine;
Ethics – impact of the religion on individual ethical decision-making; and
Community – involvement with the religious community.

Each of these six dimensions is postulated to vary according to four components: Content, Frequency, Intensity and Emotion. If we examine doctrine, for example, an individual with high religiosity could be seen to follow the doctrine of his/her religion, to do so frequently, to believe in the doctrine intensely and with conviction, and to feel a strong emotional reaction to the doctrine.

Religion can serve purely as a label, splitting people into groups. Individuals are *de facto* members of several social groups (e.g., ethnic, religious, gender), and subjectively identify with and classify themselves as members of some of these groups. According to Social Identity Theory (Tajfel, 1979), this *self-categorization* process enables the individual to structure an understanding of the social world and provides a system of orientation for self-reference and defining one's position and status in society. The categorization process simplifies the social world by accentuating similarities within groups and differences between groups, this is termed the *accentuation hypothesis*. It is the self-categorization process which enables the individual to determine in any given context which group s/he belongs to (the in-group) and those groups to which s/he does not belong (the out-groups), and as such involves the processes of perception and categorization. Social identity is defined as:

> that part of an individual's self-concept that derives from his knowledge of his membership of a social group or groups, together with the value and emotional significance attached to that membership. (Tajfel, 1979, p. 52)

In summary, therefore, it can be said that religion is defined by a belief in the supernatural who makes demands on the beliefs, thoughts, behaviour and emotional reactions of the individual. These demands can then be expressed by the behaviour predetermined by the particular religious group. Individuals can be members of a religious group, and this can form a social identity. Within groups, individuals may vary according to the type and level of religiosity.

7.2.2 The interaction between religion and ethnicity

Ethnicity can be referred to as a label defining a number of characteristics such as race, language and religion which are shared by a group of individuals (Phinney, 1990). For example, a group of Mexican Americans are considered to be of Hispanic ethnicity, sharing race, language, customs and religious beliefs. The use of ethnicity as a label defines the group and as such constitutes ethnic identity. Religion can, therefore, be seen to be embedded within ethnicity, and it has often been cited as a component of ethnicity. Geertz (1973) for example, defines ethnicity as being based on kin connections, religion, shared race, shared language and social practices. Similarly, Nash (1989) defines religion as one of the basic building blocks of ethnicity. It is evident that religion and ethnicity often coincide so that religion is a defining feature of the ethnic group, however, that is not to presume that religious identity can be subsumed by ethnic identity.

Interestingly, however, Jacobson (1997), in her study of young British Pakistanis, found that ethnicity was viewed as an attachment to a geographical location of origin and a set of customs and traditions, while religion was defined as acceptance of a set of absolute truths. Neilson (1984) and Ali (1992) found similar trends which they attributed to the emigration of religious groups from various countries, where different traditions prevailed. Such diversity in views about ethnicity has led to a re-evaluation of religion and consequently the separation of ethnicity and religion.

It is evident that young children also have issues with disentangling religion from components of ethnicity such as language and nationality (Takriti, Barrett and Buchannan-Barrow, 2006). For example, a Hindu child aged seven said 'I'm a Hindu because I speak Gujarati and go to Temple'. Similarly, an eight-year-old Muslim child said 'I'm Muslim because my mum was born in Iraq and my dad was born in Egypt'. So, it appears that although, theoretically, religion can be separated from ethnicity, in the minds of children, the two remain somewhat embedded.

Rotherham and Phinney (1987) define ethnic identity as 'one's sense of belonging to an ethnic group and the part of one's thinking, perception, feelings and behaviour that is due to ethnic group membership' (p. 13). Ethnic identity, along with racial, gender and national identity, can, therefore, be viewed as one of many socially shared identities available to an individual. Religious identity can also be postulated to exist as a social identity. Following from Rotherham and Phinney (1987), religious identity can be defined as one's sense of belonging to a religious group and the part of one's thinking, perception, feelings and behaviour that is due to religious group membership.

> **Discussion point:** What features do ethnicity, culture and religion encompass? How are they related to one another in multicultural societies such as the United Kingdom?

7.3 Prejudice and children's understanding of ethnic groups

Ethnic prejudice may be defined as:

> An organised predisposition to respond in an unfavorable manner towards people from an ethnic group because of their ethnic affiliation. (Aboud, 1988, p. 6)

It should be noted that although this definition is concerned with ethnic groups, prejudice can be directed towards any group. Aboud (1988) states that for a person to be prejudiced, they must have an underlying tendency to feel negatively towards individuals on the basis of their group membership, not on the basis of individual attributes. As such, the prejudiced or negative feelings and responses should be elicited by all members of a particular group. The predisposition should also remain relatively stable over time, allowing for situational and motivational changes.

Aboud (1988) makes a distinction between prejudice and stereotypes. Stereotypes are defined as rigid, overgeneralized beliefs about a group of people which may not be negative, whereas prejudice is always negative. It is, however, accepted that prejudice can be related to stereotypes, in that prejudiced people are likely to hold negative stereotypes about the target group. However, it is necessary to explain the formation of prejudice. To begin with, an adequate theory of prejudice must account for three main factors. First, certain groups within society are victims of prejudice more often than others. Second, there is individual variation in levels of prejudice; and finally, prejudice develops in children, and there are differences between the adult and child forms of prejudice (Aboud, 1988).

7.3.1 Theories of children's development of prejudice

The main theoretical approach which provides an account and explanation of the development of prejudice in childhood is the Social-Cognitive Developmental Theory. The following section will review this approach in some depth. However, two other theories which could also be applied in the domain are Social Reflection Theory (Allport, 1954) and Inner State Theory (Adorno, Frenkel-Brunswick, Levinson and Sanford, 1950; Ryan and Buirski, 2001) which will not be discussed here, but which readers are encouraged to review.

7.3.1.1 Social-Cognitive Developmental Theory

This approach is cognitive-constructivist (Katz, 1976; Piaget and Weil, 1951) and predicts age-related changes in prejudice as dependent upon generalized changes in cognitive structures. It is acknowledged that the environment will affect these changes but this effect is limited by the cognitive abilities of the child. According to this theory, there will be a fundamental shift in the child's thinking and reasoning around the age of seven, which coincides with the shift from preoperational to concrete operational thinking and links with the development of

Table 7.1 Development of prejudice as predicted by social-cognitive developmental theory

Age	Attitudes associated with the stage
4–7 years	Children will be egocentric and have a limited concept of ethnic groups. Any preferences are based on random personal preferences
7–10 years	Children are no longer egocentric, but sociocentric. Children focusing on their own group rather than themselves. Other groups are recognized by the way they compare with the in-group
10–15 years	Children become more integrated, understanding reciprocity, that is the understanding that members of groups can hold their own views which may differ from the group's views

Affective – Perception – Cognition	Focus of attention
Step 1 – Children are initially dominated by feelings with any prejudice being determined by emotions.	**Step 1** – Egocentrism. Evident in children under the age of 7 years.
Step 2 – Perceotion is dominant. Dissimilar people = disliked. Factors such as skin colour are basis for ethnic self-identification. Prejudice at high level.	**Step 2** – Focus of attention on groups, specifically the differences between in-groups and out-groups. In order to clarify understanding, differences are exaggerated and prejudice is high.
Step 3 – Cognition is dominant. Categorical understanding, understanding the basis of ethnicity and reciprocal understanding develop. At around 7–8 years. Prejudice declines.	**Step 3** – Greater emphasis on individuals emerges. Corresponds with a reduction in prejudice.

Figure 7.1 Aboud's theory of early ethnic preferences

prejudice. Table 7.1 shows the three-stage developmental sequence for prejudice which can be predicted.

7.3.1.2 Aboud's theory of early ethnic attitudes

Aboud (1988) suggests that the Piagetian theory does not account fully for early preferences, which do not appear to be whimsical, but common among children in the same group. She, therefore, proposes two overlapping sequences of development which are shown in Figure 7.1.

Aboud (1988) proposes that prejudice will develop in line with other cognitive developments in the child. Initially, the child is dominated by affective processes which are then overtaken by more developed cognitive processes. In addition, the child moves from being profoundly egocentric to being able to focus on groups and later to focusing on individuals within groups. The egocentrism of young children prevents them from accepting that individuals in other groups may think and feel differently from themselves and also from attending to within-group differentiation. So, it is proposed that preoperational thinkers will focus on group differences and external attributes resulting in potentially high levels of prejudice (Aboud and Skerry, 1983). Concrete operational thinkers, in contrast, will be more likely to consider internal psychological features of themselves and peers as important, leading to a reduction in prejudice (Damon and Hart, 1982).

Evidence for Aboud's position can be taken from studies which have found that prejudice correlates negatively with cognitive development. For example, Kutner (1958) classified seven-year-old children as being either high- or low- prejudiced on the basis of a racial attitude scale. Highly prejudiced children were found to be less capable of inductive reasoning. Similar findings were obtained by Clark, Hovecar and Dembo (1980). Later work by Doyle and Aboud (1995), however, did not find a correlation between racial attitude change and performance on generalized conservation tasks. Rather, the perspective-taking skills of reciprocity (the understanding that members of each ethnic group are likely to prefer their in-group) and reconciliation (the awareness that this preference for the in-group is valid) have been linked to decreases in prejudiced attitudes and also to an increase in perception of intra-group variability (Doyle and Aboud, 1995). As such, it can be suggested that prejudice is influenced by the acceptance of the legitimacy of an out-group member's views.

It has been proposed (Katz, Sohn and Zalk, 1975) that prejudice does not decline with age, but rather that with age, children become more adept at and more motivated towards hiding their socially undesirable prejudiced views. Aboud (1992) disputes this, pointing out that with age, the number of positive attributes ascribed to out-groups increases, while the number of negative attributes remains stable. Thus, it is the flexibility of ethnic attitudes, the ability to differentiate between members of the same group, which appears with age. Flexibility in ethnic cognition was found to increase at around the age of seven, and this ability to differentiate is thought to be characteristic of concrete operational thinking (Aboud, 1981; Davey, 1983; Katz and Zalk, 1974).

In line with Piaget, Aboud (1988) proposes that children will be sensitive to social factors which address their age-related concerns. As such, input from sources such as television, parents or peers will be interpreted with respect to the child's current concerns such as attachment, fear, reward or approval. However, later work by Aboud and Doyle (1996) did not find any correlation between parental attitudes, the child's perception of parental attitudes and the child's own attitudes towards ethnic groups in nine-year-old black, Chinese, white and East Indian children. Similar findings were obtained examining relationships between friends and non-friend peers (Aboud and

Doyle, 1996). The proposed shifts from egocentrism to group focus and then to individual focus (see Figure 7.1) is linked to ethnic prejudice. At the egocentric stage, the child will only like those people who fulfil their needs. At the group focus stage, the child will only like those people with whom they share group membership, and at the individual stage, other people are no longer considered purely in terms of their group membership, but also on the basis of individual attributes.

In summary, therefore, Aboud's (1988) theory proposes that when affective processes dominate the child's functioning the child will focus on the self. When perceptual processes dominate, a preoccupation with groups will occur, and when cognitive processes dominate, the focus will shift to individuals. It is suggested that higher levels of prejudice will occur during the group stage, with a reduction being expected when cognitive processes dominate, allowing the child to focus on individual variation. Individual differences in prejudice occur as a result of the child not being exposed to or not attending to information which may facilitate lower levels of prejudice, although the child is also cognitively capable of being less prejudiced.

7.4 Children's ethnic attitudes

In this section, research findings relating to children's attitudes towards other ethnic groups are discussed. The majority of research was done in the United States or Canada and was mostly carried out prior to 1980. Very little work has been conducted in this area since then. A notable exception is the work by Nesdale, Griffith, Durkin and Maass (2005) who conducted a minimal group experiment with Anglo-Australian children aged 5–12. They found an interaction between empathy and ethnic prejudice where out-group members were liked more when children felt empathy towards them.

Studies into ethnic identity in childhood used a variety of measures including the following: forced-choice measures (often involving props such as dolls) (Asher and Allen, 1969; Clark and Clark, 1947); multiple item measures, such as The Pre-School Racial Attitude Measure (PRAMI & PRAMII) (Williams, Best and Boswell, 1975a; Williams, Best, Boswell et al., 1975b) and the Katz-Zalk Projective Prejudice Test (Katz and Zalk, 1974; Zalk and Katz, 1976); continuous rating scales, such as the Social Distance Scale (Aboud, 1983; Aboud and Mitchell, 1977); and friendship measures (Whitley, Schofield and Snyder, 1984). These measures are outlined and discussed in this section in relation to empirical findings obtained on children's ethnic attitudes. It is important to note, however, that poor inter-correlations have been found between the following: Projective Prejudice Test, Intolerance Scale, Dogmatism Scale and Measure of Social Distance (all of which are assumed to measure prejudice) (Katz et al., 1975). However, unsurprisingly, given the similarity of the two tasks, a correlation of 0.3 was found with the PRAM doll technique and a modified doll task (Branch and Newcombe, 1980; 1986). From this, Aboud (1988) concludes that prejudice is a unitary construct. However, it could also be suggested that prejudice is not a unitary construct, with the different measures tapping into various factors involved in prejudice. Furthermore, it could also be hypothesized that such poor correlations cast doubt on the reliability of the various measures. In addition, it should be noted that the inter-correlations of the measures may indicate poor validity of the measures themselves. Again, this casts doubt on the suggestion that prejudice is a unitary construct.

7.4.1 White children's attitudes to other groups

Research has shown that white children from the age of three to seven express negative attitudes towards black children (Asher and Allen, 1969; Clark and Clark, 1947; Kircher and Furby, 1971; Renninger and Williams, 1966; Vaughan, 1964). Asher and Allen (1969) used a forced-choice measure in which children were presented with two puppets, one black and one white, and asked a series of simple questions such as 'Which puppet would you like to play with?', 'Which puppet looks bad?' and so on. When presented with attribute tasks, white children tend to describe black children with the negative attributes and as being the least preferred playmate. The findings were similar using Asian and Native Indian as additional out-groups (Aboud, 1977, 1980; Clark, Hovecar and Dembo, 1980; Corenblum and Wilson, 1982; Morland and Hwang, 1981). Such forced-choice measures, however, do not produce definitive results, as it cannot be determined whether children are stating their preferences for the puppet itself, and whether the preferences can be generalized to the members of the racial group that the doll represents. In addition, a false polarization effect is obtained with these measures, in that by accepting one puppet, the child is rejecting the other. This does not enable degrees of liking and disliking to be evaluated, nor does it allow mixed feelings to be expressed, for example, ambivalence or acceptance that intra-group variability exists.

Studies investigating the developmental progression of prejudice have obtained conflicting findings. It has been found that prejudice begins to decline from the age of seven (Aboud, 1980; Clark et al., 1980). However, other research has found that prejudice does not decline, but remains constant from the ages 7 to 12 (Davey, 1983). Yet other studies, in contrast, have observed a trend with children actually becoming more prejudiced at around age seven, with a reduction occurring at around ten years (George and Hoppe, 1979; Vaughan, 1964). However, there are methodological issues such as the small number of items used in measures and the possible confound between a preference for the in-group and rejecting the out-group, which may affect the findings obtained in particular studies.

Aboud and Mitchell (1977), for example, used a social distance task with multiple out-groups. Children aged 6–12 were first asked to label photographs of children according to ethnic group membership. The children were then presented with a 60cm ruler, and were given a stick figure to represent themselves. Two photographs at a time were placed at either end of the ruler and the children were asked to place their stick figure on the board in relation to the photographs to display how close they would like to be to each child. The younger children liked their own group best and disliked the out-groups, whereas the older children held less dichotomized attitudes, liking their own group less, and disliking the out-groups less. Similar findings were also obtained in earlier work (Aboud and Mitchell, 1977). However, the methodological problem with this task is the implication of dislike for the child whose photograph is not kept close to the stick figure, whereas, it is possible to like both photographs and wish to be close to both children, but having a slight preference for one over the other. This task could, therefore, lead to a false polarization of attitudes. In addition, using this method the child may be classifying the person in the picture at the individual rather than the group level. However, this method does allow several examples from each racial group to be evaluated.

7.4.2 White children's attitudes to whites

There is evidence that white children show strong in-group preference from the age of five, regardless of whether the alternative ethnic groups are Asian, black, Hispanic or Native Indian (Aboud, 1977; Asher and Allen, 1969). Nevertheless, Stephan and Rosenfield (1979) found that at around the age of seven, white children became less positive about their in-group and in general began to express positive affect for all groups. However, children's preferences were found to be subject to experimenter effects, with children interviewed by black or Hispanic interviewers expressing a preference for this ethnic group (Corenblum and Wilson, 1982; Katz and Zalk, 1974). Clark et al. (1980), however, found no experimenter effects. Thus, the findings regarding interviewer effects are contradictory and it may therefore be useful to conduct a systematic investigation into these effects.

7.4.3 Black children's attitudes to own and other groups

Kircher and Furby (1971) reviewed 36 studies of black children's attitudes which were carried out in North America and Britain where black children were the minority and in South Africa where they were the majority. Little consensus was found overall and no trends relating to whether the children were in the minority or majority group were obtained. Nevertheless, in 16 of the studies, the black children did not show a preference for their in-group and in some studies rated the out-group (whites) more positively (Asher and Allen, 1969). However, the majority of these studies used the forced-choice measure using materials such as dolls and as such should be regarded with caution for methodological reasons.

In general, younger black children (below seven years) will occasionally demonstrate out-group favouritism, which declines between the age of seven and ten (Davey, 1983; Semaj, 1980). However, this phenomenon is dependent on the particular out-group presented for comparison, with in-group favouritism being more likely if the out-group is another minority group rather than the majority (white) group (Aboud and Doyle, 1996). The degree to which children become pro-black after the age of seven appears to depend on their initial attitude, with a small shift towards being pro-black. Thus, black children who were very pro-white initially may become neutral, whereas a child who was neutral may become more pro-black (Williams et al., 1975a). It could be extrapolated from the in-group favouritism occasionally shown by minority children that they have a lower self-esteem than the majority children. Rosenberg and Simmons (1971), however, found that this was not necessarily the case.

However, Schofield (1978) suggested that black children are often not aware of their own ethnicity. The children in this study were shown photographs of children playing in a school playground, and were asked to identify a child who represented themselves and which children would be their friends. Black children were more likely to identify themselves as a white child until around the age of seven, but later they began to identify with a member of their own group. It could be, however, that the children were choosing their own character on the basis of a factor other than race. For example, it could have been because of the activity that the white child was engaged in, the people around the particular child in the photograph or because of a completely arbitrary reason.

Much of the work examining the attitudes of minority children has used multiple item measures. There are two main types of multiple item measures which have been used in the research: The Pre-School Racial Attitude Measure (PRAM & PRAMII) (Williams et al., 1975a; 1975b), and the Katz-Zalk Projective Prejudice Test (Katz and Zalk, 1974; Zalk and Katz, 1976). Both tests use photographs of two racial groups. The PRAM consists of 24 items relating to race and 12 filler items relating to gender. The items consist of questions such as: 'Here are two girls (child shown two photographs, one of a black girl and one of a white girl) one of them is an ugly girl. People do not like to look at her. Which is the ugly girl?' The intensity of attitude in the PRAM is obtained by summing the number of pro-white and anti-black (or vice versa) choices made. However, it should be noted that the use of a criterion level after which a child can be considered prejudiced is artificial. Furthermore, once again, the rejection of one group is confounded by the acceptance of another. This can be overcome by allowing the child to choose both pictures. It has been shown that when children are permitted to choose both pictures, they will indeed tend to do so (Davey, 1983; Doyle, Beaudet and Aboud, 1988). This measure does, however, allow generalizability across contexts to be assessed through using many different contexts and adjectives. Using the PRAM, attitudes towards two ethnic groups can be assessed by asking children to assign attributes to racial groups. This has been done using boxes for each ethnic group. More recent research using such measures includes that by Barrett, Wilson and Lyons (1999). Here, investigating children's attitudes to national groups has allowed the children to assign attributes to both ethnic groups by providing a 'both' box. Similarly, Takriti (2002) asked children to evaluate two religious groups separately, thus allowing the children to evaluate both groups in a similar way if they wished. An alternative method would be to give two copies of each attribute card to the child, although this may cue the child to use both cards.

The lack of consensus in the findings relating to black children's attitudes may reflect the fact that the studies have been conducted in different countries, where although the black children are still in the minority, either numerically or in terms of status or power, cultural variations may exist which could influence the findings. In addition, as Brown (1997) points out, there appeared to be a shift in the empirical findings at around 1970. Prior to 1970, a conflicting picture of attitudes held by minority children was obtained, with some children showing no preference for either the in-group or the out-group and other children showing a clear pro-out-group bias (Asher and Allen, 1969). However, subsequent to 1970, findings have emerged with minority children showing a clear preference for their in-group (Aboud, 1980; Braha and Rutter, 1980). Such changes in attitude may link to socio-political changes which were occurring around that time, such as the Civil Rights Movement in the United States, and as such this shift highlights the fact that children's attitudes do not develop in a vacuum but may be linked to changes in the social world.

7.4.4 Attitudes held by other minority groups

Hispanic children living in the United States tend to follow the same trend as black children, holding neutral or pro-white attitudes before the age of seven, and becoming more pro-Hispanic subsequently (Newman, Liss and Sherman, 1983). Studies involving Asian children have not been well documented (Aboud, 1977; Davey, 1983). Nevertheless, a trend is noted with the Asian children being pro-white in the early years, later becoming more pro-Asian and rejecting towards blacks.

7.4.5 Implications of empirical work relating to ethnicity

It can be seen that ethnic attitudes are highly dependent upon ethnic group membership. Generally, minority children do not demonstrate out-group prejudice, and in some cases have even been found to identify with the out-group, whereas white majority children tend to identify firmly with their in-group and show a marked prejudice towards out-groups. This asymmetry between the attitudes of white and black children has been shown consistently and using a variety of different techniques (Brand, Ruiz and Padilla, 1974; Jahoda, Thomson and Bhatt, 1972). It was also clearly demonstrated in Asher and Allen's (1969) study, where three- to eight-year-old black and white children showed a clear pro-white bias, which peaked at ages five to six and declining at seven to eight. However, majority of the research obtaining these findings was conducted before the mid-1970s, and a different trend has been noted in later research conducted in the 1970s, with the ambivalence previously noted in black children decreasing and an in-group preference emerging. For example, Hraba and Grant (1970) presented four- to eight-year-old children with the standard two-doll choice and found that both black and white children made pro-in-group choices, with the proportion of children doing so increasing with age (see also, Aboud, 1980; Braha and Rutter, 1980; Stephan and Rosenfield, 1979). This apparent change in children's attitudes requires further investigation. However, there have been many socio-political changes since the mid-1970s, for example, as mentioned earlier, the black civil rights movement in the United States, and this change in children's attitudes suggests that they may be affected by the wider socio-political environment.

A later study by Bennett, Dewbury and Yeeles (1991) presented white children aged 8 and 11 living in a largely white area with 24 photographs of children varying on the basis of sex, race and facial expression. The children were asked to sort the photographs in any way they wished and they were asked if there were any photographs that they liked/disliked and to explain their choices. The children neglected race and sorted mainly on the basis of facial expression and, in justification, only 3 per cent mentioned race. McGuire's (1984) distinctiveness theory would suggest that the children's focus on personal rather than group characteristics is due to the largely white population in which the children lived, with personal characteristics being more salient as a function of how distinctive the child's group is within the population. To test this, the study was replicated with white and ethnic minority children living in a multicultural area. Again, the majority of children did not refer to race, although there was a tendency to mention race in justifications by the eight-year-olds. From these studies, Bennett et al. (1991) suggest that the previous findings about ethnicity are an artefact of methodologies which denied children the opportunity to consider race in relation to individual variables.

It could be suggested that inter-ethnic contact, for example in mixed ethnic schools, could influence children's attitudes towards ethnic groups. According to the contact hypothesis (Hewstone and Brown, 1986), increased contact with members of other ethnic groups should result in a reduction in prejudice through exposure to counter-stereotypical attitudes. The majority of studies have found lower levels of prejudice in multi-ethnic schools (Davey, 1983; Friedman, 1980), although less so for children below the age of eight (Brown and Johnson, 1971; Milner, 1973). However, overall evidence for the contact hypothesis has been mixed. There is some evidence that positive affect resulting from contact with individual members of a group does not generalize to the group as a whole, with children simultaneously holding a negative attitude towards an out-group whilst holding a friend from that group in positive regard (Aronson, Blaney, Stephin, Sikes and Snapp, 1978; Davey, 1983). This could, however, be due to the overemphasis on interpersonal rather than inter-group interaction, or that the friendship is based on individualistic aspects of the friend such as loyalty or humour. Consequently, the contact hypothesis may be difficult to test empirically, in that the group dimension must be stressed, as in team games. Such situations may foster increased feelings of competitiveness leading to increased prejudice.

Hallinan and Teixeira (1987) found that the more the number of black minority group members in a classroom, the more likely it was that a black child would be nominated as a best friend by a white majority group member but this did not hold true in the opposite case (i.e., the proportion of white children did not influence the black child's best-friend nomination).

Three modifications to the contact hypothesis have been proposed: the decategorization model, redefining boundaries and individualization (Brown, 2000). Brewer and Miller (1984) proposed the decategorization model, which aims to decategorize groups by identifying new groups which cut across the old ones or by stressing the interpersonal level of identity, reducing the impact of group membership. Evidence has supported this method of reducing in-group bias with children (Bettencourt, Charlton and Kernaham, 1997; Bettencourt, Brewer, Croak and Miller, 1992). However, research into the decategorization model has focused on laboratory groups and it is not clear how effective this method of reducing prejudice would be in real-world groups, who may not find it so easy to abandon their group memberships.

It is theoretically possible to redefine category boundaries to include both the in-group and the out-group and make the new category salient (Gaertner, Dovidio, Anastasio et al., 1993). This should have the effect of reducing the perception of inter-group differences and therefore reducing inter-group bias. For example, the subcategories of Pakistani and Indian could be redefined as Asian, making the two groups share the same in-group identity. Such a strategy has been proven to increase contact between groups and decrease bias (Dovidio, Gaertner and Validzic, 1998). Again, however, the majority of work in this area has not utilized real-world groups, and as Brown (2000) points out, it may be that individuals may still revert to categorizing at the old group level. This may be especially true for minority groups, who may view the decategorizing strategy as an attempt to assimilate their group into a dominant culture.

Hewstone and Brown (1986) found support for a third approach which aims to identify out-group members as individuals rather than just out-group members, hence making the contact as positive as possible and stressing that the particular member is typical of other out-group members. Such a strategy has had positive implications for contact and reduction in bias in real-world groups (Brown, Vivian and Hewstone, 1999; Brown, Maras, Masser et al., 2000; Gonzalez and Brown, 1999).

In summary, Pettigrew (1998) suggests that a combination of all three contact strategies would be effective in reducing inter-group prejudice. He suggests that first the group interactions should be decategorized so that the personal level of analysis is evoked. The strategy advocated by Hewstone and Brown (1986) is suggested to be the next step in reducing prejudice, whereby subgroup identities are allowed to become salient. Finally, the groups should be allowed to recategorize into meaningful subgroups.

STUDY TASK

Revisit the work on ethnic attitudes and classify each of the studies according to the methodology used.
What are the advantages and disadvantages of each of the methods?

7.5 Religious identity

Religious identity can be seen as a social identity and as such can vary in salience according to situational context. It has been suggested that children are likely to follow their parents' religion, with estimates of between 40 per cent and 90 per cent of children doing so (Argyle and Beit-Hallahmi, 1975; Beit-Hallahmi and Argyle, 1997). The smaller proportion is more typical of liberal faiths where religious participation is not compulsory. Thus, such findings should be treated with caution as the meaning of being religious differs between religious groups and simply categorizing oneself as being a religious group member does not imply the holding of strong religious beliefs. However, a study by Hoge and Petrillo (1978) on the effect of peers, type and quality of church programmes and family factors on the church attendance found family factors to have the most impact with a correlation of 0.6 between church attendance in adolescents and that of their parents.

As in other areas of social understanding in children, the majority of the work investigating the development of religious identity has been based to some degree on the Piagetian framework of cognitive development in children. Harms (1944), one of the first researchers to study religious thought in childhood, studied Christian children's spontaneous drawings from age three to adolescence, and also asked the children to comment on their drawings. Three stages were derived. Stage 1 was characterized by a large degree of uniformity with children portraying God as a king or daddy, living in a house in the sky or resting on clouds. At this stage, God was viewed as a fantasy in the same way as dragons or giants, and hence this stage was termed the Fairy-Tale stage. This stage was typical of children aged three to six. Stage 2, the Realistic stage, was found in children aged 6–11 with God being portrayed in a human form. Stage 3, the Individualistic stage, appeared from adolescence and showed a wide variety of portrayals of God running from the conventional to the creative or mystical. No specific link was made between the findings of this study and Piagetian stages of cognitive development. However, it can be seen that Stage 2 links with the concrete operational stage of development with understanding of God being seen in concrete terms. This study was replicated by Tamm (1996) with a sample of 9–19-year-old Swedish participants. The degree of anthropomorphic representations of God was again found to decrease with age. Interestingly, Johnson (1961) found that six-year-old UK children were very reluctant to draw God.

Goldman (1964) established a Piagetian paradigm in the studying of religious thinking in children through the establishment of his 'Picture and Story Religious Thinking Test'. The test consisted of three pictures showing a child entering a church, a child kneeling in prayer and a child reading from a mutilated Bible. In addition, three Biblical texts were used: Moses and the burning bush, the Red Sea crossing and the temptations of Jesus. The initial sample of 200 children aged 6–18 revealed age-related stages in religious understanding. Younger children's understanding was characterized by literal interpretations, such as the burning bush being placed in water and then lit again. The next stage in understanding was the concrete stage where children made logical but limited interpretations, such as the bush being lit by an electric torch. The older children had attained formal operational thought and were, therefore, capable of symbolic interpretations such as God appearing in the bush. As such, the children's understanding is shown to become less embedded and more abstract with age.

Matthews (1966) and Godin (1968) criticized Goldman's research saying that the biblical narratives used by Goldman were particularly abstract and that by de-contextualizing the narratives and highlighting the supernatural it was very difficult for children to give a logical answer. In addition, the questions used were somewhat leading. For example: 'Supposing Moses had got over his fear and looked at God, what do you think he would have seen?' This question could lead the child to believe that Moses would have seen something and makes giving the answer indicative of formal operational thought, that Moses would not have seen anything, more difficult to express.

Goldman (1964) suggested that the development of formal operational thought would lead the adolescent to critically assess their theological understanding which would lead to a decline in positive attitude towards religious education, in this case Christianity. Forlitti and Benson (1986) found in a sample of 8165 adolescents that approximately 50 per cent claimed that their religion was very important to them. There is evidence, however, to suggest that attitude towards religion becomes less positive during adolescence (Potvin and Lee, 1982; Turner, Turner and Reid, 1980). Francis (1987) examined the attitudes of 800 children, aged between 8 and 15, towards different school subjects using bipolar adjectival pairs to evaluate the subjects. At age eight, religious education was evaluated positively. However, after the age of ten, religious education consistently occupied the lowest position in the children's relative preference of school subjects, with no similar pattern found in attitudes towards other school subjects. It was not clear from this evidence, however, if this decline correlated with the development of formal operational thought per se. Kay, Francis and Gibson (1996) tested this with a sample of 6098 participants aged 11–15. The participants completed standardized IQ tests, a test of cognitive function, and the Francis Scale of Attitude towards Christianity, a 24-item Likert scale assessing evaluative and affective attitudes towards God, Jesus, the Bible, prayer, church and the expression of Christianity in schools. No evidence was found that the appearance of formal operational thought impacted on attitudes towards Christianity.

Elkind (1961; 1962; 1963; 1964; 1970; 1971) postulated that while cognitive development does not guarantee religious development it does have a profound effect on the type and level of religious thinking that children are capable of. Elkind (1961; 1962; 1963; 1964) interviewed Jewish, Catholic and Protestant children aged between 5 and 14 about

Table 7.2 Stages of religious development as proposed by Elkind (1961)

Stage	Age	Description
1	5–7	The children had a global undifferentiated concept of religious identity. They knew that the terms referred to people and were related to God, but they were unable to choose whether the terms related to ethnicity, race or religion. The children in this stage were not aware of what constituted a religious group and had problems understanding class inclusion. Consequently, in this stage, children had a vague impression of their family's religious denomination.
2	7–9	The children in this stage had a clear understanding that the religious terms related to people, as they had a clear knowledge of concrete referents by which groups can be distinguished. The children understood group labels and could use them spontaneously. They were also capable of understanding multiple group memberships, such as being Jewish and American. This stage was dominated by a concrete conception of religion as based in behaviour. For example: you are Catholic because you go to Church.
3	10–12	Children in this stage looked for evidence of religious group membership in religious beliefs and actions, and as such their understanding had become more abstracted. These children understood that denominations were characterized by shared beliefs and understood multiple group memberships. It is at this stage that an abstract concept of religion involving belief, faith and conviction begins to emerge.

their religions using a semi-structured interview technique. The interview focused mainly on items relating to class inclusion such as 'Can cats and dogs be Jewish?' or 'Can you be Jewish and American?' Three stages of development were obtained as shown in Table 7.2.

In Elkind's 1970 paper, the relationship between religion and cognitive development was stated explicitly in terms of religion facilitating four cognitive needs. The need for conservation is met by religion in that religious belief provides an explanation of the afterlife and death. The need for representation is facilitated by religion in that an acceptance of the existence of God has been reached; children will therefore search for a representation of Him, which is a by-product of children searching for representations in general. Religion provides this representation through scriptural teaching. The need for relations is met by children attempting to relate themselves to God in the same way as they try to understand relations in other non-religious spheres, such as A + B = C. It is suggested that this need is met through worship and prayer. Finally, the need for comprehension in adolescence is met through theology. As such, it can be seen that Elkind claims a close fit between four cognitive need capacities and major elements of institutionalized religion, which develops in line with cognitive development. Elkind (1970) suggested that the child's understanding of object permanence comes to interact with the discovery that s/he and others must die. This conflict between the desire for permanence and the inevitability of death impacts fully in adolescence and is solved by religion through teaching the concept of God. Elkind suggests that the religious analogies, metaphors and abstractions which are common in religion are difficult for younger children to understand and that they interact with experience and cognitive abilities. Thus, a likely explanation for religious understanding is that it develops with age and in stages.

Long, Elkind and Spilka (1967) studied the development of the concept of prayer. Interviews were carried out with a sample of 160 children aged between 5 and 12. The interview consisted of six open-ended questions such as 'What is prayer?' and four incomplete sentences such as 'I usually pray when ...' Three stages were proposed. In Stage 1, children aged between five and seven were often unable to understand the questions and gave global and undifferentiated responses. This was assumed to reflect an almost non existent understanding of prayer. It could be suggested, however, that the children in this stage simply did not understand the questions and a different methodology could have improved their 'stage of understanding'. In Stage 2, seven- to nine-year-olds were characterized by a clear, differentiated and concrete understanding of prayer, with the goal of prayer being specific, for example, to ask for a new toy. The final stage, Stage 3, from nine years onwards was characterized by the beginnings of an abstract conception of prayer. It was suggested that each of the stages paralleled a stage of cognitive development: Stage 1 being typical of children in the preoperational stage, Stage 2 of concrete operational and Stage 3 of formal operational thought.

Fowler (1981) specified a six-stage theory of the development of religious concepts, describing how the individual's understanding of faith develops from being constructed from simple narrowly defined concepts to highly complex, multifaceted concepts. Fowler linked this to the work of Erikson (1968) and Piaget (1969). The work of Erikson (1968) would view the development of religious understanding as the by-product of the predetermined and invariant

Table 7.3 Fowler's (1981) stages of the development of religious concepts in childhood

Stage	Description
Intuitive Projective Faith	Beliefs at this stage are based on an omnipotent and magical view of God, with natural phenomena such as lightning and sunshine being seen as punishment or praise from God.
Mythic-literal faith	This stage is common in childhood, and faith is dominated by a literal acceptance of the dogma of religion and a strict adherence to the concrete symbols used in religion, such as crosses. Rules are adhered to and viewed as leading to rewards from God. This can be linked to work on moral development (Kohlberg, Levine and Hewer, 1983) with children seeing rules as fixed, non-negotiable and unchangeable, with obedience to them occurring in order to obtain rewards and avoid punishment.
Synthetic-conventional faith	Faith provides a social structure with which to deal with the complexities of life. Again, religious rules are interpreted rigidly and members of the faith community are expected to adhere to all the rules.
Individuating-reflexive faith	This stage is common during late adolescence where a struggle between loyalty to the religious community and a quest for individuality occurs. The completion of this stage requires the adolescent to personalize their religion and recognize personal responsibility to their faith.
Paradoxical-consolidative faith	Individuals recognize and appreciate the integrity and validity of other religions.
Universalizing faith	Only a few people attain this stage. People in this stage are able to live in harmony with all people.

maturation of the human being which sets the scene for acquiring knowledge and social understanding. Fowler's (1981) stages are outlined in Table 7.3. It should be noted, however, that Fowler used the term religion to refer to a life philosophy with explicit affiliation with a religious group not being a necessary requirement in the development of faith.

Berryman, Davies and Simmons (1981) criticized Fowler for combining the two approaches offered by Piaget and Erikson as they are not truly compatible, with Erikson offering a linear explanation of development whereas Piaget's approach is hierarchical in nature. In addition, Fowler's stages were derived from work using small sample sizes, where the majority of the adult sample were recruited from academic colleagues and students (Jardine and Viljoen, 1992).

A major criticism of work in this area is the limited samples of children used with much of the research having focused on Jewish children and Christian children of various denominations. As such, it can be seen that children from other religious groups, for example, Muslim and Hindu children, have been largely ignored in research. It has been suggested that this is due to researchers being committed believers in Judeo-Christian religions, leading them to neglect other religions in their research (Furnham and Stacey, 1991). It could also be suggested that at the time when much of the empirical work in this field was undertaken, minority groups were not easily accessible for research.

An exception to this is the work by Takriti et al. (2006) where Christian, Asian Muslim, Arab Muslim and Hindu children aged between 5 and 11 were interviewed about their religious beliefs and their evaluations of their own and other religious groups. All of the children correctly identified themselves as being members of their religious groups, and expressed positive attitudes towards their own religious group. However, this interview was cued, in that the children were aware of the focus of the interview and this could have increased the apparent salience of religion for the children (Case Study 1).

CASE STUDY 1: JUSTIFICATIONS GIVEN BY CHILDREN FOR RELIGIOUS GROUP MEMBERSHIP AND BELIEF IN GOD(S).

I'm a Christian because I kind of like the Bible because it doesn't seem to have any stories which are hard to believe. I was born, my mum and dad were both Christians and most of my family and friends are Christians. They all go to a church I know and they have a Sunday school afterwards. I decided that I would like to go to Sunday school because it sounded like fun... I like parties and stuff. I think it is fun because people have Christmas parties but they don't really realise what is behind it. God is great and I believe in Him, all those reasons is why I am a Christian. (Christian male, aged 11)

I can tell you that some Gods can do more things than other Gods. I've got lots of Gods. My favourite one is this little elephant one which I love the best. He has six hands, elephant head and two legs. Once they had a war against these baddie Gods. I believe this. (Hindu female, aged 6)

Source: Examples from Takriti et al. (2006)

A study by Takriti (2002) asked Christian, Muslim and Hindu children aged between 5 and 11 to rate their religious identity alongside other social identities such as age, gender and ethnicity in a non-cued context. Takriti found that religion became more important with age in this relative context. Overall, the Muslim children rated religious identity higher than the other groups, with the majority of the Muslim children rating religious identity as their most important social identity.

In summary, following work by Goldman (1964) and Elkind (1970), the majority of the research investigating religion in childhood defined it as characterized by different levels of logical thinking (Francis, 1979). The validity of the Piagetian stages is assumed and the stages are treated as normative (McGrady, 1983). Thus, the results obtained in the majority of studies have been analysed by the application of stage criteria to subjects' responses to Piagetian-style dilemmas modelled on Goldman's design (Slee, 1986). As such, research interest in religious understanding has been dominated by testing the presence and nature of religious thinking in terms of Piagetian-style stages. The majority of the results have shown religious thinking being determined by the development of cognitive structures developing from an intuitive, undifferentiated structure of thought to one bound by concrete realities and finally to abstract, reversible and logical thinking. More recent work (Takriti, 2002; Takriti et al., 2006) has moved away from this to a conceptualization of religion as part of a child's identity.

7.6 Social-psychological theories

Given that children from different religious groups appear to understand and evaluate their own religious group in differing ways, it is likely that the Piagetian-based explanations of religious and ethnic identities do not provide an adequate account of children's development in this area. We can see that in order to further research in the field of identity development in children, it is necessary to utilize theories which consider the effects of socialization and therefore group differences. There are two main theoretical approaches which could be applied to research in this area, Social Identity Theory (SIT) (Tajfel, 1979) and Self-Categorization Theory (SCT) (Oakes, Haslam and Turner, 1994; Turner, Hogg, Oakes et al., 1987). According to these approaches, individuals are *de facto* members of several social groups (e.g., ethnic, religious, gender), and subjectively identify with and classify themselves as members of some of these groups.

7.6.1 Social Identity Theory (SIT)

In terms of SIT, this self-categorization process enables the individual to structure an understanding of the social world and provides a system of orientation for understanding self-reference and defining one's position and status in society. The categorization process simplifies the social world by accentuating similarities within groups and differences between groups; this is termed the accentuation hypothesis. It is the self-categorization process which enables the individual to determine in any given context which group s/he belongs to (the in-group) and those groups to which s/he does not belong (the out-groups), and as such involves the processes of perception and categorization. Social identity is defined as:

> that part of an individual's self-concept that derives from his knowledge of his membership of a social group or groups, together with the value and emotional significance attached to that membership. (Tajfel, 1979, p. 52)

SIT postulates the motivation to evaluate the self positively, thus, in so far as group membership is significant to self-definition, the in-group will be evaluated positively. The value which any particular group membership holds is dependent upon comparison with other social groups. The accentuation hypothesis can therefore be seen to be a cognitive by-product of the motivation to achieve and maintain a positive self-esteem. In-group favouritism is not, however, an automatic result of minimal social categorization, but is seen as a function of the following:

- the degree of identification with the in-group
- the salience of the categorization
- the relevance and importance of the comparative dimension to the in-group identity
- the degree to which groups can be compared on the particular dimension
- the in-group status and the nature of the perceived differences between the groups.

It follows, therefore, that if an out-group were to be seen as superior to the in-group on a relevant and salient dimension, then out-group favouritism could be expected to occur. As such, SIT proposes that the likelihood of inter-group relationships resulting in prejudice is not solely determined by the process of categorization alone. Social categorization places behaviour into a group-based context, and the probability of prejudice occurring is then dependent on that particular inter-group relationship.

7.6.2 Self-Categorization Theory (SCT)

SCT (Oakes et al., 1994; Turner et al., 1987) may be seen as an extension to SIT. SIT does not discuss the effect of context on self-categorization, whereas SCT views categorization as a dynamic process which is highly context dependent. Any categorization is determined by the comparative relations, or comparative fit within a given context, which is termed the Principle of Meta-Contrast. This proposes that a set of items is likely to be categorized together to the extent that the differences within that set of items are less than the differences when compared with other sets. For example, a collection of fruits will more likely be classified by a perceiver as 'fruit' rather than, for example, pears and peaches if seen with vegetables than with other fruits. Normative fit also influences perception. Normative fit refers to the content of the match between the category specifications and the instances being represented. For example, the English should be more alike to each other than to the French (comparative fit) and should differ from each other on expected dimensions. For example, the French should support the French rugby team and the English, the English rugby team (normative fit). As such, groups form on the basis of inter-group differences in a manner aimed at ensuring that the differences between the groups are greater than those within them. The selective activation or salience of social categories is determined by the relative accessibility of the category and the perceiver's motivation to use the category and the fit (both normative and comparative). Accessibility is the product of past experiences, expectations, current goals, tasks and purposes, ensuring that categorization is linked to changing circumstances, goals and contexts. Fit ensures that categories are not applied despite contradictory evidence (Haslam, Oakes, Turner and McGarty, 1995).

SCT postulates that social categorizations are highly context dependent, with an individual possibly being categorized according to their gender on one occasion and in terms of their job on another occasion with no actual change in their position. According to the theory, changes in comparative context can result in changes in inter-group relationships and intra-category structure. The different levels of identity are highly dependent upon each other with social identity being dependent upon having a set of groups with which to self-categorize, and personal identity being dependent upon individual differences.

Social categorization will become more likely as inter-group differences increase and intra-group differences decrease. The accentuation principle plays a part in exaggerating inter-group differences and intra-group similarities associated with salient comparison features.

7.6.3 Social categorization, in-group and out-group relations

Stereotyping and prejudice are the outcome of social categorical perception, that is, the product of categorizing at the group level. Categories become salient through an interaction between accessibility and fit, both normative and comparative – meta-contrast. When a category becomes salient it results in the depersonalization of group members, leading to representation at the inter-group rather than the interpersonal level. As fit is linked to reality, stereotyping varies with the social context, in terms of society and the comparative context. Accentuation has the effect of minimizing within-group differences, and so group members are seen as homogeneous. However, frequently out-group members are perceived as more homogenous than in-group members. For example, Mullen and Hu (1989) conducted a meta-analysis of studies showing the out-group homogeneity effect and concluded that it was a significant though small finding. Linville, Salovey and Fischer (1986) suggested that the out-group homogeneity effect occurs as a result of the individual having more familiarity with in-group members leading to more exemplar-based knowledge of the in-group and the perception of greater out-group homogeneity. Judd and Park (1988) extended this theory with the dual-storage model, proposing that individuals hold general information or abstract summaries about groups which are then extended by exemplar information. Following this, greater out-group homogeneity can be expected as more variable abstractions are stored for in-groups which are then supplemented by more exemplar-based information, leading to a greater perception of in-group variability. The out-group homogeneity effect can be seen as the result of three factors:

- a lack of contact with the out-group (Park and Rothbart, 1982)
- a greater awareness of in-group subgroups (Judd, Ryan and Park, 1991)
- a motivation to represent the in-group more accurately (Judd and Park, 1988).

SIT would predict symmetry in judgements of the in-group and out-groups (Tajfel, 1979). SCT predicts that perceived similarity occurs to the extent that group members are categorized as members of a group within which similarity is accentuated. Group members will be perceived as variable to the extent that they are classified at a lower level of abstraction, in terms of individual personal categories between which differences are accentuated. As such, the theory predicts symmetry between in-group and out-group homogeneity in so far as both groups are evaluated in an explicitly inter-group context. The robust research findings for greater perceived out-group homogeneity can be expected to have occurred because of an asymmetry in the contexts in which the in-group and out-group were evaluated with the in-group being judged at a more interpersonal level.

SCT and SIT have been applied to religious groups. In a study of Muslims (majority group) and Hindus (minority group) in Bangladesh, Islam and Hewstone (1993) obtained support for the theories with both groups showing in-group favouritism when asked to rate both groups. However, only Muslims were found to be out-group denigrating.

Research suggests that children are capable of understanding group status differences (Vaughan, Tajfel and Williams, 1981). Combining research findings with SIT and SCT, Vaughan (1987) offers an explanation for the apparent out-group preference shown by minority children. When children from minority groups compare their in-group with the relevant out-groups, the comparison can lead to the in-group being perceived as inferior. This would result in lowering self-esteem, and the child may express a preference for the out-group.

Takriti (2002) applied SIT and SCT to religious identity with Christian and Muslim children aged between 5 and 11. The children were asked to evaluate their own and one other religious group according to positivity (how much they like the group) and homogeneity (an assessment of how similar group members are to each other). In line with the social-psychological theories, the children did rate their own group as more heterogeneous than the out-group. All of the children did also view their own group in a more positive light. This study did not find evidence for out-group denigration in the Muslim group. This tendency to out-group denigration was seen in an earlier qualitative study by Takriti et al. (2006), where Christian and Hindu children engaged in out-group denigration to a much greater extent than Muslim children. Illustrative examples of what children say about other religious groups are given below (See Case Study 2).

A link between self-esteem and religious identity has been obtained (Takriti, 2005). In particular, Muslim children, who viewed their own

> ### CASE STUDY 2: CHILDREN'S STATEMENTS ABOUT OTHER RELIGIOUS GROUPS
>
> What do children say about members of other religious groups?
>
> Their Hindu Gods are made of rocks and mud and are joined together and painted. Sometimes I look at them and think I wish I could see my God. It makes you happy when you can see your God. Indians always give their Gods food but my God can have all the food by himself because He makes all the food. It is really disgusting because they make statues of their Gods and it takes them a month to make it and then they throw it into the sea. They are stupid to believe in Gods like that. (Christian female, aged 7)
>
> Muslims are all terrorists and like to bomb people. They say that they do it because their God tells them to. My God is better because He believes in peace and love. (Christian female aged 7)
>
> I like all religions because I think it is important for people to socialize and learn from each other and things like that. I believe no-one is different although I still believe in my God. I don't judge people on what they look like or what religion they are. (Muslim male aged 10)
>
> The Muslims have a God called Allah and they have to pray five times a day. I like them and I like that they have to pray a lot. (Hindu male, aged 9)
>
> *Source*: Takriti et al., 2006.

group more positively than either Christian or Hindu children, had a higher self-esteem than either of the other two groups. SIT predicts that a motivation to view the in-group positively serves self-esteem. This does appear to be the case, especially for Muslim children.

7.7 Summary and conclusions

Overall, social-psychological theories appear to be useful in accounting for ethnic and religious identity. More research is needed, however, to assess whether they fully account for children's development, and the role of social and political factors. For example, it could be suggested that in the United Kingdom, Muslims are viewed in a negative light in the current political situation following the terror attacks of

September 11th, 2001 and July 7th, 2005 and the war in Afghanistan and Iraq. A survey of racist incidents in Leicester suggests that the United Kingdom is experiencing a rise in Islamaphobia following the terrorist attacks. Sheridan (2006) showed that religious attacks on Muslims in Leicester rose after September 11. Examples included children being verbally abused on their way to school, and Muslim passengers on buses being accused of being bombers. In Britain overall, more than 300 assaults on Muslims were reported to the police in the year following September 11th, 2001 (Fetzer and Soper, 2005). The data on the relationship between children's self-esteem and religious identity reported above (Takriti, 2005) were collected in 1998 prior to the terror attacks. Data collected in 2006, showed a decrease in Muslim children's self-esteem levels (Takriti and Takriti, 2007).

A negative outcome of group identity is prejudice against other groups. There are many theories of prejudice, and one main theme is that in order to be prejudiced, there must be an awareness of group differences. The issue of children's awareness of group differences has been an active area of research for some time, with work focusing on areas such as ethnicity, race and religion. However, the majority of the work in these areas has taken the cognitive-constructivist theory as a background, and as such offers a domain-general approach to all of children's understanding. Here, it is suggested that this approach is not appropriate for the understanding of children's religious identity and that a social-psychological perspective should be taken to allow for group differences. With the exception of the few studies outlined above, the majority of work using SCT and SIT has focused on adults, leaving the area of children's understanding primarily studied from a cognitive-developmental perspective. Thus, there is little understanding of the development of children's social understanding from a social-psychological perspective. Given that it is apparent that children from different religious and ethnic groups appear to develop their social understanding in different ways, a more social-psychological approach is suggested and more research in this area would be useful.

FURTHER READING

Aboud, F.E. (1988). *Children and prejudice.* Oxford: Blackwell.
Chryssochoou, X. (2004). *Cultural diversity: Its social psychology.* Oxford: Blackwell.
Nelson, T.D. (2006). *The psychology of prejudice.* London: Pearson.

REFERENCES

Aboud, F.E. (1977). Interest in ethnic information: A cross-cultural developmental study. *Canadian Journal of Behavioural Science*, **9**, 134–146.
Aboud, F.E. (1980). A test of ethnocentrism with young children. *Canadian Journal of Behavioural Science*, **12**, 195–209.
Aboud, F.E. (1981). Egocentrism, conformity and agreeing to disagree. *Developmental Psychology*, **17**, 791–799.
Aboud, F.E. (1983). Social and cognitive bases of ethnic identity constancy. *The Journal of Genetic Psychology*, 145(2), 217–230.
Aboud, F.E. (1988). *Children and prejudice*. London: Blackwell.
Aboud, F.E. (1992). *The developmental psychology of racial prejudice*. Paper presented at Racism and Psychiatry seminar. Jewish General Hospital, Montreal. November 13.
Aboud, F.E. and Doyle, A.-B. (1996). Parental and peer influences on children's racial attitudes. *International Journal of Intercultural Relations*, **20**, 1–13.
Aboud, F.E. and Mitchell, F.G. (1977). Ethnic role-taking: The effects of preference and self-identification. *International Journal of Psychology*, **12**, 1–17.
Aboud, F.E. and Skerry, S. (1983). The development of ethnic attitudes. *Journal of Cross Cultural Psychology*, **15**, 3–34.
Adorno, T.W., Frenkel-Brunswick, E., Levinson, D.J., and Sanford, R.N. (1950). *The authoritarian personality*. New York: Harper & Row.
Ali, Y. (1992). Muslim women and the politics of ethnicity and culture in Northen England. In G. Sahgal and N. Yuval-Davis. (Eds), *Refusing holy orders: Women and fundamentalism in Britain* (pp. 17–89). London: Virago.
Allport, G.W. (1954). *The nature of prejudice*. Reading, MA: Addison-Wesley.
Argyle, M. and Beit-Hallahmi, B. (1975). *The social psychology of religion*. London: Routledge and Kegan Paul.
Aronson, E., Blaney, N., Stephin, C., Sikes, J., and Snapp, M. (1978). *The jigsaw classroom*. Beverly Hills, CA: Sage.
Asher, S.R. and Allen, V.L. (1969). Racial preference and social comparison processes. *Journal of Social Issues*, **25**, 157–167.
Barrett, M., Wilson, H., and Lyons, E. (1999). *Self-categorization theory and the development of national identity in English children*. Poster presented at the Biennial meeting of the Society of Research in Child Development. Alburquerque, New Mexico, 15–18 April.
Beit-Hallahmi, B. and Argyle, M. (1997). *The psychology of religious behaviour, belief and experience*. London: Routledge and Kegan Paul.
Bennett, K., Heath, T., and Jeffries, R. (2007). Asylum statistics United Kingdom 2006. *Home Office Statistics Bulletin*, 21st August 2007.
Bennett, M., Dewberry, C., and Yeeles, C. (1991). A reassessment of the role of ethnicity in children's social perception. *Journal of Child Psychology and Psychiatry*, **32**(6), 969–982.
Berryman, J.W., Davies, R.E., and Simmons, H.C. (1981). Comments on the article by Eugene J. Mischey. *Character Potential*, **9**(4), 186–191.

Bettencourt, A., Charlton, K., and Kernaham, C. (1997). Numerical representations of groups in co-operative settings: Social orientation effects on ingroup bias. *Journal of Experimental Social Psychology*, **33**, 630–659.

Bettencourt, B.A., Brewer, M.B., Croak, M.R., and Miller, N. (1992). Cooperation and the reduction of intergroup bias: The role of reward structure and social orientation. *Journal of Experimental Social Psychology*, **28**, 301–309.

Braha, V. and Rutter, D.R. (1980). Friendship choice in a mixed-race primary school. *Educational Studies*, **6**, 217–223.

Branch, C.W. and Newcombe, N. (1980). Racial attitude of Black preschoolers as related to parental civil rights activism. *Merrill-Palmer Quarterly*, **26**, 425–428.

Branch, C.W. and Newcombe, N. (1986). Racial attitude development among young Black children as a function of parental attitudes: A longitudinal and cross-sectional study. *Child Development*, **57**(3), 712–721.

Brand, E.S., Ruiz, R.A., and Padilla, A.M. (1974). Ethnic identification and preference: A review. *Psychological Bulletin*, **81**, 860–890.

Brewer, M.B. and Miller, N.E. (1984). Beyond the contact hypothesis: Theoretical perspectives in desegregation. In N.E. Miller and M.B. Brewer (Eds), *Groups in conflict: The psychology of desegregation* (pp. 112–167). New York: Academic Press.

Brown, G. and Johnson, S.P. (1971). The attribution of behaviour connotations to shaded and white figures by Caucasian children. *British Journal of Social and Clinical Psychology*, **10**, 306–312.

Brown, R. (1997). *Prejudice: Its social psychology*. Oxford: Blackwell.

Brown, R. (2000). Social identity theory: Past achievements, current problems and future challenges. *European Journal of Social Psychology*, **30**(6), 745–778.

Brown, R.J., Maras, P., Masser, B., Vivian, J., and Hewstone, M. (2000). Life on the ocean wave: Testing some intergroup hypotheses in a naturalistic setting. Unpublished MS, University of Kent.

Brown, R.J., Vivian, J., and Hewstone, M. (1999). Changing attitudes through intergroup contact: The effects of membership salience. *European Journal of Social Psychology*, **29**, 741–764.

Clark, A., Hovecar, D., and Dembo, M.H. (1980). The role of cognitive development in children's explanations and preferences for skin color. *Developmental Psychology*, **16**, 332–339.

Clark, K.B. and Clark, M.P. (1947). Racial identification and preference in Negro children. In T.W. Newcomb and E.L. Hartley (Eds), *Readings in social psychology*. New York: Holt.

Corenblum, B. and Wilson, A.E. (1982). Ethnic preference and identification among Canadian Indian and White children: Replication and extension. *Canadian Journal of Behavioural Science*, **14**, 50–59.

Damon, W. and Hart, D. (1982). The development of self-understanding from infancy through adolescence. *Child Development*, **53**, 841–864.

Davey, A.G. (1983). *Learning to be prejudiced: Growing up in multi-ethnic Britain*. London: Edward Arnold.

Dovidio, J., Gaertner, S.L., and Validzic, A. (1998). Intergroup bias: Status differentiation and a common ingroup identity. *Journal of Personality and Social Psychology*, **75**, 109–120.

Doyle, A.-B. and Aboud, F.E. (1995). A longitudinal study of white children's racial prejudice as a social-cognitive development. *Merrill-Palmer Quarterly*, 4(2), 209–228.

Doyle, A.-B., Beaudet, J., and Aboud, F. (1988). Developmental patterns in the flexibility of children's ethnic attitudes. *Journal of Cross-Cultural Psychology*, **19**(1), 3–18.

Elkind, D. (1961). The child's conception of his religious denomination I: The Jewish child. *Journal of Genetic Psychology*, **99**, 209–225.

Elkind, D. (1962). The child's conception of his religious denomination II: The Catholic child. *Journal of Genetic Psychology*, **101**, 185–193.

Elkind, D. (1963). The child's conception of his religious denomination III: The Protestant child. *Journal of Genetic Psychology*, **103**, 291–304.

Elkind, D. (1964). Discrimination, seriation and numeration of size and dimensional differences in young children. *Journal of Genetic Psychology*, **104**, 275–296.

Elkind, D. (1970). The origins of religion in the child. *Review of Religious Research*, 12, 35–42.

Elkind, D. (1971). The development of religious understanding in children and adolescents. In M.P. Strommen (Ed.), *Research on religious development*. (pp. 655–685). New York: Hawthorn Books.

Erikson, E.H. (1968). *Identity: Youth and crisis*. New York: Norton.

Fetzer, J.S. and Soper, C.J. (2005). The roots of public attitudes state accommodation of European Muslims' religious practices before and after September 11th. *Journal for the Scientific Study of Religion*, **44**(2), 247–258.

Forlitti, J. and Benson, P. (1986). Young adolescents: A national study. *Religious Education*, **81**, 199–224.

Fowler, J.W. (1981). *Stages of faith: The psychology of human development and the quest for meaning*. San Francisco, CA: Harper & Row.

Francis, L.J. (1979). Research and the development of religious thinking. *Educational Studies*, **5**, 109–115.

Francis, L.J. (1987). The decline in attitudes towards religion among 8–15 year olds. *Educational Studies*, **13**(2), 125–134.

Friedman, P. (1980). Racial preferences and identifications of White elementary schoolchildren. *Contemporary Educational Psychology*, **5**, 256–265.

Furnham, A. and Stacey, B. (1991). *Young people's understanding of society*. London: Routledge and Kegan Paul.

Gaertner, S., Dovidio, J.F., Anastasio, P.A., Bachevan, B.A., and Rust, M.C. (1993). The common ingroup identity model: Recategorisation and the reduction of intergroup bias. *European Review of Social Psychology*, **4**, 1–26.

Geertz, C. (1973). The interactive revolution: Primordial sentiments and civil politics in the new states. In C. Geertz (Ed.), *The interpretation of cultures*. New York: Basic Books.

George, D.M. and Hoppe, R.A. (1979). Racial identification, preference and self concept. *Journal of Cross-Cultural Psychology*, **10**(1), 85–100.

Godin, A. (1968). Genetic development of the symbolic function: Meaning and limits of the work of R. Goldman. *Religious Education*, **63**, 439–445.

Goldman, R.J. (1964). Researches in religious thinking. *Educational Research*, 6, 139–155.

Gonzalez, R. and Brown, R. (1999). *The role of categorisation, group status and group size in mediating inter-nation attitudes in the European Union.* Paper presented to BPS Social Psychology Section Conference, Lancaster, September.

Hallinan, M. and Teixeira, R. (1987). Opportunities and constraints: Black-White differences in the formation of interracial friendships. *Child Development*, 58, 1358–1371.

Harms, E. (1944). The development of religious experience in children. *American Journal of Sociology*, **50**, 112–122.

Haslam, S.A., Oakes, P.J., Turner, J.C., and McGarty, C. (1995). Social categorisation and group homogeneity: Changes in perceived applicability of stereotype content as a function of comparative context and trait favourableness. *British Journal of Social Psychology*, **34**, 139–160.

Hewstone, M. and Brown, R. (1986). *Contact and conflict in inter-group encounters.* Oxford: Blackwell.

Hoge, D.R. and Petrillo, G.H. (1978). Determinants of church participation and attitudes among high school youth. *Journal for the Scientific Study of Religion*, **17**, 359–379.

Hraba, J. and Grant, G. (1970). Black is beautiful: A re-examination of racial preference and identification. *Journal of Personality and Social Psychology*, **16**, 398–402.

Islam, M.R. and Hewstone, M. (1993). Intergroup attributions and affective consequences in majority and minority groups. *Journal of Personality and Social Psychology*, **64**(6), 936–950.

Jacobson, J. (1997). Religion and ethnicity: Dual and alternative sources of identity among young British Pakistanis. *Ethnic and Racial Studies*, **20**(2), 238–256.

Jahoda, G., Thomson, S.S., and Bhatt, S. (1972). Ethnic identity and preferences among Asian immigrant children in Glasgow: A replicated study. *European Journal of Social Psychology*, **2**, 19–32.

Jardine, M.M. and Viljoen, H.G. (1992). Fowler's theory of faith development: An evaluative discussion. *Religious Education*, **87**(1), 77–85.

Johnson, J.E. (1961). *An enquiry into some of the religious ideas of six year old children.* Unpublished Dip. Ed. dissertation, University of Birmingham.

Judd, C.M. and Park, B. (1988). Out-group homogeneity: Judgements of variability at the individual and group levels. *Journal of Personality and Social Psychology*, **54**, 778–788.

Judd, C.M., Ryan, C.S., and Park, B. (1991). Accuracy in the judgement of in-group and out-group variability. *Journal of Personality and Social Psychology*, **61**, 366–379.

Katz, P.A. (1976). The acquisition of racial attitudes in children. In P.A. Katz (Ed.), *Towards the elimination of racism* (pp. 136–177). New York: Pergamon.

Katz, P.A. and Zalk, S.R. (1974). Doll preferences: An index of racial attitudes? *Journal of Educational Psychology*, **66**, 663–668.

Katz, P.A., Sohn, M., and Zalk, S.R. (1975). Perceptual concomitants of racial attitudes in urban grade-school children. *Developmental Psychology*, **11**(2), 135–144.

Kay, W.K., Francis, L.J., and Gibson, H.M. (1996). Attitude towards Christianity and the transition to formal operational thinking. *British Journal of Religious Education*, **19**(1), 45–55.

Kircher, M. and Furby, L. (1971). Racial preferences in young children. *Child Development*, **42**, 2076–2078.

Kohlberg, L., Levive, C., and Hewer, A. (1983). *Moral stages: A current formulation and a response to critics*. Basel: Karger.

Kutner, B. (1958). Patterns of mental functioning associated with prejudice in children. *Psychology Monographs*, **72**, 7.

Linville, P.W., Salovey, P., and Fischer, G.W. (1986). Stereotyping and perceived distributions of social characteristics: An application to ingroup-outgroup perception. In J.F. Dovidio and S.L. Gaertner (Eds), *Prejudice, discrimination and racism* (pp. 165–208). New York and Orlando, FL: Academic Press.

Loewenthal, K.M. (1994). *Mental health and religion*. London: Chapman and Hall.

Long, D., Elkind, D., and Spilka, B. (1967). The child's construction of prayer. *Journal for the Scientific Study of Religion*, **1**, 101–109.

McGrady, A.G. (1983). Teaching the Bible: Research from a Piagetian perspective. *British Journal of Religious Education*, **5**, 126–133.

McGuire, W.J. (1984). Search for the self: Going beyond self-esteem and the reactive self. In R.A. Zucker, J. Aronoff, and A.I. Rabin. (Eds), *Personality and the prediction of behaviour* (pp. 28–56). New York: Academic Press.

Matthews, H.F. (1966). *Revolution in religious education*. Washington, DC: Religious Education Press.

Milner, D. (1973). Racial identification and preference in Black British children. *European Journal of Social Psychology*, **3**, 281–295.

Morland, J.K. and Hwang, C.H. (1981). Racial/ethnic identity of preschool children. *Journal of Cross-Cultural Psychology*, **12**, 409–424.

Mullen, B. and Hu, L. (1989). Perceptions of ingroup and outgroup variability: A meta-analytic integration. *Basic and Applied Social Psychology*, **10**, 233–252.

Nash, M. (1989). *The cauldron of ethnicity in the modern world*. Chicago, IL: University of Chicago Press.

Nesdale, D., Griffith, J., Durkin, K., and Maass, A. (2005). Empathy, group norms and children's ethnic attitudes. *Journal of Applied Developmental Psychology*, **26**(6), 623–637.

Newman, M.A., Liss, M.B., and Sherman, F. (1983). Ethnic awareness in children: Not a unitary concept. *Journal of Genetic Psychology*, **143**, 103–112.

Nielson, J.S. (1984). Muslim immigration and settlement in Britain. *Research papers: Muslims in Europe. No. 21*, Birmingham: CSIC: Selly Oak Colleges.

Oakes, P.J., Haslam, S.A., and Turner, J.C. (1994). *Stereotyping and social reality*. Oxford: Basil Blackwell.

Office for National Statistics (ONS) (2000). *Labour force survey.* London: HMSO Publications.
Office for National Statistics (ONS) (2000). *Social trends.* London: HMSO Publications.
Park, B. and Rothbart, M. (1982). Perception of out-group homogeneity and levels of social categorisation: Memory for the subordinate attributes of in-group and out-group members. *Journal of Personality and Social Psychology,* **42**, 1051–1068.
Pettigrew, T.F. (1998). Intergroup contact theory. *Annual Review of Psychology,* **49**, 65–85.
Phinney, J. (1990). Ethnic identity in adolescents and adults: A review of research. *Psychological Bulletin,* **180**, 499–514.
Piaget, J. (1969). *The child's conception of the world.* Patterson, NJ: Littlefield, Adams & Co.
Piaget, J. and Weil, A.M. (1951). The development in children of the idea of a homeland and of relations to other countries. *International Social Science Journal,* **3**, 561–578.
Potvin, R.H. and Lee, C.-F. (1982). Adolescent religion: A developmental approach. *Sociological Analysis,* **43**, 131–144.
Renninger, C.A. and Williams, J.E. (1966). Black-White color connotations and racial awareness in preschool children. *Perceptual and Motor Skills,* **22**, 771–785.
Rosenberg, M. and Simmons, R.G. (1971). *Black and White in school: Trust, tension or tolerance?* Washington, DC: American Sociological Association.
Rotherham, M. and Phinney, J. (1987). Definitions and perspectives in the study of children's ethnic socialisation. In J. Phinney and M. Rotherham (Eds), *Children's ethnic socialisation: Pluralism and development.* Newbury Park, CA: Sage.
Ryan, M.K. and Buirski, P. (2001). Prejudice as a function of self-organization. *Psychoanalytic Psychology,* **18**(1), 21–36.
Schofield, J.W. (1978). An exploratory study of the Draw-A-Person as a measure of racial identity. *Perceptual and Motor Skills,* **46**, 311–321.
Semaj, L. (1980). The development of racial identification and preference: A cognitive approach. *Journal of Black Psychology,* **6**, 59–79.
Sheridan, L.P. (2006). Islamaphobia pre- and post-September 11th. *Journal of Interpersonal Violence,* **21**(3), 317–336.
Slee, N. (1986). Goldman yet again: An overview and critique of his contribution to research. *British Journal of Religious Education,* **8**, 84–93.
Stephan, W.G. and Rosenfield, D. (1979). Black self-rejection: Another look. *Journal of Educational Psychology,* **71**, 708–716.
Tajfel, H. (1979). Individuals and groups in social psychology. *British Journal of Social and Clinical Psychology,* **18**, 183–190.
Takriti, R. (2002). The development of religious identity in Christian, Hindu and Muslim children. Unpublished PhD thesis, University of Surrey.
Takriti, R. (2005). *The relationship between religiosity and self-esteem.* Poster presented at The World Psychiatric Association, Cairo, Egypt, September 2005.

Takriti, R. and Takriti, Y. (2007). The changing nature of self-esteem in Muslim children following the terror attacks of September 11th 2001 and July 7th 2005. Discussion Papers. Leeds: Leeds Metropolitan University.

Takriti, R., Barrett, M., and Buchanan-Barrow, E. (2006). Children's understanding of religion: Interviews with Arab-Muslim, Asian-Muslim, Christian and Hindu children aged 5–11 years. *Mental Health, Religion and Culture*, **9**, 29–42.

Tamm, M.E. (1996). The meaning of God for children and adolescents: A phenomenographic study of drawings. *British Journal of Religious Education*, **19**(1), 33–43.

Thouless, R.H. (1971). *An introduction to the psychology of religion*. Cambridge: Cambridge University Press.

Turner, E.B., Turner, I.F., and Reid, A. (1980). Religious attitude in two types of urban secondary school: A decade of change. *Irish Journal of Education*, **14**, 43–52.

Turner, J.C., Hogg, M.A., Oakes, P.J., Reicher, S.D., and Wetherell, M.S. (1987). *Rediscovering the social group: A self-categorisation theory*. Oxford: Blackwell.

Vaughan, G.M. (1964). The development of ethnic attitudes in New Zealand school children. *Genetic Psychology Monographs*, **70**, 135–175.

Vaughan, G.M. (1987). A social psychology model of ethnic identity development. In J.S. Phinney and M.J. Rotheran (Eds), *Children's ethnic socialization*. London: Sage.

Vaughan, G.M., Tajfel, H., and Williams, J.A. (1981). Bias in reward allocation in an intergroup and interpersonal context. *Social Psychology Quarterly*, **44**, 37–42.

Verbit, M.F. (1970). The components and dimensions of religious behaviour: Toward a reconceptualisation of religiosity. In P.E. Hammond and B. Johnson. (Eds), *American mosaic* (pp. 108–158). New York: Random House.

Wallace, A.F.C. (1966). *Religion: An anthropological view*. New York: Random House.

Whitley, B.E., Schofield, J.W., and Snyder, H.N. (1984). Peer preferences in a desegregated school: A round robin analysis. *Journal of Personality and Social Psychology*, **46**, 799–810.

Williams, J.E., Best, D.L., and Boswell, D.A. (1975a). The measurement of children's racial attitudes in the early school years. *Child Development*, **46**, 494–500.

Williams, J.E., Best, D.L., Boswell, D.A., Mattson, L., and Graves, D. (1975b). Preschool racial attitude measurement II. *Educational and Psychological Measurement*, **35**, 37–38.

Zalk, S.R. and Katz, P.A. (1976). The Katz-Zalk projective prejudice test: A measure of racial attitudes in children. *Journal of Supplement Abstract Services. Catalog of Selected Documents in Psychology*, **6**, 37–38.

# Culture in Applied Developmental Psychology

Dabie Nabuzoka and Janet M. Empson

OUTLINE

8.1 Introduction
    8.1.1 Children's development in cultural context
    8.1.2 Implications for applied developmental psychology
8.2 Application of theory and research findings
    8.2.1 Relevance of evidence from different perspectives
    8.2.2 Developmental outcomes in children's adjustment
8.3 Implications for policy and practice
    8.3.1 Approaches to learning and teaching
    8.3.2 Language use in schools
    8.3.3 Children's social adjustment
    8.3.4 Promoting children's identity in multicultural environments
8.4 Issues in applied developmental psychology and research
    8.4.1 Research with a cultural perspective
    8.4.2 Methodological issues
8.5 Conclusions
Further reading
References

8.1 Introduction

In earlier chapters you were introduced to a number of issues in relation to the role of cultural factors in the psychological development and adjustment of children. In addition, the earlier chapters demonstrated that there are various ways in which culture can be constituted, and also how it can be defined and studied. The influence of culture was illustrated in various domains of child development – cognitive, linguistic and social-emotional – and in different environments. In addition, different examples of the constitutions of culture were discussed: traditional, modern, ethnic background, religious affiliation and socioeconomic status. A number of outcomes of such cultural factors were identified in social and cognitive functioning, language development, general outcomes in psychological adjustment and the development of cultural and ethnic identity. Each one of these outcomes illustrates culture's influence on a particular domain of the psychological development of children.

As we indicated in Chapter 1, studying children's development in cultural context has become increasingly important in the modern world for a number of reasons. With globalization, people all over the world are increasing their contact with members of other cultures. Therefore, to understand differences and similarities between them is becoming increasingly relevant to governments, international agencies, professionals and businesses. Of equal importance is the need to understand the significance and relevance of cultural practices to the people concerned and others who may be affected. Within a particular society today, there are typically many cultures and subcultures and these are constituted on the basis of income, ethnicity, religion and so on. Minority groups in multicultural societies may use different child-rearing practices to those of the dominant group and their appropriateness may be questioned by those not familiar with that particular culture. It is therefore important for developmental psychologists and practitioners to understand both the reasons for differing practices and psychological outcomes associated with them.

8.1.1 Children's development in cultural context

As you also saw in earlier chapters, psychologists and researchers from other disciplines have studied child-rearing practices as a mechanism for socializing children for adult life in different cultures. Such studies have focused on specific parenting styles and psychological outcomes in the offspring and also on environmental and contextual factors as determinants of parenting goals and practices. Some studies have specifically identified ethnic and other social factors as important determinants of such goals and practices. These practices have been linked to some psychological outcomes, which include personality attributes and aspects of emotional and behavioural adjustment. Other concerns have been reflected in debates about culture's specific influence on language development and functioning, and also on cognitive and social development.

On the whole, research evidence illustrates various interactions between children's social-cognitive development and context, and supports the argument that it is important to examine children's functioning, including thinking processes, and its development in relation to the social and cultural environment and the ways in which such environments support children's activities. Language in this respect is one tool that supports such activities, mediating between culture and social as well as cognitive development. Such considerations have led to a substantial amount of research being focused on examining the link between the acquisition of different languages and aspects of cognitive functioning. This is particularly illustrated in the case of bi and multilingual development and its possible influences on cognitive functioning and aspects of psychological adjustment. Research in this area has also shown that language is one of the ways in which people assert their cultural identity, and that learning a second language can be an indicator of the acculturation process.

Identity, however, has many dimensions and can also include such things as ethnicity and religious beliefs. Understanding the development of children's cultural and ethnic identity, including religious beliefs, has become important as children born today are exposed to a greater proportion of multi-ethnic and multi-religious people for whom their cultural identity is largely defined by their religion. How children come to understand and evaluate their own and other people's cultures is of interest not only to psychologists and other professionals concerned with child development, but also to policy-makers as it has implications for group relations and addressing problems such as those related to prejudice and feelings of alienation experienced by young people from minority groups in multicultural societies.

These issues have implications both for our understanding of the various influences on children's development and also how such understanding can inform various efforts aimed at promoting the welfare of children growing up in various cultural contexts.

8.1.2 Implications for applied developmental psychology

The particular ways in which the development of children are influenced by cultural factors should be of interest not only to academics and researchers but also to practitioners concerned with the welfare of children in general and policy-makers concerned with the design and delivery of services. The applications of theoretical models in research are of importance in studying child development. The findings from such research are of relevance to the promotion of children's well-being, education and sound child-rearing practices. These considerations have been the focus of applied developmental psychology. In this chapter these are discussed in relation to some of the research findings and explanations discussed in earlier chapters.

Specifically, we focus on some of the theoretical, research and practical implications by integrating some of the empirical evidence and theoretical explanations for findings from research, and relating them to some of the social issues of today. Findings from developmental psychology and other relevant disciplines with a cultural perspective are identified as providing information which can be utilized to optimize development for children in different sociocultural contexts. In discussing these issues, there is recognition that much of the theoretical basis for the research discussed has been developed in Western, industrialized societies such as the United States and the United Kingdom. However, as we saw in Chapter 2, other perspectives like cultural psychology and indigenous psychologies have emerged. These differences in perspectives are highlighted and discussed where appropriate.

The chapter is divided into three main sections (Sections 8.2, 8.3 and 8.4). Section 8.2 is concerned with the application of theories and research findings to issues related to children's education, methods of childrearing and upbringing with implications for particular developmental outcomes, and children's psychological adjustment. Section 8.3 focuses on the implications for policy and practice as related to the provision of education, social and mental health services for children. Section 8.4 identifies a number of practical issues in applied developmental psychology and research that have implications for the discipline being attuned to the experiences of the vast majority of the world's children. This includes a discussion of some areas for focusing research efforts, methodological issues and concerns around the study of culture's influence on human development. Some specific issues and guidelines on conducting research that incorporates cultural considerations are also discussed. The chapter concludes with an overview of main issues in developmental psychology where cultural considerations are relevant, and a brief discussion of the importance of work on cultural influences on the psychological development of children.

8.2 Application of theory and research findings

In this section, we discuss issues related to applied research and focus on the application of theories and research findings to children's psychological adjustment and education, and methods of childrearing and upbringing that optimize developmental outcomes. We begin this section by discussing the use and relevance of the different perspectives of cross-cultural psychology, cultural psychology and indigenous psychologies in understanding children's development. The particular ways in which these may be used to explain developmental outcomes and children's adjustment are illustrated in some of the domains discussed in earlier chapters.

8.2.1 Relevance of evidence from different perspectives

How can we judge the utility of data from the different fields of psychology for understanding children's development? Which approach offers a better explanation of the relationship between culture and psychological development? As we saw in Chapter 2, cross-cultural psychology, cultural psychology and indigenous psychology have been presented as somewhat different fields within psychology but have a common focus on the relationship between culture and psychological development. There are, however, a number of specific theoretical and methodological features of each of these different perspectives or fields of psychology. These, as we saw in Chapter 2, include the conceptual underpinnings of each approach and the preferred methods of psychological research.

Regarding conceptual frameworks, the concern of cross-cultural psychology is the comparison of the existence and/or manifestation in a given culture of phenomena observed in another culture. We can **use** the orientation of the quantitative method of factor analysis to illustrate this approach. Factor analysis is primarily concerned with describing the variation or variance shared by the scores of people on a number of variables. This variance is referred to as 'common variance'. Another variance is that which is specific to a variable and not shared with any other variable. This together with variance that might arise from measurement errors (error variance) is known as unique variance. The total variance thus consists of a combination of common and unique variance. Similarly, different cultures can be considered as variables characterized by behaviours and psychological attributes shared by most of its people. Some of these will also be shared with other cultures while others may only apply to a particular culture. For example, the concern of cross-cultural studies on child-rearing practices would be to identify those aspects of childcare behaviours that are common between one or more cultures and/or those specific to a given culture. Such a concern is illustrated in Figure 8.1, where the circles represent three different cultures with their own child-rearing practices. The overlap between two or all of the cultures represents those aspects of childcare that are

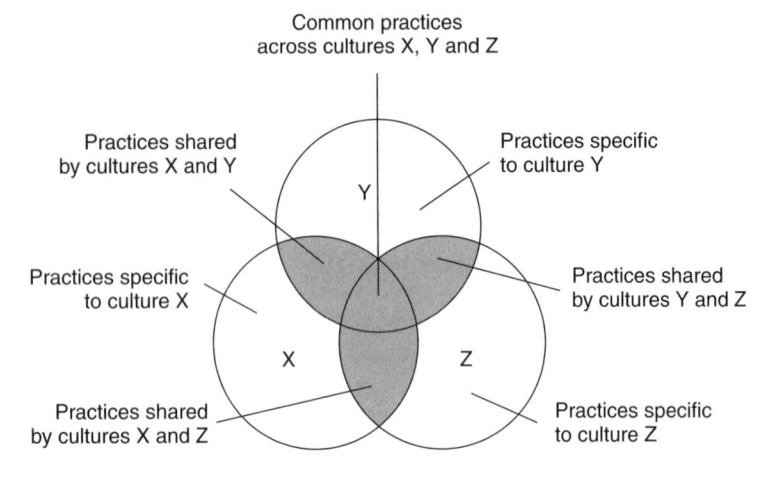

Figure 8.1 Child-rearing practices common across three cultures X, Y and Z (shaded) and those unique to each culture (unshaded)

shared (e.g., feeding and clothing the young) and thus related to common variance. The rest represent those aspects of childcare unique to a given culture (i.e., related to unique or specific variance). Data collected within this framework would be useful to those interested in identifying similarities and differences between given cultures.

The orientation of cultural- and indigenous-psychologies is different in that the main concern is to explain phenomena within a culture. Cultural psychology, on one hand, is concerned with the meaning and significance of a given phenomenon to the people of a particular culture (e.g., why do mothers in society X carry their babies on the back?), what processes give rise to it, and its implications. The main focus is thus more intra-cultural (*emic*) for cultural psychology, and intercultural (*etic*) for cross-cultural psychology. Similarly, the orientation of indigenous psychology is that the conceptualization and therefore definition of any given phenomenon is specific to a given cultural context and its people. According to this perspective, each cultural context creates its own psychological reality, and therefore, the concepts and theories of, **for example,** mainstream psychology have a particular cultural bias that reflects the society that gave rise to it. The dominance of the contribution of Western, mostly American (the United States), perspectives and theorists to the field of developmental psychology is, therefore, seen as a particular bias that limits their contribution to a full understanding of the experiences and developmental paths of children from other (majority) parts of the world. The perspective of indigenous psychology is useful in identifying perspectives or *ethnotheories* held by members of a given culture about psychological phenomena.

In terms of methodology, cultural psychology is mostly associated with the use of qualitative methods, which are also used more widely in indigenous psychology. Examples include the study of child-rearing practices and parental ethnotheories that accompany them, and the definitions of cultural phenomena in specific contexts. The former is illustrated clearly in the studies reported by Keller (2003), which used observational studies to assess infants' parenting experiences and video-based ethnographic interviews about parental ethnotheories of rural Cameroonian Nso and urban German families. Serpell's (1993) study of definitions of intelligence employed by the Chewa of Eastern Zambia (see Chapter 2) illustrates a particular focus on indigenous definition of a psychological attribute using interviews about ecologically valid but hypothetical situations and tasks about which adults could make judgements about a child's competence. In that study, the respondents were asked to explain their responses regarding the competence of individual children with reference to particular demands of the tasks in a given situation.

Thus, the emphasis on qualitative methodology employed by cultural and indigenous psychologies distinguishes these two fields from cross-cultural psychology which has tended to embrace the positivistic quantitative methodology. While arguments have been put forward regarding the merits of using one or the other method, it has been suggested that explanations of child development in cultural context should utilize either qualitative or quantitative data as appropriate to specific research questions and purposes (Berry, Poortinga, Segal and Dasen, 2002; Nsamenang, 2000).

In summary, evidence from cross-cultural psychology, concerned about comparing the existence and/or manifestation of phenomena in a given culture **with** that observed in another, is useful for identifying differences and similarities of the experiences and development of children in various cultures. Evidence from cultural psychology, on the other hand, is of relevance to those concerned about the meaning and significance of a given phenomenon to the people of a particular culture, the processes that give rise to it and its implications for that society. The focus is thus more intra-cultural for cultural psychology, and intercultural for cross-cultural psychology. Indigenous psychology, whose premise is that the conceptualization and definition of any given phenomenon is specific to a given cultural context and its people, provides evidence that is useful in identifying perspectives or ethnotheories held by members of a given culture about psychological phenomena.

8.2.1.1 Theoretical models

Conceptual approaches provide a general framework for studying the role of culture in psychological development, and interpretations of the function and significance of observed patterns of behaviour of people in a given cultural context involve the application of particular theoretical perspectives or models. As we saw in Chapter 2, there are various theoretical approaches to child socialization in different environments, which include the *ecological systems approach* of Bronfenbrenner (1979; 2005), the notion of the *developmental niche* of Super and Harkness (1986) and, more recently, the *ecological-transactional approach* of Lynch and Cicchetti (1998). Other theoretical frameworks include Kagitçibasi's (1990) *family change model*.

Each of these theoretical models emphasizes different aspects of the child's environment and of the ways in which they influence development, but all share an orientation that focuses less on internal processes underlying development and more on the role of contextual factors in shaping children's development. Thus, the ecological systems approach focuses on the structure of society and how different social contexts define the child's interactions with the world; the notion of a developmental niche emphasizes the interrelationships between the context (both physical and social), practices and the ideas that inform the practices; the ecological-transactional approach focuses on the interactions of various influences on the child (both internal and external) and how such interaction in itself has further influence on development across time; and the family change model accounts for different relationships between generations, and differing goals and aspirations, in different societies in relation to their degree of individualism or collectivism and the changes occurring in these as a society develops. Figure 8.2 illustrates the relationships between various approaches, theoretical perspectives and key concepts associated with each in studying child development.

8.2.1.2 How useful are models of culture in explaining development?

Models are representations of some selected, essential characteristics or aspects of development. They provide an operational meaning to theories that give rise to them. In this sense, the usefulness of any given model

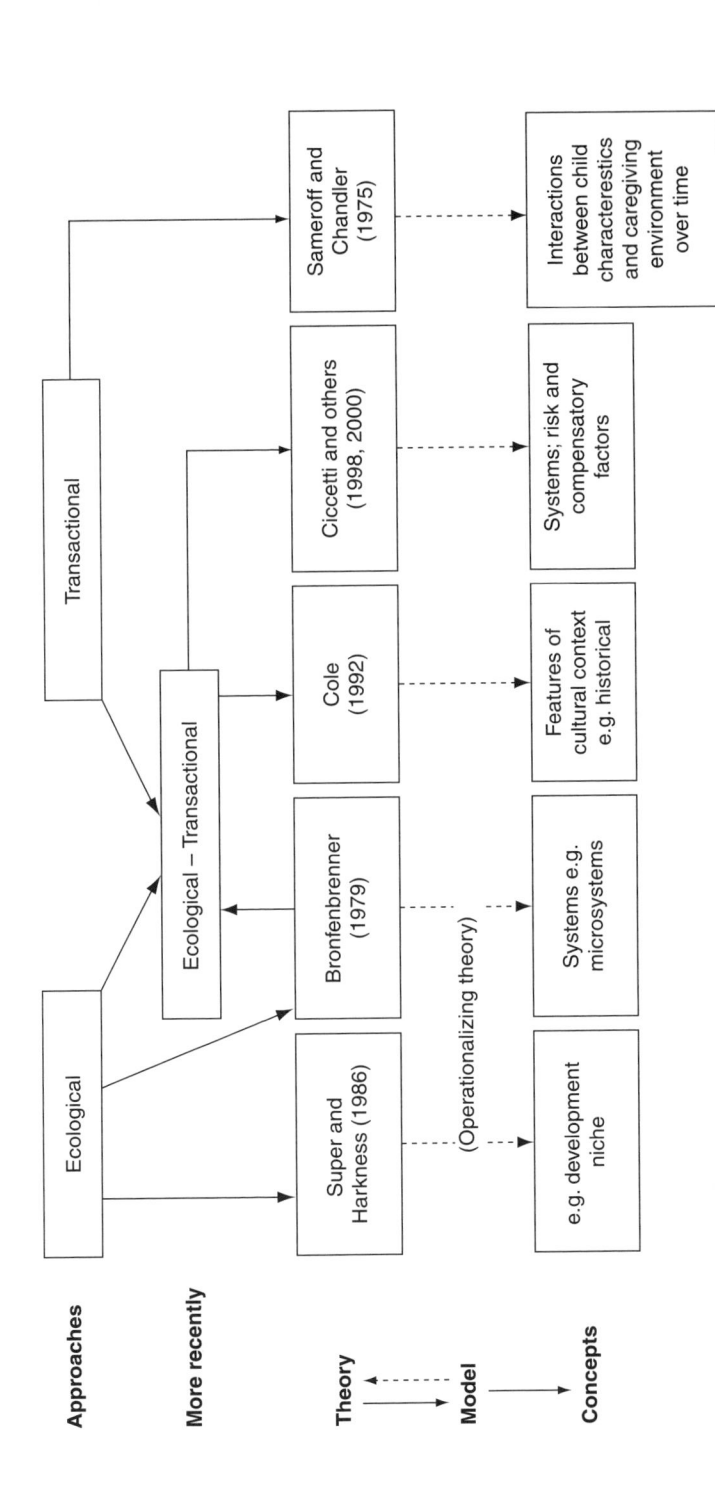

Figure 8.2 A taxonomy of approaches to child development in cultural context

can only be determined by how well it represents a particular explanation of the nature of children's development and in the light of available evidence. An issue that highlights both the differences in approaches to the relation between culture and psychological development and the validity of the conceptual frameworks used to study phenomena relates to the consistency with which obtained evidence fit a particular model. For example, one conceptual framework used extensively in cross-cultural psychology is that cultural differences in parenting and child socialization largely involve how individuals define themselves and their relationships with others, in particular the groups to which they belong. In some cultures, the core of self-definition is considered to be based on individual autonomy and separation from others and labelled 'independent self-construal' or 'idiocentrism'. In contrast, other cultures are said to define the self-concept primarily based on social embeddedness and interdependence with others comprising their in-groups ('interdependent self-construal' or 'allocentrism'). Psychologists have tended to associate the former with Western 'industrial' societies and the latter with non-Western 'traditional' societies. However, as illustrated by Jávo in Chapter 3, such categorizations may not always be accurate as some 'traditional' societies have been found to promote individualistic attributes in their young. In addition, it is recognized that individualism-collectivism at the cultural level may not necessarily correspond with idiocentrism-allocentrism at the psychological level, and that there are many different ways of being 'separate individuals', and also of being 'embedded' in social relations or groups (Kagitçibasi, 1997; 2005).

There has been some recent acknowledgement of such variations, and this has been reflected in cultural models by a number of investigators of the child-rearing goals and parental ethnotheories, who have further pointed to the multidimensionality of the attitudes, values and practices that promote independence or interdependence in different cultures (Keller, 2003). As these dimensions define the socialization of children in different cultures, it is argued that evaluations of the significance of particular child-rearing practices of different cultures should take into account the nuances of such multidimensionality (see Keller, Lamm, Abels et al., 2006). Such considerations require the application of multiple methods of studying the phenomenon of interest. In addition to utilizing a range of methods, it can be argued that explanations should draw on various perspectives including mainstream developmental psychology and other disciplines such as anthropology and sociology serving an integrative function not only within psychology but also between psychology and other disciplines.

8.2.2 Developmental outcomes in children's adjustment

In earlier chapters, cultural factors have been discussed as influencing or in some way accounting for the developmental pathways of children and the ways in which they function later as adolescents. For example, those characteristics or behavioural skills central to the functioning of society and individuals within it are emphasized in the socialization of children. Thus, there has been some focus on the extent to which 'collectivist societies' may socialize children to become 'allocentric individuals', and 'individualistic societies' socialize their young to become 'idiocentric individuals' (see Cecilie Jávo, Chapter 3, and Section 8.2.1.1 of this chapter). Other concerns have been directed at the specific effects of socialization institutions such as the school. For example, Cole (2005) and Serpell (1993; 2005) have discussed the importance of the specific effects of schooling as a mechanism of cultural transmission. Differing features of the school environment, in particular, have implications for meeting the educational needs of children of diverse cultures. These include the effects of bilingualism or the use of a non-native language as a medium of instruction.

In addition, certain factors such as disadvantage may account for children's functional limitations in some domains. Thus, the attitudes and behaviours of parents and children that occur more frequently in the stressful and impoverished conditions of low socio-economic status and/or ethnic minority status have been implicated in accounting for the greater probability of emotional and behavioural difficulties, stress and/or lower academic achievement (see Chapter 4), lower self-esteem or negative attitudes towards own ethnic identity (see Chapter 7).

However, a full understanding of variations in child-developmental progress in different sociocultural contexts requires a multi-level analysis and explanation focused on both within-child personality characteristics and behaviours which are a function of characteristics of the child and the environment. Such considerations have been demonstrated to be relevant in manifestation of shyness and behavioural inhibition, and in aggression and emotional and behavioural difficulties. For example, aggression and emotional and behavioural difficulties in children constitute major social issues in Western societies, which demonstrate the importance of taking cultural context into account when considering their aetiology and impact upon children, their families and communities. A child's ability to cope with stress will make it more or less likely that they develop emotional and behavioural difficulties and good coping strategies are associated with resilience in the child (see Chapter 4).

In this section we, therefore, outline some of these developmental outcomes and the ways in which culture plays a significant role.

8.2.2.1 Educational outcomes

Culture's influence on cognitive and language development can be demonstrated in the context of educating children in various cultural contexts. Education as a form of socialization of the young for adult roles can be considered to comprise two characteristic features: formal and informal education. Formal education, as observed by Nsamenang (2003), involves deliberate teaching or training of the young as 'a specific form of enculturation and socialization widely referred to as schooling' (p. 222). Benefits of schooling as a means of education cannot be disputed, especially in industrialized societies. However, questions have been raised about the benefits of such education, often Western-type, in the form specifically applied to less industrialized settings such as those of Africa (Nsamenang, 2003; Serpell, 1993) where it tends not to incorporate indigenous cultural and economic realities, and other psychological factors thus making the majority of its graduates ill-prepared to contribute meaningfully to their societies (Nsamenang, 2003). This problem of questionable relevance of schooling in various cultural settings, especially Africa, has been demonstrated by Serpell (1993) in a case study of children growing up in a rural community of the Chewa of Eastern Zambia. The study found that while the school system emphasized a preparation for employment in the formal and 'modern' economic sector, most of the children could not make much progress and/or found their schooling to have little application in adult life.

While teaching and learning occur both in and out of the school context, the education that is embodied in the child-rearing practices of a given culture tends to be more informal and often occurs in-context and with particular reference to a specific activity with immediately apparent relevance. Such teaching of the child, characteristic of indigenous informal education in Africa, for example, is aimed at socializing the child into responsible participation in acceptable and valued social and economic activities and includes imparting of aspects of morality and social responsibility. The lack of these features in the school curriculum in such cultures has been associated with children lacking those forms of responsibility training and cognitive development relevant to functioning in their communities leading to lack of motivation to persevere with schooling (see Serpell, 1993).

Other demonstrations of the limitations of formal schooling, but of the efficacy of learning in-context in other cultures, have been presented in studies of Brazilian street children. Nunes and her colleagues (Nunes Carraher, Carraher and Schliemann, 1985) showed that children who struggled with simple mathematical computations in the school curriculum were nonetheless highly skilled in manipulations of figures and sums when it came to dealing with various denominations of currency in the context of trading on the streets. The key factor seems to have been the learning in-context and the immediate application of skills to a relevant problem. The difficulties with mathematics encountered by Brazilian children were attributed partly to the methods of teaching characteristic of the school curriculum. While teaching methods applied to different cultures can account for differences in educational outcomes for the children involved, other aspects of the school context also have significant implications for children's school adjustment. One such factor is the language used.

As we saw in Chapter 6, the impact of language on educational outcomes has been studied in the context of the functioning of bilingual children in Western educational systems. Contrary to early research, recent research has indicated the positive effects of being bilingual on cognitive development and academic advancement (Bialystok, 2001; 2007; Kovacs and Mehler, 2009). However, there is some evidence that such children, especially those of minority or immigrant community, may experience problems in their psychological adjustment that could indirectly impact on their academic functioning (see discussion in Chapter 6). This has implications for the educational- as well as social and mental health- services in such countries.

In other cultural contexts, the effect of language on educational outcomes in the context of schooling has had to do with the use of a non-native language as a medium of instruction. Such has been the case historically in Kenya, Zambia and other former British colonies where English was introduced as a medium of instruction in the local schools. Though for the vast majority of the children such a language is unfamiliar, especially in rural areas, it was introduced as a medium of instruction from the beginning of the curriculum. The rationale and policy implications of such decisions are discussed later in Section 8.3.2. Here it will suffice to note that evaluations of the effects of this on children's learning in Zambia suggested that the use of English instead of the local language of the children's communities made learning more difficult for many children (Chishimba, 1980; Hoppers, 1981; Sekeleti, 1985; 1998). As Serpell (1993) observed:

> one consequence of requiring children to become literate in English as a precondition for understanding the rest of the curriculum has been effectively to deprive a large number of pupils of the opportunity even to sample the accumulated knowledge on offer. (p. 98)

8.2.2.2 Shyness or behavioural inhibition

Shyness or behavioural inhibition in children is a developmental outcome that is also susceptible to cultural influences. It is a stable characteristic (Rubin, Chen and Hymel, 1993) associated with likely developmental outcomes especially in Western societies. It illustrates well the influence of socialization practices as discussed in Chapter 3, and also the interaction between cultural factors and judgements as to what constitutes typical or atypical child development. Thus, shyness and behavioural inhibition can be taken to indicate difficulties in forming relationships, especially in the context of Western culture. However, parents and professionals in different cultures may interpret specific manifestations of child characteristics in different ways such that shyness is viewed as a positive quality in Eastern cultures and negatively in the West. In all, evidence on shyness or behavioural inhibition in different cultures shows that it is of importance to take ethnicity of the child and his/her family into account when considering the effects of this characteristic on the child's socialization and developmental progress. Parental and peer appraisal, expectations and behaviour with shy children differ greatly between cultural groups. Boivin, Hymel and Bukowski (1995) found that by early adolescence, in Western society, shy individuals are aware that they are lacking social skills and friendship with peers and often become lonely and depressed. In more collectivist societies like China reticent and quiet children receive encouragement and praise from teachers and parents (Ho, 1986); in addition, shy children evaluate themselves positively. Thus, shy or behaviourally inhibited children may thrive in Asian groups while they would tend to be disadvantaged in Western societies.

The practical implications of such cultural differences are that teachers and other professionals who may encourage children to 'overcome their shyness' and become more socially assertive would therefore need to be aware that this message may conflict with messages within the family and the child's community about the value of shyness as a personality trait. Related to this are cultural differences in expectations as to how children should conduct themselves when interacting with adults (Harkness and Super, 2008). An example is where immigrant children from non-Western cultures may be seen as rude for 'not looking the teacher in the eyes' when talking to them, when the children's own culture may consider it rude for them to do so!

8.2.2.3 Aggression in children and young people

Like shyness, aggression can be related to difficulty in forming relationships, and can be viewed differently in different ecological niches. For example, the prevalence of aggression as a behavioural characteristic in Western societies such as the United Kingdom has been associated with some subcultures such as gang membership and social deprivation. However, being aggressive can be considered to be adaptive in 'tough' neighbourhoods. Recently, for example, in the United Kingdom there has been much attention on what has been perceived as rising incidences of violence amongst young people, especially involving the use of knives or firearms, often attributed to social factors that create subcultures which promote the carrying and use of weapons. Peers in such contexts can play a very significant role in a child's socialization and development of attitudes towards aggressive behaviour.

There is varying ethos in different cultures regarding the desired nature of peer relationships (Schneider, Woodburn, Soteras-de Toro and Udvari, 2005). This is evidenced in the different ways in which interpersonal conflicts are managed. In the United States, as an example of an 'individualistic culture', conflict is viewed as an inevitable part of the functioning of society with its inherent tension between autonomy and integration (Rothbaum, Pott, Azuma et al., 2000). Children are encouraged to stand up for themselves, to 'give as good as you get' in physical fights, and 'don't take it lying down'. Other societies, as shown in a study in Indonesia (Markus and Lin, 1999), avoid conflict, encouraging children not to engage in problematic topics and to avoid those with whom they may encounter conflict. More harmonious group functioning will be maintained with the latter approaches, with individual achievement being greater in the former.

There are also wide variations in the degree to which children are exposed to aggression and violence. In Western society, children living in the subculture of impoverished neighbourhoods have the greatest exposure. In such cases, aggression in both boys and girls is associated with family violence and conflict between family members. The correlation between violence and low income, with the impact of poverty compounding the impact of violence, both creates and extends poverty (McInnes, 2004). The recipients of violence, especially the children, carry the costs in terms of impaired physical and mental health (McInnes, 2004). Professions dealing with children who may show high levels of violent conduct need to be aware of such sociocultural factors that may predispose the children to such behaviour.

8.2.2.4 Emotional and behavioural difficulties

Emotional and behavioural difficulties (EBD) in children pose a particular challenge for parents, teachers and other professionals. The definition of 'emotional and behavioural difficulties' as 'behaviours which are deemed to violate social norms of acceptable behaviour and are therefore undesirable' (Empson and Hamilton, 2004, p. 112) immediately incorporates the premise that what are seen as constituting EBDs will vary with the social context. Social norms of acceptable behaviour will change over time and differ from one sociocultural context to another, and these contexts also change over time. In the United Kingdom, antisocial and unacceptable behaviour in children and young people is a major concern for the government and public alike. In relation to this, many educationalists, psychologists and other public figures have voiced their concerns (see Greenfield, Leach, Bowlby et al., 2006) about the changing nature of childhood, the rise in mental health problems among children and the need for society to take action to alleviate these.

Existing cultural values and goals provide a basis whereby children's characteristics and social behaviours are judged by others to be more or less acceptable within that cultural context. These judgements will then influence how children feel about themselves and the extent to which they develop good social skills and hence function well socially. As child characteristics are viewed very differently in different cultures, then it would be expected that what is deemed to constitute EBDs would vary across the different cultures or subcultures. Behaviours such as extreme aggression would be universally seen as problematic across all cultures, but the cut-off point between problematic and non-problematic, or between normal and abnormal, will differ depending upon the overall cultural tolerance of violence in a particular society, or subculture within a society. The concept of 'normality' is a statistical one which takes into account the probability of occurrence of particular behaviours at particular developmental levels. A significant feature of the criteria for considering behaviours as abnormal is that they include the life circumstances of the child and the sociocultural setting of the family.

Interpersonal relationships are repeatedly found to be centrally involved in the aetiology and development of EBDs. The child's relationship with parents or other caregivers is of fundamental importance and these relationships may also interact with and influence the child's relationships with peers. Understanding how EBDs develop in different cultures therefore involves the examination of the particular ways parenting styles may interact with child characteristics to see if specific patterns of parenting are similarly associated with specific types of child behaviour. If so, this would make it more likely that similar interpersonal processes are involved in different cultures. Social factors can also define the nature of interpersonal relationships, thus accounting for the prevalence of EBD in some cases. For example, there is evidence that children from socially and economically deprived backgrounds in Western societies have an increased risk of developing emotional and behavioural problems (Schneiders, Drukker, van der Ende et al., 2003).

A secondary outcome of social, emotional and behavioural difficulties can be lowered academic achievement (Department for Education and Skills, 2004). The interactions between educational attainment, family income and EBDs are complex. In Western society, the cause of the link between educational failure, social, emotional and behavioural difficulties (SEBDs) and a disadvantaged home environment is frequently argued to be parents. It is argued that impoverished parents, who usually have only the statutory minimum years of education, provide a cognitively unstimulating environment for their children (Bradley, Whiteside, Mundfrom et al., 1994), which is likely to be particularly important in the preschool years. It is possible also that parenting style, which is more likely to be lacking in emotional support (Korenman, Miller and Sjaastad, 1995) and including the use of inconsistent and severe punishment in impoverished and highly stressed families, contributes to low self-esteem and lack of motivation in the children. Parenting practices have been linked with externalizing problems, especially conduct disorder (Patterson, 1982; Webster-Stratton and Herbert, 1993), which could result in affected children's lack of educational success as teachers tend to respond less positively and are more punitive with children who are demotivated and misbehave in the classroom (see also Chapter 4 for a discussion of other relevant factors).

It is important to note that similar parenting practices may have different consequences depending on the sociocultural circumstances. A case in point is the use of corporal punishment which has been associated with negative outcomes in children in Western, particularly white, middle class families, but not in ethnic minority families such as African Americans (Deater-Deckard, Dodge, Bates and Petit, 1996; Straus and Stewart, 1999) or in those of lower socio-economic status. The specific implications of cultural differences in the practice and impact of corporal punishment for policy and practice are discussed further in Section 8.3.3.1.

8.2.2.5 Stress and coping

Factors associated with adverse developmental outcomes can be offset by the resilience and coping strategies developed in specific cultural contexts. For children in various cultural groups, coping with stress is one of the main abilities which reduce the likelihood of emotional and behavioural difficulties. Different children will be exposed to different stressors, and disadvantaged children (such as those from ethnic minorities or low-income families in Western societies) may experience more stress under certain conditions than more advantaged children. While bearing in mind the importance of non-shared environmental influences, parental behaviour is an important aspect of the home environment which provides the first context in which children learn strategies for dealing with the more difficult aspects of life stresses such as major negative life events or everyday hassles. The kinds of strategy that are predominant in a particular environment will reflect the influences of the wider cultural context (Xu, Farver, Chang et al., 2006). Children's coping strategies have been described by Weisz and colleagues (1984) as falling into three categories as follows:

- Changing aspects of the situation to reduce the source of stress (primary control)
- Changing themselves to adjust to the situation (secondary control)
- Relinquish control to neither modify nor adjust (no control).

The importance that children attach to control will vary with the cultural ethos. In Western societies, control over events, feelings and so on is very important. However, highly religious people may feel less in control as a reflection of the religion they practice helping them to adjust to situations than trying to change them. Children's responses to stress and their coping strategies will thus largely reflect the social-cultural context in which their family is situated. In the Western context of a nuclear family, cohesive families characterized by positive interactions and supportive relationships are said to promote better social adjustment, a sense of security and acceptance and greater concepts of their own possibilities of control over stressful circumstances. In such contexts, children in families where they feel rejected will not be able to rely on social-support strategies of coping, nor have confidence in their own abilities to change situations to facilitate their control over them. The children of families living in poverty, whose parents are likely to express the hopelessness of achieving change and movement out of their unhappy circumstances, are likely to have this way of functioning passed on to them, so the children, too, are likely to adopt control-relinquishing strategies of coping. It must, however, be borne in mind that there will be a range of individual differences in the extent to which children in poverty will rise above their circumstances and generate adaptive solutions to problematic circumstances. The resilience of the child which facilitates adaptive behaviour involves the child characteristics of, for example, high intelligence, a positive and optimistic personality and stability of temperament.

Circumstances of children growing up in much of the majority world in developing countries are likely to be different. Relationships and circumstances in the more immediate nuclear families may not have the same impact as in the Western industrialized settings. In most non-Western (non-industrialized) settings, children can be supported by a more extended network of family members when their immediate family is faced with difficulties. However, cultural change brought about by urbanization has led to different manifestations of the impact of family problems. In most of these settings, there has been wide documentation of the problems of poverty and situations such as that of street children who show high levels of resilience and adaptability to their circumstances while being very vulnerable in many respects (see study by Aderinto, 2000).

8.3 Implications for policy and practice

In this section we focus on some of the implications of issues discussed in the previous section for policy and practice as related to the provision of education, social and mental health services for children. We begin the section with a discussion of the evolution of education policies as influenced by cultural factors and illustrating the particular applications of various theoretical perspectives from the child-centred movements influenced by Piagetian theory to activity theory reflecting the Vygotskian perspective with emphasis on learning in context. Next, our focus is on use of language in schools as applied to contexts where the medium of instruction is other than the native tongue of the majority of the children, and also in multicultural societies where bilingualism may be an issue. The implications for educational policies are discussed addressing both cognitive and social dimensions to experiences of children in such schools.

Another area of practical application from a cultural perspective is in parenting practices and the implications for understanding and dealing with cultural manifestation of child health and well-being. This is illustrated in the specific examples of shyness and behavioural inhibition, aggression, emotional and behavioural difficulties of children, and the stresses and coping strategies that may be employed by the children and their families especially in the context of social disadvantage. A specific example of an approach to parenting influenced by cultural factors is the disciplining of children. Variations across ethnic groups and socio-economic status are illustrated in the use of physical or corporal punishment to control children's behaviour and the consequences of such practices. Finally, the section focuses on the promotion of children's identity in multicultural environments, with a specific focus on ethnic and cultural identity. Implications for socio-emotional adjustment of children from ethnic minority backgrounds are discussed. An example of a programme aimed at cultivating positive cultural identities for such children is presented.

8.3.1 Approaches to learning and teaching

Different theoretical approaches have implications for policy and practice related to the provision of education services and practice in so far as they explain children's learning and cognitive development (Chapter 5). Concern regarding practical implications of these approaches relate to the extent to which cultural factors can be taken into account when designing curricula and other aspects of schooling in different societies and countries. Other issues include the implications of particular conceptual formulations such as the concept of intelligence and how effective different formulations are in accounting for cognitive (intellectual) development in different contexts; the importance of teacher and parent expectations in relation to the achievements of children from different social and ethnic groups in school; and the relationship between functioning in other domains and educational achievements.

As we have seen in earlier chapters, many children worldwide are growing up in contexts that reflect different pathways of development. The general concerns for children in less industrialized countries is that they need better access to the opportunities that families in industrial, and post-industrial societies take for granted – health-care provision and education being the two most relevant to our discussions here. The extent to which approaches to learning and teaching reflect these needs in these contexts is therefore an important issue of concern. In the wealthier societies, particularly those in Europe and the United States, interventions to facilitate optimal development in disadvantaged children have been financed by governments and non-governmental organizations (charities) since the 1960s and the early days of the Headstart Programmes in North America. Among the initial lessons learned from these interventions for children from socially disadvantaged backgrounds was the need to tackle underachievement in children at multiple levels, targeting parents and the community as well as the children; also the need to evaluate the effects of a programme of intervention over the middle to long term as well as immediately post-intervention, as 'sleeper effects' occur, in which effects become evident as many as 5–10 years post-intervention. Such effects may be due to a number of different mechanisms – developmental change or reciprocal interpersonal influences becoming greater over time for example – for different measures. In all, the different experiences of approaches to learning and teaching in both less developed countries and ameliorative programmes in industrialized settings have implications for educational policy.

8.3.1.1 Implications for educational policy

A significant influence on education practice applied in the formalized institution of the school in significant parts of the world has been Piaget's (1951) theory which, as we saw in Chapter 5, has been a key theory of cognitive development. Two features of the theory have been particularly significant for educating children. One of these is the view that children are not born with knowledge that matures with time, and that they do not simply acquire it already packaged from the outside world. Rather, children are considered to actively construct their own development by interacting with the environment. Another feature of Piaget's theory is that children's thinking is seen as being qualitatively different from that of others at different ages, including adults. In addition to the older children being more knowledgable than the younger ones, the ways in which they view and understand the world at different stages of development is different. The notion of stages is an important feature of Piaget's theory, with each successive stage involving increasing levels of organization and logical underlying structures.

Piaget's theory has been influential in the formulation of educational policy in Western countries. An example of such influence were the recommendations of the Plowden Report on primary education in England and Wales (Central Advisory Council for Education, 1967), which informed national education policies and classroom practice for a number of years. Among the key features of the report were references to the significance of developmental sequences in children, readiness for particular educational experiences, and a focus on developmental age in the provision of education. In particular, and consistent with Piaget's theory, the role of the teacher was seen as simply to allow children to engage with their environment in an active way, and to enable them have appropriate experiences at the right time to promote their capacity to learn. In addition, it was considered that education would only be effective if it took account of the stage at which the children were ready for particular educational experiences. Such considerations were consistent with the child-centred movement in educational practice.

While features of Piaget's theory associated with the child-centred movement may not have been fully adopted in non-Western educational systems (e.g., the move away from 'chalk and talk'), the notion of intellectual functioning as a purely individual ability or activity has been imported to such cultures and formalized in features of the educational system that emphasize cultivation of the individual child's mind, discovery and personal achievement. The focus is on developing the child towards the ability to think systematically about the logical relations within a problem as reflected in Piaget's (1951) final formal operations stage of cognitive development.

Such an orientation of the educational system is seen to fall short in equipping children in non-Western societies with the full range of skills and knowledge that would enable them to connect appropriately with their everyday realities and cognitions as reflected in their immediate environments (Nsamenang, 2003). It has been suggested that school curriculum in places such as Africa needs to be geared towards education that socializes children for responsible participation in acceptable and valued social and economic activities, including responsibility training and cognitive functioning (Nsamenang, 2003; Serpell, 1993). Such training has traditionally been achieved through indigenous forms of participatory learning consistent with the neo-Vygotskian sociohistorical theory (Rogoff, 2003).

8.3.1.2 Programmes for socially disadvantaged children

In industrialized societies, the failure to benefit from educational experiences has been associated with social disadvantage. There is much evidence that children from socially and economically deprived backgrounds, for example, in the United Kingdom, have an increased risk of educational failure (Department for Education and Skills, 2004) and manifesting emotional and behavioural problems (Schneiders et al., 2003). There is also a well-established relationship between socio-economic status and educational success. In the United Kingdom, the proportion of children who achieved 5 GCSE passes at grades A–C in 2002 varied from 77 per cent in the professional class to 32 per cent in children whose parents had routine occupations. In the same year, 87 per cent children with parents in professional occupations and 60 per cent with parents in routine occupations participated in post-16 education (National Statistics, UK Government online).

The interactions between educational attainment, family income and EBDs are complex. As we saw earlier, poor parents, characterized by low levels of education, do not provide stimulating environments for their children (Bradley et al., 1994), which is particularly important in the pre-school years. Entwistle, Alexander and Olson (1997) showed that while children from poor backgrounds progress in school term at a rate comparable with children from better-off homes, they fall behind in summer holidays. Other factors that have been implicated include parenting style, which is more likely to be lacking in emotional support (Korenman et al., 1995) and using inconsistent and severe punishment contributing to low self-esteem and lack of motivation in children. Parenting practices have been linked with externalizing problems, especially Conduct Disorder (Patterson, 1982; Webster-Stratton and Herbert, 1993). Conduct Disorders, in turn, result in affected children's lack of educational success in that teachers respond less positively and are more punitive with children who are demotivated and misbehave in the classroom. Children's ability to do well at school could also be handicapped by poor health status, due to inadequate housing and clothing, poor diet, and inadequate health care, all of which are associated with a life in poverty (Crooks, 1995).

In recognition of the effects of these factors on the functioning of children from disadvantaged backgrounds, programmes have been implemented at various points in the United Kingdom and the United States to support the development of children affected. Notable in the United Kingdom is the Sure Start Programme (see Case Study 1). In the United States, the positive effects of many prevention and intervention programmes such as the Perry Preschool Project (Schweinhart, Barnes, Weikart et al., 1993) have also been assessed and disseminated.

Arnold and Doctoroff (2003) point out that few of these have been specifically aimed at improving both educational and mental health outcomes for at-risk children, even though the connection between the two is clear and greater for children living in the most disadvantaged circumstances. The gains in those programmes that do address both issues seem to be more long-term, even into adulthood (Schweinhart et al., 1993).

CASE STUDY 1: THE SURE START PROGRAMME IN THE UNITED KINGDOM

The Sure Start programme was initiated by the UK Government (Department for Education and Employment, 1999) to prevent social exclusion by targeting very young children living in poverty. Sure Start augments and builds on existing services so that the support became more coordinated with better communication and information-sharing between service providers in which Health Visitors played a key role. The objectives were to eliminate or at least reduce the negative effects of social disadvantage by improving child health, social and emotional development and ability to learn, and by strengthening families and communities. The key principles include the following: involvement of local parents and carers in the design, organization and delivery of Sure Start programmes; coordination to add value; cultural sensitivity in service delivery, as ethnic minority children are those most likely to be poor so services need to be appropriate to their particular needs; avoiding stigma; providing long-lasting involvement as necessary; and ensuring that local achievements are relevant to national objectives (Eisenstadt, 2002).

Evaluations of Sure Start have shown it to be effective with many children and families, but two problems identified have been that there is a lack of take-up of services from the most disadvantaged families, and that the resources were insufficient to adequately help multi-problem families (Brown and Dillenburger, 2004). It is of importance to note that the lack of take-up is usually due to practical circumstances rather than being the result of lack of interest or concern in parents. The UK Government requires continuing evaluation of the Sure Start Programme and the last report of the National Evaluation of Sure Start (Belsky, Melhuish, Barnes et al., 2006) suggests that these efforts to improve the health and development of socially deprived children less than four years of age and their families are having only limited effects, varying with the degree of social deprivation.

8.3.2 Language use in schools

That cognitive and language development are intimately related is indisputable although, as we saw in Chapter 6, theories differ in the importance they attach to language as the facilitator of cognitive development or vice versa. For example, the language of instruction can be a very significant factor in a child's academic progress especially if it is different from the child's native language. In this section, we return to two problems identified in Section 8.2.2.1 as being associated with language use in schools: one related to the introduction of a foreign language as a medium of instruction, and the other related to the experience of bilingual children. The problem of using a foreign language as a medium of instruction in schools has been highlighted in the compulsory introduction of English in Zambian schools by the former colonial masters (Sekeleti, 1998; Serpell, 1993).

In the Zambian example, it has been observed that the rationale for the policy of using English as a medium of instruction in schools was based on 'administrative, political and economic expediency' (Sekeleti, 1998). In particular, and as a multilingual society, using a 'foreign' language as both a medium of instruction in schools and as the national language of official discourse was presented as offering a unifying effect without any particular local language being seen as favoured above others. Some argument was also presented that introducing such a language early in the educational process would have the advantage of making learning easier, consistent with the notion of a critical period of language acquisition (Lenneberg, 1967). However as we saw in Section 8.2.2.1, the evidence showed that in fact learning was made more difficult through the introduction of a language that most of the children were not familiar with (Sekeleti, 1998). It was acknowledged by the education authorities that on educational grounds, a child entering primary school was better off being instructed in their own local language, but it was considered that this needed to be balanced against the linguistic diversity of the country. Such considerations illustrate how various aspects of a culture can have a significant effect on the experiences of children that have implications for their psychological development.

The situation of children being exposed to more than one language, where the language of instruction in school is that of the majority culture, is somewhat different to that of schools using a language foreign to the majority of the children's community. However, there are similarities in that for some of the children, such as those of immigrant families in multicultural societies, the second language of the school would in many respects be 'foreign'. Thus, the difficulties that such children face regarding their academic achievements and progress may be similar to those experienced by children where a foreign language has been imposed as a medium of instruction. However, as we saw in Chapter 6, there are social and psychological implications of the experiences of bilingual children in addition to those related to educational achievement. These need to be addressed in developing policy aimed at improving the educational experiences of bilingual children.

At one level, the concern would be to improve bilingual children's access to the language of instruction. One example of an area of difficulty is that the accent of the spoken language can itself be a barrier even when the same language is supposedly familiar to both the teacher and pupil. Relatively new media such as computers have been found to have very positive effects with children with severe learning difficulties (Computer Assisted Learning) and autism. In the light of this and other considerations, provision of PCs for schools is a government priority in the United Kingdom. Education via PC in the early years can be equally attractive and facilitating for children of different ethnic groups and different degrees of confidence, and can reduce the difficulties of the spoken word such as interpreting different accents. However, there is evidence that boys and girls differ in their use of electronic communication (Light and Littleton, 1999), whereby boys seem to find PCs more attractive and enabling than girls. These differences may be narrowing with increased access to computers in schools of industrialized countries, but may nonetheless be a factor in other parts of the world.

8.3.3 Children's social adjustment

Children's social adjustment is reciprocally related to their self-concept and self-esteem, cognitive and educational functioning, and relationships with others. In many societies, particularly in Western culture, good adjustment is generally associated with a particular style of parenting – authoritative – in which parents have high expectations of their children and when control of a child's undesirable behaviour is needed, the parents provide explanations as to why discipline is required and use non-punitive methods, such as withdrawal of privileges. The affection and mutual respect between parent and child is deemed to be maintained throughout. Poor social adjustment in children is associated with parenting styles which are 'laissez-faire' or authoritarian (in which children are ignored or subject to excessive control). However, there have been some variations across different socio-economic groups and ethnic cultures as to the extent to which particular styles of parenting are favoured, and of the developmental implications associated with the different styles. A case in point that has implications for the social adjustment of children is the use of corporal or physical punishment. The question of the use of physical punishment of children and its implications for parent-child relationships and child social adjustment has been much debated for decades. This issue is discussed in the next section to highlight some of the implications for social policy in this area.

8.3.3.1 Discipline of children

A major concern of parents at home, teachers at school and communities at large is how to prevent misconduct in children, and what sanctions should be put in place when children do misbehave. One method of disciplining children that has been used worldwide is physical punishment. Surveys in the 1980s and 1990s found that over 80 per cent of parents in different countries (Chile, India, Korea, Pakistan, the United Kingdom and the United States) had used physical punishment (End Corporal Punishment's Website, 2009). In recent years there has been worldwide debate about the use of physical punishment of children. The focus of such debate has included the extent to which punitive parenting can be associated with socio-emotional and cognitive development of the children.

Those against physical punishment cite research that suggests that children who are frequently punished physically are more likely to be 'troublesome' and delinquent later on (Gershoff, 2002). It has been argued that the use of physical punishment by parents is one of the precursors of aggression in children (Leach, 1993; Newson and Newson, 1989). Newson and Newson (1989) presented evidence that frequent physical punishment can escalate into much more aggressive and violent relationships in families, and that it is associated with more aggressive and antisocial behaviour in the children as they grow through adolescence and into adulthood. There are also some suggestions of a relationship between acceptance of and frequency of use of physical punishment of children and the prevalence of violence in the culture overall (Leach, 1993).

Those favouring physical punishment argue from historical, religious and cultural perspectives. They distinguish smacking in the context of a loving family from that in generally negative and unsupportive families. Some evidence has been cited that suggests that mild physical punishment can be associated with more positive adjustment in children

(Parker and Slaby, 1983). However, what constitutes mild, moderate or severe levels of physical punishment is open to debate, especially as the same terms (such as 'smacking', 'tapping') may have different meanings in different cultural groups.

Most of the arguments about physical punishment reflect specific beliefs about the efficacy of punishing children as a means of disciplining them. A running theme in a number of chapters in this book is that cultural factors account for differences in child-rearing practices between different societies. In this respect, disciplining techniques or interventions to correct behavioural misconduct in children can be seen as aspects of culture with specific beliefs accompanying such practices. The term 'Parental ethnotheories' was used by Harkness and Super (1995; Super and Harkness, 1986) to describe parental beliefs and value systems that accompany child-rearing practices. Such beliefs and values as to the significance of specific practices are regulated by the culture and in turn regulate the development of the child. They are held by caretakers of children to guide the way they adapt the customs of childcare (i.e., child-rearing practices) to the ecological and cultural settings in which they live. Such beliefs would, therefore, be expected to accompany practices related to disciplining children.

Antecedents and effects of physical punishment. It has been suggested that use of physical or corporal punishment is associated with particular parenting styles, with high frequency and intensity of physical punishment being more likely in authoritarian than authoritative parents. Authoritarian parents are said to emphasize rule-oriented control, de-emphasizing warmth and nurturance of their children (Baumrind, 1968; 1971) while authoritative parents are more cooperative and foster shared responsibility, decision-making and independence in their children. The authoritarian parenting style and its associated harsher family climate have been linked with poorer child adjustment (Darling and Steinberg, 1993). There are suggestions that physical or corporal punishment in particular is associated with a higher incidence of behaviour problems in children (Leach, 1993; Newson and Newson, 1989), at least in highly industrialized countries of Europe and the United States.

There however are some indications that broader features of the culture in which the child is situated may be more significant in moderating the effects of physical punishment, positively or negatively. For example, and as suggested in Chapter 3, the effects of physical punishment within the United States seem to be different in different ethnic groups. A number of studies in the United States have generally found physical punishment to be more acceptable and more frequently used in African-American than Caucasian families (Deater-Deckard et al., 1996; Straus and Stewart, 1999). For example, Deater-Deckard et al. (1996) found that the negative effects of physical discipline were only evident in European-American children but not in African-American children. A possible explanation is that physical discipline is more normative in African-American families, which alters its meaning to the child (Deater-Deckard and Dodge, 1997). This suggestion could well apply to the parental belief systems also. Monyooe (1996) reported high rates of the use of physical discipline in Sub-Saharan African countries. In particular, Lansford et al. (2005) found high frequency of use of physical discipline in Kenya, where it was perceived as normative by mothers.

Deater-Deckard et al. (1996) suggested that if disciplining of children by smacking is normative in a particular culture, then the children may perceive it in a different way, not seeing it as an indication of lack of parental warmth and acceptance. Children's interpretations of the meaning of smacking is clearly of importance when considering the desirability or otherwise of physical punishment. In African-American families it has been shown that not only are parents more likely to use physical punishment, but also that authoritarian parenting (associated with physical punishment) is more effective as it is appropriate to the culture in which the child is growing up (Deater-Deckard et al., 1996). The association of physical punishment with aggression has only been found in Caucasian and not in African-American children in the United States (Deater-Deckard et al., 1996; Dietz, 2000). Similar contrasts between white and African-American children have been found with respect to internalizing behaviour problems (Stormshak, Bierman, McMahon et al., 2000) and disruptive disorders in children (Whaley, 2000).

One problem with Deater-Deckard et al.'s hypothesis about group perceptions of the acceptability of physical punishment exerting an influence on child adjustment is that attitudes in the United States and the United Kingdom are overwhelmingly in favour of parental rights to use physical punishment with their children and more than 90 per cent of parents do exercise this right (Leach, 2002; Straus and Stewart, 1999). It would also appear that attitudes do not differ markedly between ethnic groups in the context of Western societies and approval of the use of physical punishment may be normative in all groups. Differences may, however, arise in the contexts and overall climate in which it is used. In particular, the extent to which those who practise it believe in its appropriateness as a means of disciplining children.

A longitudinal study of African-American families reported by McLoyd, Kaplan, Hardaway and Wood (2007) also showed the significance of parental views and attitudes towards the use of physical punishment and child depression. They found that physical discipline administered by 'non-endorsing' mothers was more strongly associated with maternal psychological distress than physical discipline administered by 'endorsing' mothers: the relationship between spanking frequency and child-reported depressive symptoms was stronger for children of 'non-endorsing' mothers. These findings are of particular interest as they demonstrate that parents are using physical punishment even if they do not think that it is an appropriate or effective means of disciplining their children. In addition, they suggest that such negative views about physical punishment undermine any possible positive effects of the practice. Similarly, a cross-cultural study on the use of physical punishment in England and Zambia by Empson and Nabuzoka (2005) found that in both countries there was a discrepancy between belief in the effectiveness of physical punishment and behaviour in smacking their children. A substantial minority (31% in Zambia and 14% in England) who smacked their children did not believe that it worked to change their children's behaviour for the better, even though they practised it. An international study of the origin of attitudes towards physical punishment (Douglas, 2006) found that the history of one's social and cultural group is as important as one's own individual experience in understanding attitudes about hitting children.

Child characteristics may also act as a moderating influence on the effects of physical punishment on child development. Colder, Lochman and Wells (1997) found that overactive and impulsive children were at particularly high risk of showing aggression when they were exposed to harsh disciplinary practices. Similarly, impulsivity in the child has been found to be a moderating factor (Aucoin, Frick and Bodin, 2006), and corporal punishment was more likely to predict behaviour problems in children with difficult temperaments (Mulvaney and Mebert, 2007). Lerner (1993) emphasizes the mutual influences of carer, child and environmental contexts in socializing the child. There are three elements to the context: attitudes, expectations and stereotypes about children, behaviour and other attributes of carers and the physical characteristics of the settings in which the child is growing up. The forms or style and content of socialization are generally viewed as adaptive to the ecocultural setting (Berry et al., 2002) which ensures that children learn the skills necessary to live successfully in that society. These modes of socialization are constrained and encouraged by social patterns and the resources available in a particular sociocultural context. Social patterns and resources can differ greatly such as between Third World and highly industrialized countries, between socio-economic groups, ethnic background, religious affiliations and so on.

Summary and conclusions It seems to be the case, therefore, that the negative effects of physical punishment are moderated by more factors than simply parenting style: family climate and ethnicity, may all be moderators of the relationship between physical punishment of children and their suboptimal development. Some research has indicated that when physical punishment occurs in the context of a warm and nurturing family, it has less adverse effects on the child (Aucoin et al., 2006). Simons, Johnson and Conger (1994), for example, showed that the level of parental involvement also moderated the negative impact of physical punishment on child adjustment. These factors could explain some evidence that mild physical punishment can be associated with more positive adjustment in the children (Parker and Slaby, 1983). Thus, the effects of physical punishment on the psychological adjustment of children seems to be moderated by parenting styles; the broader family climate, including parental involvement; and even the severity of the punishment. The particular form in which these may be manifested will vary according to the broader culture in which it is practised.

Overall, the empirical evidence on the developmental consequences of physical punishment of children suggests a very complex situation. The effects differ in relation to the context in which this kind of punishment occurs. Significant variables include parenting style and family climate, parents' beliefs and attitudes, ethnicity, socio-economic status and child characteristics. It has been pointed out that the evidence about negative effects of physical punishment is not sufficiently clear **now** to justify widescale interventions to reduce parental reliance on this method of disciplining their children (Douglas, 2006). Overall, the evidence points to somewhat different causes and consequences of physical punishment for children from different social and cultural groups and it is important to know about these differences when intervening to reduce the use of physical punishment as a disciplinary technique within and among populations from different cultures. More positive disciplinary methods such as discussion, reasoning, ignoring, withholding privileges and time out should, however, probably be encouraged as alternatives to physical punishment in all cultural groups as they have not been found to be associated with negative consequences for children's development.

8.3.3.2 Addressing developmental difficulties

As discussed in the previous section, empirical evidence shows that parent-child relationships (and the way parents discipline their children) are intimately related to children's social and cognitive functioning, self-concept and well-being. In addition, the contexts of family functioning, such as the degree of stress experienced (e.g., through living in poverty or as a member of an ethnic minority which may also be associated with poverty) influence children's developmental progress and adjustment. When poor environments and negative family relationships coincide, there will be an elevated risk of developmental difficulties in children living in such circumstances. In such cases, research evidence can then be used to inform interventions to help children and families in difficulties in the use of evidence-based practice. Below we present an example of such an approach to intervention in the context of a small-scale Positive Play intervention.

8.3.3.2.1 Case study of a Positive Play Programme: An intervention approach for socially disadvantaged children was started in an infant school in a socially and economically deprived area in Derbyshire, England. Here many families were highly stressed and living in poverty, and 25 per cent of children had emotional and behavioural difficulties (Empson, 2006). It was evident that many of the children were starting school with such problems, including language delay, lack of social skills, depression and withdrawal, and they were unable to access the curriculum, and thus their academic progress was being impeded. Many of these children did not respond to the behaviour policies of the school and became increasingly disruptive in class and difficult to control. An early intervention, called the Positive Play Programme (PPP), was instigated by the Head Teacher and Behaviour Support at Derbyshire County Council to change the children's behaviour and avoid disaffection.

The programme was aimed at creating a safe, non-threatening environment in which an experienced play worker would establish a relationship of trust with the child so that they could work effectively together. Work was carried out on a one-to-one basis with children through a variety of media and individually chosen play activities. This allowed the child to express and communicate their feelings and difficulties. The children were engaged in activities which utilized their strengths and thus enabling them to feel good about themselves and raise their self-esteem. The focus was on using the relationship with the play worker and the activities provided to develop social skills, for example, self-control, turn-taking or sharing, or developmental skills, such as fine motor skills, to provide some of the early experiences that might have been missed at home but which are necessary for formal education. These activities were aimed at helping the children to acquire the coping skills necessary in the classroom so that they could have positive learning experiences there, and thus develop a more positive approach to school.

The children who were selected for involvement in the programme possessed one or more of the following difficulties: immaturity and difficulties settling in school; negative attitudes about school; poor social skills; having developmental delay in some respects; sad, depressed, withdrawn and isolated; needing short-term support during a difficult period; not responding to the normal behaviour policy of the school (Swanwick, Brown and Zelickman, 2002). Case studies 2 and 3 provide examples of two children who were thought by their teachers to be in need of the extra help offered by Positive Play.

CASE STUDY 2: THE CASE OF BILLY

Billy was seen to be in need of help at the age of five shortly after he started at Infant School and he soon began participating in the Positive Play Programme. He was a troubled child in many ways. He was unhappy, grumpy and self-abusive, smacking and hitting his own face, arms and legs. His difficulties could be related to his family background which held many secrets. For example, Billy's natural father was never referred to. Billy lived with his mother and his stepfather, who was mainly in employment, so the family was not living in total poverty. Billy received negative parenting from his mother. Her self-esteem was shown to be low by her demeanour when in school. She had poor eye contact, lacked confidence and emotional stability. As the school came to know Billy better, it was apparent that the mother was engaged in trying to meet her own needs at the expense of her children. She had little understanding of Billy, whose confidante was his grandfather. Following the death of his grandfather, Billy (then aged nine years) had outbursts at school. When asked if there could be any reason for this, his mother said she 'didn't think it would affect him'.

> **CASE STUDY 2 (cont'd)**
>
> When, at the age of five years, Billy had first started having one-to-one sessions in the Positive Play intervention, he could not cope with any of the demands of school and kept trying to run away. In the sessions, the initial task was to establish a trusting relationship with the play worker. Over time, this enabled Billy to start to talk through his difficulties, to identify the way in which he was treated differently from his siblings. He also engaged in tasks at which he could succeed which began to raise his self-esteem. On the last assessment, Billy had been involved in the Positive Play intervention on and off for about eight years. He no longer saw himself as a victim; he engaged with school and was the carer of his younger siblings as his mother now had a new partner with no interest in her children. Billy had to find his own way in life and learn from his mistakes. He was now self-determined and had ambitions to make something of his life.

The parents of the children taking part in the Positive Play intervention had varying degrees of involvement. All had to give their permission for their child to take part and all were invited to take part in a session or sessions with their child and play worker. Some took up the offer, but most did not. They did show their interest in other ways, by asking for progress reports from class teacher or play worker. It was considered that parents were of great importance to the success of such interventions, particularly in maintaining and further encouraging their child's interest and motivation in educational tasks. Some parents were interviewed about their child's involvement and all were very positive about the intervention.

> **CASE STUDY 3: THE CASE OF LINDA**
>
> When Linda started school, it was apparent that she was a neglected child, being poorly dressed, dirty and thin. She had problems in school straightaway with her attitudes and behaviour: she was undisciplined and unaware of boundaries, had little self-control and emotional regulation, was unable to form appropriate relationships, being mistrustful of adults, and she had no friends. Linda lived with her single mother and a younger

> **CASE STUDY 3 (cont'd)**
>
> sibling in extreme poverty. Her mother had no family to rely on for help and was socially excluded by the community in which she lived. She was also antisocial, swearing at people who she perceived to be authority figures, and her children were not appropriately socialized.
>
> When Linda began the intervention programme, it focused on teaching her social skills and how to form relationships, a massive task in a child with such negative attitudes, so she remained on the programme for the majority of her years in primary education.
>
> After moving into secondary school, Linda was being supported by the Positive Support (PS) Programme for older participants. The PS worker was helping Linda to cope with the emotional issues she was facing and which lead to emotional outbursts. The school staff found it difficult to deal with the emotional outbursts. The Programme offered the only unconditional support in her life and this enabled her to keep attending school. Now increasingly emotionally fragile due to circumstances at home, Linda was starting to repeat the behaviour of her mother and her future did not look promising.

The PPP was extended to include many schools, including secondary as well as primary schools. Evaluations of the effectiveness of the PPP showed that this combination of a safe place, a trusting relationship and individually chosen play and other activities have a positive effect in reducing maladaptive behaviour and improving positive behaviour as assessed by the Boxall Profile (Bennathan and Boxall, 1998) in primary school children (Empson, 2006). The performance on educational tasks (language and mathematics) of infant school children participating in the PPP was found to be up to the norms. In addition, different evaluations that were conducted found that the emotional and behavioural difficulties in children from very disadvantaged home backgrounds were reduced by participation in the PPP.

Key aspects of the programme were the individual attention given to the children in a situation of mutual trust between the play worker and child, and the tasks being individually suited to the child's strengths, building confidence in achievement. Children who had difficulties with language worked on that, and children who had problems with peer relationships improved their social skills and ability to work and play cooperatively with others. Children with difficulties in coping with stress did role-plays and other exercises which helped them to develop new skills and coping strategies.

However, it was observed by the staff that many children regressed during the long period of the summer holidays when they spent so much time in their difficult home environment without the support of the staff (see earlier examples of Billy and Linda). But they again made gains on restarting the intervention programme.

The Positive Play intervention was evidence-based and embedded in a range of well-established findings in the field of cognitive and social-emotional development (see Box 1 below).

BOX 1: SOME EVIDENCE SUPPORTING THE POSITIVE PLAY PROGRAMME

- The role of play in both social-emotional and cognitive development which is relevant to all societies and ethnic groups, given its evolutionary significance (Bruner, Jolly and Sylva, 1976).
- The role of the social conditions of learning, especially the part played by a more able and experienced person, often a parent, in facilitating a child's learning (Vygotsky, 1978).
- The use of 'scaffolding' (Wood, Bruner and Ross, 1976) in which a structure is provided to aid the child's learning to achieve a goal which would be beyond his unassisted efforts. The concept of 'scaffolding' is widely applied in the classroom.

These ideas were applied in the PPP sessions between the child and play worker, and are generally acknowledged to be important in encouraging optimal performance in the child. Cultural differences have been found (e.g., Rogoff, 1990) in the techniques used by mothers to help their children in problem-solving situations. Different techniques have also been found between mothers in different socio-economic groups. Thus, it is of importance for educational facilities to understand which techniques would be most effective for children in particular social and ethnic groups in enhancing their learning: which methods employed in school complement those used at home.

8.3.4 Promoting children's identity in multicultural environments

A young person's sense of positive self-concept and 'achieved' identity are core to well-being and effective socio-emotional and cognitive functioning, these being among the goals of socialization. As we saw in Chapter 7, there are various aspects to the development of children's identity in relation to ethnicity and religious affiliation. These include implications both for individual children in terms of their psychological adjustment, and for society in terms of such outcomes as the development of prejudice in multi-ethnic societies. In previous sections of this chapter relating to children's adjustment, the importance of parents and other interpersonal relationships have been emphasized. These relationships are also important for children's identity and self-esteem in different ethnic groups which may be exposed to prejudice and stigma in multicultural societies. Young children acquire particular attitudes towards different groups of people from their parents and other influential role models as they grow up through the processes of modelling, social learning and identification. This reflects learning in the microsystems of family, school and neighbourhood as described by Bronfenbrenner (2005).

The impact of societal and global events also affect children by filtering through the wider exosystems and macrosystems to influence, for example, workplace relationships between individuals of different ethnicities and religions, and discussions within families. Thus, in the 1960s, the activities of the Civil Rights Movement, and associated legislative changes in the United States created the context for dramatic changes in black children's attitudes towards their own group in a positive direction. More recently, the destruction of US planes and the twin towers of the World Trade Center in New York on September 11th, 2001 were followed by President Bush's 'war on terror' and increased tensions between the Muslim world and those of other religions. It is possible that because of this the self-esteem of Muslim children in Western society fell following September 11. There is a clear need, therefore, to investigate the implications of this for the developing identity and mental health of these children, and the processes through which world events may influence children's development in the spheres of ethnic and religious identity.

There are a number of explanations about factors that may contribute to the development of positive ethnic identity amongst children from minority groups. One of these has focused on availability of appropriate role models to which they can relate. It has been suggested that belonging to a group with devalued status evokes feelings of rejection of membership to such groups (see Harris, 1995 for an example of people with disabilities). Thus, experiences of discrimination, prejudice and racism by members of minority groups in multi-ethnic or multicultural contexts engenders feelings of rejection, by children of such groups, of their own membership to the group in question. In this sense, availability of successful and thus positive role models for such children is seen as one way of restoring their positive regard for their own membership to minority groups. The recent election, as American President, of Mr Barack Obama has been hailed as something that has cultivated a sense of pride in a number of black people. One such individual remarked on British national television on the day of the presidential inauguration: 'I can, from today, walk around with my head held high as an equal to anybody...'

CASE STUDY 4: THE ROLE MODEL PROJECT

At a secondary school in Sheffield (England), a project was conducted to introduce students to 'successful' ethnic minority individuals under the auspices of the then Sheffield Unified Multicultural Educational Service (SUMES). The 'role models' were invited from different spectrums of society at one point including a police inspector, university lecturer, banker, community worker, educational psychologist and a sports personality. Sessions were held in workshop format at least once in a term at which the 'role models' were invited to speak informally about their professions and how they had got to be where they were currently in terms of progressing in their professions. The students were invited to ask the speakers any questions regarding their careers.

Initially, the students were somewhat inhibited in initiating responses to the first talk. However, soon there were lots of questions raised, mostly around whether barriers had been experienced or any problems experienced. Almost everyone wanted to contribute to the discussions by expressing their opinions about the difficulties and, in some cases, benefits of being from an ethnic minority background. The students were clearly overjoyed to have the opportunity to chat to these role models and seemed fascinated that people like themselves could progress in society. The teachers, in their evaluation of such sessions, commented on the general attentiveness, interest and enthusiasm shown by the students in such sessions 'unlike in our normal lessons!'

Case Study 4 describes a project conducted at a secondary school in Sheffield, England, aimed at enhancing the self-esteem and motivation to pursue educational advancement by children from ethnic minority backgrounds. It has been argued, for example, in earlier literature that the British school system led black children to acquire low self-image and consequently low self-expectations in life, including the abandonment of intellectual and career goals (Coard, 1971). We have suggested elsewhere that the difficulties faced by children from ethnic minority backgrounds, which may be related to their ethnic identity, should be considered as specific special needs arising from social and/or cultural factors (Nabuzoka, 2000). Social factors in this sense relate to the structure of society and resultant interpersonal relations including racism and prejudice; cultural factors relate to the fact that skills and behaviours valued in the dominant culture may at times not relate the values of a child's culture of origin.

8.4 Issues in applied developmental psychology and research

In this section we identify a number of issues in applied developmental psychology and research that have implications for the discipline being attuned to the experiences of the vast majority of the world's children. First, we briefly outline areas of research that have implications for cultural considerations. The specific case of evaluative research conducted in different cultural settings is briefly discussed. Methodological issues and concerns that have characterized much of the psychological work in various cultures are then outlined and briefly discussed. The section concludes with an outline of some more specific methodological considerations that may inform the conduct of research that incorporates cultural considerations.

8.4.1 Research with a cultural perspective

8.4.1.1 Areas of research

Research incorporating culture in the study of human development has included efforts aimed at examining the specific ways in which culture may account for both socialization practices and developmental outcomes. Such research has focused on both the mechanisms of such influences and also the manifestation of cultural variations and similarities across different societies. Some examples of different types of research have been discussed in earlier chapters of this volume. One type of research that has not been discussed much, but has been introduced in this chapter, is that aimed at evaluating the effects of interventions or cultural change on the developing individuals. Examples of some issues raised by such 'applied' research are briefly discussed in the next section.

8.4.1.2 Evaluating programmes

Intervention programmes, by definition, in one way or another often challenge established ways of doing things and as such can be seen as often aimed at changing the 'culture' of a group of people (as in social engineering), families or individuals. As pointed out in Chapter 2, established practices with a strong cultural or subcultural basis are very difficult to change and can at times be met with strong resistance. In some cases, problems may simply arise as a result of the suggested activities being considered as falling outside the normal range of activities for a given community or society. Such difficulties were noted when evaluating the effects of a community-based programme for children with disabilities in rural communities of Zambia (Nabuzoka, 1991; 1993). In that study it was found that family – and other community – members were more likely to be actively involved in an intervention programme if it was incorporated in their day-to-day activities than if it was a completely new one. Similarly, a significant observation on the Positive Play Programme discussed above was the lack of continuity of the positive effects of this programme outside school context, for example, during summer holidays.

Evidence from the Chicago longitudinal study of minority children from low-income families (Ou, 2005) who took part in an early intervention at a Child-Parent Centre highlights the importance of social factors, such as the promotion of family-school partnerships and family involvement in early intervention programmes, in furthering educational attainment. Several pathways have been identified in a number of major early intervention studies through which the relationship between participation in intervention programme and later academic achievement is mediated. Both the Chicago intervention and the High/Scope Perry Preschool Program (Barnett, Young and Schweinhart, 1998) found that one pathway involved cognitive advantage achieved through school-related factors – classroom adjustment, lower-grade retention, intellectual gain – but other pathways involved support by families and schools. Ou (2005) argued that parental involvement in the Chicago intervention was crucial as higher aspirations by parents not only affect the child's motivation in the short term but also improve the quality of the home environment in the longer term. As Bronfenbrenner (1975) maintained, 'cognitive skills obtained through early intervention will be hard to maintain if the quality of one's home environment stays deprived' (Ou, 2005, p. 603).

In the United Kingdom, government policy has been directed towards providing improved employment, education and training opportunities for the lowest-income groups, including lone mothers, and also to provide support for parenting, for example, Sure Start schemes. However, one of the obstacles to greater success in this enterprise has been the shortage of good quality, affordable childcare. It is vitally important that government continues to increase its investment in the war on poverty and its associated difficulties so that the potential of children living in such circumstances is not wasted. An analysis of a research network in the United Kingdom (Schoon and Bartley, 2008), which also uses an ecological framework and brings together research findings from different disciplines – psychology, psychiatry, economics, geography, epidemiology and social policy – concludes that interventions need to operate on several levels including community and integrated service delivery as well as on the more micro level of the family and individual. Such evaluations of interventions of this type indicate that interventions must utilize what we know about the processes of resilience that enable some people to function well despite adversity, and also need to address the risk factors for vulnerability and the environmental and social factors that can be altered to minimize risk and enhance coping. Interventions, therefore, need to take into account possible cultural factors related to resilience and also vulnerability and susceptibility to intervention when helping groups, which include different cultural groups, to help themselves. In all, these programmes demonstrate that it is important all interventions are evaluated for their success in improving people's lives not just in the short term but also in the long term.

8.4.2 Methodological issues

One early concern in the history of cross-cultural research was that most studies tended to be predominantly atheoretical and unsystematic, simply focusing on whether a psychological attribute observed in one culture, often that of the researcher, also existed in other cultures. This has largely been attributed to a lack of appreciation of the complexities of conducting such research. Questions have often focused on the theoretical basis of much of the research conducted, methods used and ethical implications, and also on wider issues concerning the generalization of findings and the relevance of **majority** of such work. At the conceptual level, and as we saw in Chapter 2, such concerns have given rise to the emergence of the perspectives of cultural psychology and indigenous psychologies. This has led to increased use of qualitative approaches other than complete reliance on quantitative methods. In cross-cultural research, efforts at addressing such concerns have focused on examining various aspects of the research process from the generation of broad research questions, through the use of appropriate methods and data analysis techniques, to the sensitive reporting of obtained results (see Goodwin, 1996).

In the next subsections we discuss some of these features of the research process to highlight issues raised. A number of these issues relate mostly to what has been termed '*etic*' research (Berry, 1989), which is concerned with the application of one's own theories in other cultures and involving access to others through techniques such as interviews, questionnaires, and so on. As indicated earlier, '*Emic*' research, in contrast, involves the examination of culturally specific phenomena and also the development of culturally specific, indigenous theories.

8.4.2.1 Focus of research

One of the initial considerations in conducting research is to identify and clearly define which cultures and topics to investigate. As we saw in Chapter 2, there are various aspects to the concept of culture and hence problems may arise as to how exactly to define it. For example, a common approach has been to use geographical units as the basis but, in the context of migrations of people and the heterogeneity of communities within geographical regions, this has a number of associated problems such as which groups in a population should be included as part of that culture and which should be left out. Major concerns in defining which topics to study across the cultures of interest are the applicability and relevance of the topics to the cultures under investigation. This is a particularly relevant issue in cross-cultural psychology as the concern is about comparing different cultures on some psychological or behavioural attribute.

There is also the risk that the issue under investigation may be so far removed from indigenous concerns and practices that it has little relevance to those societies being compared (see Wagner, 1986). As observed by Sta. Maria (2000), 'the issue of relevance is that which characterizes the problem of research in non-Western experience' (p. 4). This not only raises ethical issues about why the research is being done at all, but may also mean that the researcher is unlikely to engage the interest of the groups targeted as participants. Goodwin (1996) points out that not only may finding willing participants be difficult if the relevance of their participation is not apparent, but also that even those respondents who actually participate may be unlikely to report or perform seriously on tasks at hand. In cultural psychology, and indigenous psychologies, the research question relates more to the meaning and significance of particular behaviours and practices. Thus, relevance of activity is the focus of research. Furthermore, in indigenous psychologies, the research questions may be formulated and examined by those participating as subjects in the research.

8.4.2.2 Suitability of research instruments

Related to the focus of research is the appropriateness of the instruments and procedures used in pursuing the aims of the study. Although a number of studies on child development in different cultures use observational and ethnographic methods, most studies use assessment procedures (including psychological tests) and questionnaires of one form or another to collect data. One issue involves the contents of those instruments and the underlying assumptions about what is being investigated. This includes the questions posed to members of other cultures who participate in the research and how responses are interpreted both by the respondent and the investigator. Greenfield (1997) has argued that a lack of agreement as to the value and meaning of particular responses can lead to cross-cultural misunderstandings that undermine the validity of psychological research. For example, a study of intelligence in different cultures would need to first establish that the definitions of intelligence in those cultures are equivalent, and if so, whether the items of the instrument used mean the same in different cultures.

In cross-cultural comparative studies, one way of ensuring that questions asked capture their intended meaning is by ensuring accurate translation of the questions into the language of the participants. Though this can be a lengthy and sometimes expensive procedure, it is deemed essential that this is done well. One of the most widely used systematic approaches is back translation. This involves a researcher preparing material in one language; a first translator translates it into the target language and a second one back into the researcher's original language, whereby the quality of the translation can be judged. This back-translation process can lead to the modification of any poorly translated terms. However, Greenfield (1997) points out that instruments reflect the value systems of their cultural origins such that even when the norms for linguistic translation have been conformed with, the same items might mean different things in different cultures.

The concern is, therefore, about how to ensure that questions asked are not only suitable and relevant to the cultures being studied, but also that they are interpreted appropriately. One suggestion for verifying the appropriateness of the questions being posed is to allow some input into the construction of the research instrument by participants from the communities under investigation, and for them to become active participants in the research (Goodwin, 1996). Such an orientation is emphasized in indigenous psychologies, and it can ensure that not only the relevant topic areas are covered (a concern discussed earlier), but also that the intended meaning is conveyed in the items of the research instruments. In this respect, a number of open-ended methods have been suggested for encouraging participant-centred designs. One example involves asking participants to produce their own questions within a broad theme, which are then used throughout the data collection (Mamali, 1982).

8.4.2.3 Conduct of research

The conduct of research can have a significant effect on the findings and hence their usefulness. One concern, especially regarding cross-cultural comparative studies, has been the extent to which the measures used and or the procedures followed can be said to represent a reliable measure of the phenomenon of interest. An essential procedure for 'refinement' of both the instruments used and the procedures to be followed is to conduct a pilot study. This often includes the 'trying out' of the translated research questions where that is the case, and/or research procedures. In some instances this can involve open-ended interviews with samples of individuals that are similar to those from the target sample, and taken from the same culture. This can be a relatively short procedure but may also include the participants in the pilot study being probed on the meaning of their answers to ensure comprehension. This process may lead to modification of the research instruments and procedures where appropriate. At this stage, an assessment can also be made of the situational factors that may affect the administration of the research instruments or the general running of the study.

The context for communication between the researcher and participants is important in cross-cultural research. Cultural conventions about communication between different groups of people can have a bearing on the research findings or observations. Conventions may vary in different cultures about communication with strangers or between adults and children. For example, there may be minimal verbalization from children in a culture where children are meant to listen and understand, not to speak in adult-child interactions (Harkness and Super, 2008). This can be misleading if the researcher is assessing the language ability of a child, or simply conducting research that relies on verbal communication. Greenfield (1997) suggests that this can be addressed by the researcher first entering a new meaning system whereby they learn about a culture's conventions about communication. This can be done using the anthropological method of ethnography, whereby the researcher has first-hand experience of the setting in which the activity of research experience occurs. This can involve participant observation, which can be supplemented by interviews and open-ended conversations. Ethnography would therefore be 'a major tool for detecting, correcting, and preventing cross-cultural misunderstandings by expanding the common cultural ground between testers and their participants' (Greenfield, 1997, p. 1122).

There is a general recognition that psychological research should be multi-method wherever possible, as culture is such a complex phenomenon with cultural differences being so easily misinterpreted. Such a multi-method approach affords a richness of analysis and understanding even though a combination of different methods may be difficult to carry out. As we saw in Chapter 2, quantitative analyses have dominated the cross-cultural literature over the years, with factor analyses being the most widely used methods of data analyses. These have been used to establish the relevance of the question schedules that have been devised in other cultures. However, a range of qualitative techniques also exist. A number of these have been developed in cultural anthropology and are often used in cultural psychology. Some of these are also suitable for some cross-cultural studies, as well as those reflecting indigenous psychology.

8.4.2.4 Communicating findings

The relevance of the research is related to the question of who constitutes the audience for the data collected. There are some ethical and social considerations involved in the dissemination of research findings and these are often complex and potentially form one of the most significant aspects of the work of the researcher. One important concern about reports of studies is the accessibility and utility of the findings for the people under investigation. A distinction can be made between theoretical (sometimes referred to as 'pure') research and applied research. The former is considered to be 'knowledge-driven' while the latter is 'decision driven' (Masters, 1984; Wagner, 1986). Knowledge-driven research involves empirical studies that are often aimed at building on findings that have been published in the literature. The audience for reports from this type of research are often academics and others who access the professional journals in which they are published. In contrast, decision-driven research is of the type that responds to some social policy issues, such as schooling and literacy in rural African communities or the impact of inclusive education on academic achievement of children with disabilities. The audience for reports from these types of research are often policy-makers. Serpell (1993) has argued that ordinary people who participate in studies should be part of the audience for any new theories or explanations about human development that are derived from such research. He has pointed out, however, that if any such new theories are to make sense as well as be acceptable and empowering to such people, they should also take account of the pre-existing ideas of those to be addressed.

Another issue relates to the extent to which the process of participating in the research can itself be a transforming process, as participants may be required to reflect on their experiences and things that have deeper and personal meanings for them. In addition, their experiences in the research process, including how the researcher treats them, may have long-lasting effects on the attitudes towards other researchers and perhaps the culture they are perceived to represent.

Issues also arise regarding the uses and interpretations of findings, especially those from cross-cultural research of the knowledge-driven variety. Of particular concern in cross-cultural psychology have been interpretations that lead to a simple, and often derogatory, summary of a culture. An example is the attempt to correlate national economic development with psychological values on such dimensions as individualism-collectivism (Hofstede, 1980), and to infer causality of the former by the latter. It has been argued that such inferences grossly underplay the complexities of cultural variation, and can have potentially damaging consequences for the cultures in question (Goodwin, 1996; Voronov and Singer, 2002). There have, therefore, been calls for some of the sensitive reporting of results obtained in different cultures (Goodwin, 1996).

8.4.2.5 Summary of methodological concerns

A concern regarding cross-cultural research has been that they have historically lacked a clear theoretical rationale as to the relevance of studies conducted. Thus, questions have often focused on the theoretical basis and the societal and cultural relevance of much of the research conducted, methods used and ethical implications, and also on wider issues concerning the generalization of findings. Efforts at addressing such concerns have given rise to the perspectives of cultural psychology and indigenous psychologies. Other concerns have focused on examining various aspects of the research process from the generation of broad research questions, through the use of appropriate methods, including the conduct of research, to the sensitive reporting of obtained results. Specific issues have included the rationale and focus of studies, and the suitability of research instruments used, including their underlying assumptions about the phenomena of interest in relation to the culture being studied. Other considerations include the conduct of research and the situational factors that may affect the findings. Finally, the relevance of the research is related to the question of who constitutes the audience for the data collected. One argument is that ordinary people who participate in studies should also be part of that audience and that research efforts should take account of the pre-existing ideas that such people may have about the phenomena of interest.

8.5 Conclusions

Psychologists and researchers from other disciplines have studied child-rearing practices as a mechanism for socializing children for adult life in different cultures. These studies have focused on specific parenting styles and psychological outcomes in the offspring and also on environmental and contextual factors as determinants of parenting goals and practices. The findings of such studies are important in informing policy-makers, practitioners and researchers about the influence of culture on human development. Studies also show that there are various ways in which culture can be constituted, and how it can be defined and examined, including its influence on the psychological development of individual children. The influence of culture can be identified in various domains of child development – cognitive, linguistic and social-emotional – and in different environments. In addition, there are different examples of the constitutions of culture as related to groups of people or societies. These include traditional, modern, ethnic background, religious affiliation and socio-economic status. A number of outcomes of such cultural factors in various domains have been identified. These findings and considerations have a number of theoretical, research and practical implications regarding the welfare of children in various cultures.

In this book, we have presented research evidence and relevant theories which explain the relationships between culture and child development in the domains of cognitive and social-emotional development, identity and the self-concept. In this final chapter we have further developed our understanding of these relationships as applied to some current social issues. The more we understand the impact of culture on children's development, the better this will inform interventions to improve life for children and families in need, and we have discussed some examples of such interventions. Of course, the evidence on the use of discipline, for example, shows that particular kinds of behaviour are appropriate for specific cultural niches and ethnic groups, and that what constitutes best practice will vary with diverse cultures. All research and any recommendations, such as that involving parenting practices therefore needs to take cultural context into account. Most of the psychological research on child development has been focused on Western industrialized societies so there is a pressing need for more research in societies of the so-called majority world, using appropriate research methodologies. Bearing these caveats in mind, in the twenty-first century, the world is facing major issues such as climate change, and globalization as people migrate from one geographical location to another, resulting in societies becoming increasingly multicultural and complex. In such circumstances, psychology that incorporates considerations of the role of culture is becoming more important as it can provide frameworks for understanding key factors and processes involved in the development of people from various backgrounds. These frameworks are increasingly becoming useful in informing policy-makers, organizations and professionals as they work to improve environments and opportunities for children and families in a range of cultural contexts. Such efforts are not only important in facilitating the provision of support that optimizes the attainment of developmental potential of all children but also contributes to enabling people from different cultures to live together in harmony.

FURTHER READING

Berry, J.W., Poortinga, Y.H., Segall, M.H., and Dasen, P.R. (1992). *Cross-cultural psychology: Research and applications*. Cambridge: Cambridge University Press.

Goodwin, R. (1996). A brief guide to cross-cultural psychological research. In J. Haworth (Ed). Psychological research: Innovative methods and strategies. London and New York: Routledge.

Paludi, M.A. (2002). *Human development in multicultural contexts: A book of readings*. Upper Saddle River, New Jersey: Prentice Hall.

Rogoff, B. (2003). *The cultural nature of human development.* Oxford: Oxford University Press.

Saraswathi, T.S. (Ed.) (2003). *Cross-cultural perspectives in human development: Theory, research and applications.* London: Sage.

Serpell, R. (1993). *The significance of schooling: Life-journeys in an African society.* Cambridge: Cambridge University Press.

Woodhead, M., Faulkner, D., and Littleton, K. (2003). *Cultural worlds of early childhood.* London and New York: Routledge and Open University.

REFERENCES

Aderinto, A.A. (2000). Social correlates and coping measures of street children: A comparative study of street and non-street children in South-Western Nigeria. *Child Abuse and Neglect,* 24(9), 1199–2000.

Arnold, D.H. and Doctoroff, G.L. (2003). The early education of socioeconomically disadvantaged children. *Annual Review of Psychology,* 54, 517–545.

Aucoin, K.J., Frick, P.J., and Bodin, S.D. (2006). Corporal punishment and child adjustment. *Journal of Applied Developmental Psychology,* 27, 527–541.

Barnett, W.S., Young, J.W., and Schweinhart, L.J. (1998). How preschool education influences long-term cognitive development and school success: A causal model. In W.S. Barnett and S.S. Boocock (Eds), *Early care and education for children in poverty: Promises, programs and long-term results* (pp. 167–184). Albany, NY: State University of New York Press.

Baumrind, D. (1968). Authoritarian vs authoritative parental control. *Adolescence,* 3, 255–272.

Baumrind, D. (1971). Current patterns of parental authority. *Developmental Psychology Monograph,* 4 (1 pt. 2), 1–103.

Belsky, J., Melhuish, E., Barnes, J., Leyland, A.H., and Romaniuk, H. (2006). Effects of Sure Start local programmes on children and families: Early findings from a quasi-experimental, cross-sectional study. *British Medical Journal,* 332, 1476–1479.

Bennathan, M. and Boxall, M. (1998) *Boxall Diagnostic Profile.* London: Nurture Group Network.

Berry, J.W. (1989). Imposed etics-emics-derived etics: The operationalization of a compelling idea. *International Journal of Psychology,* 24, 721–735.

Berry, J.W., Poortinga, Y.H., Segal, M.H., and Dasen, P.R. (2002). *Cross-cultural psychology: Research and applications.* Second Edition. New York: Cambridge University Press.

Bialystok, E. (2001). *Bilingualism in development: Language, literacy and cognition.* New York: Cambridge University Press.

Bialystok, E. (2007). Cognitive effects of bilingualism: How linguistic experience leads to cognitive change. *The International Journal of Bilingual Education and Bilingualism,* 10(3), 210–223.

Boivin, M., Hymel, S., and Bukowski, W.M. (1995). The roles of social withdrawal, peer rejection, and victimization by peers in predicting loneliness and depressed mood in childhood. *Development and Psychopathology,* 7, 765–785.

Bradley, R., Whiteside, L., Mundfrom, D., Casey, P., Kelleher, K., and Pope, S. (1994). Early indications of resilience and their relation to experiences in the home environments of low birth-weight, premature children living in poverty. *Child Development*, **65**, 346–360.

Bronfenbrenner, U. (1975). Is early intervention effective? In E.L. Struening and M. Guttentag (Eds), *Handbook of evaluation research* (pp. 519–603). Beverley Hills, CA: Sage.

Bronfenbrenner, U. (1979). *The ecology of human development: Experiments by nature and by design.* Cambridge, MA: Harvard University Press.

Bronfenbrenner, U. (Ed.) (2005). *Making human beings human: Bioecological perspectives on human development.* London: Sage.

Brown, E.A. and Dillenburger, K. (2004). An evaluation of the effectiveness of intervention in families with children with behavioural problems within the context of a Sure Start programme. *Child Care in Practice*, 10(1), 63–77.

Bruner, J.S., Jolly, A., and Sylva. K. (Eds) (1976). *Play. Its role in development and evolution.* Harmondsworth: Penguin.

Central Advisory Council for Education (1967). *Children and their primary schools.* London: HMSO (The Plowden Report).

Chishimba, M. (1980). Observations on the English Medium component of the Zambia Primary Course. *Zambia Educational Review*, 2.

Coard, B. (1971). *How the West Indian child is made educationally subnormal in the British school system.* London: New Beacon Books.

Colder, C.R., Lochman, J.E., and Wells, K.C. (1997). The moderating effects of children's fear and activity level on relations between parenting practices and child symptomatology *Journal of Abnormal Child Psychology*, **25**, 251–263.

Cole, M. (2005). Cross-cultural and historical perspectives on the developmental consequences of education. *Human Development*, **48**, 195–216.

Crooks, D. (1995). American children at risk: Poverty and its consequences for children's health, growth, and school achievement. *Yearbook of Physical Anthropology*, **38**, 57–86.

Darling, N. and Steinberg, L. (1993). Parenting style as context: An integrative model. *Psychological Bulletin*, **113**, 487–496.

Deater-Deckard, K. and Dodge, K.A. (1997). Externalizing behaviour problems and discipline revisited: Nonlinear effects and variation by culture, context and gender. *Psychological Inquiry*, **8**, 161–175.

Deater-Deckard, K., Bates, J.E., Dodge, K.A., and Petit, G.S. (1996). Physical discipline among African American and European American mothers: Links to children's externalizing behaviours. *Developmental Psychology*, **32**, 1065–1072.

Department for Education and Employment (1999). *Sure start.* London: The Stationery Office.

Department for Education and Skills (2004). *Breaking the cycle.* London: DfES.

Dietz, T. (2000). Disciplining children: Characteristics associated with the use of corporal punishment. *Child Abuse and Neglect*, **24**, 1529–1542.

Douglas, E.M. (2006). Familial violence socialization in childhood and later-life approval of corporal punishment: A cross-cultural perspective. *American Journal of Orthopsychiatry*, 76(1), 23–30.
Eisenstadt, N. (2002). Sure start: Key principles and ethos. *Child: Care, Health and Development*, **28**, 3–4.
Empson, J.M. (2006). *Evaluation of the positive Play/Positive Support Programme in Derbyshire schools*. Report for Derbyshire County Council, July.
Empson, J.M. and Hamilton, D. (2004). Emotional and behavioural difficulties. In J.M. Empson and D. Nabuzoka (Eds), *Atypical child development in context*. Basingstoke: Palgrave.
Empson, J.M. and Nabuzoka, D. (2005). Parents' views of physical punishment of children in England and Zambia. *Paper presented to the Biennial Conference of the European Society of Developmental Psychology*, Tenerife, August.
End Corporal Punishment Website (2009). http://www.endcorporalpunishment.org/pages/frame.html accessed 3/09/09.
Entwistle, D., Alexander, K., and Olson, L. (1997). *Children, schools and inequality*. Boulder, CO: Westview Press.
Gershoff, E.T. (2002). Corporal punishment by parents and associated child behaviours and experiences: A meta-Analytic and theoretical review. *Psychological Bulletin*, 128(4), 539–579.
Goodwin, R. (1996). A brief guide to cross-cultural psychological research. In J. Haworth (Ed.), *Psychological research: Innovative methods and strategies*. London and New York: Routledge.
Greenfield, P.M. (1997). You can't take it with you: Why ability assessments don't cross cultures. *American Psychologist*, **52**, 1115–1124.
Greenfield, S., Leach, P., Bowlby, R. and others (2006). Modern life leads to more depression among children. *Daily Telegraph*, 12 Sept., p. 1. http://www.telegraph.co.uk/news/1528639/Modern-life-leads-to-more-depression-among-children.html accessed 3/09/09.
Harkness, S. and Super, C.M. (Eds) (1995). *Parents' cultural belief systems: Their origins, expressions and consequences*. New York: Guildford Press.
Harkness, S. and Super, C.M. (2008). Why African children are so hard to test. In R.A. Levine and R.S. New (Eds), *Anthropology and child development: A cross-cultural reader* (pp. 182–186). Oxford: Blackwell Publishing.
Harris, P. (1995). Who am I? Concepts of disability and their implications for people with learning disabilities. *Disability & Society*, 10(3), 341–364.
Hofstede, G. (1980). *Culture's consequences: International differences in work-related values*. Beverly Hills, CA: Sage.
Hoppers, W.H. (1981). *Education in a rural society*. Lusaka: Institute for African Studies, University of Zambia.
Kagitçibasi, C. (1990). Family and socialization in cross-cultural perspective: A model of change. In J. Berman (Ed.), *Nebraska symposium on motivation, 1989: Cross-cultural perspectives* (pp. 135–200). Lincoln, NE: Nebraska University Press.

Kagitçibasi, C. (1997). Individualism and collectivism. In J.W. Berry, M.H. Segall, and C. Kagitçibasi (Eds), *Handbook of cross-cultural psychology* (Vol. 3) (pp.1–47). Boston, MA: Allyn & Bacon.

Kagitçibasi, C. (2005). Autonomy and relatedness in cultural context. Implications for self and family. *Journal of Cross-Cultural Psychology*, **20**, 1–20.

Keller, H. (2003). Socialization for competence: Cultural models of infancy. *Human Development*, **46**, 288–311.

Keller, H., Lamm, B., Abels, M., Yovsi, R., Borke, J., Jensen, H., Papalogoura, Z., Holub, C., Lo, W., Tomiyama, A.J., Su, Y., Wang, Y., and Chaudhary, N. (2006). Cultural models, socialization goals, and parenting ethnotheories: A multicultural analysis. *Journal of Cross-Cultural Psychology*, 37(2), 155–172.

Korenman, S., Miller, J., and Sjaastad, J. (1995). Long-term poverty and child development in the United States: Results from the NLSY. *Children and Youth Services Review*, **17**, 127–155.

Kovacs, A. and Mehler, J. (2009). Cognitive gains in 7-month-old bilingual infants. *Proceedings of the National Academy of Sciences*, 106(16), 6556–6560.

Lansford, J.E., Chang, L., Dodge, K.A., Malone, P.S., Oburu, P., Palmerus, K., Bacchini, D., Pastorelli, C., Bombi, A.S., Zelli, A., Tapanya, S., Chaudhary, N., Deater-Deckard, K., Manke, B., and Quinn, N. (2005). Physical discipline and children's adjustment: Cultural normativeness as a moderator. *Child Development*, 76(6), 1234–1246.

Leach, P. (1993). Should parents hit their children? *The Psychologist*, 6, 216–220.

Leach, P. (2002). You can't beat psychological input. *The Psychologist*, 15(1), 8–9.

Lenneberg, E. (1967). *Biological foundations of language*. New York: John Wiley & Sons.

Lerner, J.V. (1993). The influence of child temperamental characteristics on parent behaviour. In T. Luster and L. Okagaki (Eds), *Parenting: An ecological perspective*, Hillsdale, NJ: Lawrence Erlbaum Associates.

Light, P. and Littleton, K. (1999). *Social processes in children's learning*. Cambridge: Cambridge University Press.

Mamali, C. (1982). Democratization of social research. In P. Stringer (Ed.), *Confronting social issues: Applications of social psychology*. London: Academic Press.

Markus, H.R. and Lin, L.R. (1999). Conflictways: Cultural diversity in the meanings and practice of conflict. In D.A. Prentice and D.T. Miller (Eds), *Cultural divides: Understanding and overcoming group conflict* (pp. 302–333). New York: Russell Sage Foundation.

Masten, A.S. and Coatsworth, J.D. (1998). The development of competence in favorable and unfavorable environments. Lessons from research on successful children. *American Psychologist*, 53(2), 205–220.

Masters, J.C. (1984). Psychology, research, and social policy. *American Psychologist*, 39, 851–862.

McInnes, E. (2004). Keeping children safe. The links between family violence and poverty. Paper presented to *Because children matter: Tackling poverty together*. Uniting Missions National Conference, Adelaide, 1–3 Nov.

McLoyd, V.C., Kaplan, R., Hardaway, C.R., and Wood, D. (2007). Does endorsement of physical discipline matter? Assessing moderating influences on the maternal and child psychological correlates of physical discipline in African American families. *Journal of Family Psychology*, 21(2), 165–175.

Monyooe, L.A. (1996). Teachers' views towards corporal punishment in Lesotho schools. *Psychological Reports*, 79, 121–122.

Mulvaney, M.K. and Mebert, C.J. (2007). Parental corporal punishment predicts behaviour problems in early childhood. *Journal of Family Psychology*, 21(3), 389–397.

Nabuzoka, D. (1991). Community-based rehabilitation for disabled children in Zambia: Experiences of the Kasama District Project. *International Journal of Special Education*, 6(3), 321–339.

Nabuzoka, D. (1993). How to define, involve and assess the care unit? Experiences and research from a CBR programme in Zambia. In H. Finkenflügel (Ed.), *The handicapped community: The relation between Primary Health Care and Community-Based Rehabilitation* (pp. 73–87). Amsterdam: VU University Press

Nabuzoka, D. (2000). Specific special needs of African and African-Caribbean children: A research note. *African Centred Review*, 2, 23–33.

Newson, J. and Newson, E. (1989). *The extent of parental physical punishment in the UK*. London: Association for the Protection of All Children Ltd. (Approach).

Nsamenang, A.B. (2000). Issues in indigenous approaches to developmental research in Sub-Saharan Africa. *ISSBD Newsletter*, 1(37), 1–4.

Nsamenang, A.B. (2003). Conceptualizing human development and education in Sub-Saharan Africa at the interface of indigenous and exogenous influences. In T.S. Saraswathi (Ed.), *Cross-cultural perspectives in human development: Theory, research and applications*. London: Sage.

Nunes Carraher, T., Carraher, D.W., and Schliemann, A.D. (1985). Mathematics in the streets and in school. *British Journal of Developmental Psychology*, 3, 21–29.

Ou, S.-R. (2005). Pathways of long-term effects of an early intervention program on educational attainment: Findings from the Chicago longitudinal study. *Applied Developmental Psychology*, 26, 578–611.

Parker, R.D. and Slaby, R.G. (1983). The development of aggression. In P.H. Mussen (Ed.), *Handbook of child psychology*. Fourth Edition. *Socialization, personality and social development, vol. 4.* (pp. 547–641). New York: John Wiley & Sons.

Patterson, G.R. (1982). *Coercive family interactions*. Eugene, OR: Castalia Press.

Piaget, J. (1951). *The origin of intelligence in children*. New York: International Universities Press.

Rogoff, B. (1990). *Apprenticeship in thinking: Cognitive development in social context.* New York: Oxford University Press.

Rothbaum, F., Pott, M., Azuma, H., Miyake, K., and Weisz, J. (2000). The development of close relationships in Japan and the United States. Paths of symbiotic harmony and generative tension. *Child Development*, 71, 1121–1142.

Rubin, K.H., Chen, X., and Hymel, S. (1993). Socio-emotional characteristics of aggressive and withdrawn children. *Merrill-Palmer Quarterly*, 49, 518–534.

Schneider, B.H., Woodburn, S., Soteras-de Toro, M., and Udvari, S. (2005). Cultural and gender differences in the implications of competition for early adolescent friendship. *Merrill-Palmer Quarterly*, **51**, 163–191.

Schneiders, J., Drukker, M., van der Ende, J., Verhulst, J., van Os, J., and Nicolson, N. (2003). Neighbourhood socio-economic disadvantage and behavioural problems from late childhood into early adolescence. *Journal of Epidemiology and Community Health*, **57**, 699–703.

Schoon, I. and Bartley, M. (2008). The role of human capability and resilience. *The Psychologist*, 21(1), 24–27.

Schweinhart, L.J., Barnes, H.V., Weikart, D.P., Barnett, W.S., and Epstein, A.S. (1993). *Significant benefits: The high/scope Perry Preschool Study through age 27*. Ypsilanti, MI: High/Scope Press.

Sekeleti, C. (1985). The medium of instruction in Zambian Primary schools. Unpublished MA dissertation. Lusaka: University of Zambia.

Sekeleti, C. (1998). Medium of instruction in Zambian primary schools. *African Social Research*, 39/40, 114–139.

Serpell, R. (1993). *The significance of schooling: Life-journeys in an African society*. Cambridge: Cambridge University Press.

Serpell, R. (2005). Optimizing developmental consequences of education: Reflections on issues raised by Michael Cole. *Human Development*, **48**, 217–222.

Simons, R.L., Johnson, C., and Conger, R.D. (1994). Harsh corporal punishment versus quality of parental involvement as an explanation of adolescent maladjustment. *Journal of Marriage and the Family*, **56**, 591–607.

Sta. Maria, M. (2000). On the nature of cultural research. *International Society for the Study of Behavioural Development (ISSBD) Newsletter*, 1(37), 4–6.

Stormshak, E.A., Bierman, K.L., McMahon, R.J., Lengua, L.J., and Conduct Problems Prevention Research Group (2000). Parenting practices and child disruptive behaviour problems in early elementary school. *Journal of Clinical Child Psychology*, **29**, 17–29.

Straus, M.A. and Stewart, J.H. (1999). Corporal punishment by American parents: National data on prevalence, chronicity, severity, and duration in relation to child and family characteristics. *Clinical Child and Family Psychology Review*, **2**, 55–70.

Super, C.M. and Harkness, S. (1986). The developmental niche: A conceptualization at the interface of child and culture. *International Journal of Behavioural Development*, 9, 545–569.

Swanwick, P., Brown, S., and Zelickman, I. (2002). *Positive play. A primary school play programme*. Derby: Derbyshire County Council.

Voronov, M. and Singer, J.A. (2000). The myth of individualism-collectivism: A critical review. *The Journal of Social Psychology*, 142(4), 461–480.

Wagner, D.A. (1986). Child development research and the third world: A future of mutual interest? *American Psychologist*, 41(3), 298–301.

Webster-Stratton, C. and Herbert, M. (1993). *Troubled families – problem children.* Chichester: John Wiley & Sons.

Weisz, R.J., Rothbaum, F.M., and Blackburn, T.C. (1984). Swapping recipes for control. *American Psychologist,* **39**, 1063–1070.

Whaley, A.L. (2000). Sociocultural differences in the developmental consequences of the use of physical discipline during childhood for African Americans. *Cultural Diversity & Ethnic Minority Psychology,* 6(1), 5–12.

Wood, D., Bruner, J.S., and Ross, G. (1976). The role of tutoring in problem-solving. *Journal of Child Psychology and Psychiatry,* **17**, 89–100.

Xu, Y., Farver, J.A.M., Chang, L., Yu, L., and Zhang, Z. (2006). Culture, family contexts and children's coping strategies in peer interactions. In X. Chen, D.C. French, and B.H. Schneider (Eds), *Peer relationships in cultural context.* New York: Cambridge University Press.

Glossary

Acculturation: The process through which individuals or groups adapt to the requirements of a new culture. Also refers to changes in a cultural group or individual as a result of contact with another cultural group.

Adaptation: Changes in the behaviour repertoire of a person or group as a reaction to the demands of the ecological or social environment.

Anthropology: A discipline concerned with the study of human societies in all their variety, and in various domains (cultural, social, biological and psychological).

Attachment: An emotional bond between people that is usually powerful and long-lasting. The term is used particularly to describe the relationship between an infant and mother from which the infant derives security and is thought by many developmental psychologists to be of consequence through the entire lifespan.

Bilingualism: The ability of persons to communicate with others in at least one other language beyond their mother tongue (persons who can speak two languages are referred to as *bilinguals*).

Characteristic features: The qualities that describe a prototypical model of a word (or concept), thereby serving as the basis for the meaning of the word (or concept); these qualities will characterize many or most of the instances of the word (or concept), but not necessarily all instances.

Child-directed speech: A characteristic form of speech that adults tend to use when speaking with infants and young children, which usually involves a higher pitch, exaggerated raising and lowering of pitch and volume, and relatively simple sentence constructions; this is generally more effective than normal speech in gaining and keeping the attention of infants and young children.

Cognition: The activity of knowing and the process through which knowledge is acquired (e.g., attending, perceiving, remembering and thinking).

Cognitive anthropology: A subdiscipline of anthropology that seeks to understand the relationship between culture and the cognitive life of the group.

Cognitive development: The diverse changes in the processes of thinking, reasoning, memory and so on whereby an individual's understanding of the world changes across the lifespan as a result of maturation and experience.

Cognitive psychology: The study of how people perceive, learn, remember, and think about the world and information.

Cognitive styles: A conception of cognitive activity that emphasizes the way in which cognitive processes are organized and used, rather than the level of development of cognitive abilities.

Collectivist: An orientation characteristic of a society which emphasizes cooperative group functioning and interdependence of relationships. The individual is construed in relation to others.

Communication: The exchange of thoughts and feelings, which may include language, as well as non-verbal forms of expression, such as gestures, glances and so on (see also *language*).

Concept: An idea or a thought about something, to which various characteristics may be attached and to which various other ideas may be connected; may be used to describe either abstract or concrete ideas.

Concrete operational thinking: The third stage of Piaget's stages of cognitive development. It is characterized by a move away from egocentrism. The child remains concerned with objects and concrete terms rather than abstract ideas.

Conservation: The ability of the child to understand that certain essential features of an object remain the same even if the appearance of it changes.

Constructivist: A way of describing children's cognitive development in which they actively seek and construct knowledge and understanding of the world through interaction with the environment.

Contextualized cognition: A conception of cognitive activity that emphasizes the development and use of cognitive processes in relation to specific cultural contexts and practices.

Contextualist: Theorist or researcher who holds that a given psychological construct, such as cognitive functioning (or intelligence), cannot be understood outside its real world context.

Contextual theories: Theories of development holding that changes over the lifespan arise from the ongoing interrelationship between a changing organism and a changing world.

Core: A set of defining features of a concept, all of which are required in order for a particular example to be considered an instance of the concept (see *characteristic features*).

Cross-cultural psychology: The study of similarities and differences in individual psychological functioning in various cultural and ethnocultural groups; of the relationships between psychological variables and sociocultural, ecological and biological variables; and of ongoing changes in these variables.

Cultural bias: The situation that arises in testing when one cultural or subcultural group is more familiar with test items than another group and therefore has an unfair advantage; An indication of cross-cultural differences that are not related to the trait or concept presumably measured by an instrument (or by some other method), and that tend to distort the interpretation of these differences.

Cultural evolution: A view that cultures have changed over time in adaptation to their ecosystem and other influences.

Cultural identity: How individuals think and feel about themselves in relation to the cultural or ethnocultural group with which they are associated.

Cultural psychology: A theoretical approach that sees culture and behaviour as essentially inseparable. The approach is linked to cultural relativism and psychological anthropology.

Cultural relativism: A view that cultures should be understood in their own terms, rather than being judged by standards of other groups.

Cultural tools: The objects and skills which each society has perfected to carry on its traditions and are passed on from one generation to the next.

Cultural transmission: Process by which cultural features of a population are transmitted to its individual members (see also *socialization*).

Cultural universals: Those cultural features that are present in all societies in some form, such as language, childrearing, family and technology.

Culture: The shared way of life of a group of people, including their artefacts (such as social institutions and technology) and their symbols (such as communications and myths). It also includes a system of meanings shared by a population of people and transmitted from one generation to the next.

Culture-comparative research: A research tradition in which similarities and differences in behaviour are studied across cultures.

Culture-fair: An ideal describing something that is equally appropriate and fair for members of all cultures (cf. *cultural bias*).

Culture-relevant: A characteristic (when referring to an assessment) based on skills and knowledge that relate to the cultural experiences of the test-takers, still recognizing that the test-givers' definitions of the construct being measured may differ from the definitions of the test-takers.

Development: Long-term changes in a person's capacities and behaviour, including physical growth and skills, feelings, patterns of thinking and social relationships.

Developmental niche: The place occupied by the child within a system in which the physical and social environment, sociocultural customs of childrearing, and psychological conceptions (e.g., beliefs) of parents and other caregivers interact with the developing child.

Dual-system hypothesis: A view of bilingualism which suggests that the two languages are represented somehow in separate systems of the brain (cf. *single-system hypothesis* and *bilingualism*).

Ecocultural framework: A conceptual approach to understanding similarities and differences in human behaviour across cultures in terms of individual and group adaptation to context.

Ecological approach: Bronfenbrenner's view emphasizing that the developing person is embedded in and interacts with a series of environmental systems (comprising of microsystem, mesosystem, exosystem and macrosystem).

Ecological validity: The degree to which particular findings in one context may be considered relevant outside of that context; based on the notion that human thought processes interact with particular environmental contexts.

Ecology: The relationship between the individual or group and their physical and social environment.

Egocentrism: The inability to understand the existence or type of thoughts, feeling, beliefs, comprehensions held by another person. Egocentrism is most profound in infancy but, according to Piaget continues throughout the preoperational stage.

Emic approach: The study of behaviour in one culture, often emphasizing culture-specific aspects (cf. *etic approach*).

Enculturation: A form of cultural transmission by which a society transmits its culture and behaviour to its members by surrounding developing members with appropriate models.

Environment: Events or conditions outside of the person that are presumed to influence and are in turn influenced by the developing individual.

Equivalence: A condition for interpreting psychological data obtained from different cultures in the same way (also referred to as comparability of data); data can have structural equivalence (measuring cross-culturally the same trait), metric equivalence (measuring the same trait on scales with the same metric) and full-score equivalence (measuring the same trait on the same scale).

Ethnic attitudes: Positive or negative evaluations of individuals or groups because of their membership in a cultural or ethnocultural group.

Ethnic identity: A sense of personal identification with one's ethnic group and its values and cultural traditions.

Ethnicity: An attribute referring to a group of people who have a common national or cultural tradition. It is a label defining a number of characteristics such as race, language and religion which are shared by a group of individuals.

Ethnocentrism: A point of view that accepts one's own group's standards as the best, and judges all other groups in relation to them.

Ethnocultural group: A group living in a plural society that is derived from a heritage cultural group, but which has changed as a result of acculturation in the larger society.

Ethnopsychology: A perspective on human behaviour that is rooted in a particular cultural world view (see also *indigenous psychologies*).

Ethnotheories: Cultural beliefs and ideas which act as powerful sources of affect and motivators of behaviour.

Etic approach: The comparative study of behaviour across cultures, often assuming some form of universality of the psychological underpinnings of a behaviour or attribute (cf. *emic approach*).

Exosystem: In Bronfenbrenner's ecological approach, settings not experienced directly by the developing individual that still influence his/her development (e.g., effects of events at parents' working places on a child's development).

Externalizing problems: Where a child's behaviour involves excessive acting-out or lack of control such as aggression sufficient to cause distress and/or harm to self and others (cf. *internalizing problem*).

Formal-operational stage: Piagetian stage during which an individual becomes proficient in mentally manipulating his/her internal representations of not only concrete objects but also abstract symbols.

Gender: The socially ascribed roles (including behaviours and identities) that accompany the male and female sexes. While a person's sex is a biological given, gender is socially constructed.

General intelligence: A unified view of the level of cognitive functioning of an individual person, derived from positive correlations found between scores on a wide range of cognitive tests (especially intelligence batteries).

Genetic epistemology: A theoretical approach that proposes a sequence of stages in the development of cognitive operations from birth to maturity.

Grammar: The study of language in terms of regular patterns that relate to the functions and relationships of words in a sentence – extending broadly to the level of discourse and narrowly to the pronunciation and meaning of individual words.

Guided participation: A process by which children learn by actively participating in culturally relevant activities in which adults and other knowledgeable individuals provide support, direction and organization for children's cognitive development by building bridges between what children know and new information to be learned.

Health: A state of complete physical, mental and social well-being, and not merely the absence of disease or infirmity.

Hypothesis: A tentative proposal regarding expected consequences, such as the outcome of research.

Identity: This refers to individuals' and groups' views or sense of themselves: Personal identity concerns who one is and how one is distinct from others whereas social identity refers to a feeling of belonging to particular social groups (e.g., based on race or religion), and that these are distinct from other groups.

Income support: In the United Kingdom, this refers to payment made by the state to people on a low income.

Indigenous: Originating or occurring naturally in a particular place.

Indigenous psychologies: Different perspectives on human behaviour that are rooted in a world view of a particular culture.

Individualism: An orientation characteristic of a society which emphasizes primary concern for oneself, freedom of action for individuals, independence and self-reliance (cf. *collectivist*).

Individualism-Collectivism (I-C): A distinction between the tendencies to be primarily concerned with oneself, or with one's group.

Integration: The acculturation strategy in which people maintain their cultural heritage, and also seek to participate in the larger society.

Intelligence: The ability to learn from experience and to adapt to the surrounding environment and considered to be partly an inherited characteristic and partly acquired through experience; intelligent behaviour is adaptive, purposive and used to solve problems and predict, control and adjust to circumstances.

Internalization: A Vygotskian process whereby individuals incorporate knowledge that they gain through their interactions within a social context into themselves.

Internalizing problems: Disorders manifested through inward-turned symptoms, such as when a child's behaviour is characterized by social withdrawal with feelings of anxiety and/or depression or somatic problems, sufficient to cause difficulties in the child's functioning (cf. *externalizing problems*).

Intersubjectivity: The sharing of focus and purpose between child and more skilled others involving cognitive, social and emotional exchange.

Labelling: Attaching a label to an individual or group on the basis of characteristic(s) from which inferences are made about their capabilities, behaviours and so on, often derogatory.

Language: A symbolic system in which a limited number of signals can be combined according to rules to produce an infinite number of messages. It includes the use of an organized means of combining words in order to communicate.

Levels of analysis: A concept that allows human phenomena to be studied and interpreted by various disciplines at various levels (such as individual, cultural or ecological) without having to be reduced to explanations at a more basic level.

Lexicon: The entire set of morphemes in a given language or a given person's linguistic repertoire.

Linguistic relativity (also known as Whorfian hypothesis): The idea that there are important relationships between characteristics of a language and the ways of thinking found in speakers of that language.

Linguistic universals: Characteristic patterns of language that apply across all languages irrelevant of cultural differences.

Macrosystem: In Bronfenbrenner's ecological approach, the larger cultural or sub cultural context of development.

Majority world: The countries in which most of the world population is living. The term is often associated with so-called developing (also referred to as Third World) countries.

Malnutrition: A state resulting from insufficient food intake, and indicated by low weight and height in relation to age.

Maturation: Developmental changes that are biologically programmed by genes rather than being caused by learning, injury, illness, or some other life experience.

Median Income: The income in a population that is in the middle of the distribution of incomes.

Mediated action: An activity characterized by the relationship between the agent and the means, often involving cultural tools, by which an action is carried out.

Mesosystem: In Bronfenbrenner's ecological approach, the interrelationships between microsystems or immediate environments (e.g., ways in which events in the family affect a child's interactions at school).

Microsystem: In Bronfenbrenner's ecological approach, the immediate settings in which the person functions (e.g., the family).

Monolinguals: Persons who can speak only one language (cf. *bilingualism*).

Morpheme: One of the smallest meaningful units of language; includes single or combined sounds that denotes meaning within a given language.

Multiculturalism: A term used to refer to both the existence of, and a policy supporting the many ethnocultural groups living together in the larger society. It involves both the maintenance of diverse ethnocultural groups and the participation of these groups in the larger society.

Object permanence: The realization by the child that an object continues to exist in its absence from his/her sight or hearing.

Parental ethnotheories: A set of cultural beliefs and practices held by parents regarding the proper way to raise a child (also called parental beliefs, implicit developmental theories).

Perception: The set of psychological processes by which people recognize, organize, synthesize and give meaning (in the brain) to the sensations received from environmental stimuli (in the sense organs).

Phoneme: The smallest unit of speech sound that can be used to distinguish one meaningful utterance from another in a given language.

Population: A well-defined group that a researcher who studies a sample of individuals is ultimately interested in drawing conclusions about.

Prejudice: A general negative orientation towards a cultural or ethnocultural group other than one's own (see also *ethnocentrism*).

Preoperational thinking: The second stage of development in Piaget's stages of cognitive development. It is characterized by *egocentrism* and an inability to perceive another's point of view.

Psycholinguistics: The interdisciplinary field of psychology and linguistics in which language behaviour is examined. It includes such areas of enquiry as acquisition, nature, structure and use of language, and the psychological processes of the users.

Psychopathology: A psychological illness that is considered by the community or experts to be reflected in strange or bizarre behaviour.

Psychosocial factors: Features of the ecological and social environment that contribute to the attainment (or loss) of health.

Qualitative methodology: Approaches to research with an emphasis on the understanding of processes and meanings; often these cannot be experimentally or psychometrically examined or measured in terms of quantity, amount and so on.

Quantitative methodology: Approaches to research in which the measurement (in terms of quantity, amount or frequency) of the phenomena that are being examined is emphasized.

Relativism: A theoretical orientation that assumes that human behaviour is strongly influenced by culture, and that it can only be studied by taking a person's culture into account.

Resilience: The self-righting or recuperative capacity that allows many children to recover from early disadvantages and get back on a normal course of development.

Reversibility: Of thought in which the child understands that an action which changes the appearance of something is reversible and the attributes of the substance involved remain unaltered.

Sample: The group of individuals chosen from a population to be the subjects of a study.

Scaffolding: The process whereby an adult or a more experienced person structures the child's learning by offering help and support in problem solving, and adjusting both the kind and amount of help to the child's level of performance.

Schema: A cognitive framework for meaningfully organizing various interrelated concepts, based on previous experiences; it is a conceptual system for understanding something.

Semantics: The study of meaning in language, which involves both denotation (specific referents) and connotation (emotional overtones and other non-explicit meanings of words).

Single-system hypothesis: A view of bilingualism, which suggests that both languages are represented in just one system in the brain (cf. *dual-system hypothesis* and see *bilingualism*).

Social class: A group of people defined by socio-economic status (occupation, income and educational qualifications) and their shared customs and practices.

Social constructivist: A view of cognitive development in which the child attaches meaning to experience through its social context and hence will vary with culture and people present.

Social mobility: Opportunity for movement between social groups or statuses.

Socialization: The process of upbringing whereby a child develops the characteristics, competencies and skills needed for successful adaptation to his/her society. It is a form of cultural transmission as a process by which individuals acquire the beliefs, values and behaviours judged to be important in their society.

Socio-cognitive conflict: A state of mind created when the child has to resolve the conflict between differing perspectives on a subject, resulting in new ways of thinking.

Socio-economic status (SES): The position people hold in society based on such factors as income, level of education, occupational status and social class.

Stage in development: A distinct phase of life characterized by a unique set of mental characteristics.

Stigma: Being perceived as unworthy or disgraced with respect to a particular characteristic, circumstance or membership of a specific group.

Theory: A system of ideas, often stated as a principle, to explain or to lead to new understandings; a statement of some general principles that explain a phenomenon or a set of phenomena.

Transactional model: A model of reciprocal influences between environmental factors and the developing person over time.

Triarchic theory of human intelligence: A theoretical perspective integrating features of the internal world, the external world and the experience of an individual, which the person uses in addressing tasks requiring analytical, practical and creative intelligence.

Universalism: A theoretical orientation that considers basic psychological processes as shared characteristics of all people, and culture as influencing their development and display.

Universality: Psychological concepts, or relationships between concepts, are universal if they appear suitable for the description of the behaviour of people in any culture.

Universals in language: Characteristics thought to be found in all human languages.

Validity: The degree to which findings and interpretations have been shown to approximate a presumed state of affairs in reality, independent of the prior belief of researchers or scientists.

Values: Conceptions of what is desirable, which influence the selection of means and ends of actions: relative worth, merit or usefulness of something.

Vocabulary: A repertoire of words, formed by combining morphemes; those words known or used by a person or group.

Zone of Proximal Development (ZPD): Vygotsky's term for the difference between what a learner can accomplish independently and what s/he can accomplish with the guidance and encouragement of a more skilled partner; the range of ability between a child's existing potential ability (competence) and the child's observed ability (performance).

Author Index

Abels, M., 57, *87*, 256, *298*
Aboud, F. E., 22, *24*, 214–24, *239, 240, 242*
Abreu, G. de, 165, *173*
Adams, C., 118, *131*
Adelman, A., 101, *132*
Adelstein, A. M., 102, *137*
Aderinto, A. A., 265, *295*
Adorno, T. W., 215, *240*
Ainsworth, M. D. S., 64, *83*
Alapack, R., 69, *87*
Alexander, K., 113, 116–17, *132, 135*, 269, *297*
Ali, Y., 213, *240*
Al-Issa, I., 97, *132*
Allen, T., 96, *139*
Allen, V. L., 218–21, 223, *240*
Alliensmith, B. B., 67, *83*
Allport, G. W., 215, *240*
Allwood, C. M., 38, *51*
Amaya-Jackson, L., *139*
Ames, G. J., 153, *173*
Amin, K., 102, *132*
Anastasio, P. A., 225, *242*
Anderson, M., 80, *83*
Andries, F., *140*
Angleitner, A., *86*
Annis, R. C., 71, *84*
Arbreton, C., *140*
Argyle, M., 211–12, 226, *240*
Arnold, D. H., 116, 118, 121, *132*, 270, *295*
Aronson, E., *54*, 225, *240*
Asher, S. R., 218–21, 223, *240*
Attar, B. K., 120, *132*
Aucoin, K. J., 276–77, *295*
Azuma, H., 261, *299*

Bachevan, B. A., *242*
Bacon, M. K., 80, *83*
Baker, L., 113, *139*
Baldry, E., 109, *140*
Baldwin, N., 109, *132*

Balto, A., 77, *83*
Banaji, M. R., 180, *206*
Barnes, H. V., 269, *300*
Barnes, J., 270, *295*
Barnett, W. S., 286, *295, 300*
Barrett, M., 213, 222, *240, 246*
Barry, H., 80, *83*
Bartz, K. W., 57, *83*
Bates, E., 182, *204*
Bates, J. E., 68–69, *85, 89*, 118, *134, 136*, 264, *296*
Baumrind, D., 66–67, *83*, 274, *295*
Beach, K., 143, *173*
Beaudet, J., 222, *242*
Becker, W. C., 68, *83*
Beiser, M., 110, *132*
Beit-Hallahmi, B., 211, 226, *240*
Belsky, J., 103, 108, *132*, 270, *295*
Benjet, C., 67–68, *84*
Bennathan, M., 281, *295*
Bennett, K., 224, *240*
Bennett, M., 211, *240*
Benson, P., 228, *242*
Ben-Zeev, S., 196, *204*
Bergeman, C. S., 125, *138*
Berry, J. W., 5, *9*, 13, *24*, 31–33, 38, 40, 49, *51, 52, 53, 54*, 71–72, *84, 87, 88*, 94–96, *132*, 146, *173*, 189, *204, 205, 207*, 253, 277, 288, *294, 295, 298*
Berryman, J. W., 231, *240*
Best, D. L., 218, *246*
Bettencourt, B. A., 225, *241*
Bhatt, S., 223, *243*
Bialystok, E., 197–99, *205, 206*, 259, *295*
Bierman, K. L., 68, *90*, 275, *300*
Bijl, R. V., *140*
Bishop, A., 165, *173*
Björksten, B., *133*
Blackburn, T. C., *301*
Blanden, J., 112
Blaney, N., 225, *240*

Blount, B. G., 182, *205*
Bodin, S. D., 276, *295*
Boivin, M., 260, *295*
Boldizar, J., 119, *135*
Borke, J., 87, *298*
Boswell, D. A., 218, *246*
Botting, B., 107, *132*
Bowlby, J., 69, *84*
Bowlby, R., 262, *297*
Bowman, B. T., 94, *132*
Boxall, M., 281, *295*
Bråbäck, L., 123, *133*
Bradley, R. H., 111, 120–21, *133*, 263, 269, *296*
Bradshaw, J., 101, 105, *131, 132, 133, 137, 138*
Braha, V., 223–24, *241*
Branch, C. W., 219, *241*
Brand, E. S., 223, *241*
Braungart, J. M., 126, *133*
Brazelton, T. B., *88*
Breborowicz, A., *133*
Brewer, M. B., 81, *84*, 225, *241*
Briggs, J. L., 79, *84*
Brillion, L., *86*
Brislin, R. W., 13, *24*, 29–30, *52*
Broberg, A. G., 14, *25*
Brody, G., 114, 120, *133*
Bronfenbrenner, U., 6, *9*, 14, *24*, 41–44, *47, 52*, 94, 96, 111–12, 117, 127–30, *133*, 155, 254, 283, 287, *296*, 305, 306, 308, 309
Brooks-Gunn, J., 111, 119–20, 125, *133, 134, 136, 137, 140*
Brown, E. A., 270, *296*
Brown, G., 224, *271*
Brown, J., 168, *174*
Brown, R., 181, *205*, 223, 225, 226, *241, 243*
Brown, R. J., 226, 241
Brown, S., 279, *300*
Bruhn, K., 77, *176*
Bruner, J. S., 35–36, 49, *52*, 149–50, 160–61, 170, *173, 174, 177*, 282, *296, 301*
Buchanan, A., 114, *138*
Buchannan-Barrow, E., 213, *246*
Buck-Moss, S., 150, *173*
Buirski, P., 215, *245*

Bukowski, W. M., 260, 295
Bulusu, L., 102, *137*
Burman, E., 151, *173*
Burns, R., 93, *134*
Burtless, G., 100, *140*

Cabinet Office, 112, *134*
Campbell, S. B., 64, *84*
Carlson, V., 68, *84*, 122, *134*
Carlton, K., *241*
Carpendale, J., 172, 182, *205*
Carr, E. G., 116, *134*
Carraher, D. W., 164–65, *176*, 259, *299*
Carroll, D. W., 180–81, 184, *205*
Casey, P., 133, *296*
Caspi, A., 115, 125, *134, 136*
Castellino, D. R., 113, *136*
Cauce, A. M., 125, *137*
Ceci, S., *133*
Cervantes, R. C., 201, *205*
Chance, N. A., 79, *84*
Chandler, M. J., 41, 47, *53*, 95, 117, 127, 139, 255
Chang, L., 264, 298, 301
Chao, R., 61, 66–67, 70, *84, 85*
Chapman, M., 19, *24*
Charalambous, N., *86*
Chen, X., 38, *53*, 156, *175*, 260, *299, 301*
Chen, Y., 81, *84*
Cheyne, B., 109, *135*
Child, I. L., 80, *83*
Childs, C. P., *174*
Chirkov, V., 62, *85*
Chishimba, M., 260, *296*
Chomsky, N., 181, *205*
Chou, K.-L., 62, *85*
Christakopoulou, S., 60, *86*
Cicchetti, D., 6, *10*, 127, *131, 134, 137*, 254
Cicirelli, V. G., 168, 173
Clark, A., 217, 219–21, *241*
Clark, K. B., 218–19, *241*
Clark, M. P., 218–19, *241*
Cle, M., 143, *176*
Coard, B., 285, *296*
Coatsworth, J. D., 125, *131, 137, 298*
Cocking, R. R., 57, *85–86*

Colder, C. R., 276, *296*
Cole, M., 5, *9*, 14, *24*, 35, 37, 41, 46–47, *51, 52*, 150, 159, 170, *173, 176, 177,* 255, 257, *296*
Cole, P. M., 57, 65, *85, 89*
Cole, S. R., 150, *173*
Coll, C. G., 71, *86*, 120, *133*
Collier, V. P., 197, *205*
Conger, K. J., 17, *24*
Conger, R. D., 17, 24–25, 120, 133, 277, 300
Coon, H. M., 61, *89*
Corenblum, B., 219, 221, *241*
Correa-Chávez, M., 143, 163–64, 166, 172, *173*
Corwyn, R. F., 120, *133*
Cowen, E. L., 124–25, *141*
Craik, K. H., 39, *52*
Crain, W., 150, *173*
Crain-Thoreson, C., 116, *134*
Crawley, R., 107, *132*
Creighton, S. J., 109, *134, 138*
Creps, C., 168, *174*
Croak, M. R., 225, *241*
Crooks, D., 117, *134*, 269, *296*
Cross, D., 166, *177*
Cummins, J., 197, 199, *205*
Cutrona, C. E., 125, *134*

Dale, P. S., 116, *134*
Dalgety-Gaitan, C., 70, *85*
Damon, W., *86, 176*, 217, *241*
Darling, C. A., 121, *137*
Darling, N., 274, *296*
Das Gupta, P., 155, *173*
Dasen, P. R., *9*, 13, *24*, 31–32, *51, 52*, 94, *132, 204, 205, 207*, 253, *294, 295*
Dauncey, M., 108, *135*
Davies, R. E., 231, *240*
Davey, A. G., 217, 220–25, *241*
Davey Smith, G., 110, *139*
Davie, R., 231, *240*
Deater-Deckard, K., 68–69, *85*, 264, 275, *296, 298*
de Boer, J. B., *140*
de Haes, H. C. J. M., *140*
de Houwer, A., 189, 192, *205*
de Regt, E. B., *140*

Deci, E. L., 62, *90*
Defoe, D., 93, *134*
DeFries, J. C., 126, *138*
DeGarmo, D. S., 114, *134*
DeKlyen, M., 64, *86*
Demant-Hatt, E., 77, *85*
Dembo, M. H., 217, 219, *241*
Dennis, T. A., 65, *85*
Department for Education and Employment, 270, *296*
Department for Education and Skills, 263, 269, *296*
Department for Work and Pensions, 101, *135*
Department of Social Security, 99, *134*
Dettwyler, K. A., 59, *85*
Dewberry, C., *240*
Diaz, R. M., 196, *205*
Dietz, T., 275, *296*
Dillenburger, K., 270, *296*
Dixon, S., 59, *88*
Doctoroff, G. L., 116, 118, 121, *132*, 270, *295*
Dodge, K. A., 68–69, *85, 89*, 118, *134, 136*, 264, 275, *296, 298*
Doise, W., 152–53, *173*
Donaldson, M., 149–50, *173*
Dorling, D., 110, *139*
Dornfield, M., 68, *89*
Dosanjh, J. S., 71, *85*
Douglas, E. M., 276–77, *297*
Dovidio, J., 225, *242, 244*
Doyle, A.-B., 217–18, 221–22, *240, 242*
Draper, P., 103, *132*
Drukker, M., 263, *300*
Duffy, S., 61, *88*
Duncan, G. J., 111, 119–20, *133, 134, 136, 140*
Dunn, J., 167–69, *173, 174*
Durkin, K., 153, *174*, 218, *244*

Eccles, J., 116, *140*
Eckman, F., 191–94, *204, 205*
Edelbrock, C., 36, *53*
Edwards, C. P., 15, *24*, 26, 36, *54*
Eisenberg, N., *53*, 122, *135*
Eisenstadt, N., 270, *297*
Elbourne, D., 108, *135*
Elder, G. J., Jr., *24*

Eliot, C. W., *134*
Elkind, D., 22, *25*, 228–30, 233, *242, 244*
Emery, R., 119, *139*
Empson, J. M., 6–9, 47, *52*, 94, 103, 105, 115, 117, *135, 137,* 276, 278, 281, *297*
English, D., *139*
Entwistle, D., 113, 116, *132, 135,* 269, *297*
Epstein, A. S., *300*
Erikson, E. H., 230–31, *242*
Ervin-Tripp, S., 182, *205*
Esmonde, I., 143, *176*
European Economic Community, 98, *135* (given as acronym in both cases)
Eyberg, S. M., 67, 89
Eysenck, H. J., 145, *174*
Eysenck, M., 18, *25*, 143, *174*

Fabes, R. A., 122, *135*
Fagen, D. B., *141*
Farquhar, G., 93, *135*
Farver, J. A. M., 264, *301*
Feimer, N., 39, *52*
Feiring, C., 62, *85*
Fenton, S., 102, *135*
Fernandez, D. M., 201, *207*
Fernández, S. C., 191–92, *207, 208*
Fetzer, J. S., 239, *242*
Fischer, G. W., 236, *244*
Fitzpatrick, H., 154, *174*
Fitzpatrick, K., 119, *135*
Flor, D., 114, *133*
Flouri, E., 113–14, *135, 138*
Foets, M., *140*
Fordham, S., 122, *138*
Forgatch, M. S., 114, *134*
Forlitti, J., 228, *242*
Fowler, J. W., 230–31, *242, 243*
Francis, L. J., 228, 233, *242, 244*
Freeman, I., *135*
Freeman, M. A., 16, *25*, 81, *85*
Frenkel-Brunswick, E., 215, *240*
Frick, P. J., 276, *295*
Friedlmeier, W., 64, 67, 83, *85, 90, 91*
Friedman, P., 224, *242*
Fuligni, A., 60, *86, 174*

Fulker, D. W., 126, *133*
Fung, H., 182, *207*
Furby, L., 219, 221, *244*
Furnham, A., 232, *242*
Furth, H. G., 186, *205*

Gaertner, S. L., 225, *242, 244*
Gallimore, R., 113, *135,* 161, *177*
Garcìa Coll, C., 71, *86*
Garcia, E. E., 199–200, 202, 206
Gardner, R. C., 194–95, *206*
Gauvain, M., 7, 9, 20, *25,* 148, *172, 174*
Gaydos, G., 118, *131*
Ge, X., 25, 120, *133*
Geertz, C., 213, *242*
Georgas, J., 60, *86*
George, D. M., 220, *243*
Gerrard, M., *133*
Gerrig, R., 180, *206*
Gershoff, E. T., 68, *86,* 273, *297*
Ghuman, P. A. S., 71, *85*
Gibbons, F. X., *133*
Gibbons, J., 109, *135*
Gibson, H. M., 228, *244*
Gillham, B., 109, *135*
Glachan, M., 153, *174, 175*
Godin, A., 228, *243*
Goldenberg, C., 113, *135*
Goldman, R. J., 227–28, 233, *243, 245*
Goldsmith, D., 53
Göncü, A., 5, *9,* 14, *24, 25,* 35, 41, *52,* 131, *176*
Gonzales, N., 125, *137*
Gonzalez, R., 226, *243*
Goodnow, J. J., 164, *174*
Goodwin, R., *86,* 288–90, 292, *294, 297*
Goodz, N., 192, *206*
Gordon, D., 98–99, 103, 109, 110, *131, 135, 136, 137, 139*
Goswami, U., 149, *174*
Grant, G., 223, *243*
Graves, D., 246
Greenberg, J. M., 180, 206
Greenberg, M. T., 64, *86*
Greenfield, P. M., 31, 35, *51, 52,* 57, 60, 62, 66–67, *85, 86, 138,* 166–67, 169–71, *174,* 289–90, 291, *297*

AUTHOR INDEX

Greenfield, S., 262, *297*
Gregg, P., 112
Griffith, J., 218, *244*
Grove, K., *137*
Guerra, N. G., 120, *132*
Gumperz, J., 181, 185, *206*

Hackett, L., 67, *86*
Hackett, R., 67, *86*
Hakuta, K., 192, 196–97, 199–200, 202, *206*
Hallinan, M., 225, *243*
Hamilton, D., 262, *297*
Hanneke, C. J. M., *140*
Hardaway, C. R., 276, *299*
Harding, L. M., 110, *136*
Hargreaves, J., 109, *140*
Harkness, S., 14, 16, *25, 26*, 39, 41, 44–47, *54*, 56, 57, 58, 59, 62, *86, 90, 91*, 130, *140*, 164, *174*, 183, 187–88, *206*, 254, 255, 261, 274, 291, *297, 300*
Harms, E., 227, *243*
Harold, R., *140*
Harper, C., 101, *136*
Harris, P., 284, *297*
Harris, T. L., 96, *136*
Hart, D., 217, *241*
Harwood, R., 68, *84*
Haslam, S. A., 233, 235, *243, 244*
Hatano, G., 164, *174*
Heath, T., 211, *240*
Hedegaard, M., 143, *174*
Heine, B., *208*
Henry, B., 125, *134*
Herbert, M., 17, *26*, 263, 269, *301*
Heslop, P., *136*
Hetherington, E. M., 53, 126, *138, 139*
Hewer, A., 231, *244*
Hewstone, M., 224, 226, 237, 241, 243
Heyerdahl, S., 16, *25*, 57, 68, 69, 83, *87*
Hill, N. E., 113–14, *136*
Hillman, N., 118, *131*
Hiraga, Y., *137*
Hiruma, N., 57, *89*
Ho, D. Y. F., 260
Hodges, R. E., 96, *136*

Hoem, A., 79, *86*
Hoeymans, N., *140*
Hoff, E., 20, *25*, 182, 183, *204, 206*
Hoff-Ginsberg, E., 191–94, *204, 205*
Hofstede, G., 60, *86–87*, 292, *297*
Hoge, D. R., 226, *243*
Hogg, M. A., 233, *246*
Hogue, C. J. R., 107, *139*
Holland, D., 58, *89*
Holmes, D. L., 116
Holmes, H., 105, *133*
Homel, P., 196, *207*
Hoppe, R. A., 220, *243*
Hoppers, W. H., 260, *297*
Hou, F., 110, *132*
Hovecar, D., 217, 219, *241*
Hovey, J. D., 201, *206*
Hoyt-Meyer, L., *141*
Hraba, J., 223, *243*
Hu, L., 236, *244*
Hunter, W. M., 125, *139*
Huntsinger, C. S., 63, *87*
Huntsinger, P. R., 63, *87*
Hwang, C. H., 219, *244*
Hwang, C. P., 14, *25*
Hyman, I., 110, *132*
Hymel, S., 260, *295, 299*
Hymes, D., 181–82, *206*

Inagaki, K., 164, *174*
Inhelder, B., 149, *176*
International Society for the Study of Behavioural Development (ISSBD), *172*
Irvine, S. H., 146, *173*
Islam, M. R., 237, *243*

Jacobs, A. E., *140*
Jacobson, J., 213, *243*
Jahoda, G., 223, *243*
Jardine, M. M., 231, *243*
Jarrett, R. L., 119, *136*
Jávo, C., 5–6, 16, *25*, 57, 67–70, 79–80, 83, *87*, 256–57
Jeffries, R., 211, *240*
Jencks, C., 118, *136*
Jensen, A. R., 145, *174*
Jensen, H., *87, 298*
Johnson, C., 277, *300*

Johnson, J. E., 227, *243*
Johnson, S., 93, *136*
Johnson, S. P., 224, *241*
Joiner, R., *175*
Jolly, A., 160, *173*, 282, *296*
Jose, P. E., 63, *87*
Judd, C. M., 236, *243*
Julge, K., *133*

Kagitçibasi, Ç., 55, 61, 62–63, 81, *83, 84, 87, 88, 91*, 146, *175*, 254, 256, *297, 298*
Kaplan, R., 276, *299*
Kaplan, U., 62, *85*
Karpov, Y. V., 7, 9, 157–59, *175*
Kashoki, M., 20, *26*
Katz, P. A., 215, 217–19, 221–22, *243–44, 246*
Kawamura, T., 61, *88*
Kay, W. K., 228, *244*
Kazdin, A. E., 67–68, *84*
Keefer, C., *88*
Kelleher, K., 133, *296*
Keller, H., 39, *52*, 57–58, 60, 63, 65, *86, 87, 174*, 253, 256, *298*
Kelley, M., 67, *87*
Kelley, M. L., 70, *87*
Kemmelmeier, M., 61, *89*
Kempen, G. I. J. M., *140*
Kempson, E., 105–06, 123, *136*
Kendler, H. H., 186, *206*
Kendler, T. S., 186, *206*
Kernaham, C., 225, *241*
Kim, U., 60–61, *83, 84, 88, 91*
Kim, Y., 62, *85*
Kim-Cohen, J., 115, 126, *136*
Kircher, M., 219, 221, *244*
Kitayama, S., 61, *88*
Klebanov, P., 111, 119–20, 125, *133, 134, 136, 140*
Kleinman, J. C., 107, *139*
Klimidis, S., 71, *90*
Knuttson, A., *133*
Kobayashi-Winata, H., 70, *88*
Kohen, D. E., 125, *137*
Kohlberg, L., 231, *244*
Korenman, S., 112–13, *136*, 263, 269, *298*
Kornadt, H.-J., 57, *91*

Kovacs, A., 259, *298*
Kozulin, A., 157, *175, 208*
Kruger, A. C., 186, *208*
Kruttschnitt, C., 68, *89*
Kunsemuller, P., 65, *87*
Kuper, A., 35, *52*
Kurtines, W., 71, *90*
Kusserow, A., 81, *88*
Kutner, B., 217, *244*
Kwak, K., 70–72, *88*
Kwan, E., *198*, 205

Lamb, M. E., *9*, 14, *24, 25, 51, 52*
Lambert, W. E., 194–95, 196, 206, 207
Lambie, A., *135*
Lamm, B., 57, *87*, 256, *298*
Landsverk, J., *139*
Lansford, J. E., 113, *136*, 275, *298*
Lanza, E., 192, *206*
Larivée, S., 154–55, *175*
Larsen, J. T., 61, *88*
Larzelere, R. E., 68, *88*
Latz, S., 59, *91*
Lautrey, J., 155, *175*
Lazarus, R. S., 201, *206*
Leach, P., 262, 273–75, *297, 298*
Lee, C. F., 228, 245
Lefley, H. P., 70, *88*
Leiderman, P. H., *88*
Lemon, N., 21, *25*
Lengua, L. J., 68, *90*, 300
Lenneberg, E., 271, *298*
Leopold, W. F., 191, *206*
Lerner, J. V., 276, *298*
Lester, D., 67, *88*
LeVine, E. S., 57, *83*
LeVine, R. A., 15, *25*, 59, 64, *88, 174*, 182, *204, 206, 207, 297*
LeVine, S., 59, *88*
Levinson, D. J., 215, 240
Levinson, S. C., 185, 206
Levive, C., 231, *244*
Lewis, C., *172*, 182, *205*
Lewis, O., 95–97, 103–04, *136*
Leyland, A. H., *295*
Liang, C.-H., 182, *207*
Liaw, F., 63, *87*, 111, *133*

AUTHOR INDEX 319

Light, P., *139*, *141*, 152–54, *174*, *175*, 272, *298*
Lin, L. R., 261, *298*
Linver, M. R., 125, *137*
Linville, P. W., 236, *244*
Liss, M. B., 223, *244*
Littlejohn-Blake, S. M., 121, *137*
Littleton, K., 154, *175*, 272, *295*, *298*
Lloyd, E., 103, *131*, *137*
Lochman, J. E., 276, *296*
Locke, D. C., 79, *89*
Loewenthal, K. M., 211, *244*
Lohaus, A., *87*
Long, D., 230, *244*
Lonigan, C. J., 116, *140*
Lonner, W. J., 33, *53*, *176*
Lorenz, F. O., *24*
Loughran, F., 103, *136*
Lourenço, O., 19, *25*, 150–51, 163, *175*
Lozoff, B., 59, *91*
Lucy, J. A., 185, *206*
Luk, G., 198, 205
Luria, A. R., 35, *53*, 143, *175*, 186, *206*
Lynch, M., 6, *10*, 127, *131*, *137*, 254
Lyons, E., 222, *240*
Lytton, H., 68, *89*

Maass, A., 218, *244*
Machado, A., 19, *25*, 150–51, 163, *175*
Machin, S., 112
Madden, T., 72, *89*
Magnus, K. B., *141*
Mamali, C., 290, *298*
Mandansky, D., 36, *53*
Maras, P., 226, *241*
Marcus, R., 101, *136*
Markus, H. R., 261, *298*
Marmot, M. G., 102, *137*
Martin, M. M., 198, *205*
Martinez, C. R., 114, *134*
Mason, C. A., 125, *137*
Mason, J. M., 116, *137*
Masser, B., 226, *241*
Masten, A. S., 124–25, *131*, *137*, *298*
Masters, J. C., 292, *298*
Matthews, H. F., 228, *244*
Mattson, L., *246*
Mayer, S., 118, *136*
Maynard, A., 60, *86*, *174*

Maynard, A. E., 147, 168, 171, *174*, *175*
McAdoo, H. P., 120, *133*
McClearn, G. E., 126, *138*
McClelland, P., 112, *133*
McCormick, C. E., 116, *137*
McGarty, C., 235, *243*
McGee, R. O., 125, *134*
McGlaughlin, A., 17, *25*, 94, 103, 105, 115, *135*, *137*
McGrady, A. G., 233, *244*
McGuffin, P., 126, *138*
McGuire, W. J., 224, *244*
McInnes, E., 262, *298*
McLelland, M. M., 116
McLeod, J. D., 68, *89*, 118, *137*
McLoyd, V. C., 276, *299*
McMahon, R. J., 68, *90*, 275, *300*
Mead, G. H., 35, *53*
Mebert, C. J., 276, *299*
Meeus, W., 63, *89*
Mehler, J., 259, *298*
Melhuish, E., 270, *295*
Messer, D., *175*
Meyer, E. C., *86*
Middleton, S., 97, 106–07, *139*
Miedema, H. S., *140*
Miller, J., 112, *136*, 263, *298*
Miller, J. G., 38, *53*, 156, *175*
Miller, N., 225, *241*
Miller, N. E., 225, *241*
Miller, P. J., 182, *207*
Milner, D., 224, *244*
Mistry, A., *176*
Mitchell, F. G., 218, 220, *240*
Miyake, K., 90, *299*
Mizuta, I., 57, 64–65, *85*, *89*
Moen, P., *133*
Moffitt, T. E., 115, *134*, *136*
Mohanty, A., 189, *204*, *207*
Monyooe, L. A., 275, *299*
Moore, R., 101, *137*
Morelli, G. A., 36–37, *53*, 65, *90*
Morland, J. K., 219, *244*
Morris, R. J., 60, *91*
Morrison, F. J., 116
Morrow, V., 123, *138*
Mosier, C., 161, *176*
Mugny, G., 152–53, *173*
Mullen, B., 236, *244*

Mulvaney, M. K., 276, *299*
Mundfrom, D., 111, *133*, 263, *296*
Mundy-Castle, A. C., 170, *175*
Munroe, R. H., 57, 67, *89*
Munroe, R. L., 57, 67, *89*
Murray, F. B., 151, 153, *173*
Murry, M., *133*

Nabuzoka, D., 5–8, 47, *52*, *135*, 276, 285–86, *297*, *299*
Nandy, S., 98, *136*
Nash, M., 213, *244*
National Statistics, 210, *245*, 269
Neiderhiser, J. M., 126, *138*
Nesdale, D., 218, *244*
New, R. S., 182, *204*, *206*
Newcombe, N., 219, *241*
Newman, M. A., 223, *244*
Newson, E., 273–74, *299*
Newson, J., 273–74, *299*
Nicolson, N., *300*
Nielson, J. S., *244*
Nisbett, R. E., 145, *175*
Norman, K., 57, *88*
Normandeau, S., 154, *175*
Nowlin, P., *136*
Nsamenang, A. B., 38–40, *51*, *53*, *54*, *170*, *175*, *253*, *258*, *268*, *299*
Nunes, T., 143, 164–65, *173*
Nunes Carraher, T., 164, *175*, *176*, 259, *299*
Nurse, D., *208*

Oakes, P. J., 233, 235, *243*, *244*, *246*
Oates, J., *173*, 182, *207*
Ochs, E., 182, *207*
Office for National Statistics, 210, *245*
Office of Population Censuses and Surveys (OPCS), 101–02, *138*
Ogbu, J. U., 17, *26*, 120, 122, *138*
Ohannessian, S., 20, *26*
Okagaki, L., 170, *176*, *298*
Oller, D. K., 191–92, *207*, *208*
Olson, L., 113, *135*, 269, *297*
Ong, A., 72, *89*
Oosterwegel, A., 63, *89*
Oppenheim, C., 102, *132*
Oppenheim, D., 36, *53*
Oskal, N., 80, *89*

O'Toole, 108, *138*
Ou, S.-R., 286–87, *300*
Oyserman, D., 61, *88*, *89*

Padilla, A. M., 201, *205*, 223, *241*
Paine, R., 80, *89*
Pal, B. R., 102, *139*
Palij, M., 196, *207*
Paludetto, R., 59, *91*
Pantazis, C., 98, *131*, *136*, *137*
Papaligoura, Z., 65, *87*
Papaliou, C., *87*
Parent, S., 154, *175*
Park, B., 236, *243*, *245*
Parker, G. R., 125
Parker, R., 103, *136*
Parker, R. D., 274, 277, *299*
Parsons, S., 113, *139*
Pascual-Leone, J., *176*
Pather, E. U., 97, *138*
Patterson, G. R., 25, 67, *89*, 263, 269, *299*
Pearson, B. Z., 191–92, *207*, *208*
Pelto, P. J., 77, 80, *89*
Pemberton, S., *136*
Perner, J., 166, *176*
Perregaux, C., 189, *204*, *207*
Perret Clermont, A. N., *173*
Petrillo, G. H., 226, *243*
Pettigrew, T. F., 226, *245*
Pettit, G. S., 68–9, *85*, *89*, 118, *134*, *136*
Phinney, J., 213, 214, *245*
Phinney, J. S., 72, *84*, *89*, *246*
Piaget, J., 7–8, 18–19, *24*, *25*, *26*, *142*, 144–45, 147–52, 154–56, 163, 167, 170, 171–72, *173*, *175*, *176*, 211, 215–17, 227, 230–31, 233, *244*, *245*, 265, 267–68, *299*, *303*, *305*, *306*, *309*
Pinch, S., 107–08, *138*
Platt, L., 101, *138*
Plomin, R., 125–26, *133*, *138*
Pompeu Jr. G., 165, *173*
Poortinga, Y. H., *9*, 13, *24*, *26*, 31, 38, *51*, *52*, *54*, 60, *86*, *94*, *132*, *205*, 253, *294*, *295*
Pope, S., 133, *296*
Pott, M., 64, *90*, 261, *299*

AUTHOR INDEX

Potvin, R. H., 228, *245*
Power, T. G., 67, 70, *87, 88*
Pritchard, C., 108, *135*
Pye, C., 182–83, *207*

Querido, J. G., 67, *89*
Quilgars, D., 107–08, *138*
Quinn, N., 58, *89, 298*

Raeff, C., 62, *86, 90*
Rainwater, L., 100, *140*
Ranieri, N., 71, *90*
Ratner, H. H., 186, *208*
Reading, R., 110, *138*
Reese, L., 113, *135*
Reicher, S. D., *246*
Reid, A., 228, *246*
Reiss, D., 126, *138*
Renninger, C. A., *86*, 219, *245*
Reuchlin, M., 154, *176*
Richman, A., *88*
Ridge, T., 101, *138*
Riikjärv, M. A., *133*
Ritchie, C., 114–15, *138*
Roberts, R. E., 200–02, *207*
Robinson, D., 107, *138*
Robinson, S., 116, *134*
Rogoff, B., 7, 10, 24, 36, *53*, 143, 161–64, 166, *172, 173, 176*, 268, 282, *295, 299*
Romaine, S., 21, *26*, 189, *204, 207*
Romaniuk, H., *295*
Romero, A. J., 200–2, *207*
Rønning, J. A., 16, *25*, 57, 68–69, *87*
Rooney, M., *135*
Rosenberg, M., 221, *245*
Rosenfield, D., 220, 224, *245*
Rosenthal, D., 71, *90*
Ross, G., 149–50, *177*, 282, *301*
Rothbart, M., 236, *245*
Rothbaum, F., 64–65, *90*, 261, *299*
Rothbaum, F. M., *301*
Rotherham, M., 214, *245*
Rowley, D., 107, *139*
Rubin, K. H., 260, *299*
Rudmin, F. W., 68, *87*
Ruiz, R. A., *241*
Runyan, D. K., 125, *139*
Rust, M. C., *242*

Rutter, D. R., 223–24, *241*
Rutter, M., 122, *139*
Ryan, C. S., 236, *243*
Ryan, M. K., 215, *245*
Ryan, R., 62, *85*
Ryan, R. M., 62, *90*

Sacker, A., 113, *139*
Sagi, A., 64, *91*
Salgado de Snyder, N., 201, *205*
Salovey, P., 236, *244*
Sam, D. L., 72, *84*
Sameroff, A. J., 41, 47, *53*, 95, 117, 127, *139*, 255
Sanchez, J. I., 201, *207*
Sanford, R. N., 215, *240*
Sapir, E., 184–85, *207*
Save the Children, 98, *139*
Saxe, G. B., 143, *176*
Schäfermeier, E., 57, *90*
Schaffer, H. R., 124, *139*, 149, 162–63, *176*
Schieffelin, B., 182, *207*
Schliemann, A. D., 164–65, *176*, 259, *299*
Schneider, B. H., 261, *300, 301*
Schneiders, J., 263, 269, *300*
Schoendorf, K. C., 107, *139*
Schofield, J. W., 218, 221, *245, 246*
Schoon, I., 113, *139*, 287, *300*
Schumann, J., 193–94. *207, 208*
Schwarz, B., 57, 66, 83, *90*
Schweinhart, L. J., 269–70, 286, *295, 300*
Scribner, S., 143, *176*
Sealand, N., 120, *133*
Segall, M. H., *9*, 13–14, *24, 26*, 31–33, 38, *51, 52, 53*, 84, 87, *94*, 132, *205, 294, 298*
Seitamo, L., 77, *90*
Sekeleti, C., 260, 271, *300*
Semaj, L., 221, *245*
Serpell, R., 19, *26*, 33–34, 39–40, *53*, *54*, 113, *139*, 145, 147, 165, 170, *176*, 179, 184, *208*, 253, 257–58, 260, 268, 271, 292, *295, 300*
Shaffer, D. R., 15, *26*
Shakespeare, W., 93, *139*
Shanahan, M., 118, *137*

Shaw, D., 119, *139*
Shaw, G. B., 93, *139*
Shaw, M., 110, *139*
Shaw, N. J., 102, *139*
Shepard, S. A., 122, *135*
Sherbak, J., 60, *91*
Sheridan, L. P., 239, *245*
Sherman, F., 223, *244*
Shropshire, J., 97, 106–07, *139*
Shweder, R. A., 31, 35, *54*, *174*, *207*
Sikes, J., 225, *240*
Silva, P. A., *134*
Simmons, H. C., 231, *240*
Simmons, R. G., 221, *245*
Simons, R. L., 24, *133*, 277, *300*
Singer, J. A., 292, 300
Singh, G. K., 107, *139*
Sinha, D., 38, 41, *54*
Sjaastad, J., 112, *136*, 263, *298*
Skelton, T., 96, *139*
Skerry, S., 217, *240*
Slaby, R. G., 274, 277, *299*
Slee, N., 233 – as Sleem, *245*
Slobin, D., 182, *205*
Smeeding, T. M., 100, *140*
Smith, J., 111, *140*
Smith, R. S., 122, 125, *140*
Snapp, M., 225, *240*
Snyder, H. N., 218, *246*
Socolar, R. R. S., 125, *139*
Soderstrom, M., 183, *208*
Sohn, M., 217, *244*
Sonnenschein, S., 113, *139*
Soper, C. J., 239, *242*
Soteras-de Toro, M., 261, *300*
Spearman, C., 145, *176*
Spencer, N., 109, *132*
Spilka, B., 230, *244*
Sprangers, M., 123, *140*
Sroufe, L. A., 122, *134*
Sta. Maria, M., 288, *300*
Stacey, B., 232, *242*
Steinberg, L., 103, *132*, 274, *296*
Stephan, W. G., 220, 224, *245*
Stephin, C., 225, *240*
Sternberg, K. J., 14, *25*
Sternberg, R. J., 7, *10*, 144–47, 170–72, *173*, *174*, *176*, *177*, 197, *206*, *208*

Stewart, J. H., 264, 275, *300*
Stormshak, E. A., 68, *90*, 275, *300*
Straus, M. A., 264, 275, *300*
Strodtbeck, F., 32, *54*
Sue, D., 79, *90*
Sue, D. W., 79, *90*
Sulzby, E., *137*
Super, C. M., 14, 16, *25*, *26*, 39, 41, 44–47, *54*, 56–59, 62, *86*, *90*, *91*, 130, *140*, 164, *174*, 187–88, *206*, 254–55, 261, 274, 291, *297*, *300*
Suzuki, L. K., 62, 66–67, *86*
Swanwick, P., 279, *300*
Sylva, K., 160, *173*, 282, *296*
Szapocznik, J., 71, *90*

Taeschner, T., 191, *208*
Tajfel, H., 212, 233–34, 236–37, *245*, *246*
Takriti, R., 8, 213, 222, 232–33, 237–39, *245*
Takriti, Y., 239, *246*
Tamm, M. E., 227, *246*
Tanner, G., 109, *135*
Taska, L. S., 62, *85*
Taylor, A., 115, *136*
Taylor, J. G., 116, *134*
Teale, W. H., *137*
Teixeira, R., 225, *243*
Tharp, R., 161, *177*
Thompson, G. G., 192, *208*
Thompson, M., 116, *132*
Thomson, S. S., 223, *243*
Thouless, R. H., 212, *246*
Tijhuis, M. A. R., *140*
Tolan, P. H., 120, *132*
Tomasello, M., 151, *177*, 186, *208*
Tousignant, M., 97, 110, *132*
Townsend, P., 99, *136*, *140*
Triandis, H. C., 62, *83*, *84*, *88*, *91*
Trommsdorff, G., 57, 64, 67, *85*, *90*, *91*
Troutman, B. R., 125, *134*
Tseng, H.-M., 70, *87*
Tulviste, P., 19, *26*
Turner, E. B., 228, *246*
Turner, I. F., 228, *246*
Turner, J. C., 233, 235, *243*, *244*, *246*

AUTHOR INDEX

Udvari, S., 261, *300*
Umbel, V. M., 192, *208*
United Nations, 99, *140*

Validzic, A., 225, *242*
Valsiner, J., 146, *177*
van Agt, H. M. E., *140*
van der Ende, J., 263, *300*
van der Vijver, F. J. R., 13, *26*, *54*
Van IJzendoorn, M. H., 64, *91*
van Os, J., *300*
van Tijen, N., 62, *86*
Vasar, M., *133*
Vaughan, G. M., 219–20, 237, *246*
Vedder, P., 72, *84*
Verbit, M. F., 212, *246*
Verhulst, J., *300*
Vernon, P. E., 33, *54*
Viljoen, H. G., 231, *243*
Vinden, P., 167, *177*
Vinson, T., 109, *140*
Vivian, J., 226, *241*
Voelker, S., *87*
Vollebergh, W., 63, *89*
Volterra, V., 191, *208*
Voronov, M., 292, *300*
Vygotsky, L. S., 7, *9*, 18–19, *26*, 35, *54*, 144, 147–48, 150–51, 155–61, 163, 167, 171–72, *175*, *177*, 186, *208*, 282, 312

Wachs, T. D., 61, *91*
Wagner, D. A., *175*, 288, 292, *300*
Wallace, A. F. C., 211, *246*
Warner, T. D., 67, *89*
Watson, J., 166, *177*
Watson, P. J., 60, *91*
Watt, N., 112, *140*
Webster-Stratton, C., 17, *26*, 64, 67–68, *91*, 263, 269, *301*
Weikart, D. P., 269, *300*
Weil, A. M., 215, *245*
Weisz, J., 64, *90*, *299*
Weisz, R. J., 264, *301*
Wellman, H. M., 166, *174*, *177*
Wells, K. C., 276, *296*
Werner, E., 130, *140*
Werner, E. E., 122, 125, *140*

Wertsch, J. V., 19, *26*, 162, 170, *177*
Wetherell, M. S., *246*
Wethington, E., 112, *133*
Whaley, A. L., 275, *301*
Whitbeck, L. B., *24*
White, R. W., 122, *140*
Whitehurst, G. J., 116, *140*
Whiteside, L., 111, *133*, 263, *296*
Whiting, B. B., 15, *24*, *26*, 36, *54*
Whiting, J., 32, *54*
Whitley, B. E., 218, *246*
Whorf, B. L., 184–85, *208*, *308*
Wiley, A. R., 182, *207*
Williams, J. A., 237, *246*
Williams, J. E., 218, 219, 221–22, *245*, *246*
Wilson, A. E., 219, 221, *241*
Wilson, H., 222, *240*
Wimbush, D. D., 67, *87*
Wingfield, A., 116, *140*
Witkin, H. A., 33, *54*
Wolf, A. W., 59, *91*
Wolff, E. H., 189, *208*
Wood, D., 149–50, 160–61, *177*, 276, 282, *299*, *301*
Woodburn, S., 261, *300*
Woodhead, M., 131, *139*, *141*, 295
Work, W. C., 124–25, *141*
www.endcorporalpunishment.org, 273, *297*
www.statistics.gov.uk/nugget.asp?id=1003, *141*
Wyman, P. A., 124–25, *141*

Xu, Y., 264, *301*

Yang, K. S., 31, *51*, *54*
Yeeles, C., 224, *240*
Yoon, K., *83*, *84*, *88*, *91*, 116, *140*
Young, J. W., 286, *295*
Yovsi, R., *87*, *298*
Yu, L., *301*
Yu, S. M., 107, *139*

Zahn-Waxler, C., 57, 65, *85*, *89*
Zalk, S. R., 217–18, 221–22, *244*, *246*
Zelickman, I., 279, *300*
Zhang, Z., *301*

Subject Index

academic functioning, 110, 112–113, 116
accentuation hypothesis, 212
acculturation, 69–72, 97, 194–195
activity theory, 160–163
Africa, 170, 187, 258, 268, 275
aggression, 77, 261–262
applied developmental psychology, 249–251
Asian, 102, 171, 225
aspirations, 113–114
attachment, 64–65, 124

Bangladeshi, 101
behavioural inhibition, 260–261
bilingualism, 21–22, 189–193, 259, 272
    outcomes of, 196–199
Brazil, 259

child abuse and neglect, 108, 109, 110
childrearing, 15–17, 57
cognition, 142
cognitive development, 18–20, 142
collaboration, 154, 172
context of child development, 12
Costa Rica, 103
cross-cultural psychology, 13–15, 31–35, 251
cultural anthropology, 49
cultural-context approach, 19, 46–47
cultural identity, 22, 200, 210
cultural psychology, 14, 31, 35–38, 252–254
cultural transmission, 30, 95
culture, 28–31

developmental difficulties, 278–280
developmental niche, 14, 44–46, 130
discipline, 67–68, 76–77, 78, 118, 273–278
    corporal punishment, 273–278
    physical punishment, 68

ecological model, 41–44, 127–130
ecological transactional model, 47, 127, 129

education, 258–260
    academic achievement, 111, 263, 269
    schooling, 170, 258–259
emotional and behavioural difficulties (EBD), 117–118, 262–264
emotional contexts, 64–65, 118–119, 167–168
environment, 14, 20, 30, 41–47, 65, 126, 224, 264
ethnicity, 56, 95, 101, 102, 120, 210, 213–214, 216–224
ethnography, 49, 291
ethnotheories, 44, 45, 58–60
exosystem, 42

factor analysis, 251
family change model, 62–63
feeding practices, 59, 75–76

globalization, 13, 248

home environment, *116–117, 120*, 263

identity, 226-227, 234, *249, 283***
immigrants, 71, 190
independence, 74–75
indigenous
    cultures, 80
    psychology, 15, 31, 38–40, 252–254
    studies, 79
individualism-collectivism, 16, 60–62, 80–81, 256
infant-directed speech, 59, 182–183
infant mortality, 107–108
intelligence, 39–40, 143, 144–147
    IQ, 111, 114
    social intelligence, 170
    technological intelligence, 170
intergenerational continuities, 103
intervention, 262, 285–287
    community-based programmes, 286

intervention – *continued*
  Positive Play Programme, 278–282
  studies, 285–287
  Sure Start Programme,
    269–270, 287
Inuit, 79, 81

Japanese culture, 61

Kenya, 187–188, 200, 259
  Kokwet community, 187–188

language, 271–272
  acquisition, 20, 181, 193–195
  development, 181
  significance, 179–180
  socialization, 182–183, 196
  structure, 180–181
Latino, 201–202
linguistic relativity, 184–186
  language and thought, 184–186
  Sapir-Whorf hypothesis, 185

macrosystem, 43
majority world, 12
malnutrition, 110
Mayan, *36–37*, 168
mediation, 156, 157, 158, 162
mesosystem, 42
methodology, 253, 287–293
microsystem, 41
minority groups, 13
models, 254

neighbourhood, 118, 119–120
Norwegian culture, 72–73

Pakistani, 101, 213
parenting, 17, 56, 66–67, 68, 104, 263
peer influences, 95–96
perceptual skills, 33–34
physical development, 107
Piaget's theory, 18–19, 147–152, 153, 171, 215, 217, 227–228, 267–268
  Neo-Piagetian, theory, 152–155
play, 76
prejudice, 214–215, 217–228, 236, 239
  stereotypes, 214–215, 236

psycholinguistics, 182
psychological tools, 156, 159, 172

qualitative methods, 49
quantitative methods, 48

reliability, 48
religion, 210, 211, 227
religious identity, 22, 226
resilience, 122–127
role models, 283–285

Sámi culture, 72–73
scaffolding, 160–161
  guided participation, 161–162
sibling relationships, 168
sleeping arrangements,
    36–37, 76, 78
social cognition, 164–167, 168
social constructivist, 155
social engagement, 163, 165–166
social identity, 212
social interaction, 153
social psychological theories,
    233–239
socialization, 15–17, 20, 56
sociocultural theory,
    155, 156–159
socio-economic status, 114, 116
  aspirations, 113, 114, 115
  poverty, 93, 97–104
  social class, 107
  social mobility, 112
South Africa, 221
stages of development,
    227, 229, 231
subculture, 95, 96
supernatural, 212

theoretical models, 254–256
thought processes, 21, 150, 179,
    184–186, 199
traditional societies, 78

United Kingdom, 93–94, 96–97, 99,
    100, 105, 108, 109, 112, 152, 168,
    269, 272, 287
  Britain, 100, 112

United Kingdom – *continued*
  England, 108, 200
United States (of America), 94, 112, 166, 171, 218, 252, 267, 269, 275
universals, 32, 33

validity, 48
vocabulary, 191, 192

Vygotsky's theory, 19, 147, 155, 171–172
  Neo-Vygotskians, 157, 159

Zambia, 34, 39, 98–99, 165, 258, 276, 286
  Chewa, 258
Zinacantec, 168
zone of proximal development, *160*, 161